# CONTENTS

Printed by Butler Tanner and Dennis Maps by The XYZ Digital Map Company

# WHO'S WHO IN SCOTLAND'S GARDENS




42a North Castle Street,
Edinburgh EH2 3BN
T: 0131 226 3714
E: info@scotlandsgardens.org
W: www.scotlandsgardens.org


## BANKERS

Adam & Company plc, 25 St Andrew Square, Edinburgh EH2 1AF

## SOLICITORS

Turcan Connell, Princes Exchange, Earl Grey Street, Edinburgh EH3 9EE

## AUDITORS

Douglas Home & Co, 47-49 The Square, Kelso TD5 7HW


ISSN 0967-831X
ISBN 978-0-901549-28-0

Getty Images ©

As the President of Scotland's Gardens, I must congratulate the garden owners for surviving a very cold and wet spring to triumph with the most glorious displays in a wonderfully sunny and warm summer. I am sure the gardens gave an enormous amount of pleasure to many visitors over the long summer days.

Every year, there is something new to enjoy. I would like to congratulate all those involved with the success of the Fife Garden Trail that took place in May and June involving nine gardens. I look forward to hearing about all the Garden Trails which are planned for 2014.

I am delighted that so many local and nationwide charities benefit from the hard work of all who take part. My thanks go to the garden owners, the volunteers and gardeners who ensure the programme's success – and of course to all the enthusiastic and knowledgeable visitors.

I wish everyone all the very best good fortune and gardening weather for 2014!

Camilla

# CHAIRMAN'S MESSAGE

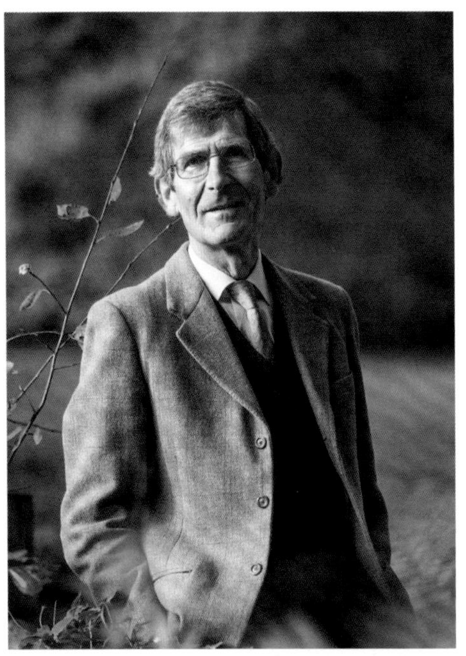

My first year in office was blighted by a memorably cold and wet summer but in contrast my second year was blessed with the warmest and sunniest summer for very many years. What a difference warm sunshine makes to our sense of wellbeing, to the gardens which are opened for us and to visitor numbers. Although we had fewer gardens opening in 2013 our garden gate takings were broadly unchanged on those of the previous year. Therefore, could I extend my thanks to our garden openers who produced such colourful gardens for us and who laid the foundations for another successful year, to our district and area organisers and to other volunteers for their hard work on our behalf.

Over the last year Paddy Scott and I have been travelling around Scotland meeting our garden openers, our organisers and volunteers. I have very much enjoyed hearing their views and ideas on how we can continue to develop and evolve Scotland's Gardens to ensure that it remains an attractive organisation and proposition to our constituents. In the light of comments made, we have begun an exercise to review our constitution which remains very largely unchanged from its original 1931 format. I have been very encouraged by the goodwill afforded to us by our garden openers and local volunteers. Without that goodwill we could not and would not raise funds for charity. It remains vital that we build on that goodwill by ensuring that we remain topical with our constituents.

In my role as Chairman, I have one huge weakness in that I have no control over the weather. It makes such a difference to us; warm sunny summers bring out the best in both the gardens and visitors and of course our net garden takings, whilst the converse is true of cold and wet ones. However I do know that we are in good heart and whatever the weather, 2014 will be another year to remember. We have a number of new gardens and trails opening for us as well as those of our loyal and regular supporters. Whether you are a garden owner, a volunteer or a visitor could I welcome you to our Guidebook and wish you a contented 2014 season of growing and giving.

Mark Hedderwick
Chairman

# SPONSORS

We would like to acknowledge and thank the following organisations that will be sponsoring Scotland's Gardens in 2014. Their support is invaluable and enables us to maximise the funds we give to our beneficiary charities.

## Investec Wealth & Investment

## Corney & Barrow

## D C Thomson & Co

## Lycetts

## Rettie & Co

## Savills (L&P) Ltd

## The Edinburgh International Conference Centre

In addition we would like to say how grateful we are to the many private donors who have given us their support.

# WHAT HAPPENS TO THE MONEY RAISED?

All garden owners who participate in the Scotland's Gardens programme are able to nominate a charity of their choice to receive 40% of the funds raised at their openings. 226 different worthy charities will be supported in this manner in 2014 and these vary from small local ones to several large well known organisations. Examples include:

- Alzheimers Scotland
- Artlink Central
- British Heart Foundation
- Cancer Research
- Chest Heart and Stroke Scotland
- Children's Hospice Association
- Colliston Youth Club
- Erskine Hospital
- Gardening Leave
- Help for Heroes
- Highland Hospice
- Lamp of Lothian
- Lord Arthur Community
- Macmillan Cancer Support
- Marie Curie Cancer Care
- Mary's Meals
- Montrose Guides
- Port Logan Hall
- RNLI
- Riding for the Disabled
- Sandpiper Trust
- SSPCA
- St Columba's Hospice
- St Andrew Episcopal Church Strathtay
- Strathcarron Hospsice
- Survival International

60%, net of expenses, of the funds raised at each garden is given to Scotland's Gardens beneficiaries:

- Maggie's Cancer Caring Centres
- The Queen's Nursing Institute Scotland
- The Gardens Fund of the National Trust for Scotland
- Perennial

Information on these organisations is provided on the following pages.

Several garden owners who open their garden on a regular basis and generously support Scotland's Gardens give a donation and the net sum is split between Scotland's Gardens beneficiaries.

In this book details of the charities nominated by the Garden Owners are provided and those gardens giving a donation are also indicated.

# BENEFICIARY MESSAGES

## maggie's

As yet another summer comes to a close, I am sure we will all be very grateful for the magnificent sunshine and the lovely balmy evenings we have had throughout 2013. I hope that all the members of Scotland's Gardens have had a wonderful summer and lots of opportunities to show off all the beautiful blooms so lovingly grown throughout the season.

I would like to take this opportunity to thank you all for your most welcome support of Maggie's in Scotland, again this year. As we grow from strength to strength, with our centres, including the brand new building in Aberdeen, I would like to say a heartfelt thank you to everyone for the support we have received year on year.

Your generosity continues to develop and enhance our support to people with cancer. In 2013 we added to our programme by having therapeutic gardening offered at many of our centres.

Maggie's Centres are now supporting people in Aberdeen, Dundee, Edinburgh, Fife, Glasgow, Inverness, Lanarkshire, and from early 2015, Forth Valley. All of our centres benefit from Scotland's Gardens donations.

With warmest regards,

Laura Lee
Chief Executive
Maggie's Centres

Please call 0300 123 1801 or visit **www.maggiescentres.org** for more information.

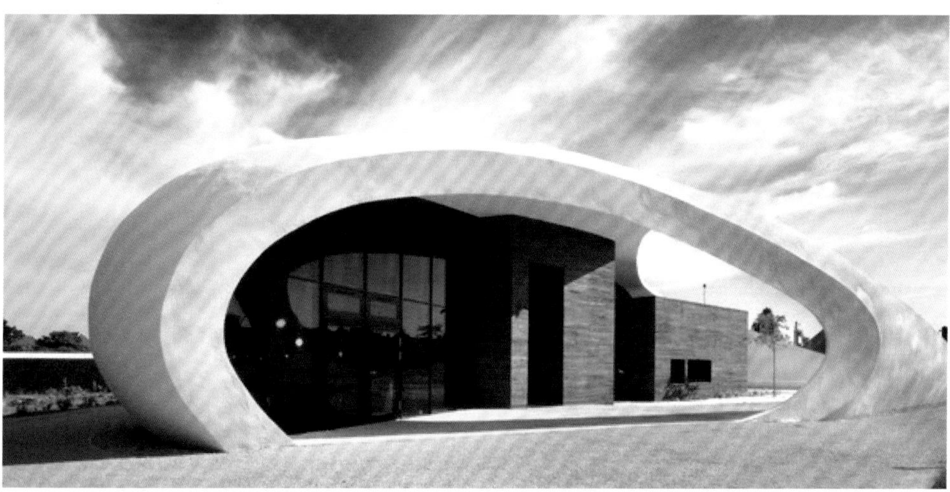

Maggie's latest centre in Scotland, which opened September 2013, at Aberdeen Royal Infirmary.

Qnis
THE QUEEN'S NURSING INSTITUTE SCOTLAND
Promoting Excellence in Community Nursing across Scotland


On behalf of the Queen's Nursing Institute Scotland I would like to thank all of the garden owners, and their visitors, for their on-going support. The link between The Queen's Nursing Institute Scotland and Scotland's Gardens goes back many years. In the early years, the donations we received from garden openings were used to support retired Queen's Nurses who were often without pensions, and with no family. Over the years, your donations have helped us to achieve so much.

In these days of the much loved NHS, some may wonder what our role now is and why we still need your support. The work of a community nurse is often undervalued and misunderstood. Many of us don't know exactly what a community nurse is - however, 90% of all care is provided in the community. Whilst the modern day community nurse doesn't work under the same conditions as the original Queen's Nurse, they still work in challenging situations and the NHS cannot provide for everything they might need. The original form of the Queen's Nursing Institute Scotland provided for the education and training of the Nurses, and we still adhere to that principle today – in 2012, we helped 11 nurses further their education and professional development by funding vocational courses. To help promote innovation and excellence, we funded four projects ranging from "Case Supervision in Community Midwifery" to " Mindfullness in Long Term Conditions". We brought 138 community nurses together at four conferences to help share advances in technology within healthcare. We also recognise and reward the dedication of our community nurses – last year we presented 79 Long Service Awards to individuals who had devoted over 21 years to nursing within the community.

Despite the fact that there have been no new Queen's Nurses since the 1970's, we continue to support over 500 retired Queen's Nurses across Scotland by providing them with welfare, companionship and fellowship.

All of this work has been done with the financial support we have received from Scotland's Gardens – thank you.

Lifelong learning - District Nurses updating their knowledge on end of life care

the National Trust for Scotland

a place for everyone

On behalf of the National Trust for Scotland's Gardens Community I would like to thank all of Scotland's Gardens owners for their ongoing support to the National Trust for Scotland in general and its gardens portfolio in particular. We really appreciate the financial (and other) support which you provide and which enables so much of the work that goes on in our gardens. Our gardens continue to flourish and grow and prove popular with our visitors, providing perfect places to escape from the pressures of daily life and contemplate the past. We are grateful to those people who support our work and the work of Scottish Gardens by continuing to visit and enjoy the places in our care.

In 2013 twenty-four of our gardens supported Scotland's Gardens, opening on 35 different occasions throughout the year at which we hosted daffodil teas at Brodie; an Evening Encounter at Broughton House; Pruning and wildlife gardening workshops at Crathes and Greenbank, respectively; Romancing the Rose at Drum Castle and an opening at Haddo House garden in support of Scotland's Gardens, the first for a few years.

In 2014 we have planned over 50 events and activities to coincide with the opening of our properties in support of Scotland's Gardens including: a new autumn produce sale at the Pineapple and the ever popular guided walks at Culzean, Drum and Leith Hall as well as events at Broughton House and Kellie – just to name a few.

Through the School of Heritage Gardening, in part supported by Scotland's Gardens, the Trust continues to play an important part in developing future gardeners. There is a high quality framework to support gardener training in our gardens across the country, with student placements at Threave Garden, Crathes Castle, Kellie Castle, Branklyn Garden, Falkland Palace and Pitmedden Garden.

Inverewe Garden

Thanks to your generous financial donation, visitors can enjoy our gardens at all times of year and see the results of the hard work and expertise of our dedicated garden staff, who conserve these beautiful places for everyone to enjoy.

Kate Mavor
Chief Executive

## PERENNIAL IS 175 YEARS OLD!

We are celebrating our 175th birthday in 2014. The Gardeners' Benevolent Institution was established in 1839 to provide pensions for retired gardeners. A group of nurserymen were uncomfortable that their head gardeners, often a key, long-serving member of household staff, could end up in the workhouse after their service and their tied accommodation came to an end.

The group financed a plan to support their staff and families into old age; and the Gardeners' Benevolent Institution was founded in January 1839. In 1840 the first pension of £75 was shared among three beneficiaries.

### 175 years later

175 years on we are living in very different times, yet Perennial continues to support those in the industry who are in need. Last year, for the first time we helped more than 1,000 individuals and their families cope and move on from a range of issues. It is not just the long-term unemployed and single parent families who need our help, it is even those who are in work.

Low-income working families are now struggling to put sufficient food on the table, and they need our help in ever growing numbers too. To safeguard these vital services we need your support.

Perhaps you could make a commitment to raise £175 for our 175th year, attend one of our special birthday events at gardens throughout the summer or join us at the flower shows across the country?

If you would like to help us and feel you could spare time this year to rally colleagues and friends to raise money and awareness of Perennial, please visit www.perennial.org.uk or contact us on 01372 373962.

THE ALNWICK
GARDEN

one

Project Part-Financed by the European Union
European Regional Development Fund

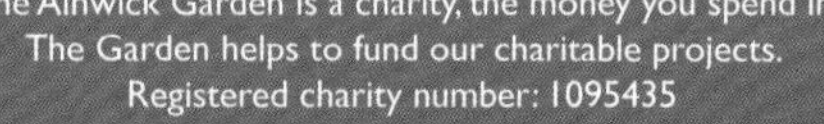

NSP
Northumberland
Strategic Partnership

EUROPEAN UNION

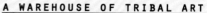

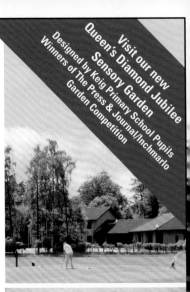

Logan

# NEW GARDENS FOR 2014

## Aberdeenshire

Dunlugas
Knockmuir

## Angus

33 Ireland Street
Ninewells Community Garden
The Garden Cottage
West Scryne Farm

## Berwickshire

Swinton Mill House
Wellfield

## Caithness, Sutherland, Orkney & Shetland

33 Hillside Road (Orkney Trail)
Dalkeith Polytunnel (Orkney Trail)
Kierfold (Orkney Trail)
Stenwood (Orkney Trail)
The Community Garden (Orkney Trail)
The Quoy of Houton (Orkney Trail)
Thurso Gardens

## Dumfriesshire

Dalgonar

## East Lothian

Blackdykes (East Lothian Trail)
Birrell's House (East Lothian Trail)
Frostineb (East Lothian Trail)
Longniddry Gardens
Stevenson Steading (East Lothian Trail)

Damnaglaur Garden, Wigtownshire

Swinton Mill House, Berwickshire

Brooklands, Kirkcudbrightshire

Anwoth Old Schoolhouse, Kirkcudbrightshire

## Edinburgh & West Lothian

4 Harelaw Road

## Fife

Blair Adam House (see entry for Greenhead Farm)
Helensbank
Kenly Green Farm (Fife Garden Festival)
Kinaldy (Fife Garden Festival)
Rofsie Arts Garden (Fife Garden Festival)
Seaview (Fife Garden Festival)
Southern Hemisphere Botanics (Fife Garden Festival)
Strathkinness Community Trust (Fife Garden Festival)
The Cottage (Fife Garden Festival)
Wemyss Castle Gardens
Wormit Village Gardens

## Glasgow & District

Watch Us Grow

## Isle of Arran

Hazelbank

## Kincardine & Deeside

14 Arbeadie Avenue
Fasque House

## Kirkcudbrightshire

Anwoth House
Anwoth Old Schoolhouse
Brooklands
Netherhall
The Limes

## Lanarkshire

Covington House
Lindsaylands

## Lochaber & Badenoch

Arisaig House
Roshven House

Fasque House, Kincardineshire

Bruntlands Bungalow, Moray & Nairn

Lindsaylands, Lanarkshire

Covington House, Lanarkshire

## Moray & Nairn

1 Sanquhar Drive
Bruntlands Bungalow
Newbold House

## Perth & Kinross

Cloichfoldich
Hollytree Lodge
Kincarrathie House
Little Tombuie
Mill of Fyall Cottage
Pitnacree House
Tullichettle
Wester House of Ross

## Renfrewshire

Newmills Cottage

## Ross, Cromarty, Skye & Inverness

Highland Liliums

## Stirlingshire

Buchlyvie Gardens
Dun Dubh
Dunblane Community Gardens
Little Broich
The Pineapple

## Wigtownshire

Balker Farmhouse
Damnaglaur Gardens
Lochnaw Castle

Hollytree Lodge, Stirlingshire

Dun Dubh, Stirlingshire

Dunblane Community Gardens, Stirlingshire

Arbeadie Avenue, Kincardineshire

# SNOWDROP OPENINGS

Snowdrops remain as popular as ever and several properties will be opening in February and March to enable visitors to enjoy the stunning displays of these flowers. Once again VisitScotland will be supporting the openings with their heavily marketed Snowdrop Festival which has become an important part of their successful Winter White campaign.

The following properties will be opening and most will be participating in the Snowdrop Festival:

### Aberdeenshire

Bruckhills Croft

### Angus

Dunninald
Gagie House
Lawton House
Pitmuies Gardens

### East Lothian

Shepherd House

### Fife

Cambo House
Lindores House

### Kincardine & Deeside

Ecclesgreig Castle

### Kirkcudbrightshire

Brooklands

Kailzie Gardens

## Lanarkshire

Cleghorn

## Midlothian

Kevock Garden

## Peeblesshire

Dawyck Botanic Garden
Kailzie Gardens

## Perth & Kinross

Braco Castle
Cluny House
Kilgraston School
Rossie House

## Renfrewshire

Ardgowan

## Ross, Cromarty, Skye & Inverness

Abriachan Garden Nursery

## Stirlingshire

Gargunnock House
Kilbryde Castle
The Linns
West Plean House

## Wigtownshire

Castle Kennedy & Gardens
Craichlaw
Dunskey Garden and Maze
Logan Botanic Garden

**We are very keen to add more snowdrop gardens in 2015 so please let us know if you would like to share your snowdrops with us next year.**

Shepherd House, Snowdrop Theatre

Eccelsgreig Castle

# FIFE GARDEN FESTIVAL 7 - 8 JUNE 2014

**The Fife Committee of Scotland's Gardens are proud to present to you their third celebration of the best in Fife gardens.**

Cedar Cottage, Craigrothie, Fife

2014's gorgeous gardens stretch from the Forth in the south-west to the North Sea coast beyond St Andrews, and the majority of the 10 gardens are opening their gates to us all for the first time. Each garden offers a fascinating glimpse of the diversity of human creativity and is completely unique.

There is something for everyone: rolling acres and pocket handkerchiefs; exciting structures and glorious confusion; horticultural gems and colourful cottage favourites; country houses, cottage gardens and community gardens, gardens created fresh from fields and farmyards, or rediscovered and reinvented. All are special in their own way.

Choose your gardens, choose your route, enjoy the rolling countryside of Fife and above all enjoy the experience.

Look after the inner self with teas, coffees and cakes along the way, buy some plants and do visit some of the best of Fife's small businesses.

Fairbairn, Craigrothie, Fife

Old Inzievar House, Fife

Kenly Green Farm, Fife

Rofsie, Fife

## Opening times

Saturday 7 & Sunday 8 June
11:00am – 5:00pm

## Admission

£20.00 for all gardens.
Accompanied children under 16 free.

Tickets (limited in number) are available only in advance from **www.fifegardenfestival.org.uk** by credit card or by cheque payable to Scotland's Gardens from S. Lorimore, Willowhill, Forgan, Newport on Tay, Fife DD6 8RA.

Seaview, Boarhills, Fife

Kinaldy, Fife

The Cottage, Boarhills, Fife

Southern Hemisphere Botanics, Fife

Strathkinness Community Garden, Fife

# EAST LOTHIAN GARDEN TRAIL 17 - 21 JUNE 2014

**Scotland's Gardens is proud to announce another new initiative – the East Lothian Garden Trail 2014.**

This trail provides an opportunity to see several gardens in close proximity over a day or days, making it worthwhile to come from afar. Ten gardens, none of which can be described as small, will be open at specific times from Tuesday 17 to Saturday 21 June – with all gardens open 1:00pm to 6:00pm on Friday 20 and Saturday 21 June.

East Lothian gardens tend to be at their best in June – and not simply as testimony to the late Christopher Lloyd's adage that 'any fool can have a garden which looks good in June' – but because spring tends to come later to this part of Scotland. So, in the inland gardens and those on high exposed ground, the trail should be an opportunity to see late rhododendrons and azaleas, primula, and blue Himalayan poppies; while the coastal gardens should boast roses and burgeoning herbaceous borders. But above all, an opportunity to see such splendid plants in a mix of settings, some many generations old, some relatively recent; both coastal and inland; both rugged and manicured – and with those who created the gardens on hand. Picking the brains of the owner, or custodian – for many of these gardens are but held in custody for the next generation – must surely be one of the highlights of wandering around the fruits of someone else's labours.

## Opening times

All gardens: Friday 20 and Saturday 21 June 1:00pm - 6:00pm.

Selected gardens open at specific times from Tuesday 17 to Saturday 21 June. Please see **www.eastlothiantrail.org.uk** for further details.

Birrell's House, Main Street, Innerwick

Blackdykes, North Berwick

Bowerhouse with Bowerhouse Walled Garden, Dunbar

Congalton House, North Berwick

## Admission

£20.00 for all 10 gardens by prepaid ticket only. Accompanied children under 16 free.

Tickets (limited in number) are available only in advance from **www.eastlothiantrail.org.uk** or by cheque payable to Scotland's Gardens from Bill Alder, Granary House, Kippielaw, Haddington EH41 4PY.

A brochure describing the gardens and providing a map, opening times, directions and details of plant stalls, teas, and wheelchair access will be sent with each ticket.

## Beneficiary charities

60% of the net proceeds of the trail to Scotland's Gardens beneficiary charities, the remainder split equally between Leuchie House and the Lamp of Lothian Trust.

Inwood, Carberry, Musselburgh

Redcliffe, Whittinghame, Haddington

Frostineb, by Fala, Pathhead

Stevenson Steading, Haddington

Humbie Dean, Humbie

Stobshiel House, Humbie

# ORKNEY GARDEN TRAIL JUNE & JULY 2014

The Orkney Garden Trail is an exciting new addition to Scotland's Gardens 2014 programme and we are delighted to have gardens opening for us in Orkney once again after quite some time.

On each of 4 Sundays in June and July 6 gardens, new to Scotland's Gardens, will be opening their gates to the public. They are all very different, but provide the visitor with wonderful examples of what can be achieved by gardeners in this northerly island with its harsh climate. Seaside, village, town and community gardens are all represented.

## Beneficiary charities

40% of the proceeds from the Orkney Garden Trail will go to the Friends of the Neuro Ward at Aberdeen Royal Infirmary, the net remaining to Scotland's Gardens beneficiary charities.

## Opening times

Sundays 22, 29 June and 6, 13 July
10:00am to 6:00pm

## Admission

£10.00 for entry to all 6 gardens.
Accompanied children under 12 free.
Repeat visits to a garden £2.50.

Tickets available by cash or cheque from Quoy of Houton, or from Scapa Travel, 11 Bridge Street, Kirkwall KW15 1HR.

Tickets may be reserved in advance by emailing c.kritchlow258@btinternet.com or scapa@barrheadtravel.com.

For further details visit **www.orkneygardentrail.org.uk**.

Stenwood, Finstown

The Quoy of Houton, Orphir

Community Garden, Finstown

33 Hillside Road, Stromness

Kierfold House, Sandwick

Dalkeith Polytunnel, Grimbister, Kirkwall

# CORSOCK HOUSE

I have always thought that Corsock garden is a rather magical place – probably because it has been lavished with much love, attention and imagination over many years. However, when Corsock House was bought by my grandparents-in-law, Peter and Rhona Ingall, in 1951 it was a post-war ruin of a garden which was being sold by a timber merchant, tree by tree. The Ingalls rescued many magnificent 19th century trees, including two splendid split-leaf beeches, several Wellingtonia, Douglas firs and Irish yews. Over the years the garden has been restored, extended and embellished with architectural features (largely due to my father-in-law, Micky Ingall) making a spectacular 20 acre garden.

Micky was the architect of the garden. He was the visionary behind the garden's Arcadian landscaping - clearing underneath the ancient trees and building the temples and bridges clothed with rhododendrons, azaleas, bluebells and candelabra primulas. He spent much time sculpting views and brashing trees to open up the vistas. A good example is seen as you first enter the 2 acre water garden through a cathedral-like avenue of firs. One of the first major tasks Micky undertook was to dig out the various ponds, starting with those in the water garden.

After you have passed the vivid maples, elegant katsura trees and rhododendrons in the water garden you meander through to the Mill Pond. The focal point of the Mill Pond is an ornamental bridge, inspired by that at Kenwood House, which hides the spillway leading to the hydroelectric system which was installed, rather innovatively, in 1905.

Above the Mill Pond you can see our "wedding wood". When my husband, Alastair, and I married in 2008 we had a "wedding list" of around 200 ornamental trees, which included maples, copper beeches, crab apple trees, cherry trees and kousa dogwoods. We recently added a similar number of species conifers.

The path from there leads you along the burn past the other ponds, through the bluebell wood, past sweeps of azaleas and rhododendrons, over several bridges and culminates in the 40 acre loch. My favourite bridge is the one designed by Alastair which was inspired by the Mathematical Bridge at Cambridge where he studied engineering (and where we met).

Woodland garden

Woodland garden

Rhododendron loderi

Rhododendron lacteum

Entrance to walled garden

Corsock garden is a paradise for rhododendron lovers, who are always excited by some of the special varieties in the garden, particularly the creamy yellow R. Lacteum, the pale pink R. Phaeochrysum and the blush-coloured R. Sutchuenense. My favourite is the R. Loderii, whose scent reminds me of marshmallows. The rhododendrons provide a dazzling display of flowers from April, if the frosts are kind, until the end of June when the bright white R. Polar Bear delights us.

Many of the rhododendrons are from George Forrest's 1930s expeditions to the Himalayas and the variety is amazing. My mother-in-law, Jane, is expert at pointing out the lavish variety to our children: from the tiny leaves of the R. Impeditum to the giant ones of R. Fictolacteum; the pink bells of R. Orbiculare to the brown velvet indumentum of R. Taliense or R. Charles Lemon.

Micky was always keen to emphasise how lucky he had been to have inherited a Scottish Baronial house by David Bryce and such a magnificent garden. We now have the privilege of stewarding and enjoying Corsock garden as it evolves. We are fortunate enough to have two wonderful and dedicated gardeners, Jim Laurie and Harry Cliff, who have a combined experience at Corsock of over 60 years, as well as our woodsman, Paul Durnan.

Micky's last project was to build a Doric temple inside the walled garden which is reflected in a canal and flanked by some stunning fountains, sculpture and a pair of ornamental gates by local blacksmith Adam Booth. Our next project is to develop the planting to compliment these wonderful features.

Corsock garden will be open this year as part of Scotland's Gardens for the 62nd time. Our hope is that our children and many other people will continue to enjoy this majestic garden for many years to come.

Alexandra Ingall

# PLANT HERITAGE IN SCOTLAND

Plant Heritage is a conservation charity which has just celebrated 35 years of conserving cultivated plants in the UK. It is easy to understand why the conservation of wild plants is so essential as their habitats are constantly under threat - but garden plants?

Unfortunately they, too, are always under threat. Many of the small, independent nurseries have disappeared, leaving no records and often few plants. Fashions change, plants fall out of favour and, in some cases, out of cultivation. Whilst one can always revive a fashion in clothes, when a plant has gone out of cultivation, it is lost forever.

The amazing variety of plants to be seen in the wonderful gardens of Scotland is a joy and something that has to be protected and conserved, not forgetting, too, plants for which, increasingly, medical uses are being identified.

'Rosie North" - one of Madeleine Tinson's National Collection of Mylnefield Lillies

Madeleine Tinson explains the finer points of a Mylnefield Lily, Parkhead

## Practical Measures

Plant Heritage has three major conservation strategies, the Threatened Plants Project, the Plant Guardian's Scheme and the National Collections Scheme.

The overall aims of the **Threatened Plants Project** are to:

- track down those cultivated plant varieties which have become rare or threatened
- search living collections to find records of those which are still alive and well
- take expert advice on the value of each in terms of its garden, historical and economic merits
- develop conservation plans with partner organisation for the most worth varieties.

Some members are keen to become actively involved in conservation, but for one reason or another, cannot establish a National Collection. The **Plant Guardian's Scheme** is for them. A plant guardian grows a small number of plants assessed as threatened by the Threatened Plants Project, thereby doing their bit for the future.

When the Threatened Plants team searches living collections to find records, their initial port of call is often one of the collections within the **National Plant Collections® Scheme** set up and administered by Plant Heritage. These are living libraries of individual species, cared for by dedicated specialist growers. They are to be found in cottage gardens, the gardens of the great and the good, in National Trust for Scotland gardens and in Scottish botanical gardens. There are some 50 National Collections in Scotland, watched over by the collection holders, HQ and one of the five Scottish Plant Heritage groups, Ayr and Arran, Dumfries and Galloway, Grampian and Tayside, South East Scotland and Strathclyde.

## Your local group

In addition to watching over the National Collections in their area, the groups put on talks, organise visits and run plant sales. The visits often involve something special - maybe a garden not usually open to the public or a private conducted tour of a garden by the head gardener. For some groups, the plant sale is the main activity of the year, one that involves a great deal of planning in order to have enough out of the ordinary plants of high quality to meet the needs of loyal customers.

For more information about the charity and about your local group, go to **www.nccpg.com** or simply google Plant Heritage.

Galanthus 'Heffalump' from Catherine Erskine's National Collection at Cambo

Paeonia tenuifolia from Mr and Mrs R J Mitchell's National Collection, Kingscroft, Elie, Fife

# Blair Castle and Gardens

Blair Castle sits at the heart of Atholl Estate's breathtaking landscape in Highland Perthshire. Recently restored to its original Georgian design, Hercules Garden is a 9 acre walled garden of fruit trees, vegetables and herbaceous borders, complete with a large landscaped pond, Chinese bridge and a trail of contemporary and 18th Century sculpture. The gardens also feature a peaceful woodland grove that boasts some of Britain's tallest and finest trees, a whimsical Gothic folly, Red Deer Park and the ruins of St Brides Kirk, the final resting place of Jacobite leader Bonnie Dundee.

Tel: 01796 481207 Email: bookings@blair-castle.co.uk Web: www.blair-castle.co.uk
Blair Castle, Blair Atholl, Pitlochry, Perthshire, PH18 5TL

# SCONE PALACE

THE CROWNING PLACE OF SCOTTISH KINGS

- Over 100 acres of landscaped grounds to explore, with historic built heritage
- 19th C Pinetum and Plant Hunters' Pavilion
- Birthplace of David Douglas
- Veteran Trees including the original David Douglas Fir
- Ericaceous Plantings providing glorious Spring colour and Woodland Walks
- The Unique Murray Star Maze

**NEW *for 2014***

- The Kitchen Garden, providing fresh produce for our Old Servants' Hall Coffee Shop
- Browse around our plant sales, Food Shop and Gift Shop
- Open 1 April - 31 October, 7days from 9.30am
- Chilli Festival 20th and 21st September

*t:* 01738 552300
*e:* visits@scone-palace.co.uk
www.sconepalace.co.uk

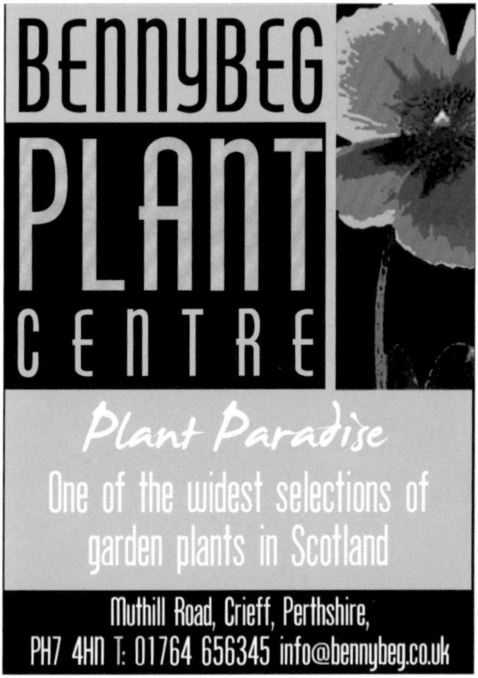

# GARDENS OPEN ON A SPECIFIC DATE

## February

**To be announced**

| | |
|---|---|
| Kirkcudbrightshire | Danevale Park, Crossmichael |

**Saturday 15 February**

| | |
|---|---|
| Kincardine & Deeside | Crathes Castle Garden, Banchory |
| Wigtownshire | Dunskey Gardens and Maze, Portpatrick |

**Sunday 16 February**

| | |
|---|---|
| Kirkcudbrightshire | Brooklands, Crocketford |
| Renfrewshire | Ardgowan, Inverkip |
| Wigtownshire | Dunskey Gardens and Maze, Portpatrick |

**Saturday 22 February**

| | |
|---|---|
| Angus | Dunninald, Montrose |
| East Lothian | Shepherd House, Inveresk |
| Wigtownshire | Dunskey Gardens and Maze, Portpatrick |

**Sunday 23 February**

| | |
|---|---|
| Angus | Dunninald, Montrose |
| East Lothian | Shepherd House, Inveresk |
| Lanarkshire | Cleghorn, by Lanark |
| Perth & Kinross | Kilgraston School, Bridge of Earn |
| Stirlingshire | Kilbryde Castle, Dunblane |
| Wigtownshire | Dunskey Gardens and Maze, Portpatrick |

## March

**Saturday 1 March**

| | |
|---|---|
| Angus | Dunninald, Montrose |

**Sunday 2 March**

| | |
|---|---|
| Angus | Dunninald, Montrose |
| Kincardine & Deeside | Ecclesgreig Castle, St Cyrus |
| Midlothian | Kevock Garden, Lasswade |
| Peeblesshire | Kailzie Gardens, Peebles |
| Stirlingshire | West Plean House, by Stirling |

**Thursday 6 March**

| | |
|---|---|
| Perth & Kinross | Rossie House, Forgandenny |

**Friday 7 March**

| | |
|---|---|
| Fife | Lindores House, by Newburgh |

**Sunday 9 March**

| | |
|---|---|
| Angus | Lawton House, Inverkeilor |
| Stirlingshire | The Linns, Sheriffmuir |

## April

**Thursday 10 April**

| | |
|---|---|
| Perth & Kinross | Rossie House, Forgandenny |

**Friday 11 April**

| | |
|---|---|
| Wigtownshire | Claymoddie Garden, Whithorn |

**Saturday 12 April**

| | |
|---|---|
| Moray & Nairn | Brodie Castle, Brodie |

**Sunday 13 April**

| | |
|---|---|
| East Lothian | Winton House, Pencaitland |
| Fife | Cambo House, Kingsbarns |
| Moray & Nairn | Brodie Castle, Brodie |
| Perth & Kinross | Megginch Castle, Errol |

**Thursday 17 April**

| | |
|---|---|
| Ross, Cromarty, Skye & Inverness | Dundonnell House, Dundonnell |

**Saturday 19 April**

| | |
|---|---|
| Glasgow & District | Holmwood, Cathcart |

**Sunday 20 April**

| | |
|---|---|
| Aberdeenshire | Westhall Castle, Oyn |
| Glasgow & District | Holmwood, Cathcart |

**Monday 21 April**

| | |
|---|---|
| Ross, Cromarty, Skye & Inverness | Brackla Wood, Culbokie |

**Wednesday 23 April**

| | |
|---|---|
| Ross, Cromarty, Skye & Inverness | Brackla Wood, Culbokie |

**Friday 25 April**

| | |
|---|---|
| Ross, Cromarty, Skye & Inverness | Brackla Wood, Culbokie |

**Saturday 26 April**

| | |
|---|---|
| Aberdeenshire | Leith Hall Garden, Huntly |

**Sunday 27 April**

| | |
|---|---|
| Argyll | Benmore Botanic Garden, Dunoon |
| Dunbartonshire | Kilarden, Rosneath |
| Edinburgh & West Lothian | 101 Greenbank Crescent, Edinburgh |
| Edinburgh & West Lothian | Dean Gardens , Edinburgh |
| Fife | Rofsie Arts Garden, by Collessie |

## May

**Thursday 1 May**

| | |
|---|---|
| Perth & Kinross | Rossie House, Forgandenny |

**Saturday 3 May**

| | |
|---|---|
| Aberdeenshire | Castle Fraser Garden, Sauchen |
| Argyll | Kames Bay, Kilmelford |
| Lochaber & Badenoch | Canna House Walled Garden, Isle of Canna |

**Sunday 4 May**

| | |
|---|---|
| Aberdeenshire | Castle Fraser Garden, Sauchen |
| Angus | Brechin Castle, Brechin |
| Argyll | Kames Bay, Kilmelford |
| Dumfriesshire | Portrack House, Holywood |
| Edinburgh & West Lothian | Redcroft, Edinburgh |
| Isle of Arran | Brodick Castle & Country Park, Brodick |
| Perth & Kinross | Branklyn Garden, Perth |
| Stirlingshire | Kilbryde Castle, Dunblane |

**Friday 9 May**

| | |
|---|---|
| Dumfriesshire | Drumpark, Irongray |
| Isle of Arran | Hazelbank, Pirnmill |

**Saturday 10 May**

| | |
|---|---|
| Angus | 3 Balfour Cottages, Menmuir |
| East Lothian | Shepherd House, Inveresk |
| Edinburgh & West Lothian | Roscullen, Edinburgh |
| Fife | Falkland's Small Gardens, Falkland |
| Isle of Arran | Hazelbank, Pirnmill |

**Sunday 11 May**

| | |
|---|---|
| Angus | Dalfruin, Kirriemuir |
| Argyll | Arduaine Garden, Oban |
| Dunbartonshire | Ross Priory, Gartocharn |
| East Lothian | Shepherd House, Inveresk |
| East Lothian | Tyninghame House, Dunbar |
| Edinburgh & West Lothian | Roscullen, Edinburgh |
| Fife | Falkland's Small Gardens, Falkland |
| Kirkcudbrightshire | Threave Garden, Castle Douglas |
| Perth & Kinross | Hollytree Lodge, Muckhart |
| Stirlingshire | Roman Camp Country House Hotel and Orchardlea House Gardens, Callendar |
| Stirlingshire | The Pass House, Kilmahog |
| Wigtownshire | Balker Farmhouse, Stranraer |

**Wednesday 14 May**

| | |
|---|---|
| Stirlingshire | Thorntree, Arnprior |

**Thursday 15 May**

| | |
|---|---|
| Perth & Kinross | Rossie House, Forgandenny |

**Friday 16 May**

| | |
|---|---|
| Dumfriesshire | Drumpark, Irongray |

**Saturday 17 May**

| | |
|---|---|
| Edinburgh & West Lothian | Redcroft, Edinburgh |

**Sunday 18 May**

| | |
|---|---|
| Angus | Dunninald, Montrose |
| Dunbartonshire | Shandon Gardens, Shandon |
| Edinburgh & West Lothian | Moray Place and Bank Gardens, Edinburgh |
| Fife | Northwood Cottage, Newport-on-Tay |
| Fife | St Monans Village Gardens, St Monans |
| Fife | Tayfield, Forgan |
| Fife | Willowhill, Forgan |
| Kirkcudbrightshire | Netherhall, Glenlochar |
| Moray & Nairn | Newbold House, Forres |
| Perth & Kinross | Briglands House, Rumbling Bridge |
| Renfrewshire | Duchal, Kilmacolm |
| Stirlingshire | Dun Dubh, Aberfoyle |
| Wigtownshire | Logan House Gardens, Port Logan |

**Wednesday 21 May**

| | |
|---|---|
| Ross, Cromarty, Skye & Inverness | Inverewe Garden and Estate, Poolewe |

**Friday 23 May**

| | |
|---|---|
| Dumfriesshire | Drumpark, Irongray |

**Saturday 24 May**

| | |
|---|---|
| Angus | Gallery, Montrose |
| Argyll | Maolachy's Garden, Lochavich |
| Argyll | Strachur House Flower & Woodland Gardens, Strachur |
| Fife | Tayport Gardens, Tayport |
| Perth & Kinross | Wester House of Ross, Comrie |
| Ross, Cromarty, Skye & Inverness | Oldtown of Leys Garden, Inverness |

**Sunday 25 May**

| | |
|---|---|
| Angus | 33 Ireland Street, Carnoustie |
| Angus | West Scryne Farm, Carnoustie |
| Argyll | Crarae Garden, Inveraray |
| Argyll | Maolachy's Garden, Lochavich |
| Argyll | Strachur House Flower & Woodland Gardens, Strachur |
| Ayrshire | Gardening Leave, SAC Auchincruive |
| Dumfriesshire | Cowhill Tower, Holywood |
| Fife | Tayport Gardens, Tayport |
| Fife | Wemyss Castle Gardens, Coaltown of Wemyss |
| Kincardine & Deeside | Woodend House, Banchory |

| | |
|---|---|
| Kirkcudbrightshire | Corsock House, Corsock |
| Lochaber & Badenoch | Aberarder, Kinlochlaggan |
| Lochaber & Badenoch | Ardverikie, Kinlochlaggan |
| Peeblesshire | Haystoun, Peebles |
| Perth & Kinross | Wester House of Ross, Comrie |
| Renfrewshire | Carruth, Bridge of Weir |
| Ross, Cromarty, Skye & Inverness | Aultgowrie Mill, Aultgowrie, Urray |
| Stirlingshire | Buchlyvie Gardens, Buchlyvie |
| Stirlingshire | The Linns, Sheriffmuir |
| Wigtownshire | Logan Botanic Garden, Port Logan |

**Wednesday 28 May**

| | |
|---|---|
| Aberdeenshire | Cruickshank Botanic Gardens, Aberdeen |
| Ross, Cromarty, Skye & Inverness | House of Gruinard, Laide, by Achnasheen |

**Thursday 29 May**

| | |
|---|---|
| Aberdeenshire | Leith Hall Garden, Huntly |
| Fife | Special Evening Openings, South Flisk and Willowhill |
| Perth & Kinross | Rossie House, Forgandenny |

**Saturday 31 May**

| | |
|---|---|
| Fife | Earlshall Castle, Leuchars |
| Fife | Newton Mains and Newton Barns, Auchtermuchty |

## June

**Sunday 1 June**

| | |
|---|---|
| Aberdeenshire | Dunlugas, Turriff |
| Aberdeenshire | Kildrummy Castle Gardens, Alford |
| Aberdeenshire | Tillypronie, Tarland |
| Angus | Cortachy Castle, Cortachy |
| Ayrshire | Borlandhills, Dunlop |
| East Lothian | Stenton Village, East Lothian |
| Edinburgh & West Lothian | The Glasshouses at the Royal Botanic Garden, Edinburgh |
| Fife | Lindores House, by Newburgh |
| Fife | Newton Mains and Newton Barns, Auchtermuchty |
| Fife | Northwood Cottage, St Fort Farm, Newport-on-Tay |
| Perth & Kinross | Pitcurran House, Abernethy |
| Ross, Cromarty, Skye & Inverness | Novar, Evanton |
| Stirlingshire | Arndean, by Dollar |
| Wigtownshire | Claymoddie Garden, Whithorn |

**Wednesday 4 June**

| | |
|---|---|
| Perth & Kinross | Tullichettle, Comrie |
| Ross, Cromarty, Skye & Inverness | Inverewe Garden and Estate, Poolewe |

**Thursday 5 June**

| | |
|---|---|
| Fife | Special Evening Openings, South Flisk and Willowhill |
| Ross, Cromarty, Skye & Inverness | Dundonnell House, Dundonnell, Little Loch Broom |

**Saturday 7 June**

| | |
|---|---|
| Ayrshire | Holmes Farm, Drybridge |
| Caithness, Sutherland, Orkney & Shetland | Amat, Ardgay |
| East Lothian | Dirleton Village, North Berwick |
| Fife | Fife Garden Festival |
| Glasgow & District | Kew Terrace Secret Gardens, Glasgow |
| Perth & Kinross | Blair Castle Gardens, Blair Atholl |

**Sunday 8 June**

| | |
|---|---|
| Aberdeenshire | Birken Cottage, Burnhervie |
| Ayrshire | Holmes Farm, Drybridge |
| Berwickshire | Swinton Mill House, Coldstream |
| Caithness, Sutherland, Orkney & Shetland | Amat, Ardgay |
| Dumfriesshire | Dunesslin, Dunscore |
| Dumfriesshire | Newtonairds Lodge, Newtonairds |
| East Lothian | Dirleton Village, North Berwick |
| East Lothian | Inveresk Village, Musselburgh |
| Edinburgh & West Lothian | Rocheid Garden, Edinburgh |
| Fife | Fife Garden Festival |
| Glasgow & District | Crossburn, Milngavie |
| Kincardine & Deeside | Inchmarlo House Garden, Inchmarlo |
| Perth & Kinross | Explorers Garden, Pitlochry |
| Ross, Cromarty, Skye & Inverness | Field House, Belladrum |
| Stirlingshire | Dunblane Community Gardens, Dunblane |
| Stirlingshire | The Linns, Sheriffmuir |

**Wednesday 11 June**

| | |
|---|---|
| Perth & Kinross | Tullichettle, Comrie |
| Ross, Cromarty, Skye & Inverness | Gorthleck , Stratherrick |

**Thursday 12 June**

| | |
|---|---|
| Fife | Special Evening Openings, South Flisk and Willowhill |
| Kirkcudbrightshire | Broughton House Garden, Kirkcudbright |

**Saturday 14 June**

| | |
|---|---|
| Edinburgh & West Lothian | Dr Neil's Garden, Duddingston Village |
| Fife | Blebo Craigs Village Gardens |
| Lochaber & Badenoch | Arisaig House, Beasdale, Arisaig |
| Midlothian | Kevock Garden, Lasswade |
| Moray & Nairn | Carestown Steading, Deskford, Buckie |
| Ross, Cromarty, Skye & Inverness | Hugh Miller's Birthplace Cottage & Museum, Cromarty |

**Sunday 15 June**

| | |
|---|---|
| Angus | Letham Village, Letham |
| Ayrshire | 1 Burnside Cottages, Sundrum |

| | |
|---|---|
| Berwickshire | Wellfield, Horndean |
| Caithness, Sutherland, Orkney & Shetland | Keldaberg, Cunningsburgh |
| East Lothian | Longniddry Gardens |
| Edinburgh & West Lothian | Dr Neil's Garden, Duddingston Village |
| Ettrick & Lauderdale | 2 Whytbank Row, Clovenfords |
| Fife | Blebo Craigs Village Gardens |
| Glasgow & District | Greenbank Garden, Clarkston |
| Kincardine & Deeside | Kincardine, Kincardine O'Neil |
| Lanarkshire | Dippoolbank Cottage, Carnwath |
| Midlothian | Kevock Garden, Lasswade |
| Perth & Kinross | The Old Manse, Caputh |
| Stirlingshire | Stirling Gardens |
| Wigtownshire | Castle Kennedy and Gardens, Stranraer |

**Tuesday 17 June**

| | |
|---|---|
| East Lothian | East Lothian Garden Trail |

**Wednesday 18 June**

| | |
|---|---|
| East Lothian | East Lothian Garden Trail |
| Perth & Kinross | Tullichettle, Comrie |

**Thursday 19 June**

| | |
|---|---|
| East Lothian | East Lothian Garden Trail |

**Friday 20 June**

| | |
|---|---|
| East Lothian | East Lothian Garden Trail |

**Saturday 21 June**

| | |
|---|---|
| Caithness, Sutherland, Orkney & Shetland | Keldaberg, Cunningsburgh |
| East Lothian | East Lothian Garden Trail |
| Ross, Cromarty, Skye & Inverness | Rhuba Phoil Forest Gardens, Isle of Skye |

**Sunday 22 June**

| | |
|---|---|
| Angus | Edzell Village & Castle, Edzell |
| Ayrshire | Gardens of West Kilbride and Seamill |
| Caithness, Sutherland, Orkney & Shetland | Keldaberg, Cunningsburgh |
| Caithness, Sutherland, Orkney & Shetland | Orkney Garden Trail |
| Dumfriesshire | Dalgonar |
| East Lothian | Gifford Village |
| Edinburgh & West Lothian | Merchiston Cottage, Edinburgh |
| Ettrick & Lauderdale | Harmony Garden, Melrose |
| Ettrick & Lauderdale | Laidlawstiel, Clovenfords |
| Ettrick & Lauderdale | Priorwood Gardens, Melrose |
| Fife | Culross Palace Garden, Culross |
| Fife | Greenhead Farm and Blair Adam House |
| Fife | Wormit Village Gardens |
| Kincardine & Deeside | Ecclesgreig Castle, St Cyrus |
| Lanarkshire | Allium Croft, Braehead |
| Lochaber & Badenoch | Craigmore Mill, Nethybridge |

| | |
|---|---|
| Midlothian | The Old Sun Inn, Newbattle |
| Perth & Kinross | Bonhard Garden, Perth |
| Perth & Kinross | Carig Dhubh, Bonskeid |
| Perth & Kinross | Hollytree Lodge, Muckhart |
| Renfrewshire | Newmills Cottage, nr Lochwinnoch |
| Ross, Cromarty, Skye & Inverness | House of Aigas and Field Centre, by Beauly |
| Stirlingshire | Settie, Kippen |
| Stirlingshire | Thorntree, Arnprior |
| Wigtownshire | Woodfall Gardens, Glasserton |

**Monday 23 June**

| | |
|---|---|
| Ross, Cromarty, Skye & Inverness | Coiltie Garden, Divach |

**Tuesday 24 June**

| | |
|---|---|
| Ross, Cromarty, Skye & Inverness | Coiltie Garden, Divach |

**Wednesday 25 June**

| | |
|---|---|
| Perth & Kinross | Tullichettle, Comrie |
| Ross, Cromarty, Skye & Inverness | Coiltie Garden, Divach |

**Thursday 26 June**

| | |
|---|---|
| Aberdeenshire | Leith Hall Garden, Huntly |
| Ross, Cromarty, Skye & Inverness | Coiltie Garden, Divach |

**Friday 27 June**

| | |
|---|---|
| Ross, Cromarty, Skye & Inverness | Coiltie Garden, Divach |

**Saturday 28 June**

| | |
|---|---|
| Argyll | The Shore Villages, by Dunoon |
| Fife | Crail: Small Gardens in the Burgh |
| Kirkcudbrightshire | The Limes, Kirkcudbright |
| Moray & Nairn | Cuddy's Well, Clephanton |
| Perth & Kinross | The Bield at Blackruthven, Tibbermore |
| Ross, Cromarty, Skye & Inverness | Coiltie Garden, Divach |

**Sunday 29 June**

| | |
|---|---|
| Argyll | The Shore Villages, by Dunoon |
| Ayrshire | 10 Grange Terrace with The Allotments of Annanhill Park, Kilmarnock |
| Berwickshire | Lennel Bank, Coldstream |
| Caithness, Sutherland, Orkney & Shetland | Orkney Garden Trail |
| Caithness, Sutherland, Orkney & Shetland | Pentland Firth Gardens, Dunnet |
| East Lothian | Tyninghame House, Dunbar |
| Fife | Crail: Small Gardens in the Burgh |
| Fife | Earlshall Castle, Leuchars |
| Isle of Arran | Dougarie |
| Kirkcudbrightshire | Brooklands, Crocketford |
| Kirkcudbrightshire | Cally Gardens, Gatehouse of Fleet |
| Midlothian | Broomieknowe Gardens, Lasswade |

| | |
|---|---|
| Moray & Nairn | Cuddy's Well, Inverness |
| Perth & Kinross | Cloichfoldich, Strathtay |
| Perth & Kinross | Pitnacree House, Pitnacree |
| Ross, Cromarty, Skye & Inverness | Coiltie Garden, Divach |
| Stirlingshire | Bridge of Allan Gardens, Bridge of Allan |

**Monday 30 June**

| | |
|---|---|
| Ross, Cromarty, Skye & Inverness | Coiltie Garden, Divach |

## July

**Tuesday 1 July**

| | |
|---|---|
| Ross, Cromarty, Skye & Inverness | Coiltie Garden, Divach |

**Wednesday 2 July**

| | |
|---|---|
| Caithness, Sutherland, Orkney & Shetland | The Castle & Gardens of Mey, Mey |
| Ettrick & Lauderdale | Carolside , Earlston |
| Peeblesshire | Portmore, Eddleston |
| Ross, Cromarty, Skye & Inverness | Coiltie Garden, Divach |
| Stirlingshire | Row House, Dunblane |

**Thursday 3 July**

| | |
|---|---|
| Ross, Cromarty, Skye & Inverness | Coiltie Garden, Divach |

**Friday 4 July**

| | |
|---|---|
| Ross, Cromarty, Skye & Inverness | Coiltie Garden, Divach |

**Saturday 5 July**

| | |
|---|---|
| Angus | Airlie Castle, by Kirriemuir |
| Ross, Cromarty, Skye & Inverness | Coiltie Garden, Divach |
| Roxburghshire | Corbet Tower, Morebattle |

**Sunday 6 July**

| | |
|---|---|
| Aberdeenshire | Bruckhills Croft, Rothienorman |
| Aberdeenshire | Leith Hall Garden, Huntly |
| Berwickshire | Angus Cottage, Preston |
| Berwickshire | Cumledge Mill House, Duns |
| Caithness, Sutherland, Orkney & Shetland | Bighouse Lodge, by Melvich |
| Caithness, Sutherland, Orkney & Shetland | Orkney Garden Trail |
| Isle of Arran | Brodick Castle & Country Park, Brodick |
| Kincardine & Deeside | Findrack, Torphins |
| Kirkcudbrightshire | Seabank, Merse Road, Rockcliffe |
| Ross, Cromarty, Skye & Inverness | Coiltie Garden, Divach |

**Wednesday 9 July**

| | |
|---|---|
| Ettrick & Lauderdale | Carolside , Earlston |
| Peeblesshire | Portmore, Eddleston |
| Ross, Cromarty, Skye & Inverness | House of Gruinard, Laide |

**Saturday 12 July**

| | |
|---|---|
| Aberdeenshire | Middle Cairncake, Cuminestown, Turriff |
| Angus | Gallery, Montrose |
| Perth & Kinross | Wester Cloquhat, Bridge of Cally |
| Roxburghshire | St Boswells Village Gardens |

**Sunday 13 July**

| | |
|---|---|
| Aberdeenshire | Middle Cairncake, Cuminestown |
| Ayrshire | Cairnhall House, Ochiltree |
| Berwickshire | Anton's Hill and Walled Garden, Leitholm |
| Caithness, Sutherland, Orkney & Shetland | Orkney Garden Trail |
| Dumfriesshire | Newtonairds Lodge, Newtonairds |
| Edinburgh & West Lothian | 4 Harelaw Road, Edinburgh |
| Fife | Logie House, Crossford |
| Kincardine & Deeside | Douneside House, Tarland |
| Kirkcudbrightshire | Southwick House, Southwick |
| Lanarkshire | Covington House, Thankerton |
| Lanarkshire | Lindsaylands, Biggar |
| Moray & Nairn | 1 Sanquhar Drive, Forres |
| Moray & Nairn | 10 Pilmuir Road West, Forres |
| Moray & Nairn | Newbold House, Forres |
| Peeblesshire | Drumelzier Old Manse, Drumelzier |
| Roxburghshire | Yetholm Village Gardens |

**Monday 14 July**

| | |
|---|---|
| Kirkcudbrightshire | Southwick House, Southwick |

**Tuesday 15 July**

| | |
|---|---|
| Ayrshire | Culzean, Maybole |
| Kirkcudbrightshire | Southwick House, Southwick |

**Wednesday 16 July**

| | |
|---|---|
| Caithness, Sutherland, Orkney & Shetland | The Castle & Gardens of Mey, Mey |
| Ettrick & Lauderdale | Carolside , Earlston |
| Kirkcudbrightshire | Southwick House, Southwick |
| Peeblesshire | Portmore, Eddleston |
| Stirlingshire | Thorntree, Arnprior |

**Thursday 17 July**

| | |
|---|---|
| Kirkcudbrightshire | Southwick House, Southwick |

**Friday 18 July**

| | |
|---|---|
| Kirkcudbrightshire | Southwick House, Southwick |

**Saturday 19 July**

| | |
|---|---|
| Argyll | Caol Ruadh, Colintraive |
| Roxburghshire | Newcastleton Village Gardens |

**Sunday 20 July**

| | |
|---|---|
| Angus | The Walled Garden at Logie, Kirriemuir |
| Argyll | Caol Ruadh, Colintraive |
| Ayrshire | Kilmaurs Village Gardens, Kilmaurs |
| Berwickshire | Netherbyres, Eyemouth |
| Caithness, Sutherland, Orkney & Shetland | Lea Gardens, Tresta |
| Edinburgh & West Lothian | Hunter's Tryst, Edinburgh |
| Fife | Northwood Cottage, St Fort Farm |
| Fife | Willowhill, Forgan |
| Kincardine & Deeside | Mill of Benholm Project, Benholm |
| Kirkcudbrightshire | Anwoth House, Anwoth |
| Kirkcudbrightshire | Anwoth Old Schoolhouse, Anwoth |
| Lanarkshire | Dippoolbank Cottage, Carnwath |
| Midlothian | Pomathorn Gardens, Penicuik |
| Peeblesshire | 8 Halmyre Mains, West Linton |
| Perth & Kinross | Auchleeks House, Calvine |
| Roxburghshire | West Leas, Bonchester Bridge |
| Wigtownshire | Damnaglaur Gardens, Drummore |

**Tuesday 22 July**

| | |
|---|---|
| Stirlingshire | Gean House, Alloa |

**Wednesday 23 July**

| | |
|---|---|
| Ettrick & Lauderdale | Carolside , Earlston |
| Peeblesshire | Portmore, Eddleston |

**Saturday 26 July**

| | |
|---|---|
| Caithness, Sutherland, Orkney & Shetland | House of Tongue, Tongue, Lairg |
| Caithness, Sutherland, Orkney & Shetland | Keldaberg, Cunningsburgh |
| East Lothian | Greywalls, Gullane |
| Edinburgh & West Lothian | 45 Northfield Crescent, Longridge |
| Edinburgh & West Lothian | 9 Braid Farm Road, Edinburgh |
| Kincardine & Deeside | Crathes Castle Garden, Banchory |
| Lochaber & Badenoch | Glenkyllachy Lodge, Tomatin |

**Sunday 27 July**

| | |
|---|---|
| Aberdeenshire | Birken Cottage, Burnhervie |
| Aberdeenshire | Glenkindie House, Glenkindie |
| Argyll | Ardchattan Priory, North Connel |
| Argyll | Crarae Garden, Inveraray |
| Caithness, Sutherland, Orkney & Shetland | Keldaberg, Cunningsburgh |
| Caithness, Sutherland, Orkney & Shetland | Langwell, Berriedale |
| Edinburgh & West Lothian | 45 Northfield Crescent, Longridge |
| Edinburgh & West Lothian | 9 Braid Farm Road, Edinburgh |
| Fife | Balcaskie, Pittenweem |
| Fife | Kellie Castle Garden, Pittenweem |
| Kincardine & Deeside | Mallamauch, Banchory |
| Kirkcudbrightshire | Glensone Walled Garden, Southwick |

| | |
|---|---|
| Lanarkshire | Wellbutts, Elsrickle |
| Lochaber & Badenoch | Glenkyllachy Lodge, Tomatin |
| Midlothian | Newhall, Carlops |
| Perth & Kinross | Croftcat Lodge, Grandtully |
| Perth & Kinross | Kincarrathie House, Perth |
| Ross, Cromarty, Skye & Inverness | House of Aigas and Field Centre, by Beauly |
| Stirlingshire | The Tors, Falkirk |
| Wigtownshire | Lochnaw Castle, Lochnaw, by Leswalt |

**Wednesday 30 July**

| | |
|---|---|
| Ettrick & Lauderdale | Carolside , Earlston |
| Peeblesshire | Portmore, Eddleston |
| Stirlingshire | Row House, Dunblane |

**Thursday 31 July**

| | |
|---|---|
| Aberdeenshire | Leith Hall Garden, Huntly |

## August

**Saturday 2 August**

| | |
|---|---|
| Aberdeenshire | Pitscurry Project, Whiteford |
| Argyll | Melfort House Kitchen Garden, Kilmelford |

**Sunday 3 August**

| | |
|---|---|
| Aberdeenshire | Pitscurry Project, Whiteford |
| Argyll | Melfort House Kitchen Garden, Kilmelford |
| Ayrshire | Glen Gardens of Largs |
| Caithness, Sutherland, Orkney & Shetland | Thurso Gardens |
| Dunbartonshire | Geilston Garden, Cardross |
| Glasgow & District | Kilsyth Gardens, Kilsyth |
| Glasgow & District | Watch Us Grow, Palacerigg Country Park |
| Kincardine & Deeside | Glenbervie House, Drumlithie |
| Moray & Nairn | Castleview, Auchindoun |
| Moray & Nairn | Glenrinnes Lodge, Dufftown |
| Peeblesshire | Glen House, Innerleithen |
| Perth & Kinross | Drummond Castle Gardens, Crieff |
| Perth & Kinross | The Walled Garden, Perth |
| Ross, Cromarty, Skye & Inverness | Woodview, Highfield |

**Monday 4 August**

| | |
|---|---|
| Aberdeenshire | Pitscurry Project, Whiteford |

**Tuesday 5 August**

| | |
|---|---|
| Aberdeenshire | Pitscurry Project, Whiteford |

**Wednesday 6 August**

| | |
|---|---|
| Aberdeenshire | Pitscurry Project, Whiteford |
| Peeblesshire | Portmore, Eddleston |

**Thursday 7 August**

| | |
|---|---|
| Aberdeenshire | Pitscurry Project, Whiteford |

**Friday 8 August**

| | |
|---|---|
| Aberdeenshire | Pitscurry Project, Whiteford |

**Saturday 9 August**

| | |
|---|---|
| Aberdeenshire | Pitscurry Project, Whiteford |
| Ayrshire | Kirkmuir Cottage, Stewarton |
| Caithness, Sutherland, Orkney & Shetland | Keldaberg, Cunningsburgh |

**Sunday 10 August**

| | |
|---|---|
| Aberdeenshire | Pitmedden Garden, Ellon |
| Aberdeenshire | Pitscurry Project, Whiteford |
| Caithness, Sutherland, Orkney & Shetland | Keldaberg, Cunningsburgh |
| Dunbartonshire | Queen Street Gardens, Helensburgh |
| Fife | Falkland Palace and Garden, Falkland |
| Kirkcudbrightshire | Crofts, Kirkpatrick Durham |
| Kirkcudbrightshire | Threave Garden, Castle Douglas |
| Peeblesshire | West Linton Village Gardens |
| Ross, Cromarty, Skye & Inverness | Aultgowrie Mill, Aultgowrie, Urray |
| Wigtownshire | Balker Farmhouse, Stranraer |

**Wednesday 13 August**

| | |
|---|---|
| Lochaber & Badenoch | Canna House Walled Garden, Isle of Canna |
| Peeblesshire | Portmore, Eddleston |

**Thursday 14 August**

| | |
|---|---|
| Ross, Cromarty, Skye & Inverness | Dundonnell House, Dundonnell |

**Saturday 16 August**

| | |
|---|---|
| Caithness, Sutherland, Orkney & Shetland | The Castle & Gardens of Mey, Mey |

**Sunday 17 August**

| | |
|---|---|
| Aberdeenshire | Haddo House, Methlick |
| Angus | Ninewells Community Garden |
| Dunbartonshire | 8 Laggary Park, Rhu |
| Kirkcudbrightshire | Cally Gardens, Gatehouse of Fleet |
| Lanarkshire | Culter Allers, Coulter |
| Ross, Cromarty, Skye & Inverness | Cardon, Balnafoich, Farr |
| Stirlingshire | Killearn Village Gardens |

**Wednesday 20 August**

| | |
|---|---|
| Peeblesshire | Portmore, Eddleston |
| Stirlingshire | Thorntree, Arnprior |

**Sunday 24 August**

| | |
|---|---|
| Aberdeenshire | Tillypronie, Tarland |
| Stirlingshire | Rowberrow, Dollar |

**Wednesday 27 August**

| | |
|---|---|
| Peeblesshire | Portmore, Eddleston |

**Thursday 28 August**

| | |
|---|---|
| Aberdeenshire | Leith Hall Garden, Huntly |

**Sunday 31 August**

| | |
|---|---|
| Aberdeenshire | Haddo House, Methlick |
| Perth & Kinross | Mill of Fyall Cottage, Alyth |
| Stirlingshire | The Pineapple, nr Airth |

## September

**Sunday 7 September**

| | |
|---|---|
| Kincardine & Deeside | Fasque House, Fettercairn |
| Lochaber & Badenoch | Roshven House, Lochailort |
| Moray & Nairn | Gordonstoun, Duffus |

**Thursday 11 September**

| | |
|---|---|
| Ross, Cromarty, Skye & Inverness | Dundonnell House, Dundonnell |

**Sunday 14 September**

| | |
|---|---|
| Stirlingshire | Dun Dubh, Aberfoyle |

**Sunday 21 September**

| | |
|---|---|
| Kincardine & Deeside | Drum Castle Garden, Drumoak |
| Stirlingshire | Gargunnock House, Gargunnock |

**Sunday 28 September**

| | |
|---|---|
| Aberdeenshire | Kildrummy Castle Gardens, Alford |

## October

**Sunday 5 October**

| | |
|---|---|
| Peeblesshire | Dawyck Botanic Garden, Stobo |
| Stirlingshire | Little Broich, Kippen |

**Sunday 19 October**

| | |
|---|---|
| Kincardine & Deeside | Inchmarlo House Garden, Inchmarlo |

**Saturday 25 October**

| | |
|---|---|
| Fife | Northwood Cottage, St Fort Farm |

**Sunday 26 October**

| | |
|---|---|
| Fife | Northwood Cottage, St Fort Farm |

## December

**Saturday 6 December**

| | |
|---|---|
| Aberdeenshire | Leith Hall Garden, Huntly |

# GLORIOUS GARDENS OPEN BY ARRANGEMENT

Our garden owners look forward to welcoming you to these fabulous gardens which are listed on pages 65 to 68.
Please do not hesitate to contact them.

Laundry Cottage, Aberdeenshire

Kirkside of Lochty, Angus

Parkhead, Perthshire

Carnell, Ayrshire

Laverockdale House, Edinburgh

Craichlaw, Wigtownshire

# GARDENS OPEN BY ARRANGEMENT

## Aberdeenshire

| | |
|---|---|
| Bruckhills Croft, Rothienorman | 1 March - 31 March |
| Grandhome, Danestone | 1 April - 31 October |
| Greenridge, Cults | 1 July - 31 August |
| Hatton Castle, Turriff | On request |
| Knockmuir, Auchry | 30 June - 25 August |
| Laundry Cottage, Culdrain | On request |
| Middle Cairncake, Cuminestown | 14 July - 10 August |
| Tillypronie, Tarland | 2 January - 31 December |
| Westfield Lodge, Aberdeen | 26 July - 1 August |

## Angus

| | |
|---|---|
| Gallery, Montrose | 1 May - 30 September |
| Kirkside of Lochty, Menmuir | 1 March - 31 October |
| Kirkton House, Kirkton of Craig | 1 May - 30 September |
| The Garden Cottage, Dunnichen | 1 May - 31 August |

## Argyll

| | |
|---|---|
| Drim na Vullin, Lochgilphead | 17 May - 31 May |

## Ayrshire

| | |
|---|---|
| Carnell, by Hurlford | 1 May - 15 September |

## Berwickshire

| | |
|---|---|
| Anton's Hill and Walled Garden, Leitholm | On request |
| Lennel Bank, Coldstream | On request |
| Netherbyres, Eyemouth | 1 May - 31 August |

## Caithness, Sutherland, Orkney & Shetland

| | |
|---|---|
| Caergarth, Scatness | 15 June - 31 August |
| Cruisdale, Sandness | 1 March - 31 October |
| Gerdi, Hillswick | 1 July - 31 August |
| Highlands, East Voe | 1 March - 31 October |
| Keldaberg, Cunningsburgh | 1 June - 31 August |
| Langwell, Berriedale | On request |
| Nonavaar, Levenwick | 1 March - 12 September |
| Norby, Burnside | 1 March - 31 October |

## Dumfriesshire

| | |
|---|---|
| Grovehill House , Burnhead | 1 April - 30 September |

## Dunbartonshire

| | |
|---|---|
| Parkhead, Rosneath | On request |

## East Lothian

| | |
|---|---|
| Bowerhouse, Dunbar | 14 April - 27 September |
| Humbie Dean, Humbie | 17 April - 31 July |
| Stobshiel House , Humbie | 17 June - 21 June |

## Edinburgh & West Lothian

| | |
|---|---|
| 101 Greenbank Crescent, Edinburgh | 1 March - 31 October |
| 61 Fountainhall Road, Edinburgh | 1 August - 31 October |
| Hunter's Tryst, Edinburgh | On request |
| Laverockdale House, Edinburgh | 1 August - 31 August |
| Rocheid Garden, Edinburgh | On request |

## Fife

| | |
|---|---|
| Barham, Bow of Fife | 1 April - 31 July |
| Earlshall Castle, Leuchars | On request |
| Glassmount House, by Kirkcaldy | 1 April - 30 September |
| Helensbank, Kincardine | 1 June - 30 June |
| Kirklands, Saline | 1 April - 30 September |
| Logie House, Crossford | 1 April - 30 September |
| Northwood Cottage, Newport-on-Tay | 1 May - 31 October |
| Rosewells, Pitscottie | 1 April - 30 September |
| South Flisk, Blebo Craigs | 1 May - 30 June |
| Strathairly House, Upper Largo | 1 April - 31 August |
| Teasses Gardens, near Ceres | On request |
| The Tower, Wormit | 1 April - 30 September |
| Willowhill, Forgan | 2 June - 29 August |
| Wormiston House, Crail | 1 April - 30 September |

## Glasgow & District

| | |
|---|---|
| Kilsyth Gardens, Kilsyth | 1 April - 30 September |

## Kincardine & Deeside

| | |
|---|---|
| 14 Arbeadie Avenue, Banchory | 1 June - 31 July |

## Kirkcudbrightshire

| | |
|---|---|
| Barholm Castle, Gatehouse of Fleet | 1 February - 1 September |
| Corsock House, Corsock | 1 April - 30 June |
| Cosy Cottage, Borgue | 1 July - 31 August |

| | |
|---|---|
| Steadstone, Dalbeattie | 1 January - 30 November |
| Stockarton, Kirkcudbright | 1 April - 31 August |
| The Mill House at Gelston, Gelston | 13 July - 14 September |
| The Waterhouse Gardens at Stockarton, Kirkcudbright | 1 April - 30 September |

## Lanarkshire

| | |
|---|---|
| Baitlaws, Lamington | 1 June - 31 August |
| Biggar Park, Biggar | 1 May - 31 July |
| Carmichael Mill, Hyndford Bridge | On request |
| The Scots Mining Company House, Biggar | On request |

## Lochaber & Badenoch

| | |
|---|---|
| Ard-Daraich, Ardgour | On request |

## Midlothian

| | |
|---|---|
| Newhall, Carlops | 1 May - 31 August |

## Moray & Nairn

| | |
|---|---|
| 10 Pilmuir Road West, Forres | 1 June - 30 August |
| Bruntlands Bungalow, Elgin | 1 May - 30 September |

## Peeblesshire

| | |
|---|---|
| Portmore, Eddleston | 1 June - 30 September |
| Stobo Japanese Water Garden, Stobo | 1 May - 31 October |

## Perth & Kinross

| | |
|---|---|
| Briglands House, Rumbling Bridge | 1 March - 30 June |
| Briglands House, Rumbling Bridge | 1 October - 31 December |
| Carig Dhubh, Bonskeid | 15 May - 15 October |
| Croftcat Lodge, Grandtully | 15 May - 15 October |
| Easter Meikle Fardle, Meikleour | On request |
| Little Tombuie, Killiechassie, Aberfeldy | 15 May - 15 October |
| Parkhead House, Perth | 1 June - 31 August |

## Ross, Cromarty, Skye & Inverness

| | |
|---|---|
| Brackla Wood, Culbokie, Dingwall | 1 April - 30 September |
| Dundonnell House, Little Loch Broom | 1 April - 30 November |
| Dunvegan Castle and Gardens, Isle of Skye | 6 January - 31 March and 16 October - 31 December |
| House of Aigas and Field Centre, by Beauly | 1 March - 25 October |
| Leathad Ard, Upper Carloway, Isle of Lewis | 1 April - 30 September |
| The Lookout, Kilmuir | On request |

## Roxburghshire

| | |
|---|---|
| Lanton Tower, Jedburgh | On request |
| West Leas, Bonchester Bridge | On request |

## Stirlingshire

| | |
|---|---|
| Arndean, by Dollar | 15 May - 15 June |
| Camallt, Fintry | 1 April - 15 May |
| Duntreath Castle, Blanefield | On request |
| Kilbryde Castle, Dunblane | 15 February - 31 October |
| Milseybank, Bridge of Allan | 1 April - 31 May |
| Tamano, by Braco | 29 September - 12 October |
| The Tors, Falkirk | 1 May - 30 September |

## Wigtownshire

| | |
|---|---|
| Castle Kennedy and Gardens, Stranraer | 1 November - 31 December |
| Claymoddie Garden, Whithorn | 1 April - 30 September |
| Craichlaw, Kirkcowan | On request |
| Dunskey Gardens and Maze, Portpatrick | 2 February - 15 March |
| Woodfall Gardens, Glasserton | On request |

# GARDENS OPEN ON A REGULAR BASIS

## Aberdeenshire

| | |
|---|---|
| Fyvie Castle, Fyvie | 1 July - 31 October |

## Angus

| | |
|---|---|
| Dunninald, Montrose | 28 June - 27 July not Mondays |
| Gagie House, Duntrune | 23 February - 25 May |
| Pitmuies Gardens, Guthrie | 1 February - 16 March & 1 April - 31 October |

## Argyll

| | |
|---|---|
| Achnacloich, Connel | 29 March - 1 November Saturdays |
| An Cala, Ellenabeich | 1 April - 31 October |
| Ardchattan Priory, North Connel | 1 April - 31 October |
| Ardkinglas Woodland Garden, Cairndow | 1 January - 31 December |
| Ardmaddy Castle, by Oban | 1 January - 31 December |
| Barguillean's "Angus Garden", Taynuilt | 1 January - 31 December |
| Benmore Botanic Garden, Benmore | 1 March - 31 October |
| Crinan Hotel Garden, Crinan | 1 May - 31 August |
| Druimneil House, Port Appin | 17 April - 31 October |
| Fairwinds, Dunoon | 1 April - 31 October |
| Inveraray Castle Gardens, Inveraray | 1 April - 31 October |
| Kinlochlaich House Gardens, Appin | 1 January - 31 December<br>but closed Sundays & Mondays October - March |
| Oakbank, Ardrishaig | 1 May - 31 October |

## Berwickshire

| | |
|---|---|
| Bughtrig, near Leitholm | 1 June - 1 September |

## Caithness, Sutherland, Orkney & Shetland

| | |
|---|---|
| 15 Linkshouse , Mid Yell | 3 July - 7 August Thursdays |
| Caergarth, Scatness | 15 June - 31 August open most days -check first |
| Holmlea, Mid Yell | 6 July - 10 August Sundays |
| Lea Gardens, Tresta | 1 April - 31 October not Thursdays |
| Nonavaar, Levenwick | 1 March - 12 September Thursdays & Fridays |
| The Castle & Gardens of Mey, Mey | 7 May - 30 September but not 28 July - 9 August |

## Dunbartonshire

| | |
|---|---|
| Glenarn, Rhu | 21 March - 21 September |

## East Lothian

| | |
|---|---|
| Inwood, Carberry | 1 May - 30 August Tuesdays, Thursdays & Saturdays |
| Shepherd House, Inveresk | 18 February - 27 February Tuesday & Thursdays & 22 April - 10 July Tuesday & Thursdays |

## Edinburgh & West Lothian

| | |
|---|---|
| Newliston, Kirkliston | 1 May - 4 June not Mondays & Tuesdays |

## Fife

| | |
|---|---|
| Cambo House, Kingsbarns | 1 January - 31 December |
| Glassmount House, by Kirkcaldy | 1 April - 30 September Monday to Friday |
| Willowhill , Forgan | 4 June - 27 August Wednesdays |

## Kincardine & Deeside

| | |
|---|---|
| Drum Castle Garden, Drumoak | 2 July - 30 July |

## Lochaber & Badenoch

| | |
|---|---|
| Ardtornish, by Lochaline | 1 January - 31 December |

## Peeblesshire

| | |
|---|---|
| Dawyck Botanic Garden, Stobo | 1 February - 30 November |
| Kailzie Gardens, Peebles | 1 January - 31 December |

## Perth & Kinross

| | |
|---|---|
| Ardvorlich, Lochearnhead | 1 May - 1 June |
| Blair Castle Gardens, Blair Atholl | 1 April - 31 October |
| Bolfracks, Aberfeldy | 1 April - 31 October |
| Braco Castle, Braco | 1 March - 31 October |
| Cluny House, Aberfeldy | 1 January - 31 December |
| Dowhill, Cleish | 1 May - 31 May |
| Drummond Castle Gardens, Crieff | 1 May - 31 October |
| Glenbeich, Lochearnhead | 21 July - 3 August |
| Glendoick, by Perth | 1 April - 31 May |
| Glenericht House, Blairgowrie | 1 January - 31 December |

## Ross, Cromarty, Skye & Inverness

| | |
|---|---|
| Abriachan Garden Nursery, Loch Ness Side | 1 February - 30 November |
| Applecross Walled Garden, Strathcarron | 15 March - 31 October |
| Attadale, Strathcarron | 31 March - 31 October not Sundays |
| Balmeanach House, Struan | 5 May - 31 October Mondays & Thursdays |
| Brackla Wood, Culbokie | 21 May - 25 June Wednesdays |
| Clan Donald Skye, Armadale | 1 January - 31 December |
| Dunvegan Castle and Gardens, Isle of Skye | 1 April - 15 October |
| Highland Liliums, Kiltarlity | 1 January - 31 December |

| | |
|---|---|
| Leathad Ard, Upper Carloway | 2 June - 30 August not Friday & Sunday also not Wednesday & Thursday 6/7 August |
| Leckmelm Shrubbery & Arboretum, by Ullapool | 1 April - 31 October |
| Oldtown of Leys Garden, Inverness | 1 January - 31 December |
| The Lookout, Kilmuir, North Kessock | 1 May - 30 September Saturdays & Sundays |

## Roxburghshire

| | |
|---|---|
| Floors Castle, Kelso | 18 April - 31 October - check website for special closing days |
| Monteviot, Jedburgh | 1 April - 30 October |

## Stirlingshire

| | |
|---|---|
| Gargunnock House, Gargunnock | 1 February - 16 March daily & 14 April - 13 June weekdays |

## Wigtownshire

| | |
|---|---|
| Ardwell House Gardens, Ardwell | 1 April - 30 September |
| Castle Kennedy and Gardens, Stranraer | 1 February - 16 March weekends only |
| Castle Kennedy and Gardens, Stranraer | 1 April - 30 October |
| Claymoddie Garden, Whithorn | 1 April - 30 September Fridays, Saturdays & Sundays |
| Dunskey Gardens and Maze, Portpatrick | 18 April - October |
| Glenwhan Gardens, Dunragit | 1 April - 31 October |
| Logan Botanic Garden, Port Logan | 15 March - 31 October |

# PLANT SALES

| | | |
|---|---|---|
| **Fife** | | |
| Cambo House Spring Plant and Craft Fair, Kingsbarns | Sunday 13 April | 11:00am - 4:00pm |
| **Renfrewshire** | | |
| Kilmacolm Plant Sale, Kilmacolm | Saturday 19 April | 10:00am - 12:30pm |
| **Dunbartonshire** | | |
| Glenarn Plant Sale, Rhu | Sunday 4 May | 2:00pm - 5:00pm |
| **Stirlingshire** | | |
| Kilbryde Castle, Dunblane | Sunday 4 May | 2:00pm - 5:00pm |
| **Midlothian** | | |
| Vogrie Plant Sale (with Midlothian Council), Gorebridge | Saturday 24 May | 10:00am - 4:00pm |
| **Dunbartonshire** | | |
| 8 Laggary Park Plant Sale, Rhu | Sunday 15 June | 2:00pm - 5:00pm |
| **Fife** | | |
| Freuchie Plant Sale and the Garden at Karbet | Sunday 15 June | 12:00pm - 4:00pm |
| **Dunbartonshire** | | |
| Hill House Plant Sale, Helensburgh | Sunday 7 September | 11:00am - 4:00pm |
| **Renfrewshire** | | |
| St Fillan's Episcopal Church Plant Sale, Kilmacolm | Saturday 13 September | 10:00am - 12:30pm |
| **Stirlingshire** | | |
| Gargunnock House, Gargunnock | Sunday 21 September | 2:00pm - 5:00pm |
| **Fife** | | |
| Hill of Tarvit Plant Sale and Autumn Fair, Cupar | Sunday 5 October | 10:30am - 4:00pm |

*Escape to Auchlochan Village to see our beautifully landscaped grounds, mature woodlands, spectacular gardens and expansive lochs.*

# Auchlochan Gardens

Escape to Auchlochan Garden Village to see our beautifully landscaped grounds, mature woodlands, spectacular gardens and lochs.

The gardens at Auchlochan are its undoubted glory, offering a wide range of attractions to visitors, walkers and residents alike.

Laid out over a 50 acre estate, the gardens feature not only the lochs that gave the village its name, but stunning herbaceous borders, terrace gardens, rhododendron beds and heather gardens. Along the River Nethan valley, the gardens merge with mature woodland which feature our prominent Sequoiadendron giganteum - giant Redwoods - which are native to California.

At Auchlochan's heart is the delightful 1.5 acre walled garden. Built around 1900, the garden was originally designed as a source of fruit and vegetables for the estate. Under the care of the current gardening team it has been transformed into a show garden.

The Auchlochan grounds attract many visitors - there is a 4 Star B&B and self catering accommodation available all year round - and enjoy a relaxing cup of tea or coffee or even lunch in our bistro, at the same time.

ngs gardens open for charity
OVER 3,800 GARDENS OPEN FOR CHARITY IN ENGLAND AND WALES
The Nook, Cumbria Image: Val Corbett
For more information telephone 01483 211535 or visit our website www.ngs.org.uk
The National Gardens Scheme registered charity number 1112664

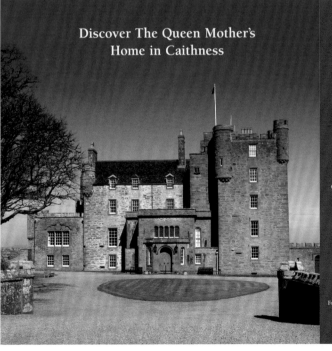

# GENERAL INFORMATION

### MAPS
A map of each district is provided at the start of each section. These show the location of gardens as per the postal codes provided. Directions can be found in the garden descriptions.

### HOUSES
Houses are not open unless specifically stated; where the house or part of the house is open, an additional charge is usually made.

### TOILETS
Private gardens do not normally have outside toilets. For security reasons owners have been advised not to admit visitors into their houses.

### PHOTOGRAPHY
No photographs taken in a garden may be used for sale or reproduction without the prior permission of the garden owner.

### CHILDREN
Children are always welcome but must be accompanied by an adult. Children's activities are often available at openings.

### CANCELLATIONS
All cancellations will be posted on our website www.scotlandsgardens.org

 New in 2014
 Teas
Cream teas
 Homemade teas
 Dogs on a lead allowed
 Wheelchair access
 Accommodation
 Plant stall
Scottish Snowdrop Festival

# MAP OF DISTRICTS

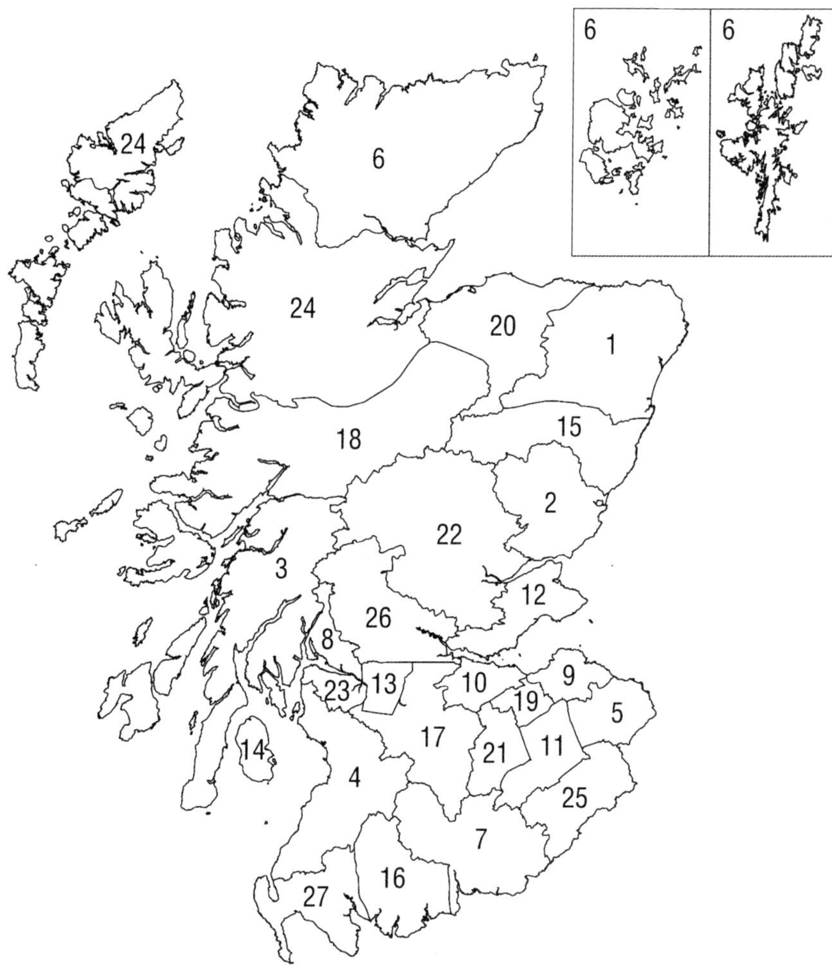


1. Aberdeenshire
2. Angus
3. Argyll
4. Ayrshire
5. Berwickshire
6. Caithness, Sutherland, Orkney & Shetland
7. Dumfriesshire
8. Dunbartonshire
9. East Lothian
10. Edinburgh & West Lothian
11. Ettrick & Lauderdale
12. Fife
13. Glasgow & District
14. Isle of Arran
15. Kincardine & Deeside
16. Kirkcudbrightshire
17. Lanarkshire
18. Lochaber & Badenoch
19. Midlothian
20. Moray & Nairn
21. Peeblesshire
22. Perth & Kinross
23. Renfrewshire
24. Ross, Cromarty, Skye & Inverness
25. Roxburghshire
26. Stirlingshire
27. Wigtownshire

# ABERDEENSHIRE



## District Organiser

| | |
|---|---|
| Mrs V Walters | Tillychetly, Alford AB33 8HQ |

## Area Organisers

| | |
|---|---|
| Mrs H Gibson | 6 The Chanonry, Old Aberdeen AB24 1RP |
| Mrs F G Lawson | Asloun, Alford AB33 8NR |
| Mrs Jan Oag | Old Balgove, Oldmeldrum, Inverurie AB51 0AX |
| Mrs Penny Orpwood | Middle Cairncake, Cuminestown, Turriff AB53 5YS |
| Mrs A Robertson | Drumblade House, Huntly AB54 6ER |
| Mrs F M K Tuck | Stable Cottage, Allargue, Gorgarff AB36 8YP |

## Treasurer

| | |
|---|---|
| Mr A H J Coleman | Templeton House, Arbroath DD11 4QP |

## Gardens open on a specific date

| | | | |
|---|---|---|---|
| Westhall Castle, Oyne | Sunday 20 April | 1:00pm | - 4:00pm |
| Leith Hall Garden, Huntly | Saturday 26 April | 7:00pm | |
| Castle Fraser Garden, Sauchen | Saturday 3 May | 11:00am | - 4:00pm |
| Castle Fraser Garden, Sauchen | Sunday 4 May | 11:00am | - 4:00pm |
| Cruickshank Botanic Gardens, Aberdeen | Wednesday 28 May | 6:30pm | - 8:30pm |
| Leith Hall Garden, Huntly | Thursday 29 May | 7:00pm | |
| Dunlugas, Turriff | Sunday 1 June | 2:00pm | - 5:00pm |
| Kildrummy Castle Gardens, Alford | Sunday 1 June | 10:00am | - 5:00pm |
| Tillypronie, Tarland | Sunday 1 June | 2:00pm | - 5:00pm |
| Birken Cottage, Burnhervie | Sunday 8 June | 2:00pm | - 5:00pm |
| Leith Hall Garden, Huntly | Thursday 26 June | 7:00pm | |
| Bruckhills Croft, Rothienorman | Sunday 6 July | 12:00pm | - 5:00pm |
| Leith Hall Garden, Huntly | Sunday 6 July | 12:00pm | - 4:00pm |
| Middle Cairncake, Cuminestown | Saturday 12 July | 12:30pm | - 5:00pm |
| Middle Cairncake, Cuminestown | Sunday 13 July | 12:30pm | - 5:00pm |
| Birken Cottage, Burnhervie | Sunday 27 July | 2:00pm | - 5:00pm |
| Glenkindie House, Glenkindie | Sunday 27 July | 2:00pm | - 5:00pm |
| Leith Hall Garden, Huntly | Thursday 31 July | 7:00pm | |
| Pitscurry Project, Whiteford | Saturday 2 August | 10:00am | - 3:00pm |
| Pitscurry Project, Whiteford | Sunday 3 August | 10:00am | - 3:00pm |
| Pitscurry Project, Whiteford | Monday 4 August | 10:00am | - 3:00pm |

| | | |
|---|---|---|
| Pitscurry Project, Whiteford | Tuesday 5 August | 10:00am - 3:00pm |
| Pitscurry Project, Whiteford | Wednesday 6 August | 10:00am - 3:00pm |
| Pitscurry Project, Whiteford | Thursday 7 August | 10:00am - 3:00pm |
| Pitscurry Project, Whiteford | Friday 8 August | 10:00am - 3:00pm |
| Pitscurry Project, Whiteford | Saturday 9 August | 10:00am - 3:00pm |
| Pitmedden Garden, Ellon | Sunday 10 August | 6:00pm - 8:00pm |
| Pitscurry Project, Whiteford | Sunday 10 August | 10:00am - 3:00pm |
| Haddo House, Methlick | Sunday 17 August | 11:00am - 5:00pm |
| Tillypronie, Tarland | Sunday 24 August | 2:00pm - 5:00pm |
| Leith Hall Garden, Huntly | Thursday 28 August | 7:00pm |
| Haddo House, Methlick | Sunday 31 August | 11:00am - 5:00pm |
| Kildrummy Castle Gardens, Alford | Sunday 28 September | 10:00am - 5:00pm |
| Leith Hall Garden, Huntly | Saturday 6 December | 1:00pm - 4:00pm |

## Gardens open regularly

| | | |
|---|---|---|
| Fyvie Castle, Turriff | 1 July - 31 October | 9:00am - Dusk |

## Gardens open by arrangement

| | | |
|---|---|---|
| Bruckhills Croft, Rothienorman | 1 March - 31 March | 01651 821596 |
| Grandhome, Danestone | 1 April - 31 October | 01224 722202 |
| Greenridge, Cults | 1 July - 31 August | 01224 860200 or F: 01224 860210 |
| Hatton Castle, Turriff | On request | 01888 562279 |
| Knockmuir, Turriff | 30 June - 25 August | 01888 514814 |
| Laundry Cottage, Culdrain | On request | 01466 720768 |
| Middle Cairncake, Turriff | 14 July - 10 August | 01888 544432 |
| Tillypronie, Tarland | 2 January - 31 December | 01339 881529 M: 07796 946309 |
| Westfield Lodge, Milltimber | 26 July - 1 August | 07435 969628 |

## Key to symbols

 New in 2014
 Teas
 Cream teas
 Homemade teas
 Dogs on a lead allowed
 Wheelchair access
 Accommodation
 Plant stall
 Scottish Snowdrop Festival

## Garden locations

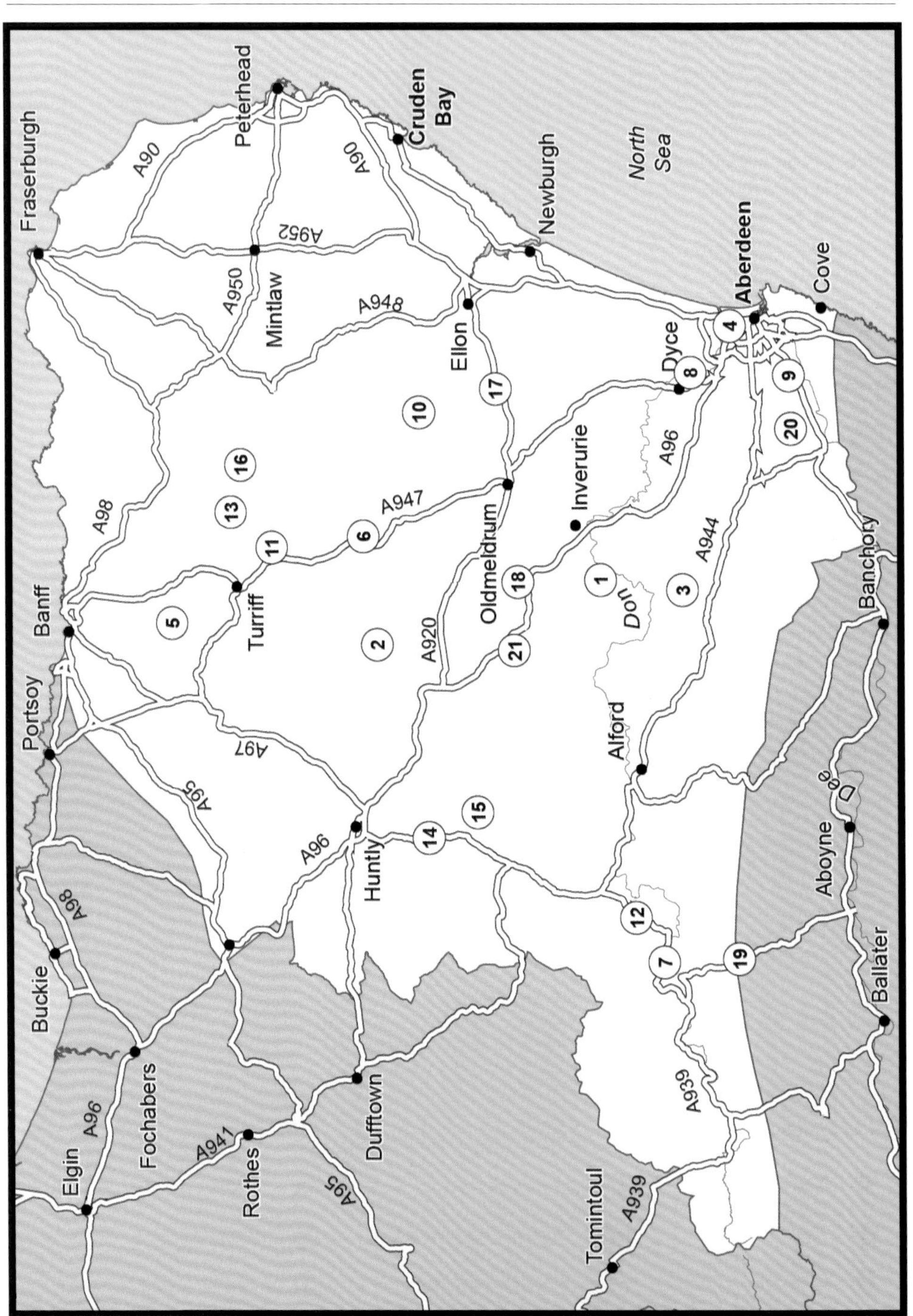

## BIRKEN COTTAGE

Burnhervie, Inverurie AB51 5JR

**Clare and Ian Alexander T: 01467 623013**

This steeply sloping garden of just under 1 acre is packed with plants. It rises from a wet streamside gully and woodland, past sunny terraces and a small parterre, to dry flowery banks.

**Directions:** Burnhervie is about 3 miles west of Inverurie. Leave Inverurie by the B9170 (Blackhall Road) or B993 (St James' Place).

Disabled Access:
None

Opening Times:
Sunday 8 June
2:00pm - 5:00pm
Sunday 27 July
2:00pm - 5:00pm

Admission:
£4.00

Charities:
Friends of Anchor receives 40%, the net remaining to SG Beneficiaries.

## BRUCKHILLS CROFT

Rothienorman, Inverurie AB51 8YB

**Paul and Helen Rushton T: 01651 821596**

**E: helenrushton1@aol.com**

A slate built croft-house surrounded by an informal country cottage garden with numerous flower borders, an orchard and a productive fruit and vegetable patch with polytunnel. Flowers range from the tiny Primula scotica to the giant Himalayan Lily. Below the main garden is a wildflower meadow and pond which attracts a great deal of wildlife. You can relax on the decking overlooking the fledgling River Ythan or try out the labyrinth.

**Other Details:** New for 2014: we are open for the Scottish Snowdrop Festival, when you are welcome to come and see our collection of over 90 different types of Snowdrop arranged in small groups throughout the garden. Please phone to arrange viewing as parking is limited and weather variable during March.

**Directions:** At Rothienorman take the B9001 north, just after Badenscoth Nursing Home turn left, after 1 mile you will be directed where to park depending if it is the Winter or Summer opening.

Disabled Access:
Partial

Opening Times:
Sunday 6 July
12:00pm - 5:00pm
By arrangement
1 March - 31 March
for the Snowdrop Festival.

Admission:
£4.00, children free

Charities:
Advocacy Service Aberdeen receives 20%, Befriend a Child, Aberdeen receives 20%, the net remaining to SG Beneficiaries.

## CASTLE FRASER GARDEN

Sauchen, Inverurie AB51 7LD
**The National Trust for Scotland T: 0844 493 2164**
**E: castlefraser@nts.org.uk www.nts.org.uk**

Castle Fraser's designed landscape and parkland is the work of Thomas White in 1794. Castle Fraser, one of the most spectacular of the Castles of Mar, has a traditional walled garden of trees, shrubs and herbaceous plantings, a medicinal and culinary border and organically grown fruit and vegetables. You can stroll through the woodland garden with its azaleas and rhododendrons or take the young at heart to the Woodland Secrets adventure playground and trails.

**Other Details:** A sale of herbaceous plants lifted straight from the garden and a raffle to win the Castle Fraser Gardeners for a day's work in your garden.

**Directions:** Near Kemnay, off A944.

Disabled Access:
Partial

Opening Times:
Saturday 3 May
11:00am - 4:00pm
Sunday 4 May
11:00am - 4:00pm

Admission:
Donations welcome

Charities:
Donation to SG Beneficiaries.

## CRUICKSHANK BOTANIC GARDENS

23 St. Machar Drive, Aberdeen AB24 3UU
**Cruickshank Botanic Garden Trust/Aberdeen University**
**www.abdn.ac.uk/botanic-garden/**

An evening tour with the Curator, Mark Paterson and Head Gardener, Richard Walker. The garden comprises: a sunken garden with alpine lawn, a rock garden built in the 1960s complete with waterfalls and pond system, a long unbroken herbaceous border, a formal rose garden with drystone walling, and an arboretum. It has a large collection of flowering bulbs and rhododendrons, and many unusual shrubs and trees including two mature Camperdown Elms. It is sometimes known as The Secret Garden of Old Aberdeen.

**Other Details:** National Plant Collection®: Baptisia, Zanthoxylum, Nomocharis.

**Directions:** Come down St Machar Drive over the mini-roundabout, just before the first set of traffic lights turn left into the Cruickshank Garden car park. The pedestrian Garden entrance is off the Chanonry.

Disabled Access:
Partial

Opening Times:
Wednesday 28 May
6:30pm - 8:30pm

Admission:
£5.00 per person, includes tea/coffee and biscuits

Charities:
Cruickshank Botanic Gardens Trust receives 40%, the net remaining to SG Beneficiaries.

## DUNLUGAS

Turriff AB53 4NL
**Mrs J Stancioff**

Impressive groups of azaleas and rhododendrons brighten the secluded and romantic gardens by the River Deveron laid out more than 70 years ago. Beautiful old trees border paths that lead beside a burn to woodland ponds edged with primula and blue meconopsis. Beyond is a large walled garden with colourful flower borders and vegetable beds. A unique feature is a Mughal garden patterned on ancient Persian pleasure parks.

**Directions:** Turn off B9025 at east side of Turriff Bridge, 4 miles along on left.

Disabled Access:
Partial

Opening Times:
Sunday 1 June
2:00pm - 5:00pm

Admission:
£4.00, children under 12 free

Charities:
Friends of Turriff Community Hospital receives 40%, the net remaining to SG Beneficiaries.

## FYVIE CASTLE

Fyvie, Turriff AB53 8JS
**The National Trust for Scotland T: 01651 891363 or 01651 891266**
**E: gthomson@nts.org.uk www.nts.org.uk**

An 18th century walled garden now developed as a garden of Scottish fruits and vegetables. There is also the American garden, Rhymer's Haugh woodland garden, a loch and parkland to visit. Expert staff are always on hand to answer any questions. Learn about the collection of Scottish fruits and their cultivation, and exciting projects for the future. Visit the newly created produce sales stall. Everything grown using organic methods.

**Other Details:** Large fresh produce stall selling a wide selection of organic fruit and vegetables. Proceeds to be donated to Scotland's Gardens.

**Directions:** Off A947 8 miles SE of Turriff and 25 miles NW of Aberdeen.

Disabled Access:
Full

Opening Times:
1 July - 31 October
9:00am - Dusk

Admission:
Fyvie Castle: £12.00, family £28.50, concessions £8.50
Garden and Grounds: free
N.B. Prices correct at time of going to print.

Charities:
Donation to SG Beneficiaries from sales of produce stall.

## GLENKINDIE HOUSE

Glenkindie, Alford AB33 8SU
**Mr and Mrs J P White**

Large country garden containing herbaceous borders, hedges and topiary surrounded by mature conifers and hardwoods.

**Directions:** On the A97 Alford/Strathdon road, 12 miles west of Alford.

Disabled Access:
Full

Opening Times:
Sunday 27 July
2:00pm - 5:00pm

Admission:
£4.00, concessions £3.00, children free

Charities:
Willow Foundation receives 40%, the net remaining to SG Beneficiaries.

## GRANDHOME

Danestone, Aberdeen AB22 8AR
**Mr and Mrs D R Paton T: 01224 722202**
**E: davidpaton@btconnect.com**

18th century walled garden, incorporating rose garden (replanted 2010); policies with daffodils, tulips, rhododendrons, azaleas, mature trees and shrubs.

**Directions:** From north end of North Anderson Drive, continue on A90 over Persley Bridge, turning left at Tesco roundabout. 1¾ miles on left, through the pillars on a left hand bend.

Disabled Access:
Partial

Opening Times:
By arrangement
1 April - 31 October

Admission:
£4.00, concessions £3.00

Charities:
Children 1st receives 40%, the net remaining to SG Beneficiaries.

## GREENRIDGE

Craigton Road, Cults AB15 9PS
**BP Exploration T: 01224 860200 or Fax 01224 860210**
**E: greenrid@bp.com**

Large secluded garden surrounding 1840 Archibald Simpson house. For many years winner of Britain in Bloom 'Best Hidden Garden'. The garden has mature specimen trees and shrubs, a kitchen garden and sloping walled rose garden and terraces.

**Directions:** Will be advised when booking.

Disabled Access:
Partial

Opening Times:
By arrangement
1 July - 31 August

Admission:
£3.50

Charities:
Cancer Research Scotland receives 40%, the net remaining to SG Beneficiaries.

## HADDO HOUSE

Methlick, Ellon AB41 7EQ
**The National Trust for Scotland T: 0844 493 2179**
**E: haddo@nts.org.uk www.nts.org.uk**

The Haddo Terrace Garden's geometric flower beds and fountain are being transformed through a lavish restoration. Meet the gardeners and learn about this exciting project. Visitors will also enjoy the secluded glades and knolls. A magnificent avenue of lime trees leads to adjacent Haddo Country Park with its lakes, monuments, walks and wildlife.

**Other Details:** Meet our expert Head Gardener in the courtyard.
Guided garden walks at 12:00pm, 2:00pm and 4:00pm.
Evening walks at 7:00pm include light refreshments.
Bookings can be made for the evening tours by phone or email.

**Directions:** Off B999 near Tarves, at 'Raxton' crossroads, 19 miles north of Aberdeen, 4 miles north of Pitmedden and 10 miles NW of Ellon. Cycle: 1 mile from NCN 1 Bus: Stagecoach Bluebird from Aberdeen bus station T: 01224 212666, c. 4 miles walk.

Disabled Access:
Partial

Opening Times:
Sunday 17 August
11:00am - 5:00pm
Sunday 31 August
11:00am - 5:00pm

Admission:
Guided tours at 12:00pm, 2:00pm and 4:00pm £4.00
Evening walks at 7:00pm £6.00

Charities:
Donation to SG Beneficiaries.

## HATTON CASTLE

Turriff AB53 8ED
**Mr and Mrs D James Duff T: 01888 562279**
**E: jjdgardens@btinternet.com**

Two acre walled garden featuring mixed borders and shrub roses with yew and box hedges and alleys of pleached hornbeam. Also, a kitchen garden, fan trained fruit trees, a lake and woodland walks.

**Other Details:** Teas and lunch parties available by arrangement.

**Directions:** On A947, 2 miles south of Turriff.

Disabled Access:
Full

Opening Times:
By arrangement on request

Admission:
£5.00, children free

Charities:
Juvenile Diabetes Research Foundation receives 40%, the net remaining to SG Beneficiaries.

## KILDRUMMY CASTLE GARDENS

Alford AB33 8RA
**Kildrummy Garden Trust T: 01975 571203**
**www.kildrummy-castle-gardens.co.uk**

April shows the gold of the lysichitons in the water garden and the small bulbs naturalised beside the copy of the 14th century Brig o' Balgownie. Rhododendrons and azaleas from April (frost permitting). September/October brings colchicums and brilliant colour with acers, fothergillas and viburnums.

**Directions:** On A97, 10 miles from Alford, 17 miles from Huntly. Car park free inside hotel main entrance. Coaches park up at hotel delivery entrance.

Disabled Access:
Partial

Opening Times:
Sunday 1 June
10:00am - 5:00pm
Sunday 28 September
10:00am - 5:00pm

Admission:
£4.50, concessions £4.00, children free

Charities:
Aberdeen Branch Multiple Sclerosis Society receives 40%, the net remaining to SG Beneficiaries.

## KNOCKMUIR

Auchry, Turriff AB53 5UR
**Mr and Mrs Ian Hamilton T: 01888 514814**
**E: rona_hamilton@hotmail.co.uk**

With easy access, our garden can be found in a countryside setting surrounded by farmland. When we purchased the property it had a well structured garden with many mature plants; however a large area was laid to lawn. During the last few years it has evolved with the addition of a vegetable garden, an additional greenhouse and polytunnel. There are also herbaceous beds, annual bedding, shrubs, trees, a rockery, a wildlife pond and a wild flower area beside a small burn.

**Directions:** Situated near Turriff on the B9170 between the A947 and Cuminestown.

Disabled Access:
Partial

Opening Times:
By arrangement
30 June - 25 August

Admission:
£3.00, children free

Charities:
All proceeds to SG Beneficiaries.

## LAUNDRY COTTAGE

Culdrain, Gartly, Huntly AB54 4PY
**Simon and Judith McPhun T: 01466 720768**
**E: simon.mcphun@btinternet.com**

An informal, cottage-style garden of about 1½ acres. Upper garden around the house of mixed borders, vegetables and fruit. Steep grass banks to the south and east are planted with native and non-native flowers, specimen trees and shrubs. Narrow grass paths, not suitable for wheelchairs, lead down to the River Bogie.

**Directions:** 4 miles south of Huntly on A97.

Disabled Access:
Partial

Opening Times:
By arrangement on request

Admission:
£3.00, children free

Charities:
Amnesty International receives 40%, the net remaining to SG Beneficiaries.

## LEITH HALL GARDEN

Huntly AB54 4NQ

**The National Trust for Scotland T: 01464 831148**

**E: tkeyworth@nts.org.uk www.nts.org.uk**

A Gardeners' Question Time, an open day, a workshop and a series of evening guided tours with the Head Gardener. The west garden was made by Charles and Henrietta Leith-Hay around the beginning of the 20th century. In summer the magnificent zigzag herbaceous and serpentine catmint borders provide a dazzling display. A lot of project work is on-going in the garden including a rose catenary along with large borders being redeveloped in a Gertrude Jekyll style and a Laburnum archway with spring interest borders.

**Other Details:** Gardeners' Question Time, workshops and tours include refreshments. July open day offering music, plant sales, and guided walks.

**Directions:** On B9002 1 mile west of Kennethmont.

Disabled Access:
Partial

Opening Times:
Saturday 26 April 7:00pm
Gardeners' Question Time
Thursday 29 May 7:00pm
Tour with Head Gardener
Thursday 26 June 7:00pm
Tour with Head Gardener
Sunday 6 July
12:00pm - 4:00pm
Thursday 31 July 7:00pm
Tour with Head Gardener
Thursday 28 August 7:00pm
Tour with Head Gardener
Saturday 6 December
1:00pm - 4:00pm
Holly wreath making workshop

Admission:
26 April: £5:00
Last Thursday in May, June, July and August: £5:00
6 July: entry to the garden and guided walk £5:00
for garden entry only £3:00, children free
December workshop: £15:00 including tea/coffee

Charities:
Donation to SG Beneficiaries.

## MIDDLE CAIRNCAKE

Cuminestown, Turriff AB53 5YS

**Mr and Mrs N Orpwood T: 01888 544432**

The garden has been planned and planted by the owners over the last 7 years. Features include a kitchen garden with soft fruit and vegetables and a polytunnel as well as a greenhouse, herbaceous beds, heathers, water garden and a walled rose garden.

It is a windy site with light, sandy soil. The walls have been built with stone dug from the garden.

**Directions:** Middle Cairncake is on the A9170 between New Deer and Cuminestown. It is clearly signposted.

Disabled Access:
Partial

Opening Times:
Saturday 12 July
12:30pm - 5:00pm
Sunday 13 July
12:30pm - 5:00pm
Also by arrangement
14 July - 10 August

Admission:
£3.00

Charities:
RNLI receives 40%, the net remaining to SG Beneficiaries.

## PITMEDDEN GARDEN

Ellon AB41 7PD

**The National Trust for Scotland T: 0844 493 2177**

**E: sburgess@nts.org.uk www.nts.org.uk**

Join Property Manager / Head Gardener Susan Burgess for an exclusive evening walk in the tranquil setting of Pitmedden's historic walled garden. Enjoy the sights and scents of an evening stroll along the colourful herbaceous borders and boxwood parterres and hear about the planning and preparation which goes into creating and presenting this highly acclaimed formal garden.

**Other Details:** Self-catering accommodation available. At the conclusion of the walk there will be a further opportunity for discussion and gardening advice over tea, coffee and homemade shortbread.

**Directions:** On A920, 1 mile west of Pitmedden village and 14 miles north of Aberdeen.

Disabled Access:
Partial

Opening Times:
Sunday 10 August
6:00pm - 8:00pm

Admission:
£15.00 admission includes exclusive evening walk and refreshments.

Charities:
Donation to SG Beneficiaries.

## PITSCURRY PROJECT

Whiteford, Pitcaple, Inverurie AB51 5DY

**Aberdeenshire Council T: 01467 681773**

Aberdeenshire Council, together with PEP Ltd and local industry have created a 6 acre garden providing work experience for adults with learning disabilities. The gardens are fully accessible and are divided into several themed areas: sensory, heritage, wildlife and production. There are also displays of sculpture, art and crafts, hand crafted garden furniture and recycling activities.

**Directions:** The site is located next to Pitcaple Quarry which is sign-posted from most local junctions. Be wary of using the postcode in a satnav as it covers a number of properties.

Disabled Access:
Full

Opening Times:
2 -10 August
10:00am - 3:00pm

Admission:
£4.00

Charities:
Pitcaple Environmental Project receives 40%, the net remaining to SG Beneficiaries.

## TILLYPRONIE

Tarland AB34 4XX

**The Hon Philip Astor T: 01339 881529, M: 07796 946309**

Late Victorian house for which Queen Victoria laid the foundation stone, with superb views over the Dee valley. Herbaceous borders, heather beds, water garden and rockery with alpines. Golden Jubilee garden containing trees, shrubs and plants of a golden texture. Fine collection of trees, including recently planted acers and a well-established pinetum with rare specimens. Fruit garden and greenhouses. In June there is a wonderful show of azaleas, rhododendrons and spring heathers.

**Other Details:** Plant stall June opening only.

**Directions:** Off A97 between Ballater and Strathdon.

Disabled Access:
Partial

Opening Times:
Sunday 1 June
2:00pm - 5:00pm
Sunday 24 August
2:00pm - 5:00pm
By arrangement
2 January - 31 December

Admission:
£5.00, children £2.00

Charities:
All proceeds to SG Beneficiaries.

## WESTFIELD LODGE

Contlaw Road, Milltimber, Aberdeen AB13 0EX

**Mr and Mrs L. Kinch T: 07435 969628**

**E: fraserdesigner@aol.com**

The gardens at Westfield are unique in that they are completely 'new' gardens, first laid out formally in the 1990s and gradually improved and reworked since that date. The commitment and investment of the Kinch family has allowed this peaceful and beautiful site to be transformed into the horticultural oasis you see today. The current Head Gardener James Fraser is responsible for the design and execution of many of the stunning features within the garden, such as the Reflection Pond, the Boathouse and the Tropical House. James has brought a flair and passion to Westfield which has elevated the garden to a higher level. The team at Westfield work extremely hard year-round to ensure that the gardens and grounds are kept in immaculate condition.

**Directions:** On North Deeside Rd (A93), at Milltimber turn into Contlaw Rd. Cont. circa 1 mile; turn right into single track road signed Westfield. From A944 turn off at Mason Lodge onto B979, over Carnie Crossroads, turn 2nd left signed Contlaw, take 1st left and follow road for almost 1 mile. Westfield turning is on left.

Disabled Access:
Partial

Opening Times:
By arrangement
26 July - 1 August
for pre-arranged groups only

Admission:
£8.00 includes refreshments

Charities:
CLAN Aberdeen receives 40%, the net remaining to SG Beneficiaries.

## WESTHALL CASTLE

Oyne, Inverurie AB52 6RW

**Mr Gavin Farquhar and Mrs Pam Burney T: 01224 214301**

**E: enquiries@ecclesgreig.com**

Set in an ancient landscape in the foothills of the impressive foreboding hill of Bennachie. A circular walk through glorious daffodils with outstanding views. Interesting garden in early stages of restoration, with large groupings of rhododendrons and specimen trees. Westhall Castle is a 16th century tower house, incorporating a 13th century building of the bishops of Aberdeen. There were additions in the 17th, 18th and 19th centuries. The castle is semi-derelict, but stabilised from total dereliction. A fascinating house encompassing 600 years of alteration and additions.

**Directions:** Marked from the A96 at Old Rayne and from Oyne Village.

Disabled Access:
Partial

Opening Times:
Sunday 20 April
1:00pm - 4:00pm

Admission:
£4.00, children free

Charities:
Bennachie Guides receives 40%, the net remaining to SG Beneficiaries.

# ANGUS



## District Organiser

| | |
|---|---|
| Mrs Terrill Dobson | Logie House, Kirriemuir DD8 5PN |

## Area Organisers

| | |
|---|---|
| Mrs Helen Brunton | Cuthlie Farm, Arbroath DD11 2NT |
| Mrs Katie Dessain | Lawton House, Inverkeilor, by Arbroath DD11 4RU |
| Mrs Jeanette Ogilvie | House of Pitmuies, Guthrie DD8 2SN |
| Mrs Rosanne Porter | West Scryne, By Carnoustie DD7 6LL |
| Mrs Sue Smith | Balintore House, Balintore, by Kirriemuir DD8 5JS |
| Mrs Gladys Stewart | Ugie-Bank, Ramsay Street, Edzell DD9 7TT |
| Mrs Annabel Stormonth Darling | Lednathie, Glen Prosen, Kirriemuir DD8 4RR |
| Mrs Tracey Williams | Alma Lodge, 51 Duncan Road, Letham DD8 2PN |

## Treasurer

| | |
|---|---|
| Mrs Mary Stansfeld | Dunninald, By Montrose DD10 9TD |

## Gardens open on a specific date

| | | |
|---|---|---|
| Dunninald, Montrose | Saturday 22 February | 12:00pm - 5:00pm |
| Dunninald, Montrose | Sunday 23 February | 12:00pm - 5:00pm |
| Dunninald, Montrose | Saturday 1 March | 12:00pm - 5:00pm |
| Dunninald, Montrose | Sunday 2 March | 12:00pm - 5:00pm |
| Lawton House, Inverkeilor | Sunday 9 March | 2:00pm - 5:00pm |
| Brechin Castle, Brechin | Sunday 4 May | 2:00pm - 5:00pm |
| 3 Balfour Cottages, Menmuir | Saturday 10 May | 1:00pm - 5:00pm |
| Dalfruin, Kirriemuir | Sunday 11 May | 2:00pm - 5:00pm |
| Dunninald, Montrose | Sunday 18 May | 2:00pm - 5:00pm |
| Gallery, Montrose | Saturday 24 May | 2:00pm - 5:00pm |
| 33 Ireland Street, Carnoustie | Sunday 25 May | 2:00pm - 5:00pm |
| West Scryne Farm, Carnoustie | Sunday 25 May | 2:00pm - 5:00pm |
| Cortachy Castle, Cortachy | Sunday 1 June | 2:00pm - 6:00pm |
| Letham Village, Letham | Sunday 15 June | 12:00pm - 6:00pm |
| Edzell Village & Castle, Edzell | Sunday 22 June | 2:00pm - 5:00pm |
| Airlie Castle, Airlie, By Kirriemuir | Saturday 5 July | 2:00pm - 5:00pm |
| Gallery, Montrose | Saturday 12 July | 2:00pm - 5:00pm |
| The Walled Garden at Logie, Kirriemuir | Sunday 20 July | 2:00pm - 5:00pm |
| Ninewells Community Garden, Dundee | Sunday 17 August | 2:00pm - 5:00pm |

## Gardens open regularly

| | | |
|---|---|---|
| Dunninald, Montrose | 28 June - 27 July (not Mons) | 1:00pm - 5:00pm |
| Gagie House, Duntrune | 23 February - 25 May | 10:00am - 5:00pm |
| Pitmuies Gardens, Guthrie | 1 February - 16 March | |
| | & 1 April - 31 October | 10:00am - 5:00pm |

## Gardens open by arrangement

| | | |
|---|---|---|
| Gallery, Montrose | 1 May - 30 September | 01674 840550 |
| Kirkside of Lochty, Menmuir | 1 March - 31 October | 01356 660431 |
| Kirkton House, Kirkton of Craig | 1 May - 30 September | 01674 673604 |
| The Garden Cottage, Dunnichen | 1 May - 31 August | 01307 818392 |

Dunninald, Angus

## Key to symbols

| | | | | | |
|---|---|---|---|---|---|
|  | New in 2014 |  | Homemade teas |  | Accommodation |
|  | Teas |  | Dogs on a lead allowed |  | Plant stall |
|  | Cream teas |  | Wheelchair access |  | Scottish Snowdrop Festival |

## Garden locations

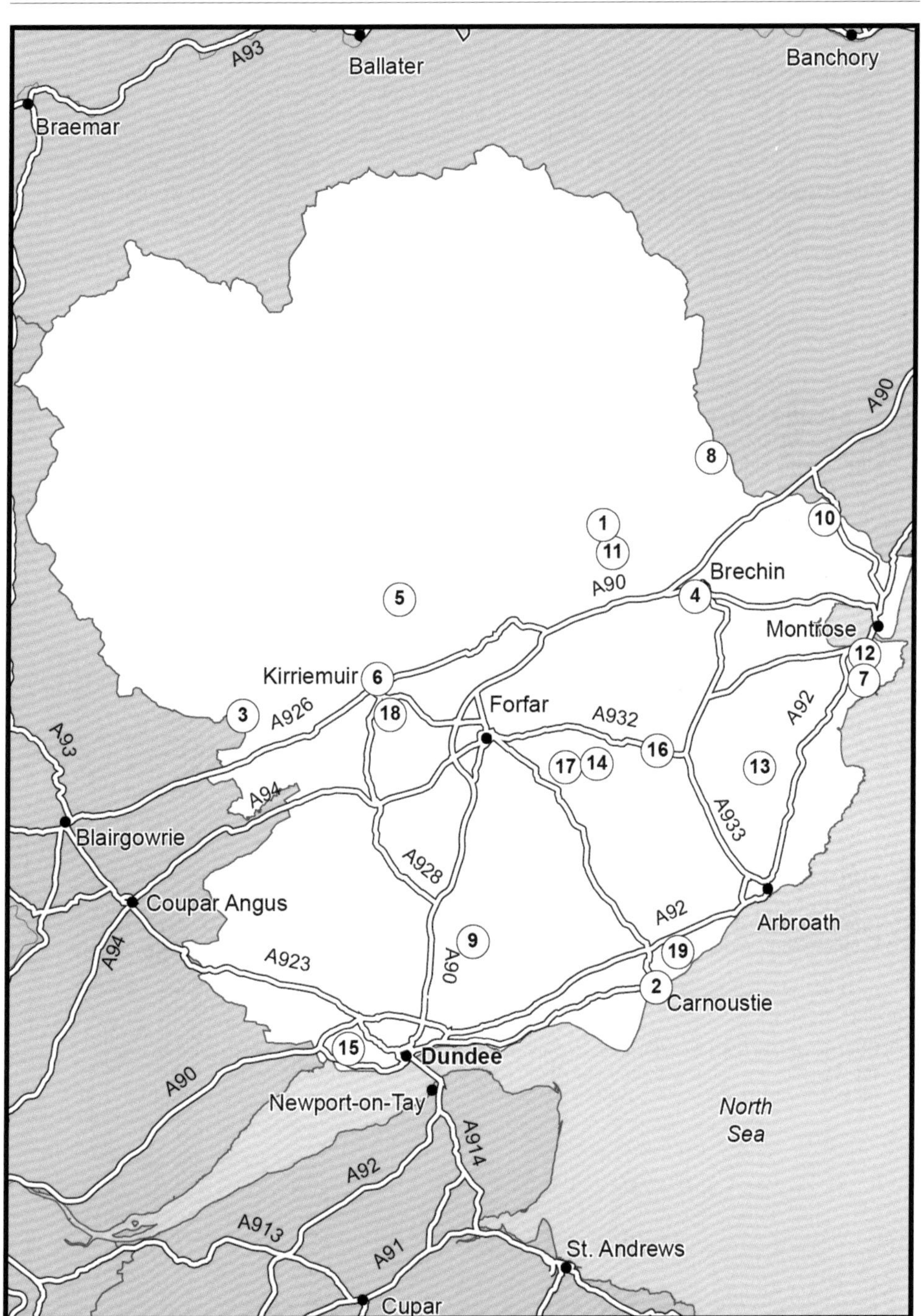

## 3 BALFOUR COTTAGES

Menmuir DD9 7RN

**Dr Alison Goldie and Mark A Hutson T: 01356 660280**

**E: alisongoldie@btinternet.com www.angusplants.co.uk**

Small cottage garden packed with rare and unusual plants. It comprises various 'rooms', containing myriad plants from potted herbs, spring bulbs and alpines in a raised bed, to a 'jungle' with a range of bamboos. Many other interesting plants include Primula, Hosta, Meconopsis, Fritillaria, Trillium, Allium, a large display of bonsai and Auriculas.

**Other Details:** National Plant Collection®: Primula auricula (alpine)

**Directions:** Leave the A90 two miles south of Brechin and take the road to Menmuir (3.5 miles). At the T-junction turn right and it is in the first group of cottages on your left (175 yards).

Disabled Access:
None

Opening Times:
Saturday 10 May
1:00pm - 5:00pm

Admission:
£3.00, under 16 free

Charities:
RAF Wings Appeal receives 40%, the net remaining to SG Beneficiaries.

## 33 IRELAND STREET (WITH WEST SCRYNE FARM)

Carnoustie DD7 6AS

**Miss Dorothy Fyffe**

A mature garden with an eclectic mix of herbaceous plants, trees and shrubs with a good display of spring bulbs.

**Other Details:** Teas served at Church Hall, Carnoustie Panbride Church, Arbroath Road, Carnoustie which is 2 minutes walk from Ireland Street.

**Directions:** 33 Ireland Street is near the railway station.

Disabled Access:
Full

Opening Times:
Sunday 25 May
2:00pm - 5:00pm

Admission:
£4.00 for entry to both gardens, accompanied children free

Charities:
Carnoustie Panbride Church receives 40%, the net remaining to SG Beneficiaries.

## AIRLIE CASTLE

Airlie, By Kirriemuir DD8 5NG

**Lord and Lady Ogilvy**

**E: office@airlieestates.com www.airlieestates.com**

An 18th century walled garden with topiary and herbaceous borders, laburnum arch and river walk.

**Directions:** Take B951 from Kirriemuir signposted Glen Isla. Pass Kinnordy Loch and then turn left signposted Airlie and Alyth. Keep on for 3.5 miles, pass Mains of Airlie farm on left. Entrance to castle is just beyond on the right.

Disabled Access:
None

Opening Times:
Saturday 5 July
2:00pm - 5:00pm

Admission:
£4.00, accompanied children free

Charities:
Maggie's Centre Dundee receives 40%, the net remaining to SG Beneficiaries.

## BRECHIN CASTLE

Brechin DD9 6SG

**The Earl and Countess of Dalhousie T: 01356 624566**

**E: mandyferries@dalhousieestates.co.uk www.dalhousieestates.co.uk**

The uniquely curving walls of the garden at Brechin Castle are just the first of many delightful surprises in store. The luxurious blend of ancient and modern plantings is the second. Find charm and splendour in the wide gravelled walks, secluded small paths and corners. May sees the rhododendrons and azaleas hit the peak of their flowering to wonderful effect; and with complementary under-planting and a framework of great and beautiful trees to set the collection in the landscape. This is a lovely garden at any time of year and a knockout in the spring.

**Other Details:** Dogs on leads please.

**Directions:** A90 southernmost exit to Brechin, 1 mile past Brechin Castle Centre, castle gates on right.

Disabled Access:
Partial

Opening Times:
Sunday 4 May
2:00pm - 5:00pm

Admission:
£4.00, OAPs £3.00, accompanied children free

Charities:
Dalhousie Day Care receives 20%, Unicorn Preservation Society receives 20%, the net remaining to SG Beneficiaries.

## CORTACHY CASTLE

Cortachy, by Kirriemuir DD8 4LX

**The Earl and Countess of Airlie T: 01575 570108**

**E: office@airlieestates.com www.airlieestates.com**

Cortachy Castle, a 16th century castellated house is the jewel in the crown for the spectacular specimen trees of the fine American garden which encompasses the Castle within a parkland setting. It is worth paying particular attention to the small ceramic plaques at the base of the trees. The formal Scottish walled garden, complete with contemporary and traditional planting schemes, provides another hidden gem. The gravelled pathways encourage you to explore from the formal borders to the natural areas of the delightful pond with spectacular displays of candelabra primulas and Meconopsis. Viewing across the pond your eyes are drawn to the elegant sculpture with stone sourced from Jaipur and the recent additions by the family to mark notable occasions include the Jardiniere and Pagoda.

**Other Details:** Pipe band and ice cream.

**Directions:** B955 out of Kirriemuir 5 miles.

Disabled Access:
None

Opening Times:
Sunday 1 June
2:00pm - 6:00pm

Admission:
£5.00, accompanied children free

Charities:
Glenisla Highland Games receives 40%, the net remaining to SG Beneficiaries.

## DALFRUIN

Kirktonhill Road, Kirriemuir DD8 4HU

**Mr and Mrs James A Welsh**

A well-stocked connoisseur's garden of about ⅓ of an acre situated at the end of a short cul-de-sac. There are many less common plants like varieties of trilliums, meconopsis (blue poppies), tree peonies (descendants of ones collected by George Sherriff and grown at Ascreavie), dactylorhiza and codonopsis. There is a scree and collection of ferns. Vigorous climbing roses, Kiftsgate and Paul's Himalayan Musk, grow over pergolas. Interconnected ponds encourage wildlife.

**Other Details:** Good plant stall which may include trilliums, meconopsis and tree peonies. Teas served at St Mary's Episcopal Church.

**Directions:** From centre of Kirriemuir turn left up Roods. Kirktonhill Road is on left near top of hill. Please park on Roods or at St Mary's Episcopal Church. Disabled parking only in Kirktonhill Road.

Disabled Access:
Full

Opening Times:
Sunday 11 May
2:00pm - 5:00pm

Admission:
£3.00, accompanied children free

Charities:
St Mary's Episcopal Church receives 40%, the net remaining to SG Beneficiaries.

## DUNNINALD

Montrose DD10 9TD

**The Stansfeld Family T: 01674 672031**

**E: visitorinformation@dunninald.com www.dunninald.com**

Dunninald is a family home built in 1824, set in policies developed during the 17th and 18th centuries. It offers many attractive features to the visitor including a beech avenue planted around 1670. Snowdrops in spring and bluebells in May carpet the woods and wild garden. At its best in July, the highlight of Dunninald is the walled garden with traditional mixed borders, vegetables, soft fruits, fruit trees and a greenhouse.

**Other Details: Sunday 18 May Bluebell Sunday**: Teas, plant stall with all proceeds to Scotland's Gardens and 6th Montrose Brownies.
Castle open 28 June to 27 July (except Mondays) 1:00pm-5:00pm.
Groups welcome throughout the year, by arrangement.

**Directions:** Two miles south of Montrose, signposted off A92 Arbroath/Montrose road (turning marked Usan).

Disabled Access:
Partial

Opening Times:
Sat/Sun 22 & 23 February and Sat/Sun 1 & 2 March
12:00pm - 5:00pm
for the Snowdrop Festival
Sunday 18 May 2:00pm - 5:00pm for Bluebell Sunday
28 June - 27 July except Mons
1:00pm - 5:00pm

Admission:
£4.00, accompanied children free

Charities:
Donation to SG Beneficiaries.

## EDZELL VILLAGE & CASTLE

Edzell DD9 7TT

**The Gardeners of Edzell & Historic Scotland**

Walk round several fabulous and different gardens in Edzell village including those of Edzell Castle.

**Directions:** On B966.

Disabled Access:
None

Opening Times:
Sunday 22 June
2:00pm - 5:00pm

Admission:
£4.00, accompanied children free

Charities:
Stracathro Cancer Care Fund UK receives 40%, the net remaining to SG Beneficiaries.

## GAGIE HOUSE

Duntrune, by Dundee DD4 0PR
**France and Clare Smoor T: 01382 380207**
**E: smoor@gagie.com www.gagie.com**

A 1 mile springtime woodland walk in a delightful secluded dell along the Sweet Burn and its artesian ponds. Also a semi-wild pond garden in the policies of early 17th century Gagie House. Naturalised and more recent plantations of snowdrops followed by daffodils, bluebells, hellebores, erythroniums, primroses and candelabra primulas. Snowdrops are at their best from late February to mid-March.

**Other Details:** Rustic do-it-yourself tea facilities in farm building.

**Directions:** From A90 about 2 miles north of Dundee take turning to east signposted Murroes. Continue for 2 miles, wood on left, sharp right bend ahead; turn left along far side of wood, signpost Gagie; follow this road through stone gateposts at end (marked Private Road). Car park immediately to right.

Disabled Access:
None

Opening Times:
23 February - 25 May
10:00am - 5:00pm
includes opening for the Snowdrop Festival
1 February - 16 March

Admission:
£4.00, accompanied children free

Charities:
Donation to SG Beneficiaries

## GALLERY

Montrose DD10 9LA
**Mr John Simson T: 01674 840550**
**E: galleryhf@googlemail.com**

The redesign and replanting of this historic garden have preserved and extended its traditional framework of holly, privet and box. A grassed central alley, embellished with circles, links themed gardens, including a fine collection of old roses, yellow and blue floral borders of the entrance garden and the fountain and pond in the formal white garden. A walk through the woodland garden, home to rare breed sheep, with its extensive border of mixed heathers, leads to the river North Esk. From there rough paths lead both ways along the bank.

**Directions:** From A90 south of Northwater Bridge take exit to Hillside and next left to Gallery & Marykirk. From A937 west of rail underpass follow signs to Gallery and Northwater Bridge.

Disabled Access:
Partial

Opening Times:
Saturday 24 May
2:00pm - 5:00pm
Saturday 12 July
2:00pm - 5:00pm
By arrangement
1 May - 30 September

Admission:
£4.00, accompanied children free

Charities:
Practical Action receives 40%, the net remaining to SG Beneficiaries.

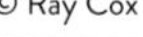

## KIRKSIDE OF LOCHTY

Menmuir, by Brechin DD9 6RY
**James & Irene Mackie T: 01356 660431**

The garden contains a large collection of plants, several rare and unusual, also many different varieties of ferns. It is approached by a strip of woodland and expands into various compartments in an overall area of 2 acres, part of which is cultivated as a flowering meadow.

**Other Details:** Groups welcome. No dogs allowed.

**Directions:** Two miles south of Brechin leave the A90 and take the road to Menmuir. After a further 2 miles, pass a wood on the left and a long beech hedge in front of the house.

Disabled Access:
None

Opening Times:
By arrangement
1 March - 31 October

Admission:
£4.00, accompanied children free

Charities:
All proceeds to SG Beneficiaries

## KIRKTON HOUSE

Kirkton of Craig, Montrose DD10 9TB
**Campbell Watterson T: 01674 673604**
**E: campbellkirktonhouse@btinternet.com**

A regency manse set in over 2 acres of garden. The walled garden includes herbaceous borders, a sunken garden, lime allee, statuary and formal rose garden. The wild garden includes a pond and waterlilies. There is also a large flock of Jacobs sheep in the adjoining glebe.

**Directions:** One mile south of Montrose, off A92 at the Balgove turn-off.

Disabled Access:
Partial

Opening Times:
By arrangement
1 May - 30 September

Admission:
£3.50, accompanied children free

Charities:
All proceeds to SG Beneficiaries.

## LAWTON HOUSE

Inverkeilor, by Arbroath DD11 4RU
**Katie & Simon Dessain**

Woodland garden of beech trees carpeted with snowdrops and crocuses in spring set around a Georgian House. There is also a walled garden planted with fruit trees and vegetables.

**Directions:** Take B965 between Inverkeiler and Friockheim. Turn right at sign for Angus Chain Saws. Drive approximately 200 metres, then take second right into drive with green gate.

Disabled Access:
Partial

Opening Times:
Sunday 9 March
2:00pm - 5:00pm
for the Snowdrop Festival

Admission:
£3.00, accompanied children free

Charities:
Julia Thomson Memorial Trust receives 40%, the net remaining to SG Beneficiaries.

## 14 LETHAM VILLAGE

Letham DD8 2PD

**Letham Gardening Club**

Be inspired by the diverse range of gardens from cottage style to shady gardens to small gardens and those newly developed by keen gardeners. Several new gardens added this year.

**Other Details:** Tickets and maps available in village with teas and plant stall at Letham Church Hall in the village centre.

**Directions:** From north take A90 exiting for Forfar town centre, then take A932 towards Arbroath and pickup signs to Letham. From south via Dundee take B978 Kellas/Wellbank Road, pick up signs.

Disabled Access:
Partial

Opening Times:
Sunday 15 June
12:00pm - 6:00pm

Admission:
£4.00, accompanied children free.

Charities:
Choice of charity to be confirmed and will receive 40%, the net remaining to SG Beneficiaries.

## 15 NINEWELLS COMMUNITY GARDEN

within the Arboretum at Ninewells Hospital, Dundee DD2 1UB

**Ninewells Community Garden Volunteers**

**E: ninewellsgarden@gmail.com**

Featured as one of Beechgrove Garden's 2013 community gardens, this therapeutic and community garden includes herbaceous plants, fruit and vegetables, sensory garden and medicinal herb garden in an accessible environment. The mission of the garden is to promote physical activity and good health through gardening. The garden is a charity supported by volunteers and available to the public, local groups, hospital staff and patients.

**Directions:** Located within the grounds of Ninewells Hospital arboretum, near the Maggie's Centre. Follow Scotland's Gardens yellow signs from hospital entrance.

Disabled Access:
Full

Opening Times:
Sunday 17 August
2:00pm - 5:00pm

Admission:
£3.00, accompanied children free.

Charities:
Ninewells Community Garden receives 40%, the net remaining to SG Beneficiaries.

## 16 PITMUIES GARDENS

House of Pitmuies, Guthrie, By Forfar DD8 2SN

**Mr and Mrs Ruaraidh Ogilvie**

Two semi-formal walled gardens adjoin the 18th century house and shelter long borders of herbaceous perennials, superb delphiniums, old fashioned roses and pavings with violas and dianthus. Spacious lawns, river and lochside walks beneath fine trees. A wide variety of shrubs with good autumn colour. Interesting picturesque turreted doocot and 'Gothick' wash-house. Myriad spring bulbs include carpets of crocus following the massed snowdrops.

**Directions:** A932. Friockheim 1½ miles.

Disabled Access:
Partial

Opening Times:
1 February - 16 March
10:00am - 5:00pm
for the Snowdrop Festival
1 April - 31 October
10:00am - 5:00pm

Admission:
£5.00, accompanied children free

Charities:
Donation to SG Beneficiaries.

## THE GARDEN COTTAGE

Dunnichen DD8 2NX

**Nora Craig T: 01307 818392**

This half acre garden was an orchard at one time but by 1974 only 2 apples remained together with 4 mature deciduous trees and a cottage. Mown grass covered rather less than a third of the area and this has been developed to surround large beds in which a few small trees, several shrubs, hardy herbaceous plants, grasses, ferns and bulbs intermingle. Narrow paths criss-cross the plantings inviting the curious to discover many unusual plants.

**Other Details:** In 2013 the sole surviving apple, Annie Elizabeth, cropped well and Eucryphia x Nymansay was decked with huge white flowers. A 70 yard, 9 ft high stone wall provides shelter for several climbers.

**Directions:** Four miles south-east of Forfar on the 9128. Bear left ¼ mile after Kingsmuir to Letham. On entering Dunnichen turn left immediately, the cottage is on the right and is signposted.

Disabled Access:
None

Opening Times:
By arrangement
1 May - 31 August

Admission:
£3.50, accompanied children free

Charities:
Scotland's Charity Air Ambulance receives 40%, the net remaining to SG Beneficiaries.

## THE WALLED GARDEN AT LOGIE

Logie House, Logie, Kirriemuir DD8 5PN

**Terrill and Gavin Dobson**

**www.angusherbalists.co.uk**

This Herbalists' garden is set amid an 18th century walled garden and large Victorian greenhouse within Logie's organic farm. Featuring more than 150 herbs, the physic garden is divided into 8 rectangles including medicinal herbs for different body systems. All the herbs are labelled with a brief description of actions to help novices learn more about this ancient art. The garden also features a herbaceous border and productive fruit and vegetable garden.

**Directions:** From the A926 leaving Kirriemuir, fork left at Beechwood Place onto the single track road (or if approaching Kirrie take sharp left after "Welcome to Kirriemuir sign"). Take the first left and follow signs to The Walled Garden.

Disabled Access:
Partial

Opening Times:
Sunday 20 July
2:00pm - 5:00pm

Admission:
£3.00, accompanied children free

Charities:
Trellis receives 40%, the net remaining to SG Beneficiaries.

## WEST SCRYNE FARM (WITH 33 IRELAND STREET)

Carnoustie DD7 6LL

**Mrs Rosanne Porter**

An informal garden with bulbs, azaleas, rhododendrons, many shrubs, roses, clematis, herbaceous border, small rock garden and patio, arches of laburnum and honeysuckle, productive vegetable plot, all encircling farmhouse.

**Other Details:** Teas and home baking served in Newton of Panbride Church Hall, 2 minutes walk from 33 Ireland Street garden.

**Directions:** 'Scryne' signposted on A92 between Arbroath and Muirdrum. 33 Ireland Street is 3 miles from Scryne in Carnoustie.

Disabled Access:
Full

Opening Times:
Sunday 25 May
2:00pm - 5:00pm

Admission:
£4.00 for entry to both gardens, accompanied children free

Charities:
Carnoustie Panbride Church receives 40%, the net remaining to SG Beneficiaries.

# ARGYLL



## District Organiser

| | |
|---|---|
| Minette Struthers | Ardmaddy Castle, Balvicar, by Oban PA34 4QY |

## Area Organisers

| | |
|---|---|
| Mrs Grace Bergius | Craignish House, Ardfern, Lochgilphead, Argyll PA31 8QN |
| Mrs G Cadzow | Duachy, Kilninver, Oban PA34 4RH |
| Mrs Mary Lindsay | Dal an Eas, Kilmore, Oban PA34 4XU |
| Mrs P McArthur | Bute Cottage, Newton, Strachlachan PA27 8DB |

## Treasurer

| | |
|---|---|
| Minette Struthers | Ardmaddy Castle, Balvicar, by Oban PA34 4QY |

## Gardens open on a specific date

| | | | | |
|---|---|---|---|---|
| Benmore Botanic Garden, Dunoon | Sunday 27 April | 10:00am | - | 6:00pm |
| Kames Bay, Kilmelford | Saturday 3 May | 1:00pm | - | 5:00pm |
| Kames Bay, Kilmelford | Sunday 4 May | 1:00pm | - | 5:00pm |
| Arduaine Garden, Oban | Sunday 11 May | 9:30am | - | 5:00pm |
| Maolachy's Garden, Lochavich | Saturday 24 May | 2:00pm | - | 5:00pm |
| Strachur House Flower & Woodland Gardens, Strachur | Saturday 24 May | 1:00pm | - | 5:00pm |
| Crarae Garden, Inveraray | Sunday 25 May | 10:00am | - | 5:00pm |
| Maolachy's Garden, Lochavich, by Taynuilt | Sunday 25 May | 2:00pm | - | 5:00pm |
| Strachur House Flower & Woodland Gardens, Strachur | Sunday 25 May | 1:00pm | - | 5:00pm |
| The Shore Villages, by Dunoon | Saturday 28 June | 1:00pm | - | 5:00pm |
| The Shore Villages, by Dunoon | Sunday 29 June | 1:00pm | - | 5:00pm |
| Caol Ruadh, Colintraive | Saturday 19 July | 2:00pm | - | 5:00pm |
| Caol Ruadh, Colintraive | Sunday 20 July | 2:00pm | - | 5:00pm |
| Ardchattan Priory, North Connel | Sunday 27 July | 12:00pm | - | 4:00pm |
| Crarae Garden, Inveraray | Sunday 27 July | 10:00am | - | 5:00pm |
| Melfort House Kitchen Garden, Kilmelford | Saturday 2 August | 2:00pm | - | 5:00pm |
| Melfort House Kitchen Garden, Kilmelford | Sunday 3 August | 2:00pm | - | 5:00pm |

## Gardens open regularly

| | | | | |
|---|---|---|---|---|
| Achnacloich, Connel | 29 Mar - 1 Nov (Sats only) | 10:00am | - | 4:00pm |
| An Cala, Ellenabeich | 1 April - 31 October | 10:00am | - | 6:00pm |
| Ardchattan Priory, North Connel | 1 April - 31 October | 9:30am | - | 5:30pm |

| Garden | Dates | Opening | | Closing |
|---|---|---|---|---|
| Ardkinglas Woodland Garden, Cairndow | 1 January - 31 December | Dawn | - | Dusk |
| Ardmaddy Castle, by Oban | 1 January - 31 December | 9:00pm | - | Dusk |
| Barguillean's "Angus Garden", Taynuilt | 1 January - 31 December | 9:00am | - | Dusk |
| Benmore Botanic Garden, Dunoon | 1 March - 31 October | 10:00am | - | 6:00pm |
| Crinan Hotel Garden, Crinan | 1 May - 31 August | Dawn | - | Dusk |
| Druimneil House, Port Appin | 17 April - 31 October | Dawn | - | Dusk |
| Fairwinds, Dunoon | 1 April - 31 October | 9:00am | - | 6:00pm |
| Inveraray Castle Gardens, Inveraray | 1 April - 31 October | 10:00am | - | 5:45pm |
| Kinlochlaich House Gardens, Appin | 1 January - 31 December (but closed Suns & Mons, October - March) | 9:30am | - | 4:30pm |
| Oakbank, Ardrishaig | 1 May - 31 October | 10:30am | - | 5:30pm |

## Gardens open by arrangement

| Garden | Dates | Telephone |
|---|---|---|
| Drim na Vullin, Lochgilphead | 17 May - 31 May | 01546 602615 |

Druimneil, Argyll

## Key to symbols

 New in 2014

 Teas

 Cream teas

 Homemade teas

 Dogs on a lead allowed

 Wheelchair access

 Accommodation

 Plant stall

 Scottish Snowdrop Festival

## Garden locations

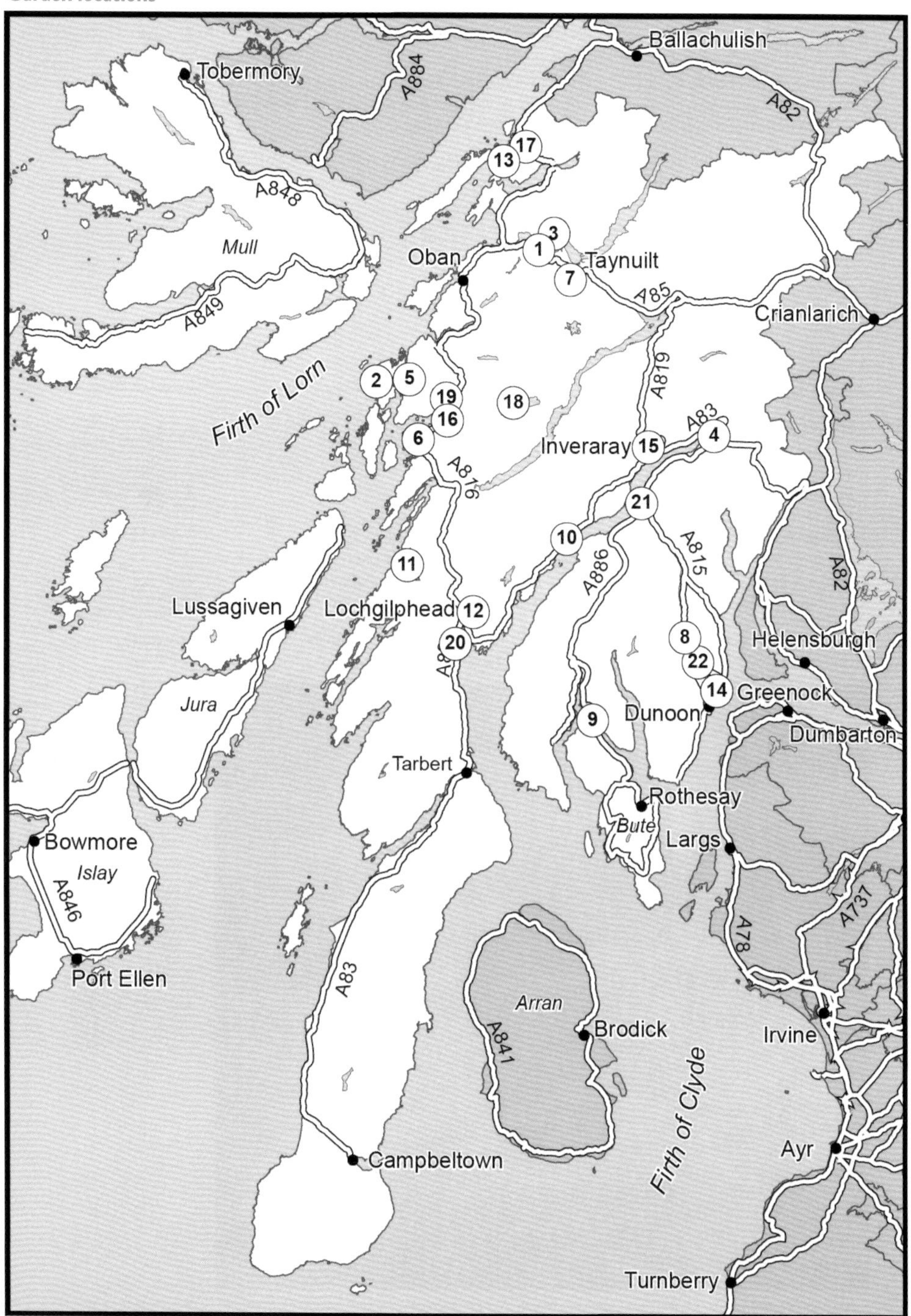

## ACHNACLOICH

Connel, Oban PA37 1PR
**Mr T E Nelson T: 01631 710796**
**E: charlie_milne@msn.com**

Scottish baronial house by John Starforth of Glasgow. Succession of wonderful bulbs, flowering shrubs, rhododendrons, azaleas, magnolias and primulas. Woodland garden with ponds above Loch Etive. Good autumn colours.

**Directions:** Three miles east of Connel on A85. Parking on the right at the bottom of the drive.

Disabled Access:
Partial

Opening Times:
29 March - 1 November
10:00am - 4:00pm
Saturdays only

Admission:
£4.00

Charities:
All proceeds to SG Beneficiaries.

## AN CALA

Ellenabeich, Isle of Seil PA34 4RF
**Mrs Thomas Downie T: 01852 300237**
**www.gardens-of-argyll.co.uk**

A wonderful example of a 1930s designed garden, An Cala sits snugly in its horseshoe shelter of surrounding cliffs. A spectacular and very pretty garden with streams, waterfall, ponds, many herbaceous plants as well as azaleas, rhododendrons and cherry trees in spring. Archive material of Mawson's design found recently.

**Directions:** Proceed south from Oban on Campbeltown road for 8 miles, turn right at Easdale sign, a further 8 miles on B844; garden between school and village.

Disabled Access:
Partial

Opening Times:
1 April - 31 October
10:00am - 6:00pm

Admission:
£3.50

Charities:
Cancer Research UK receives 40%, the net remaining to SG Beneficiaries.

## ARDCHATTAN PRIORY

North Connel PA37 1RQ
**Mrs Sarah Troughton T: 01796 481355**
**E: sh.troughton@virgin.net www.ardchattan.co.uk**

Beautifully situated on the north side of Loch Etive. In front of the house there is a rockery, extensive herbaceous and rose borders, with excellent views over the loch. West of the house there are shrub borders and a wild garden, numerous roses and many different varieties of sorbus providing excellent autumn colour. The Priory, founded in 1230, is now a private house. The ruins of the chapel and graveyard, with fine early stones, are in the care of Historic Scotland and open with the garden.

**Other Details: Sunday 27th July**: Garden Fete - soup lunches, homemade teas, stalls including plant stall and other attractions.

**Directions:** Oban 10 miles. From north, left off A828 at Barcaldine onto B845 for 6 miles. From East/Oban on A85, cross Connel Bridge and turn first right, proceed east on Bonawe Road. Well signposted.

Disabled Access:
Partial

Opening Times:
Sunday 27 July
12:00pm - 4:00pm
1 April - 31 October
9:30am - 5:30pm

Admission:
£4.00, children 16 and under are free

Charities:
Donation to SG Beneficiaries.

## ARDKINGLAS WOODLAND GARDEN

Cairndow PA26 8BH
**Ardkinglas Estate T: 01499 600261**
**www.ardkinglas.com**

In a peaceful setting overlooking Loch Fyne the garden contains one of the finest collections of rhododendrons and conifers in Britain. This includes the tallest tree in Britain, a 'Grand Fir' measured at over 64 metres as well as many other champion trees. Gazebo with unique "Scriptorium" based around a collection of literary quotes. Woodland lochan, ancient mill ruins and many woodland walks. Visit Scotland 3* garden.

**Other Details:** Champion Trees: includes tallest tree in Britain. Nearby The Tree Shop – garden centre café offers fabulous food.

**Directions:** Entrance through Cairndow village off A83 Loch Lomond/Inveraray road.

Disabled Access:
Partial

Opening Times:
1 January - 31 December
Dawn - Dusk

Admission:
£4.50, children under 16 free

Charities:
Donation to SG Beneficiaries.

## ARDMADDY CASTLE

by Oban PA34 4QY
**Mr and Mrs Charles Struthers T: 01852 300353**
**E: ardmaddycastle@btinternet.com www.gardens-of-argyll.co.uk**

Ardmaddy Castle gardens, in a most spectacular setting, are shielded to the north by mature woodlands, carpeted with bluebells and daffodils and protected from the Atlantic winds by the elevated Castle. The Walled Garden is full of magnificent rhododendrons, some huge, an increasing collection of rare and unusual shrubs and plants, the 'Clock Garden' with its cutting flowers, fruit and vegetables grown with labour saving formality, all within dwarf box hedging. Beyond, a woodland walk, with its amazing hydrangea climbing to 60 feet, leads to the water gardens - in early summer a riot of candelabra primulas, irises, rodgersias and other damp loving plants and grasses. Lovely autumn colour. A garden for all seasons.

**Other Details:** Plant stalls and veg and summer fruits in season. Toilet suitable for disabled. Six self-catering cottages, details can be found at www.ardmaddy.com.

**Directions:** Take A816 south of Oban for 8 miles. Turn right B844 to Seil Island/ Easdale. Four miles on, take Ardmaddy road for further 2 miles.

Disabled Access:
Full

Opening Times:
1 January - 31 December
9:00pm - Dusk

Admission:
£4.00, children free

Charities:
Donation to SG Beneficiaries.

## ARDUAINE GARDEN

Oban PA34 4XQ

**The National Trust for Scotland T: 0844 493 2216**

**E: mwilkins@nts.org.uk www.nts.org.uk**

Outstanding 20 acre coastal garden created over 100 years ago on the south facing slope of a promontory separating Asknish Bay from Loch Melfort. This remarkable hidden paradise, protected by tall shelterbelts and influenced favourably by the North Atlantic Drift, grows a wide variety of plants from all over the globe. Internationally known for the rhododendron species collection, the garden also features magnolias, camellias, azaleas and other wonderful trees and shrubs, many being tender and rarely seen. A broad selection of perennials, bulbs, ferns and water plants ensure year-long interest.

**Other Details:** Garden staff walks at 11:00am and 2:30pm. Teas available in local hotel.

**Directions:** Off A816 Oban-Lochgilphead, sharing an entrance with the Loch Melfort Hotel.

Disabled Access:
Partial

Opening Times:
Sunday 11 May
9:30am - 5:00pm

Admission:
£6.00 including NTS members.
N.B. These prices are correct at time of going to print.

Charities:
Donation to SG Beneficiaries.

## BARGUILLEAN'S "ANGUS GARDEN"

Taynuilt PA35 1HY

**The Josephine Marshall Trust T: 01866 822333**

**E: info@barguillean.co.uk www.barguillean.co.uk**

Nine acre woodland garden around an 11 acre loch set in the Glen Lonan hills. Spring flowering shrubs and bulbs, extensive collection of rhododendron hybrids, deciduous azaleas, conifers and unusual trees. The garden contains a large collection of North American rhododendron hybrids from famous contemporary plant breeders. Some paths can be steep. Three marked walks from thirty minutes to one and a half hours.

**Other Details:** Self catering accommodation in comfortable wing of Main House. Coach tours by appointment.

**Directions:** Three miles south off A85 Glasgow/Oban road at Taynuilt; road marked Glen Lonan; 3 miles up single track road; turn right at sign.

Disabled Access:
None

Opening Times:
1 January - 31 December
9:00am - Dusk

Admission:
£3.00, children under 14 free

Charities:
Donation to SG Beneficiaries.

## BENMORE BOTANIC GARDEN

Benmore, Dunoon PA23 8QU

**Regional Garden of the Royal Botanic Garden Edinburgh T: 01369 706261**

**E: benmore@rbge.org.uk www.rbge.org.uk**

World famous for magnificent conifers and its extensive range of flowering trees and shrubs, including over 250 species of rhododendron. From a spectacular avenue of Giant Redwoods numerous marked walks lead, via a formal garden and pond, through hillside woodlands to a dramatic viewpoint overlooking the Eachaig valley and the Holy Loch. The newly restored Benmore Fernery is open from 11:00 am, closing an hour before the Garden closes.

**Other Details:** Guided tours Tuesdays, Wednesdays, Thursdays and Sundays at 2:00pm.

**Directions:** Seven miles north of Dunoon or 22 miles south from Glen Kinglass below Rest and Be Thankful pass. On A815.

Disabled Access:
Partial

Opening Times:
Sunday 27 April
10:00am - 6:00pm
1 March - 31 October
10:00am - 6:00pm

Admission:
£6.00, concessions £5.00, children under 16 free (prices include a small donation to the Garden. For admission prices without donation please check our website)

Charities:
Donation to SG Beneficiaries.

## 9 CAOL RUADH

Colintraive PA22 3AR
**Mr and Mrs C Scotland**

Delightful seaside garden on the old B866 shore road looking out over Loch Riddon and the Kyles of Bute in this very beautiful corner of Argyll. Also has the additional attraction of a unique outdoor sculpture park featuring works from a variety of Scottish artists.

**Directions:** Turn right off A886 Strachur - Colintraive onto B866 about 2½ miles before Colintraive. From Dunoon take A815 north about 3½ miles, left on to B836 and then left on to A886.

Disabled Access:
None

Opening Times:
Saturday 19 July
2:00pm - 5:00pm
Sunday 20 July
2:00pm - 5:00pm

Admission:
£6.00 includes tea

Charities:
All proceeds to SG Beneficiaries.

## 10 CRARAE GARDEN

Inveraray PA32 8YA
**The National Trust for Scotland T: 0844 4932210**
**E: nprice@nts.org.uk www.nts.org.uk**

A spectacular 50 acre garden in a dramatic setting. Crarae has a wonderful collection of woody plants centred on the Crarae Burn, which is spanned by several bridges and tumbles through a rocky gorge in a series of cascades. A wide variety of shrubs and trees chosen for spring flowering and autumn colour grow in the shelter of towering conifers. The lush naturalistic planting and rushing water give the garden the feel of a valley in the Himalayas.

**Other Details:** National Plant Collection®: Nothofagus (Southern Beech). This collection is the most northerly of its type in the UK. Champion Trees: Abies, Acer and Chamaecyparis.
Price includes behind the scenes guided walk by our expert staff.
Sturdy footwear is recommended.

**Directions:** On A83 10 miles south of Inveraray.

Disabled Access:
Partial

Opening Times:
Sunday 25 May
10:00am - 5:00pm
Sunday 27 July
10:00am - 5:00pm

Admission:
£6.50 including NTS members.
N.B. Prices correct at time of going to print.

Charities:
Donation to SG Beneficiaries.

## 11 CRINAN HOTEL GARDEN

Crinan PA31 8SR
**Mr and Mrs N Ryan T: 01546 830261**
**E: nryan@crinanhotel.com www.crinanhotel.com**

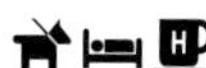

Small rock garden with azaleas and rhododendrons created into a steep hillside over a century ago with steps leading to a sheltered, secluded garden with sloping lawns, herbaceous beds and spectacular views of the canal and Crinan Loch.

**Other Details:** Raffle of painting by Frances Macdonald (Ryan), tickets at coffee shop, art gallery and hotel. Homemade teas available in coffee shop.

**Directions:** Lochgilphead A83, then A816 to Oban, then A841 Cairnbaan to Crinan.

Disabled Access:
None

Opening Times:
1 May - 31 August
Dawn - Dusk

Admission:
By donation

Charities:
Feedback Madagascar receives 40%, the net remaining to SG Beneficiaries.

## DRIM NA VULLIN

Blarbuie Road, Lochgilphead PA31 8LE
**Mr and Mrs Robin Campbell Byatt T: 01546 602615**
**E: byatt.drim@virgin.net**

Drim na Vullin, originally a mill, and its woodland garden have been owned by the same family since 1829. Most of the development of the garden was landscaped and planted in the 1950s by Sybil Campbell OBE, Britain's first female professional magistrate, assisted by Percy Cane, the garden designer. It lies along a cleft formed by the Cuilarstitch Burn with a spectacular waterfall at the top. Mature species and hybrid rhododendrons, magnolias, azaleas and other shrubs are under a canopy of mostly native trees. The present owners' planting brings the developed area to about 5 acres.

**Directions:** A83 to Lochgilphead. At the top of main street in front of parish church, turn right up Manse Brae. The garden is ⅓ mile up the hill on the left. Beyond the houses on the left a high fence leads to Drim na Vullin's entrance. Please park on the road.

Disabled Access:
None

Opening Times:
By arrangement
17 - 31 May
2.00pm - 5.00pm

Admission:
£3.00

Charities:
Christchurch Episcopal Church, Lochgilphead receives 40%, the net remaining to SG Beneficiaries.

## DRUIMNEIL HOUSE

Port Appin PA38 4DQ
**Mrs J Glaisher (Gardener: Mr Andrew Ritchie) T: 01631 730228**
**E: druimneillhouse@btinternet.com**

Large garden overlooking Loch Linnhe with many fine varieties of mature trees and rhododendrons and other woodland shrubs. Nearer the house, an impressive bank of deciduous azaleas is underplanted with a block of camassia and a range of other bulbs. A small Victorian walled garden is currently being restored.

**Other Details:** Teas normally available. Lunch by prior arrangement.

**Directions:** Turn in for Appin off A828 (Connel/Fort William Road). Two miles, sharp left at Airds Hotel, second house on right.

Disabled Access:
None

Opening Times:
17 April - 31 October
Dawn - Dusk

Admission:
By donation

Charities:
All proceeds to SG Beneficiaries.

## FAIRWINDS

14 George Street, Hunter's Quay, Dunoon PA23 8JU
**Mrs Carol Stewart T: 01369 702666**
**E: carol.argyll@talk21.com**

This mature garden was created in the fifties from a small orchard. The present owner is constantly trying to add colour and interest for all seasons. Spring brings a flourish of spring flowers, rhododendrons and azaleas. Trees of all kinds display their constantly changing shades throughout the year and in autumn the acers and copper beech are at their very best. Around every corner there is yet another plant of interest, a goldfish pond or a swing.

**Other Details:** Please call if coming from a distance. Teas on request.

**Directions:** On A815. Enter Dunoon on loch side road, right up Cammesreinach Brae just before the Royal Marine Hotel opposite W Ferries terminal. The Brae becomes George Street, Fairwinds is on left.

Disabled Access:
Full

Opening Times:
1 April - 31 October
9:00am - 6:00pm

Admission:
£2.50, children free

Charities:
The Cowal Hospice receives 40%, the net remaining to SG Beneficiaries.

## INVERARAY CASTLE GARDENS

Inveraray PA32 8XF
**The Duke and Duchess of Argyll T: 01499 302203**
**E: enquiries@inveraray-castle.com www.inveraray-castle.com**

Rhododendrons and azaleas abound and flower from April to June. Very fine specimens of Cedrus deodars, Sequoiadendron wellingtonia, Cryptomeria japonica, Taxus baccata and others thrive in the damp climate. The 'Flag-Borders' on each side of the main drive with paths in the shape of Scotland's national flag, the St. Andrew's Cross, are outstanding in spring with Prunus "Ukon" and "Subhirtella" and are underplanted with rhododendrons, Eucryphias, shrubs and herbaceous plants giving interest all year.

**Other Details:** Tearoom open for teas, coffees, homebaking and light lunches. Only guide dogs allowed.

**Directions:** Inveraray is 60 miles north of Glasgow on the banks of Loch Fyne on the A83 with a regular bus service from Glasgow and 15 miles from Dalmally on A819.

Disabled Access:
Partial

Opening Times:
1 April - 31 October
10:00am - 5:45pm

Admission:
£4.00

Charities:
Donation to SG Beneficiaries.

## KAMES BAY

Kilmelford PA34 4XA
**Stuart Cannon T: 01852 200205**
**E: stuartcannon@kames.co.uk**

The garden and house were first established from a wild hillside in 1982. The garden and woodland were extended in 2001. It is principally a spring garden with ornamental trees, rhododendrons and azaleas, some of the rhodies are from Arduaine and Ardanasaig gardens, as well as other friends' gardens. A pond was created while landscaping the hill to provide a flatter area for a shed and greenhouse. There are some pleasant walks in the woodland with wild primroses, violets, and other wild flowers, with various seats to rest and enjoy the special views over Loch Melfort and the Islands to the west.

**Other Details:** Some grass paths - suitable walking shoes are recommended as access is up a steep drive.

**Directions:** On A816 Oban to Lochgilphead road opposite Kames Bay and the fish farm. 2½ miles south of Kilmelford and 2½ miles north of Arduaine.

Disabled Access:
None

Opening Times:
Saturday 3 May
1:00pm - 5:00pm
Sunday 4 May
1:00pm - 5:00pm

Admission:
£4.00

Charities:
St Columba's Church receives 40%, the net remaining to SG Beneficiaries.

## KINLOCHLAICH HOUSE GARDENS

Appin PA38 4BD
**Mr and Mrs D E Hutchison and Miss F M M Hutchison T: 07881 525754**
**E: gardens@kinlochlaich-house.co.uk www.kinlochlaichgardencentre.co.uk**

Walled garden incorporating the Western Highlands' largest Nursery Garden Centre. Amazing variety of plants growing and for sale. Extensive grounds with woodland walk, spring garden, vegetable gardens, fruit polyhouse and formal garden. Extensive display of rhododendrons, azaleas, trees, shrubs and herbaceous, including many unusuals - Embothrium, Davidia, Magnolia, Eucryphia and Tropaeolum.

**Other Details:** Self-catering accommodation.
We do not sell teas but are happy to make you one if possible.

**Directions:** On the A828 in Appin. Oban 18 miles south, Fort William 27 miles north. The entrance is next to the Police Station.

Disabled Access:
Partial

Opening Times:
1 January - 31 December
9:30am - 4:30pm
(but closed Sundays and Mondays October - March)

Admission:
£2.50, accompanied children free

Charities:
Appin Village Hall receives 40%, the net remaining to SG Beneficiaries.

## MAOLACHY'S GARDEN

Lochavich, by Taynuilt PA35 1HJ
**Georgina Dalton T: 01866 844212**

Three acres of Woodland Garden with a tumbling burn, created in a small glen over 30 years. At an altitude of 450 feet and 2 weeks behind the coast we have a shorter growing season. By not struggling to grow tender or late species we can enjoy those that are happy to grow well here. Early rhodies, masses of daffodils in many varieties, bluebells, wild flowers and azaleas, primulas and irises. Herbaceous blooms flower on into summer's greenery. Productive vegetable patch and tunnel.

**Other Details:** The main path is gravelled, but some others are narrow, steep and not for the faint hearted! Sensible shoes are recommended.

**Directions:** A816 to Kilmelford. Turn uphill between the shop and church, signed Lochavich 6, steep twisty road with hairpin bend shortly after leaving village. Check for passing places. Maolachy Drive is 4 miles from village. Cross 3 cattle grids; after the 3rd **ignore the forestry tracks** to left and right. Continue downhill towards Loch Avich, Maolachy is up on the left, first house after Kilmelford. **Ignore satnav.**

Disabled Access:
None

Opening Times:
Saturday 24 May
2:00pm - 5:00pm
Sunday 25 May
2:00pm - 5:00pm

Admission:
£3.50

Charities:
Hope Kitchen -Oban receives 40%, the net remaining to SG Beneficiaries.

## MELFORT HOUSE KITCHEN GARDEN

Kilmelford, by Oban PA34 4XD
**Yvonne Anderson**
**E: yvonne@melforthouse.co.uk www.melforthouse.co.uk**

Melfort house is a family home and country house dinner, bed and breakfast on the shores of Loch Melfort, set in a mature 2 acre garden with specimen trees, a water feature and a variety of rhododendron and azaleas. In the quest for the most exquisite tastes and flavours for our table we were inspired to 'grow our own'. Two years ago the kitchen garden was born. Now over 40 types of vegetables are grown from seed, including rarer heritage seed varieties, in a 54 feet long polytunnel. Whatever the weather, the polytunnel has become a place to relax and enjoy the colour, texture and aromas of the whole growing experience from seed to plate.

**Directions:** Leave A816 Oban to Lochgilphead road in the village of Kilmelford. Turn west following sign for "Melfort 1¼ " for just over 1 mile. Immediately after the stone bridge turn right through stone pillars and then bear left into our drive.

Disabled Access:
Full

Opening Times:
Saturday 2 August
2:00pm - 5:00pm
Sunday 3 August
2:00pm - 5:00pm

Admission:
£3.00

Charities:
Local Kilmelford charities will receive 40%, the net remaining to SG Beneficiaries.

## OAKBANK

Ardrishaig PA30 8EP
**Helga Macfarlane T: 01546 603405**
**E: helgamacfarlane@onetel.com www.gardenatoakbank.blogspot.com**

This unusual and delightful garden was formed by clearing some 3 acres of hillside and creating a series of paths that wind amongst a varied collection of trees, shrubs, bulbs and wild flowers. There are several small ponds, many wonderful wood carvings, an active visiting population of red squirrels and a viewpoint overlooking Loch Fyne to the Isle of Arran. The garden also has huge appeal for children with lots to explore, including a secret garden.

**Directions:** On the Tarbert side of Ardrishaig: entry to the garden is at the junction of Tarbert Road (A83) and Oakfield Road and immediately opposite the more southerly Scottish Water lay-by.

Disabled Access:
None

Opening Times:
1 May - 31 October
10:30am - 5:30pm

Admission:
£3.00, children free

Charities:
Diabetes UK receives 40%, the net remaining to SG Beneficiaries.

## STRACHUR HOUSE FLOWER & WOODLAND GARDENS
Strachur PA27 8BX
**Sir Charles and Lady Maclean**

Directly behind Strachur House the flower garden is sheltered by magnificent beeches, limes, ancient yews and Japanese maples. There are herbaceous borders, a burnside rhododendron and azalea walk and a rockery. Old fashioned and species roses, lilies, tulips, spring bulbs and Himalayan poppies make a varied display in this informal haven of beauty and tranquillity. The garden gives onto Strachur Park, laid out by General Campbell in 1782, which offers spectacular walks through natural woodland with two hundred-year-old trees, rare shrubs and a lochan rich in native wildlife.

**Other Details:** Teas available at the Post Office.

**Directions:** Turn off A815 at Strachur House Farm entrance. Park in farm square.

Disabled Access:
Full

Opening Times:
Saturday 24 May
1:00pm - 5:00pm
Sunday 25 May
1:00pm - 5:00pm

Admission:
£3.50

Charities:
CLASP receives 40%, the net remaining to SG Beneficiaries.

## THE SHORE VILLAGES
by Dunoon PA23 8SE
**The Gardeners of The Shore Villages**

**19-20 Graham's Point**, Kilmun (Mr and Mrs A McClintock)
**Dunclutha**, Strone (Mr and Mrs R Aldam)
**Belhaven**, Blairmore (Mr and Mrs J Hampson)
**Saltire House**, Blairmore (Mr and Mrs I McEwan)
**4 Swedish Houses**, Ardentinny (E Connell)
**5 Swedish Houses**, Ardentinny (Mr and Mrs B Waldapfel)
**Garden Cottage**, Ardentinny (Mr and Mrs A McLundie).

Seven very different gardens on a 7 mile stretch off the A880, overlooking the Holy Loch, the Clyde and Loch Long. Gardening for wildlife, colour combinations and for low maintenance, with terracing, sculpture, wildflower meadows and ponds, herbaceous borders and trees from seed. Some gardens are on steep slopes with limited disabled access.

**Other Details:** Several plant stalls. Teas at Dunclutha, Strone.
Tickets, with information sheet, can be purchased at all gardens.

**Directions:** Approaching Dunoon from the north on the A815, take the left hand turning for Kilmun and follow the yellow arrows.

5 Swedish Houses

Dunclutha House

Disabled Access:
Partial

Opening Times:
Saturday 28 June
1:00pm - 5:00pm
Sunday 29 June
1:00pm - 5:00pm

Admission:
£4.00, accompanied children free

Charities:
All proceeds to SG Beneficiaries.

# AYRSHIRE

Scotland's Gardens 2014 Guidebook is sponsored by **INVESTEC WEALTH & INVESTMENT**

## District Organiser

| | |
|---|---|
| Mrs R F Cuninghame | Caprington Castle, Kilmarnock KA2 9AA |

## Area Organisers

| | |
|---|---|
| Mrs Glen Collins | Grougarbank House, Kilmarnock KA3 6HP |
| Mrs Michael Findlay | Carnell, By Hurlford, Kilmarnock KA1 5JS |
| Mrs John MacKay | Pierhill, Annbank KA6 5AW |
| Mrs A J Sandiford | Harrowhill Cottage, Kilmarnock KA3 6HX |
| Ms Heidi Stone | 3 Noddsdale Cottage, Brisbane Glen Rd, Largs KA30 8SL |

## Treasurer

| | |
|---|---|
| Brigadier A J Sandiford | Harrowhill Cottage, Kilmarnock KA3 6HX |

## Gardens open on a specific date

| | | |
|---|---|---|
| Gardening Leave, SAC Auchincruive | Sunday 25 May | 12:00pm - 4:00pm |
| Borlandhills, Dunlop | Sunday 1 June | 2:00pm - 5:00pm |
| Holmes Farm, By Irvine | Saturday 7 June | 1:00pm - 5:00pm |
| Holmes Farm, By Irvine | Sunday 8 June | 1:00pm - 5:00pm |
| 1 Burnside Cottages, Sundrum | Sunday 15 June | 2:00pm - 5:00pm |
| Gardens of West Kilbride and Seamill | Sunday 22 June | 1:00pm - 5:00pm |
| 10 Grange Terrace & The Annanhill Park Allotments | Sunday 29 June | 2:00pm - 5:00pm |
| Cairnhall House, Ochiltree | Sunday 13 July | 2:00pm - 5:00pm |
| Culzean, Maybole | Tuesday 15 July | 9:30am - 5:00pm |
| Kilmaurs Village Gardens | Sunday 20 July | 1:30pm - 4:30pm |
| Glen Gardens of Largs | Sunday 3 August | 2:00pm - 5:00pm |
| Kirkmuir Cottage, Stewarton | Saturday 9 August | 1:00pm - 5:00pm |

## Gardens open by arrangement

| | | |
|---|---|---|
| Carnell, by Hurlford | 1 May - 15 September | 01563 884236 |

## Key to symbols

| | | |
|---|---|---|
| New in 2014 | Homemade teas | Accommodation |
| Teas | Dogs on a lead allowed | Plant stall |
| Cream teas | Wheelchair access | Scottish Snowdrop Festival |

## Garden locations

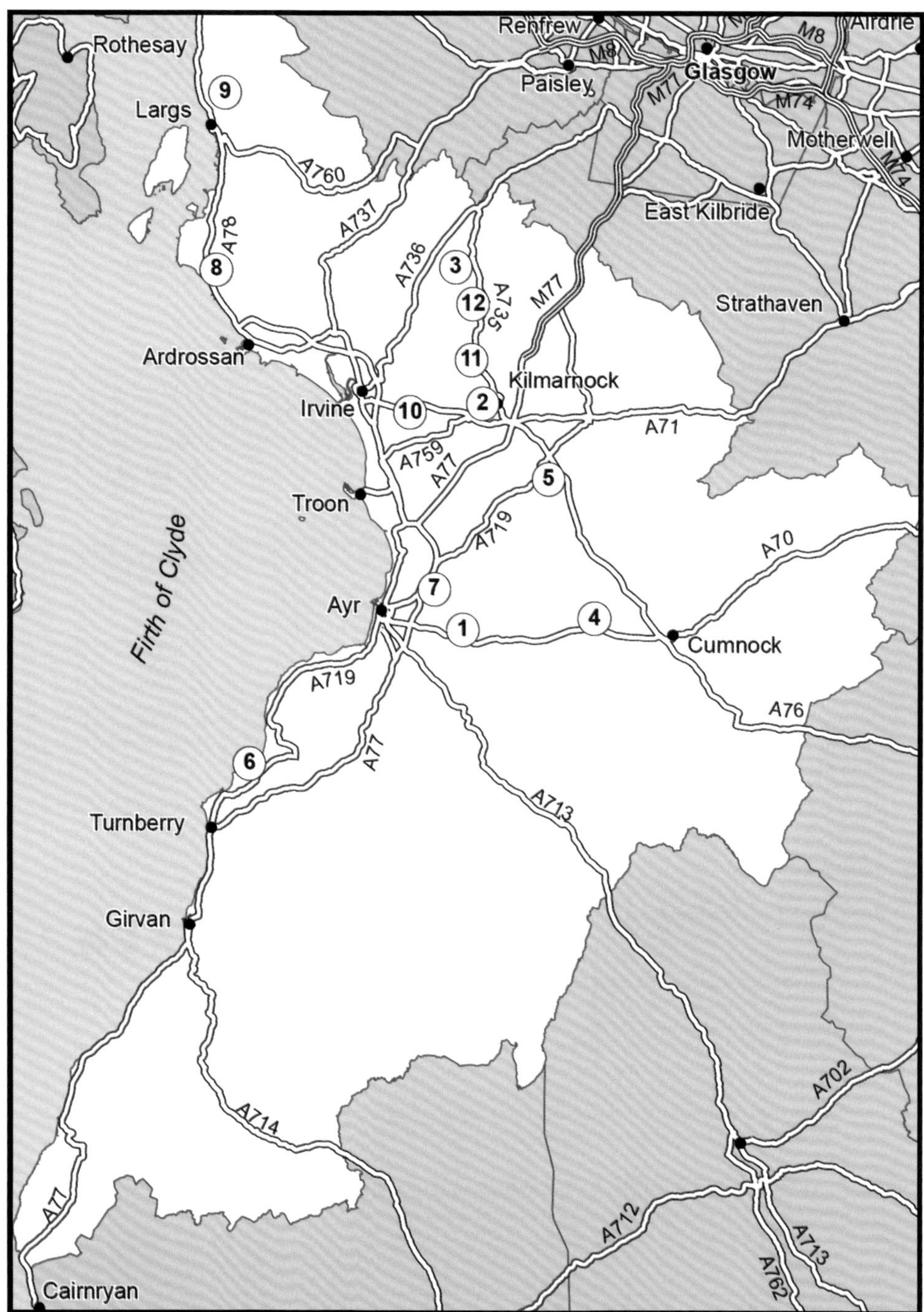

## 1 BURNSIDE COTTAGES

Sundrum, Coylton KA6 5JX
**Carol Freireich**

A sheltered Cottage Garden of 1.3 acres. Organically cultivated, native trees and many wild flowers encourage wide varieties of bird and insect life. A stream runs through a small wood, an old orchard with newer plantings of varieties chosen to tolerate northern conditions, a pond, vegetable garden and ornamental plantings all with plenty of places to sit.

**Directions:** Three miles from Ayr on the A70, signed left at Sundrum Castle Caravan Park, go up the road for ¾ mile and then left down dirt track where there is limited parking.
OR continue to Coylton first left at Barclauch Drive round to the right, park at Woodhead Road and walk for 5 minutes to the garden. Look for signposts.
Bus 45 or 48 Ayr/Cumnock to foot of Barclaugh Drive and follow signed route.

Disabled Access:
Partial

Opening Times:
Sunday 15 June
2:00pm - 5:00pm

Admission:
£4.00, children under 12 free

Charities:
Marie Curie Cancer Care (Ayrshire) receives 40%, the net remaining to SG Beneficiaries.

## 10 GRANGE TERRACE AND ALLOTMENTS OF ANNANHILL PARK

Kilmarnock KA1 2JR
**Mr & Mrs Iain Linton and The Annanhill Park Association**

**10 Grange Terrace:** This south facing established garden has a diversity of well-chosen shrubs and herbaceous borders. A vegetable plot with soft fruit and top fruit trees complete a delightful triangular garden.
**Annanhill Park Association Allotments:** The former walled garden to Annanhill Park has been most successfully turned into allotments by the Annanhill Park Association in 2013. Well stocked plots are complemented by colourful huts.

**Other Details:** Tickets available at 10 Grange Terrace.

**Directions:** From A77 Bellfield interchange take the A71 dual carriageway marked Irvine to first roundabout and take Crosshouse exit. Over a small roundabout directing to Hospital (B7081) and at T-junction turn right to Kilmarnock Town Centre, past Annanhill Park/Golf Course through set of lights, turn right off Irvine Road before filling station into Grange Terrace.
Route will be yellow signposted to both gardens.

Disabled Access:
Partial

Opening Times:
Sunday 29 June
2:00pm - 5:00pm

Admission:
£4.00, children under 12 free

Charities:
Annanhill Allotment Society receives 40%, the net remaining to SG Beneficiaries.

## BORLANDHILLS

Brecknabraes Road, Dunlop KA3 4BU
**Professor and Mrs Michael Moss**

This is an exciting hilltop garden created over the last 16 years, with hidden corners and magnificent views of Arran. It contains a surprising variety of habitats ranging from a bog garden with gunnera, primula and great clumps of irises to dry sheltered corners with fine displays of bulbs in late spring, magnolias, rhododendrons, azaleas and meconopsis. Roses and clematis scramble through hedges and over the buildings. There are herbaceous borders with many unusual Himalayan plants grown mostly from seed. In the heart of the garden there are large vegetable plots and two polytunnels with a great variety of produce that provide for the family throughout the year.

**Directions:** From the centre of Dunlop down Main Street, turn left at the Church into Brecknabraes Road (right is the B706 to Beith) and the garden is 0.7 miles on the left.

Disabled Access:
Partial

Opening Times:
Sunday 1 June
2:00pm - 5:00pm

Admission:
£4.00

Charities:
Send a Cow receives 40%, the net remaining to SG Beneficiaries.

## CAIRNHALL HOUSE

Mauchline Road, Ochiltree KA18 2QA
**Ian and Sarah Hay**

A nature lover's garden created over 8 years from a thistle-filled field into an organic 2 acre garden of extensive flower beds, large pond and vegetable plot, a clematis meadow (new in 2013) and laburnum tunnel all designed to appeal to insects, butterflies, birds and people.

**Other Details:** Drop off at house for the infirm only - driver to park as below.

**Directions:** From A70 into Ochiltree where road forks to Cumnock, turn left up Mauchline Road. Drive is 150 yards on left. Please note parking is limited. Cemetery car park nearby option. See drop off info above.

Disabled Access:
Partial

Opening Times:
Sunday 13 July
2:00pm - 5:00pm

Admission:
£4.00, children free

Charities:
MND Scotland receives 20%, Vegfam receives 20%, the net remaining to SG Beneficiaries.

## CARNELL

by Hurlford KA1 5JS
**Mr & Mrs John Findlay and Mr & Mrs Michael Findlay T: 01563 884236**
**E: carnellestates@aol.com www.carnellestates.com**

The 16th century Peel Tower looks down over a 10 acre garden which has featured in the "Beechgrove Garden", "Country Life", "The Good Gardens Guide" as well as Suki Urquhart's book "The Scottish Gardener". Carnell has a traditional walled garden with a 100 yard long herbaceous border, as well as a rock and water garden, gazebo with Burmese statues, lawns and many other features of interest. Herbaceous, rose and phlox borders are in full bloom during July.

**Other Details:** Teas may be available by prior booking, contact Mrs Michael Findlay (details above).

**Directions:** From A77 (Glasgow/Kilmarnock) take A76 (Mauchline/Dumfries) then right on to the A719 to Ayr for 1½ miles.

Disabled Access:
Partial

Opening Times:
By arrangement
1 May - 15 September
for garden tours, minimum of 10 persons

Admission:
£4.00, children under 12 free

Charities:
Donation to SG Beneficiaries.

## CULZEAN

Maybole KA19 8LE
**The National Trust for Scotland T: 0844 493 2148**
**E: culzean@nts.org.uk www.nts.org.uk**

A major Scottish attraction and a perfect day out for all the family. Robert Adam's romantic 18th century masterpiece is perched on a cliff high above the Firth of Clyde. The Fountain Garden lies in front of the castle with terraces and herbaceous borders reflecting its Georgian elegance. The extensive country park offers beaches and rockpools, parklands, gardens, woodland walks and adventure playground. It contains fascinating restored buildings contemporary with the castle.

**Other Details:** Castle and estate open - see NTS website for details. Restaurant has homemade wine from Culzean. The tour starts from the walled garden at 2:00pm and includes behind the scenes.

**Directions:** Twelve miles south of Ayr on A719, 4 miles west of Maybole.
Bus: Stagecoach, Ayr/Girvan via Maidens (No 60) to entrance. One mile walk downhill from stop to Castle/Visitor Centre.

Disabled Access:
Partial

Opening Times:
Tuesday 15 July
9:30am - 5:00pm

Admission:
Normal admission applies. £2.00 (including NTS members) for special guided walk with the Head Gardener

Charities:
Donation to SG Beneficiaries.

## GARDENING LEAVE

c/o Gardens Unit, SAC Auchincruive KA6 5HW

**Gardening Leave T: 01292 521444**
**E: admin@gardeningleave.org**

Small, walled terrace garden located within the grounds of Auchincruive Estate in Ayrshire run by a charity which provides sessions of horticultural therapy to veterans of the Armed Forces. The garden houses vegetable beds, poppy collection and a quiet reflective corner. The charity is also in the process of restoring an 84 metre long Victorian Greenhouse known as the 'Stovehouse'. Part of the Stovehouse is open for use and teas and coffee will be served there.

**Other Details:** Pre-booked tickets are available, please email or phone Gardening Leave for details. Tickets can also be purchased on the day.

**Directions:** From Whitletts roundabout outside Ayr, follow B743 to Mauchline, bypass the signposted entrance to the Auchincruive Estate SAC. Continue for approximately ¾ mile and take next on right.

Disabled Access:
Partial

Opening Times:
Sunday 25 May
12:00pm - 4:00pm

Admission:
£4.00, children under 12 free

Charities:
Gardening Leave receives 40%, the net remaining to SG Beneficiaries.

## GARDENS OF WEST KILBRIDE AND SEAMILL

KA23

**The Gardeners of West Kilbride and Seamill**

Opening again 2 summers later, a selection of gardens in this seaside town will show a variety of styles and planting.

**Other Details:** Tickets and maps marked with gardens opening, disabled access, etc. available at the Village Hall.

**Directions:** Heading from Dalry take B781 for 7 miles. Alternatively take the A78 south for 8 miles from Largs or the A78 north for 7 miles from Kilwinning. Signposted to Village Hall.

Disabled Access:
Partial

Opening Times:
Sunday 22 June
1:00pm - 5:00pm

Admission:
£4.00, children under 12 free

Charities:
Choice of charity to be decided and will receive 40%, the net remaining to SG Beneficiaries.

## GLEN GARDENS OF LARGS

Largs KA30 8SL

**The Very Rev. Dr. Idris S Jones & Dr Alison Jones and Heidi Stone**
**T: 01475 673155**
**E: heidi-stone@sky.com**

**27 Donald Wynd**, The Rise KA30 8TH: A beautifully crafted, layered garden with many specimen plants and creative ideas for colour and form.
**3 Noddesdale Cottages**, Brisbane Glen Road KA30 8SL: A wildlife garden where you can sit and enjoy delicious strawberry cream teas surrounded by wonderful country views.

**Other Details:** Tickets available at 27 Donald Wynd.
Teas and plant stall at 3 Noddesdale Cottages.

**Directions:** A78 south from Greenock and north from Irvine.
Route will be yellow signposted to each garden.

Disabled Access:
Partial

Opening Times:
Sunday 3 August
2:00pm - 5:00pm

Admission:
£3.50, children free

Charities:
Save The Children receives 40%, the net remaining to SG Beneficiaries.

## HOLMES FARM

Drybridge, By Irvine KA11 5BS
**Mr Brian A Young T: 01294 311210**
**E: yungi@fsmail.net**

A plantsman's garden created by a confirmed plantaholic. Meandering paths guide the eye through plantings predominantly herbaceous, with small trees and shrubs. Some plant collections are housed permanently in polytunnels. The garden opening will hopefully be timed for peak bloom of some of the 400 iris in the garden. Some areas of the garden are currently undergoing a partial replant and redesign.
Plant nursery with a wide selection of plants from the garden and a gift shop too!

**Directions:** Holmes is the only farm between Drybridge and Dreghorn on B730.

Disab
None

Opening Times:
Saturday 7 June
1:00pm - 5:00pm
Sunday 8 June
1:00pm - 5:00pm

Admission:
£4.00

Charities:
Crossmichael and Parton Playgroup receives 40%, the net remaining to SG Beneficiaries.

## KILMAURS VILLAGE GARDENS

Kilmaurs KA3 2QS
**The Gardeners of Kilmaurs**

Following a successful first opening in 2013, there will be some new gardens, one with the owner's own sculpture and another delightful one built around the site of an early group of collegiate buildings with original doocot and woodland. Other openings include, a very elegant modern one with a pond feature, a garden with clever use of specimen Acers in pots and further planters of fruit, vegetables and flowers which are grown for the table, the flower show and to encourage wild life in 2 adjacent gardens. Whilst others show inspired mixed planting of trees, shrubs, herbaceous and alpines in traditional Scottish garden style.

**Other Details:** Teas, tickets & maps showing shortcuts and paths around this historic conservation village available at Maxwell Church Hall, Crosshouse Rd KA3 2SA.

**Directions:** From M77 north take B751 turnoff at Fenwick for Kilmaurs.
From A77 from east and south A71 Irvine and turn off to Crosshouse, Knockentiber on B751. Yellow signposted from A735 and B751.

Disabled Access:
Partial

Opening Times:
Sunday 20 July
1:30pm - 4:30pm

Admission:
£4.00, children under 12 free

Charities:
Charity to be advised and will receive 40%, the net remaining to SG Beneficiaries.

## KIRKMUIR COTTAGE

Stewarton KA3 3DZ
**Mr and Mrs Brian Macpherson**

A one and a half acre garden which includes a pond, woodland area, formal borders, lawns and many ornamental features.

**Directions:** From M77 take B778 to Stewarton. At traffic lights turn left, and continue to mini roundabout. Turn right at mini roundabout signposted B778 Kilwinning. Continue for 100 yards under the railway bridge, take immediate left at war memorial. Parking for Kirkmuir Cottage will be well signposted.

Disabled Access:
Full

Opening Times:
Saturday 9 August
1:00pm - 5:00pm

Admission:
£3.50, accompanied children free

Charities:
Capability Scotland receives 40%, the net remaining to SG Beneficiaries.

# ERWICKSHIRE



## District Organiser

| | |
|---|---|
| Mrs F Wills | Anton's Hill, Coldstream TD12 4JD |

## Area Organisers

| | |
|---|---|
| Mrs Carolyn Innes | Boon House, Boon, Lauder TD2 6SB |
| Mrs S Wight | Wellfield, Horndean, Berwick-upon-Tweed TD15 1XJ |

## Treasurer

| | |
|---|---|
| Mr F Wills | Anton's Hill, Coldstream TD12 4JD |

## Gardens open on a specific date

| | | |
|---|---|---|
| Swinton Mill House, Coldstream | Sunday 8 June | 1:00pm - 5:00pm |
| Wellfield, Horndean | Sunday 15 June | 11:00am - 4:00pm |
| Lennel Bank, Coldstream | Sunday 29 June | 10:30am - 5:00pm |
| Angus Cottage, Preston | Sunday 6 July | 10:30am - 3:00pm |
| Cumledge Mill House, Duns | Sunday 6 July | 10:30am - 3:00pm |
| Anton's Hill and Walled Garden, Leitholm | Sunday 13 July | 2:00pm - 5:30pm |
| Netherbyres, Eyemouth | Sunday 20 July | 2:00pm - 5:30pm |

## Gardens open regularly

| | | |
|---|---|---|
| Bughtrig, Near Leitholm | 1 June - 1 September | 11:00am - 5:00pm |

## Gardens open by arrangement

| | | |
|---|---|---|
| Anton's Hill and Walled Garden, Leitholm | On request | 01890 840203 |
| Lennel Bank, Coldstream | On request | 01890 882297 |
| Netherbyres, Eyemouth | 1 May - 31 August | 01890 750337 |

## Key to symbols

 New in 2014

 Teas

 Cream teas

 Homemade teas

 Dogs on a lead allowed

 Wheelchair access

 Accommodation

 Plant stall

 Scottish Snowdrop Festival

## Garden locations

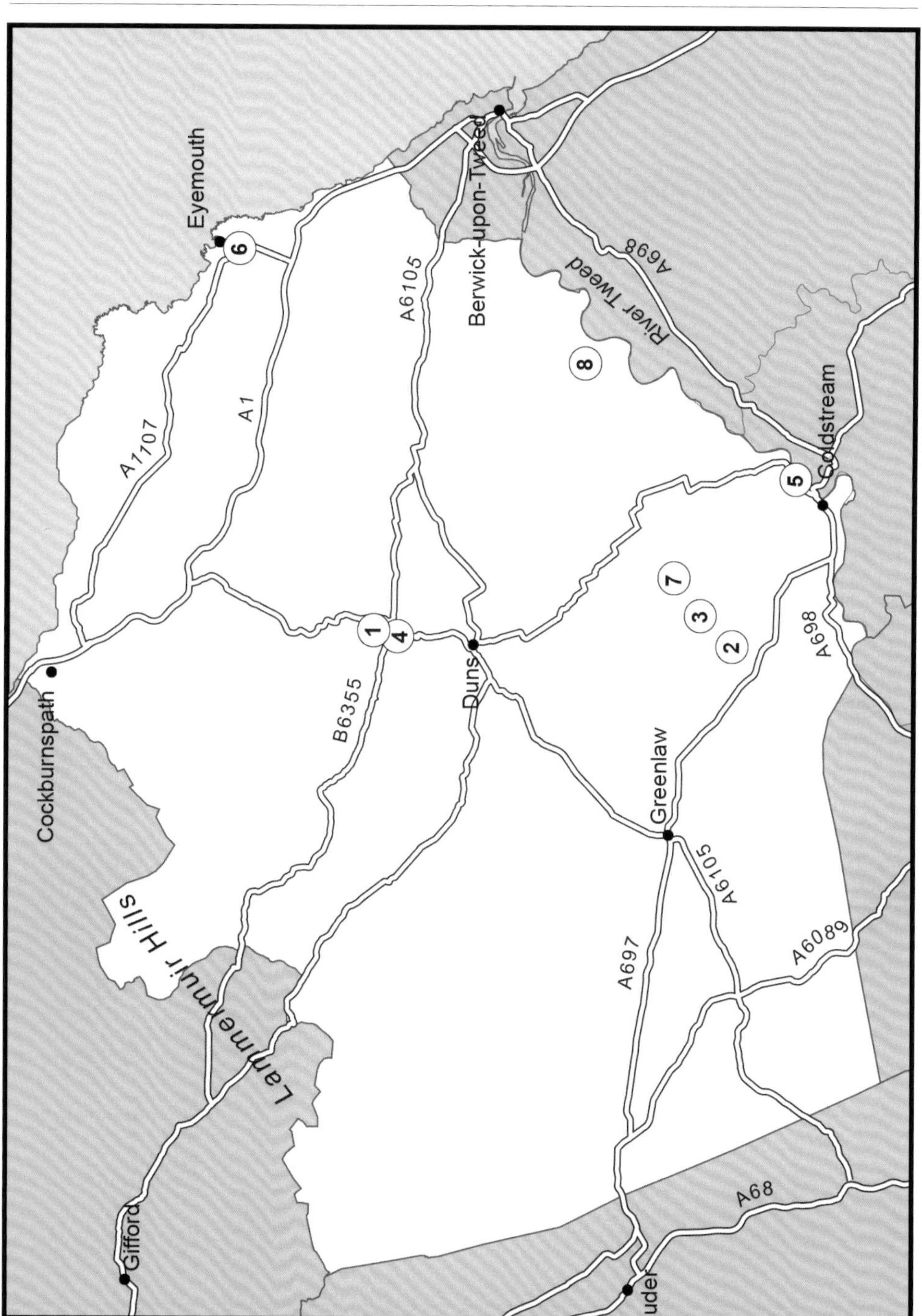

## ANGUS COTTAGE (WITH CUMLEDGE MILL HOUSE)

Preston, Duns TD11 3TQ
**Mr and Mrs R Eggo**

A charming garden with interesting shrubs and long curving herbaceous border, full of perennials, climbing roses and clematis. Gravel garden with small pond.

**Other Details:** Teas served in Preston Village Hall.

**Directions:** Preston Village is 2 miles north of Duns on the Duns - Grantshouse Road. Angus Cottage is on the right on entry to the village from Duns and will be signed.

**Disabled Access:**
Full

**Opening Times:**
Sunday 6 July
10:30am - 3:00pm

**Admission:**
£4.00 for entry to both gardens.

**Charities:**
Macmillan Cancer Support receives 40%, the net remaining to SG Beneficiaries.

## ANTON'S HILL AND WALLED GARDEN

Leitholm, Coldstream TD12 4JD
**Mr and Mrs F Wills, Alec West and Pat Watson T: 01890 840203/468**
**E: cillawills@antonshill.co.uk**

Well treed mature garden which has been improved and added to since 1999. There are woodland walks with over 20 different varieties of oaks. A stumpery, well planted pond, shrubberies and herbaceous borders. Topiary elephant family of yew, shrub rose walk, leads to new Acer glade with Martagon lilies. There is a further pond planted with dogwood and Gunnera with a hosta island. A restored, organic, walled garden and greenhouse with an apple and pear orchard containing a growing collection of over 230 varieties.

**Other Details:** Dogs are not allowed in the walled garden.

**Directions:** Signposted off B6461 west of Leitholm.

**Disabled Access:**
Full

**Opening Times:**
Sunday 13 July
2:00pm - 5:30pm
Also open by arrangement on request

**Admission:**
£4.00, children free

**Charities:**
"Oakfield Ltd" Home for people with special needs, Northants. receives 40%, the net remaining to SG Beneficiaries.

## BUGHTRIG

Near Leitholm, Coldstream TD12 4JP
**Mr and Mrs William Ramsay T: 01890 840777**
**E: ramsay@bughtrig.co.uk**

A traditional hedged Scottish family garden with an interesting combination of herbaceous plants, shrubs, annuals and fruit. It is surrounded by fine specimen trees which provide remarkable shelter.

**Other Details:** Small picnic area.

**Directions:** ¼ mile east of Leitholm on B6461.

**Disabled Access:**
Partial

**Opening Times:**
1 June - 1 September
11:00am - 5:00pm

**Admission:**
£4.00, children under 18 £1.00

**Charities:**
Donation to SG Beneficiaries.

## CUMLEDGE MILL HOUSE (WITH ANGUS COTTAGE)

Duns TD11 3TD

**Mr William Laidlaw**

The garden is surrounded by an attractive new wall, a good backdrop for the herbaceous borders, mature trees and spacious lawns. The garden enclosed part of a former blanket factory, which was run by the owner's family 1850s - 1970s.

**Other Details:** Teas served in Preston Village Hall.

**Directions:** Preston Village is 2 miles north of Duns on the Duns - Grantshouse Road. Cumledge Mill House is located between the village and the River Whiteadder, opposite white mill cottages.

Disabled Access:
Full

Opening Times:
Sunday 6 July
10:30am - 3:00pm

Admission:
£4.00 for entry to both gardens.

Charities:
Macmillan Cancer Support receives 40%, the net remaining to SG Beneficiaries.

## LENNEL BANK

Coldstream TD12 4EX

**Mrs Honor Brown T: 01890 882297**

Lennel Bank is a terraced garden overlooking the River Tweed, consisting of wide borders packed with shrubs and perennial planting, some unusual. The water garden, built in 2008, is surrounded by a rockery and utilises the slope ending in a pond. There is a small kitchen garden with raised beds in unusual shapes. Different growing conditions throughout the garden from dry, wet, shady and sun lend themselves to a variety of plants, which hopefully enhance the garden's interest.

**Directions:** On A6112 Coldstream to Duns road, 1 mile from Coldstream.

Disabled Access:
None

Opening Times:
Sunday 29 June
10:30am - 5:00pm
Also by arrangement on request

Admission:
£4.00, children free

Charities:
British Heart Foundation receives 40%, the net remaining to SG Beneficiaries.

## NETHERBYRES

Eyemouth TD14 5SE

**Col. S J Furness T: 018907 50337**

A unique 18th century elliptical walled garden. Annuals, roses, herbaceous borders, fruit and vegetables in summer.

**Directions:** Half a mile south of Eyemouth on A1107 to Berwick.

**Disabled Access:**
Full

**Opening Times:**
Sunday 20 July
2:00pm - 5:30pm
Also by arrangement
1 May - 31 August

**Admission:**
£4.00, concessions £3.00, children under 12 free

**Charities:**
Gunsgreen House Trust receives 40%, the net remaining to SG Beneficiaries.

## SWINTON MILL HOUSE

Swinton Mill, Coldstream TD12 4JS

**Mr and Mrs HF Mitchell T: 01890 840 530**

**E: pmemitchell@hotmail.com**

Traditional family garden containing a wide mix of herbaceous plants and shrubs. The garden has an annual flower meadow and woodland walks with an interesting selection of trees. There is also a small ornamental pond. A newly created orchard (2005) has apples, pears, plums, cobnuts and medlars.

**Other Details:** Delicious homemade teas available. Home of the Border Beekeepers Association Apiary, members will be on hand to offer beekeeping advice and there will be honey for sale.

**Directions:** Swinton Mill Crossroads 2 miles east of Leitholm on the B6461

**Disabled Access:**
Full

**Opening Times:**
Sunday 8 June
1:00pm - 5:00pm

**Admission:**
£3.50

**Charities:**
Swinton and Fogo Church receives 40%, the net remaining to SG Beneficiaries.

## WELLFIELD

Horndean, Berwick-upon-Tweed TD15 1XJ

**Mrs Susan Wight T: 01289 382 384**

**E: swellfield@btinternet.com**

An informal, fairly young garden of about 1½ acres set in a quiet hamlet. An old paddock has been transformed to create a cottage-style garden with mixed borders, raised beds and fruit with contrast hedging to create boundaries. A large grassy bank leads to a wildlife pond surrounded by native and non-native flowers, specimen trees and shrubs. Pretty, informal herbaceous beds surround the house. Narrow paths and steps in some areas make this unsuitable for wheelchair access.

**Directions:** Horndean is 8 miles west of Berwick-upon-Tweed. From Berwick take the B6461 road (to Kelso) and turn left after 8 miles. Horndean is half a mile from the B6461 and Wellfield is at the lowest point of the hamlet.

**Disabled Access:**
Partial

**Opening Times:**
Sunday 15 June
11:00am - 4:00pm

**Admission:**
£4.00

**Charities:**
Macmillan Cancer Support receives 40%, the net remaining to SG Beneficiaries.

# CAITHNESS, SUTHERLAND ORKNEY & SHETLAND



## District Organiser

| | |
|---|---|
| Mrs Judith Middlemas | 22 Miller Place, Scrabster, Thurso KW14 7UH |

## Area Organisers

| | |
|---|---|
| Mrs Caroline Critchlow | The Quoy of Houton, Orphir, Orkney KW17 2RD |
| Mrs Kathy Greaves | Caregarth, Scatness, Virkie ZE3 9JW |
| Mrs Mary Leask | VisitShetland, Market Cross, Lerwick ZE1 0LU |
| Mr Steve Mathieson | VisitShetland, Market Cross, Lerwick ZE1 0LU |
| Mrs Jonny Shaw | Amat, Ardgay, Sutherland IV24 3BS |

## Treasurer

| | |
|---|---|
| Mr Chris Hobson | Braeside, Dunnet, Caithness KW14 8YD |

## Gardens open on a specific date

| | | | | |
|---|---|---|---|---|
| Amat, Ardgay | Sat & Sun 7/8 June | 2:00pm | - | 5:00pm |
| Pentland Firth Gardens, Dunnet | Sunday 29 June | 1:00pm | - | 5:00pm |
| The Castle & Gardens of Mey, Mey | Wednesday 2 July | 10:00am | - | 5:00pm |
| Bighouse Lodge, by Melvich | Sunday 6 July | 2:30pm | - | 5:30pm |
| The Castle & Gardens of Mey, Mey | Wednesday 16 July | 10:00am | - | 5:00pm |
| House of Tongue, Tongue, Lairg | Saturday 26 July | 2:00pm | - | 6:00pm |
| Langwell, Berriedale | Sunday 27 July | 1:00pm | - | 5:00pm |
| Thurso Gardens | Sunday 3 August | 1:00pm | - | 5:00pm |
| The Castle & Gardens of Mey, Mey | Saturday 16 August | 10:00am | - | 5:00pm |

## Gardens open regularly

| | | | | |
|---|---|---|---|---|
| The Castle & Gardens of Mey, Mey | 7 May-30 Sep: ex 28 Jul-9 Aug | 10:00am | - | 5:00pm |

## Gardens open by arrangement

| | | |
|---|---|---|
| Langwell, Berriedale | On request | 01593 751278/751237 |

## Key to symbols

| | | | | | |
|---|---|---|---|---|---|
|   | New in 2014 |  | Homemade teas |  | Accommodation |
|  | Teas |  | Dogs on a lead allowed |  | Plant stall |
|  | Cream teas |  | Wheelchair access |  | Scottish Snowdrop Festival |

## Garden locations

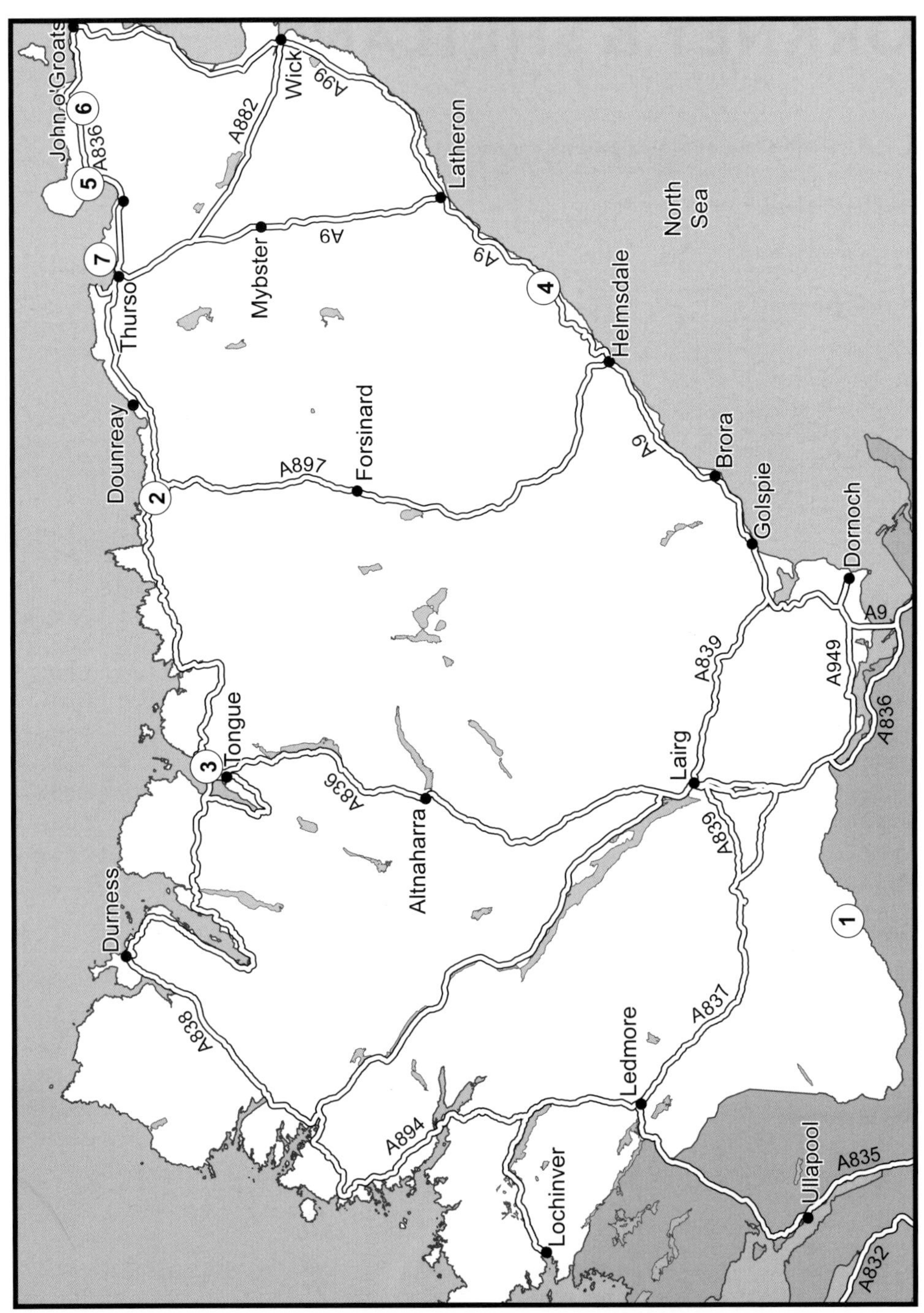

## AMAT

Ardgay IV24 3BS
**Jonny and Sara Shaw**
**E: saraamat@btinternet.com**

Riverside garden set in Amat forest. Herbaceous borders and rockery set in large lawn looking onto salmon pool. Old and new rhododendrons with woodland and river walk plus large specimen trees in policies.

**Other Details:** Teas £2.50.

**Directions:** Take road from Ardgay to Croick 9 miles. Turn left at red phone box and the garden is 500 yards on the left.

Disabled Access:
Partial

Opening Times:
Saturday 7 June
2:00pm - 5:00pm
Sunday 8 June
2:00pm - 5:00pm

Admission:
£4.50

Charities:
Gardening Leave receives 20%, Croick church receives 20%, the net remaining to SG Beneficiaries.

## BIGHOUSE LODGE

by Melvich KW14 7YJ
**Bighouse Estate**
**E: info@bighouseestate.com www.bighouseestate.com**

Bighouse Lodge is situated on the north coast of Sutherland at the mouth of the River Halladale. The 2 acre walled garden, originally laid out in 1715, consists of a central axis leading to a charming bothy with lawn, herbaceous borders, a sunken garden and 4 separate conceptual gardens behind the hedgerows. Each garden contains a sculpture to reflect the aspects of the Bighouse Estate namely the River, the Forest, the Strath and the Hill. The garden has recently been restored and is now a most interesting place to visit.

**Other Details:** Teas £3.00.

**Directions:** Off A836 ½ mile East of Melvich.

Disabled Access:
Partial

Opening Times:
Sunday 6 July
2:30pm - 5:30pm

Admission:
£4.00. Children under 12 £1.00

Charities:
RNLI receives 40%, the net remaining to SG Beneficiaries.

## HOUSE OF TONGUE

Tongue, Lairg IV27 4XH
**The Countess of Sutherland**
**E: ginrik@btopenworld.com**

17th century house on Kyle of Tongue. Walled garden with herbaceous borders, lawns, old fashioned roses, vegetables, soft fruit and small orchard.

**Other Details:** Teas £3.50

**Directions:** Half a mile from Tongue village. House just off main road approaching causeway. Well signposted.

**Disabled Access:**
Partial

**Opening Times:**
Saturday 26 July
2:00pm - 6:00pm

**Admission:**
£4.00, children £1.00

**Charities:**
Children 1st receives 40%, the net remaining to SG Beneficiaries.

## LANGWELL

Berriedale KW7 6HD
**Welbeck Estates T: 01593 751278/751237**
**E: macanson@hotmail.com**

A beautiful and spectacular old walled garden with outstanding borders situated in the secluded Langwell Strath. Charming wooded access drive with a chance to see deer.

**Directions:** A9 Berriedale 2 miles.

**Disabled Access:**
Partial

**Opening Times:**
Sunday 27 July
1:00pm - 5:00pm
Also by arrangement on request

**Admission:**
£4.00, children free

**Charities:**
RNLI receives 40%, the net remaining to SG Beneficiaries.

## PENTLAND FIRTH GARDENS

Britannia Hall, Dunnet KW14 8YD
**The Pentland Firth Gardeners T: 01847 851757**

With panoramic views of the Pentland Firth, these gardens show what is possible when gardening on the exposed northern coast of Scotland. Two old favourites, one with a rock garden and herb wheel, greenhouse and container-grown vegetables, the other with a good selection of trees, a pond and vegetable garden. A third new 1¾ acre country garden with duck pond, chickens, a polytunnel for fruit and vegetables and containers of bedding. All gardens have a good variety of hardy plants and shrubs to enjoy.

**Other Details:** Transport required in order to visit all gardens. Teas are available at Britannia Hall.

**Directions:** Start at Britannia Hall, Dunnet KW14 8YD where a map of gardens will be available on payment of admission fee.

**Disabled Access:**
Partial

**Opening Times:**
Sunday 29 June
1:00pm - 5:00pm

**Admission:**
£4.00, children under 12 free

**Charities:**
Mary Ann's Cottage - Caithness Heritage Trust receives 40%, the net remaining to SG Beneficiaries.

## THE CASTLE & GARDENS OF MEY

Mey KW14 8XH

**The Queen Elizabeth Castle of Mey Trust T: 01847 851473**

**E: enquiries@castleofmey.org.uk www.castleofmey.org.uk**

Originally a Z plan castle bought by the Queen Mother in 1952 and then restored and improved. The walled garden and the East Garden were also created by the Queen Mother. An animal centre has been established over the last 3 years and is proving very popular with all ages.

**Other Details:** Tearoom, shop and animal centre. Castle opens 10:20am and last entries are at 4:00pm.
*Please check Castle website as dates subject to change.

**Directions:** On A836 between Thurso and John O'Groats.

Disabled Access:
Partial

Opening Times:
Wednesday 2 July
10:00am - 5:00pm
Wednesday 16 July
10:00am - 5:00pm
Saturday 16 August
10:00am - 5:00pm
7 May - 30 September
10:00am - 5:00pm
Closed 28 July - 9 August inclusive*

Admission:
£11.00, concessions £9.75, children £6.50, family £29.00.
Grounds and garden £6.50, family £19.00

Charities:
Help the Aged receives 40%, the net remaining to SG Beneficiaries.

## THURSO GARDENS

KW14 8NR

**Thurso Gardeners T: 01847 893467**

Springpark House is hosting 2 small town gardens. Another chance to see Springpark's walled garden with collection of farming and household memorabilia, vegetable garden and polytunnel with good wheelchair access to all parts. The town gardens offer a good variety of interesting shrubs, roses and herbaceous plants. One has a small collection of bonsai and limited wheelchair access, the other is designed to support bees and butterflies and is not wheelchair accessible.

**Other Details:** Start at Springpark House where a map of the 2 other gardens will be available on payment of admission fee.
Teas £2.00 at Springpark.

**Directions:** In Thurso turn off the Catletown road at Mount Pleasant Road, continue up the hill until you see Laurie Terrace (last road on right) and house is at end on left.

Disabled Access:
Partial

Opening Times:
Sunday 3 August
1:00pm - 5:00pm

Admission:
£4.50

Charities:
Caithness Samaritans receives 10%, Starlight receives 10%, Cancer Research UK receives 20%, the net remaining to SG Beneficiaries.

## Garden locations

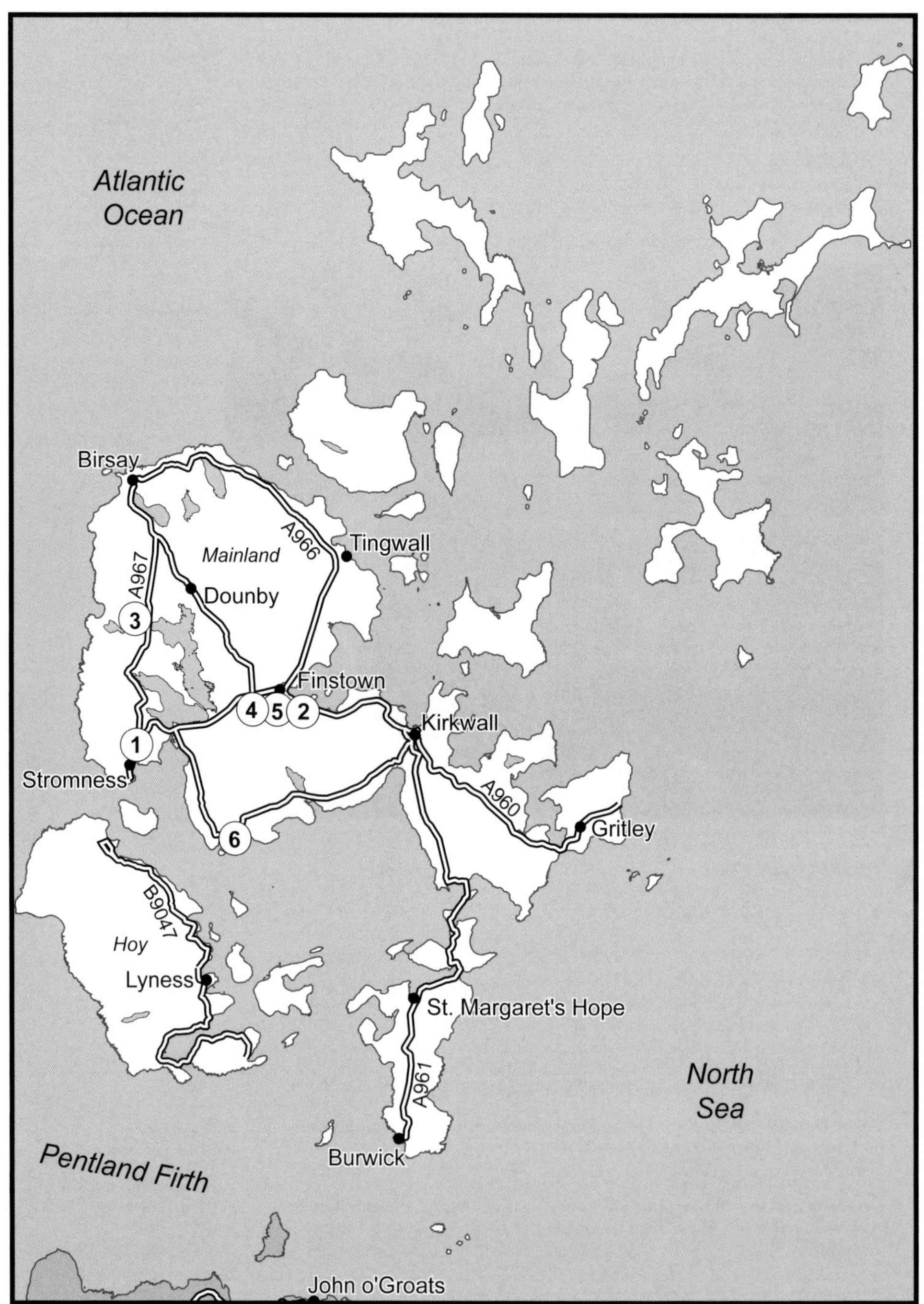

## ORKNEY GARDEN TRAIL

Orkney
**The Gardeners of Orkney**
**www.orkneygardentrail.org.uk**

1 **33 HILLSIDE ROAD:** Stromness KW16 3HR (Mr David Walker)
An informal garden of approx. ½ an acre created from a field over the past 20 years. Situated on a gentle slope its features include dry stone walls and terracing, a pond, a large variety of trees and shrubs and many cottage garden perennials.
**Directions:** On Hillside Road approx. 100 yards past the swimming pool on the opposite side of the road.

2 **DALKEITH POLYTUNNEL**: Grimbister, Kirkwall KW15 1TT (Olive Robertson)
The Polytunnel is 70 metres long, 24 metres wide and 3 metres high and is used to grow produce for our own use. In good weather it can have 3 growing seasons over the summer months. A variety of vegetables flourish including cabbages, cauliflower, peas and tomatoes. "I have enjoyed gardening and horticulture for over 25 years and have won most points in the East Mainland Show for the past 2 years".
**Directions:** A965 to Finstown, look for Esson garage and turn up the old Finstown Road. Approx. 1 mile out of village, the poly tunnel is clearly visible from the road.

3 **KIERFOLD**: Sandwick KW16 3JE (Mr and Mrs E Smith)
A walled Victorian garden, whose layout has remained largely unchanged for 100 years, although the planting has changed in line with each owner's taste. The garden is packed with geraniums, grasses, euphorbia and irises. The protection of the wall and tree shelter belt has created a calm and warm environment in which many unusual and rare plants are found.
**Directions:** Leaving Stromness turn left onto A967/A966. Take B9056 sign posted Skara Brae. On reaching Skaill Loch take the 2nd right onto B9057 to Dounby. Kierfold is the first house on the right.

4 **STENWOOD**: Finstown KW17 2JX (Mr and Mrs J Wood)
A garden of about 1 acre on a north facing slope. Starting at the bottom, visitors can wander through a number of interlinked areas featuring a wide range of perennial plants, primulas, roses, shrubs and rhododendrons.
**Directions:** Turn up the Heddle Road in the centre of Finstown (at the church) and the garden is situated approximately 300 metres on the left.

5 **THE COMMUNITY GARDEN**: Finstown KW17 2JX
The garden has a stunning variety of features from miniature shrub and primula lined valleys and beautiful perennial flower bordered burns. There are large herbaceous flower beds around lawned areas. The public have access to this area at all times.
**Directions:** Almost directly opposite Stenwood up the land and first right.

6 **THE QUOY OF HOUTON**: Orphir KW17 2RD (Mrs Caroline Critchlow)
An historic walled garden a stone's throw away from the sea and completely restored in 2008. The garden is planted to withstand winds in excess of 100 mph and features drystone walling features, raised beds and a 60 foot water rill. The planting reflects its coastal location and is planted in the cottage garden style encouraging bees and butterflies. There is a separate walled vegetable garden and fruit cage which supplies the house and B&B guests.
**Directions:** A964 from Kirkwall to Houton. Take ferry turning, straight across at first junction following tarmac road to a 2 storey yellow house across the bay.

**Other Details:** For further details visit www.orkneygardentrail.org.uk
**Kierfold House:** Self catering holiday cottage available
(T: 01856 841583 or E: fiona@kierfold-house.co.uk).
**The Quoy of Houton:** Cream teas and plant stall. 4* gold B&B and 5* self catering available (T: 01856 811237 or E: c.kritchlow258@btinternet.com).

Disabled Access:
None

Opening Times:
Sunday 22 June
9:30am - 6:30am
Sunday 29 June
9:30am - 6:30pm
Sunday 6 July
9:30am - 6:30pm
Sunday 13 July
9:30am - 6:30pm

Admission:
£10.00 for entry to all six gardens. Accompanied children under 12 free. Tickets available by cash or cheque from Quoy of Houton, or
Scapa Travel, 11 Bridge Street, Kirkwall KW15 1HR.
Tickets may be reserved in advance by emailing c.kritchlow258@btinternet.com.
or scapa@barrheadtravel.com
Repeat visits to a garden £2.50.

Charities:
Friends of Neuro Ward ARI receives 40%, the net remaining to SG Beneficiaries.

## Gardens open on a specific date

| | | | | |
|---|---|---|---|---|
| Keldaberg, Cunningsburgh | Sunday 15 June | 2:00pm | - | 4:00pm |
| Keldaberg, Cunningsburgh | Saturday 21 June | 2:00pm | - | 4:00pm |
| Keldaberg, Cunningsburgh | Sunday 22 June | 2:00pm | - | 4:00pm |
| Lea Gardens, Tresta | Sunday 20 July | 2:00pm | - | 7:00pm |
| Keldaberg, Cunningsburgh | Saturday 26 July | 2:00pm | - | 4:00pm |
| Keldaberg, Cunningsburgh | Sunday 27 July | 2:00pm | - | 4:00pm |
| Keldaberg, Cunningsburgh | Saturday 9 August | 2:00pm | - | 4:00pm |
| Keldaberg, Cunningsburgh | Sunday 10 August | 2:00pm | - | 4:00pm |

## Gardens open regularly

| | | | | |
|---|---|---|---|---|
| 15 Linkshouse , Mid Yell | 3 July - 7 August (Thurs) | 10:00am | - | 7:00pm |
| Caergarth, Scatness | 15 June - 31 Aug (most days) | 11:00am | - | 5:00pm |
| Holmlea, Mid Yell | 6 July - 10 August (Suns) | 10:00am | - | 7:00pm |
| Lea Gardens, Tresta | 1 April - 31 Oct (not Thurs) | 2:00pm | - | 5:00pm |
| Nonavaar, Levenwick | 1 Mar- 12 Sept (Thurs & Fris) | 2:00pm | - | 5:00pm |

## Gardens open by arrangement

| | | |
|---|---|---|
| Caergarth, Scatness | 15 June - 31 August | 01950 460576 |
| Cruisdale, Sandness | 1 March - 31 October | 01595 870739 |
| Gerdi, Hillswick | 1 July - 31 August | 01806 503776 |
| Highlands, East Voe | 1 March - 31 October | 01595 880526 |
| Keldaberg, Cunningsburgh | 1 June - 31 August | 01950 477331 |
| Nonavaar, Levenwick | 1 March - 12 September | 01950 422447 |
| Norby, Burnside | 1 March - 31 October | 01595 870246 |

Cruisdale, Sandness, Shetland

## Key to symbols

 New in 2014

 Teas

Cream teas

 Homemade teas

 Dogs on a lead allowed

 Wheelchair access

 Accommodation

 Plant stall

 Scottish Snowdrop Festival

## Garden locations

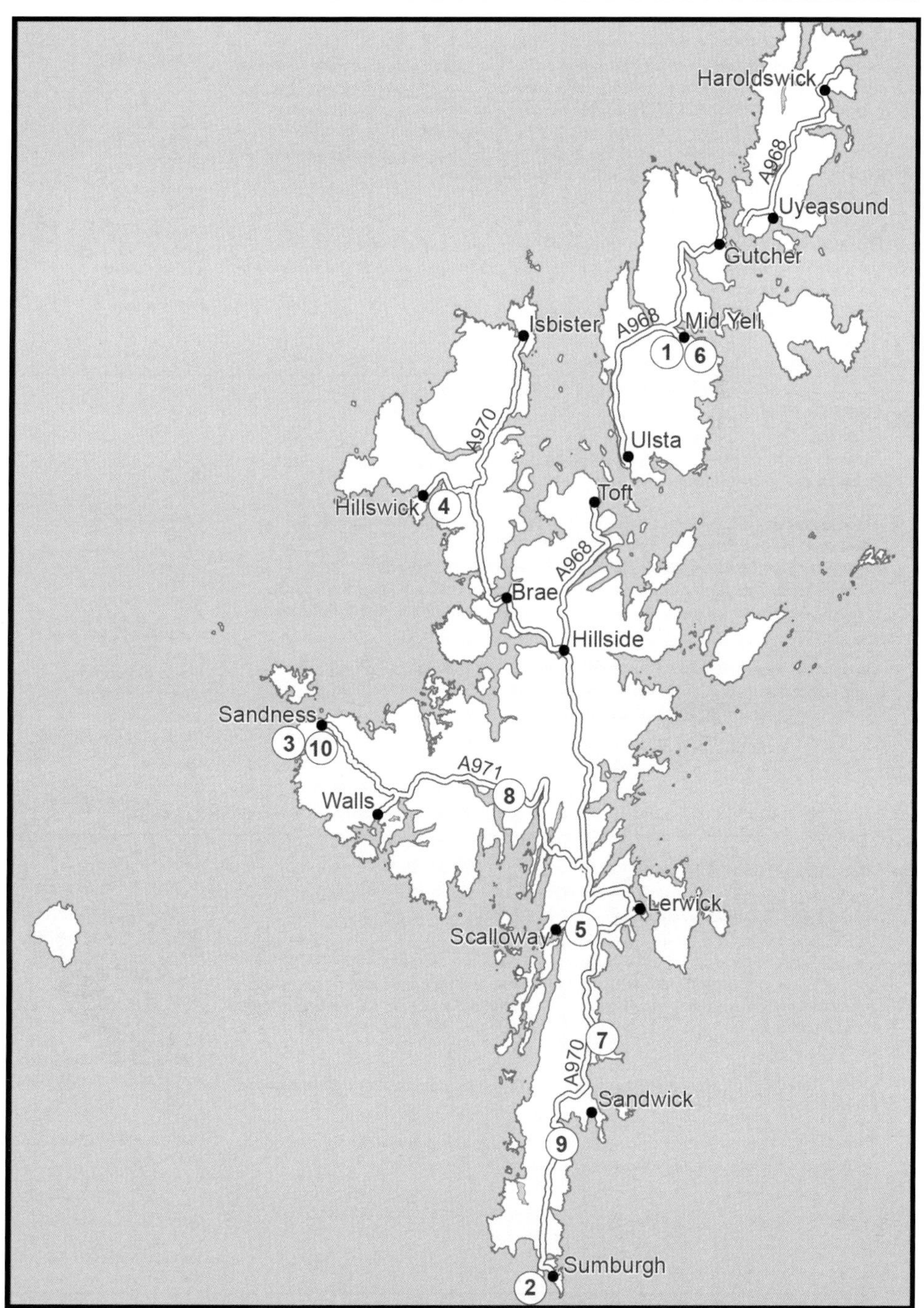

## 15 LINKSHOUSE

Mid Yell ZE2 9BP
**Mr Charlie Inkster T: 01957 702049**
**E: cjinkster@btinternet.com**

A small cottage garden with a greenhouse full of plants and colour, a pond complete with fountain and water lilies, and a small aviary with canaries and finches. The garden is well established with trees, bushes and a good variety of plants giving plenty of colour. Fuschias are a favourite providing a good selection of different varieties both in the garden and in the greenhouse. Also in the greenhouse are many varieties of streptocarpus adding to the colourful display.

**Other Details:** Small aviary.

**Directions:** In Yell head north on the A968, turn right to Mid Yell. Drive down through Mid Yell and turn towards Linkshouse Pier. The garden is at the far end of the row of white cottages.

Disabled Access:
None

Opening Times:
3 July - 7 August
10:00am - 7:00pm
Thursdays

Admission:
£3.00

Charities:
Yell for Cancer Support receives 40%, the net remaining to SG Beneficiaries.

## CAERGARTH

Scatness, Virkie ZE3 9JW
**Mr and Mrs M Greaves T: 01950 460576**
**E: kathy.caergarth@btinternet.com**

The creation of this ½ acre garden began in 2013. It has 360 degree sea views of Sumburgh Head lighthouse, Fair Isle, Fitful Head and Virkie landscapes. Some areas have been successfully established with new raised strawberry bed and fruit bushes added. The garden is set out with a herbaceous border, lawn, rose garden, meadow, vegetable gardens, shrubbery, wildlife pond and pool, with a poly tunnel and greenhouse.

**Directions:** South A970 to Sumburgh Airport, over the runway take the road signposted Scatness. Caergarth is 100 yards on the left. Look for SG signs on corner and green fence with OPEN sign.

Disabled Access:
Partial

Opening Times:
15 June - 31 August
11:00am - 5:00pm
open most of these days check for OPEN sign or phone first.
Also by arrangement
15 June - 31 August

Admission:
£3.00

Charities:
Macmillan Nurses receives 40%, the net remaining to SG Beneficiaries.

## CRUISDALE (WITH NORBY)

Sandness ZE2 9PL
**Alfred Kern T: 01595 870739**

The garden is in a natural state with many willows, several ponds and a variety of colourful hardy plants that grow well in the Shetland climate. It is a work in progress, started about 7 years ago and growing bigger over the years with more work planned.

**Other Details:** If Norby garden is closed, ticket will be valid to visit the garden on another day.

**Directions:** In Sandness, on the west side of Shetland. Opposite the school, on the right hand side with a wind generator in the field.

Disabled Access:
None

Opening Times:
By arrangement
1 March - 31 October
visitors must phone first due to the remote location.

Admission:
£5.00 ticket for Cruisdale and Norby
£3.00 for Cruisdale alone

Charities:
WRVS receives 20%, Survival International receives 20%, the net remaining to SG Beneficiaries.

## GERDI

Hillswick ZE2 9RW

**Alison Charleson T: 01806 503776**

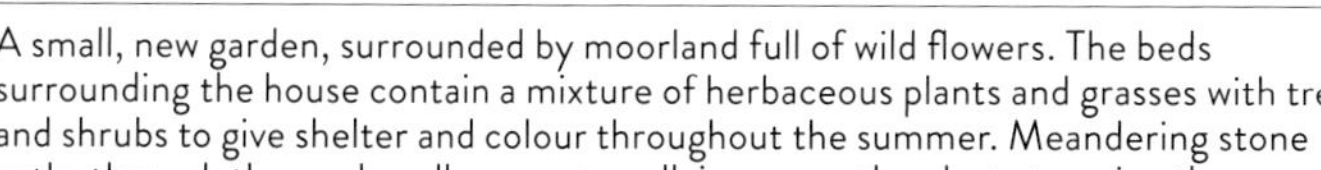

A small, new garden, surrounded by moorland full of wild flowers. The beds surrounding the house contain a mixture of herbaceous plants and grasses with trees and shrubs to give shelter and colour throughout the summer. Meandering stone paths through the garden allow you to walk in among the plants to enjoy them up close.

**Other Details:** Make a day of it and explore the dramatic Eshaness cliff scenery, then have teas, lunch or dinner all available at nearby Hillswick Hotel and at the Braewick Cafe in Eshaness. Local shop with petrol.

**Directions:** Follow the A970 north from Lerwick to Hillswick, continuing on past the public hall and Stucca. Gerdi is a pale blue wooden chalet on the left just before the Hillswick Hotel.

Disabled Access:
None

Opening Times:
By arrangement
1 July - 31 August

Admission:
£3.00

Charities:
All proceeds to SG Beneficiaries.

## HIGHLANDS

East Voe, Scalloway ZE1 0UR

**Sarah Kay T: 01595 880526**

**E: info@easterhoull.co.uk**

The garden is in 2 parts. The upper garden includes a rockery built with large rocks and a wide selection of plants. The lower garden is on a steep slope with a spectacular sea view over village of Scalloway. Path to lead visitors around. Wide selection of plants, pond and vegetable patch.

**Other Details:** Please phone first to avoid disappointment.

**Directions:** Follow A970 main road towards village of Scalloway. Near the top of the hill, take a sharp turn to the left, signpost Easterhoull Chalets, follow road stopping at greenhouse.

Disabled Access:
None

Opening Times:
By arrangement
1 March - 31 October

Admission:
£3.50

Charities:
Yorkhill Childrens Charity receives 40%, the net remaining to SG Beneficiaries.

## HOLMLEA

Mid Yell ZE2 9BT

**John and Sandra Robertson T: 01957 702062**

The garden has a greenhouse, conservatory and drystane dyke, with a mixture of flowers, shrubs and vegetables. Enjoy wandering around admiring the variety of different shrubs and herbaceous plants interspersed with colourful annuals, then see the plot of mixed vegetables before moving on into the greenhouse where tomatoes, cucumber and peppers grow.

**Other Details:** Waterwheel and Boathouse

**Directions:** Once on the island of Yell, head for Mid Yell, going down to Linkshouse Pier. From there, go up past the shop about 150yds. Holmlea is right on the corner with garage and basement.

Disabled Access:
Partial

Opening Times:
Sundays 6 July - 10 August
10:00am - 7:00pm

Admission:
£3.00

Charities:
Parkinsons Disease Society of the UK receives 40%, the net remaining to SG Beneficiaries.

## KELDABERG

Cunningsburgh ZE2 9HG
**Mrs L Johnston T: 01950 477331**
**E: linda.keldaberg@btinternet.com**

A 'secret garden' divided into 4 areas. A beach garden of grasses, flowers and driftwood. The main area is a sloping perennial border leading down to a greenhouse, vegetable plot, up to a decked area with containers and exotic plants including agaves, pineapple lilies, cannas and gunneras. The new part has trees, raised vegetable beds, a rockery, retaining walls and an arbour to rest in. There is a pond complete with goldfish, golden orf and koi plus aquatic plants, and a water lily.

**Other Details:** Teas available at the local hall on Sundays.

**Directions:** On the A970 south of Lerwick is Cunningsburgh, take the Gord junction on the left after passing the village hall. Continue along the road to the first house past the Kenwood sign.

Disabled Access:
Partial

Opening Times:
Sunday 15 June
Saturday 21 June
Sunday 22 June
Saturday 26 July
Sunday 27 July
Saturday 9 August
Sunday 10 August
all dates 2:00pm - 4:00pm
Also by arrangement
1 June - 31 August
must phone in advance to avoid disappointment

Admission:
£3.00

Charities:
Chest Heart & Stroke Scotland receives 40%, the net remaining to SG Beneficiaries.

## LEA GARDENS

Tresta ZE2 9LT
**Rosa Steppanova T: 01595 810454**

Lea Gardens, started in the early 1980s, now covers almost 2 acres. The plant collection, the largest north of Inverewe Gardens, consists of 1,500 different species and cultivars from all over the world, including phyto-geographic elements of collections of plants from New Zealand, South Africa and South America. Planted to provide all-year-round interest it has been divided into a variety of habitats: woodland and shade, borders, wetland, raised beds, and acid and lime lovers. A winner of the 2011 Shetland Environmental Award.

**Other Details:** On 20 July entrance tickets will be valid for other visits. If you are unable to visit at our opening times please phone to check if we can open at an alternative time for you.

**Directions:** From Lerwick take A970 north, turn left at Tingwall onto A971 past Weisdale along Weisdale Voe and up Weisdale hill. Coming down, Lea Gardens is on your right surrounded by trees.

Disabled Access:
Partial

Opening Times:
Sunday 20 July
2:00pm - 7:00pm
for Scotland's Gardens
1 April - 31 October
2:00pm - 5:00pm
Closed Thursdays

Admission:
£4.00

Charities:
Donation to SG Beneficiaries.

## NONAVAAR

Levenwick ZE2 9HX
**James B Thomason T: 01950 422447**

This is a delightful country garden, sloping within drystone walls, overlooking magnificent coastal views. It contains ponds, terraces, areas of lawn, trees, bushes, varied perennials, annuals, vegetable garden and greenhouse.

**Other Details:** Arts and Crafts studio.

**Directions:** Head south from Lerwick. Turn left at Levenwick sign soon after Bigton turnoff. Follow road to 3rd house on left after Midway stores. Park where there is a 'Garden Open' sign.

© Andrea Jones

Disabled Access:
None

Opening Times:
Thursdays and Fridays
1 March - 12 September
2:00pm - 5:00pm
Also by arrangement
1 March - 12 September
Must phone first

Admission:
£3.00

Charities:
Cancer Research receives 40%, the net remaining to SG Beneficiaries.

## NORBY (WITH CRUISDALE)

Burnside, Sandness ZE2 9PL
**Mrs Gundel Grolimund T: 01595 870246**
**E: gislinde@tiscali.co.uk**

A small but perfectly formed garden and a prime example of what can be achieved in a very exposed situation. Blue painted wooden pallets provide internal wind breaks and form a background for shrubs, climbers and herbaceous plants, while willows provide a perfect wildlife habitat. There are treasured plants such as chionocloa rubra, pieris, Chinese tree peonies, and a selection of old-fashioned shrub roses. Narrow raised beds contain salads and herbs decorated by beach finds.

**Other Details:** If Cruisdale garden is closed, ticket will be valid to visit the garden on another date.

**Directions:** At Sandness, take road to Norby, turn right at Methodist Church, 'Burnside' at end.

Disabled Access:
None

Opening Times:
By arrangement
1 March - 31 October
visitors must phone before visit due to remote location

Admission:
£5.00 ticket for Norby and Cruisdale
£3.00 for Norby alone

Charities:
Survival International receives 20%, WRVS receives 20%, the net remaining to SG Beneficiaries

# DUMFRIESSHIRE

Scotland's Gardens 2014 Guidebook is sponsored by **INVESTEC WEALTH & INVESTMENT**

## District Organiser

| | |
|---|---|
| Mrs Sarah Landale | Dalswinton House, Dalswinton, Auldgirth DG2 0XZ |

## Area Organisers

| | |
|---|---|
| Mrs Fiona Bell-Irving | Bankside, Kettleholm, Lockerbie DG11 1BY |
| Mrs Liz Mitchell | Drumpark, Irongray, Dumfriesshire DG2 9TX |

## Treasurer

| | |
|---|---|
| Mr Harold Jack | The Clachan, Newtonairds DG2 0JL |

## Gardens open on a specific date

| | | |
|---|---|---|
| Portrack House, Holywood | Sunday 4 May | 12:00pm - 5:00pm |
| Drumpark, Irongray | Friday 9 May | 10:00am - 4:00pm |
| Drumpark, Irongray | Friday 16 May | 10:00am - 4:00pm |
| Drumpark, Irongray | Friday 23 May | 10:00am - 4:00pm |
| Cowhill Tower, Holywood | Sunday 25 May | 2:00pm - 5:00pm |
| Dunesslin, Dunscore | Sunday 8 June | 2:00pm - 5:00pm |
| Newtonairds Lodge, Newtonairds | Sunday 8 June | 5:00pm - 9:00pm |
| Dalgonar, Dunscore | Sunday 22 June | 2:00pm - 5:00pm |
| Newtonairds Lodge, Newtonairds | Sunday 13 July | 2:00pm - 5:00pm |

## Gardens open by arrangement

| | | |
|---|---|---|
| Grovehill House , Burnhead | 1 April - 30 September | 01848 331637 |

## Key to symbols

 New in 2014
 Homemade teas
 Accommodation
 Teas
 Dogs on a lead allowed
 Plant stall
Cream teas
 Wheelchair access
 Scottish Snowdrop Festival

## Garden locations

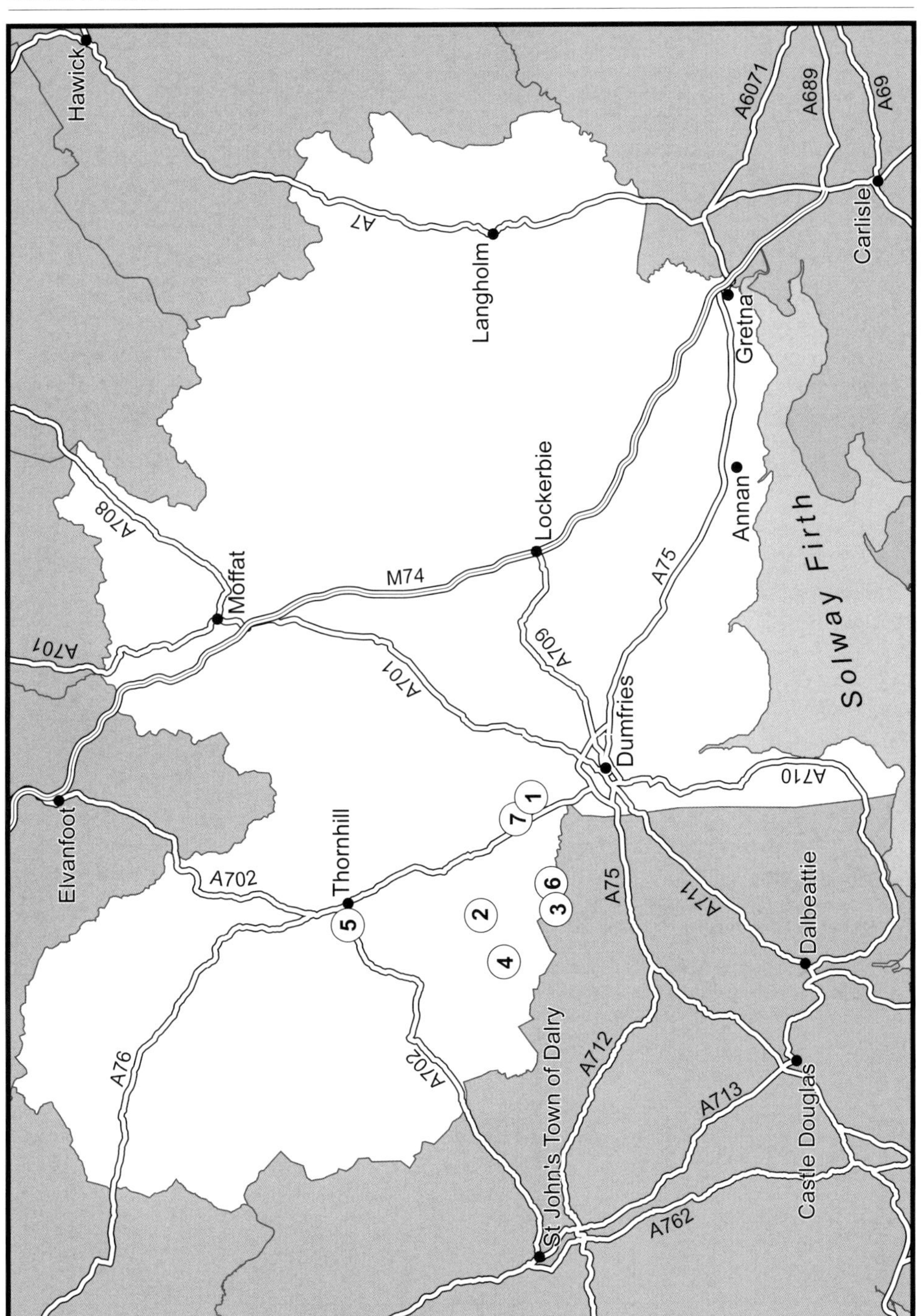

## COWHILL TOWER

Holywood DG2 0RL

**Mr and Mrs P Weatherall T: 01387 720304**

Interesting walled garden. There are also topiary animals, birds and figures and a beautiful woodland walk. Splendid views from lawn down the Nith valley. A variety of statues from the Far East.

**Directions:** Holywood 1½ miles off A76, 5 miles north of Dumfries.

Disabled Access:
Partial

Opening Times:
Sunday 25 May
2:00pm - 5:00pm

Admission:
£4.00, children £0.50

Charities:
Maggie's Cancer Caring Centres receives 40%, the net remaining to SG Beneficiaries.

## DALGONAR

Dunscore DG2 0SS

**Judge and Mrs William Crawford T: 01387 820339**

There are well-wooded policies with woodland paths and a traditional walled garden containing an unusual and beautiful sundial.

**Directions:** Half a mile north west of Dunscore, Dumfriesshire on the B729 road to Moniaive. Entrance through black gates on north side of road.

Disabled Access:
Partial

Opening Times:
Sunday 22 June
2:00pm - 5:00pm

Admission:
£4.00

Charities:
Dunscore Church receives 20%, Compassion in World Farming receives 20%, the net remaining to SG Beneficiaries.

## DRUMPARK

Irongray DG2 9TX

**Mr and Mrs Iain Mitchell T: 01387 820323**

Well contoured woodland garden and extensive policies with mature azaleas, rhododendrons and rare shrubs among impressive specimen trees. Water garden with primulas and meconopsis. Victorian walled garden with fruit trees and garden produce. There is also a beautiful herbaceous border. All set in a natural bowl providing attractive vistas.

**Directions:** From Dumfries by-pass, head north on A76 for ½ mile, turn left at signpost to "Lochside Industrial Estates" and immediately right onto Irongray Road; continue for 5 miles; gates in sandstone wall on left (½ mile after Routin' Brig).

Disabled Access:
Partial

Opening Times:
Friday 9 May
10:00am - 4:00pm
Friday 16 May
10:00am - 4:00pm
Friday 23 May
10:00am - 4:00pm

Admission:
£4.00, children free

Charities:
Loch Arthur Community (Camphill Trust) receives 40%, the net remaining to SG Beneficiaries.

## DUNESSLIN

Dunscore DG2 0UR

**Iain and Zara Milligan T: 01387 820345**

Set in the hills with good views, the principal garden consists of a series of connecting rooms filled with herbaceous plants. There is a substantial rock garden with alpines and unusual plants and a hill walk to view 3 cairns by Andy Goldsworthy.

**Directions:** From Dunscore, follow road to Corsock. Approximately 1½ miles further on, turn right at post box, still on road to Corsock and at small crossroads ½ mile on, turn left.

Disabled Access:
None

Opening Times:
Sunday 8 June
2:00pm - 5:00pm

Admission:
£4.00

Charities:
Alzheimer Scotland receives 40%, the net remaining to SG Beneficiaries.

© Allan Pollok-Morris

## GROVEHILL HOUSE

Burnhead, Thornhill DG3 4AD

**Mr and Mrs Allen & Penelope Paterson T: 01848 331637**

Two-acre plantsman's garden designed for year-round interest. The steep site has been terraced to offer sheltered borders and garden 'rooms'. Small productive walled garden. There are fine views down the Nith Valley and to the surrounding hills.

**Directions:** In Burnhead on the A702. Approximately 1 mile, coming from Thornhill. House on left on steep corner with sandstone lodge and red phone box opposite.

Disabled Access:
None

Opening Times:
By arrangement
1 April - 30 September

Admission:
£3.00

Charities:
Loch Arthur Community (Camphill Trust) receives 40%, the net remaining to SG Beneficiaries.

## NEWTONAIRDS LODGE

Newtonairds DG2 0JL
**Mr and Mrs J Coutts**
**www.newtonairds-hostasandgarden.co.uk**

An interesting 1.2 acre plantsman's garden punctuated with topiary, trees and shrubs, surrounding a 19th century listed baronial lodge. The National Collection is integrated with a further 150 other hosta varieties on a natural terraced wooded bank.

**Other Details:** National Plant Collection®: Hosta Plantaginea hybrids and cultivars. There will be wine and nibbles available at the evening opening on 8 June.

**Directions:** From Dumfries take A76 north. At Holywood take B729 (Dunscore). After 1 mile turn left (Morrinton). After 3 miles red sandstone lodge is on right, behind black iron railings.

**Disabled Access:**
Partial

**Opening Times:**
Sunday 8 June
5:00pm - 9:00pm
Sunday 13 July
2:00pm - 5:00pm

**Admission:**
£4.00 for both openings

**Charities:**
June: Peter Pan Moat Brae Trust receives 40%
July: Dumfries North West Free Meals Project receives 40%, the net remaining to SG Beneficiaries.

## PORTRACK HOUSE

Holywood DG2 0RW
**Charles Jencks**
**www.charlesjencks.com**

Original 18th century manor house with Victorian addition; octagonal folly library. Twisted undulating landforms and terraces designed by Charles Jencks as "The Garden of Cosmic Speculation"; lakes designed by Maggie Keswick; rhododendrons, large new greenhouse in a geometric kitchen garden of the Six Senses; Glengower Hill plantation and view; woodland walks with Nonsense Building (architect: James Stirling); Universe cascade and rail garden of the Scottish Worthies; interesting sculpture including that of DNA and newly completed Comet Bridge.

**Other Details:** There are ongoing repairs to the garden this year and the tennis court is under construction as a metaphysical garden called Anti Entropy. We hope this will not detract from your visit.

**Directions:** Holywood 1½ miles off A76, five miles north of Dumfries.

**Disabled Access:**
Partial

**Opening Times:**
Sunday 4 May
12:00pm - 5:00pm

**Admission:**
£6.00

**Charities:**
Maggie's Cancer Caring Centres receives 40%, the net remaining to SG Beneficiaries.

# DUNBARTONSHIRE



## District Organiser

| | |
|---|---|
| Mrs K Murray | 7 The Birches, Shandon, Helensburgh G84 8HN |

## Area Organisers

| | |
|---|---|
| Mrs M Greenwell | Avalon, Shore Rd, Mambeg Garelochhead G84 0EN |
| Mrs R Lang | Ardchapel, Shandon, Helensburgh G84 8NP |
| Mrs R Macaulay | Denehard, Garelochhead G84 0EL |
| Mrs S Miller | 8 Laggary Park, Rhu G84 8LY |
| Mrs M Rogers | Station House, Station Road, Tarbet G83 7DA |
| Mrs J Theaker | 19 Blackhill Drive, Helensburgh G84 9AF |

## Treasurer

| | |
|---|---|
| Mrs S Miller | 8 Laggary Park, Rhu G84 8LY |

## Gardens open on a specific date

| | | |
|---|---|---|
| Kilarden, Rosneath | Sunday 27 April | 2:00pm - 5:00pm |
| Ross Priory, Gartocharn | Sunday 11 May | 2:00pm - 5:00pm |
| Shandon Gardens, Shandon | Sunday 18 May | 2:00pm - 5:00pm |
| Geilston Garden, Cardross | Sunday 3 August | 1:00pm - 5:00pm |
| Queen Street Gardens, Helensburgh | Sunday 10 August | 2:00pm - 5:00pm |
| 8 Laggary Park, Rhu | Sunday 17 August | 2:00pm - 5:00pm |

## Gardens open regularly

| | | |
|---|---|---|
| Glenarn, Glenarn Road, Rhu | 21 March - 21 September | Dawn - Dusk |

## Gardens open by arrangement

| | | |
|---|---|---|
| Parkhead, Rosneath | On request | 01436 831448<br>or (preferred) E:<br>imckellaris@gmail.com |

## Plant sales

| | | | | |
|---|---|---|---|---|
| Glenarn Plant Sale, Glenarn Road, Rhu | Sunday 4 May | 2:00pm | - | 5:00pm |
| 8 Laggary Park Plant Sale, Rhu | Sunday 15 June | 2:00pm | - | 5:00pm |
| Hill House Plant Sale, Helensburgh | Sunday 7 September | 11:00am | - | 4:00pm |

Laggary Park, Rhu, Dunbartonshire

## Key to symbols

 New in 2014

 Teas

 Cream teas

 Homemade teas

 Dogs on a lead allowed

 Wheelchair access

 Accommodation

 Plant stall

 Scottish Snowdrop Festival

## Garden locations

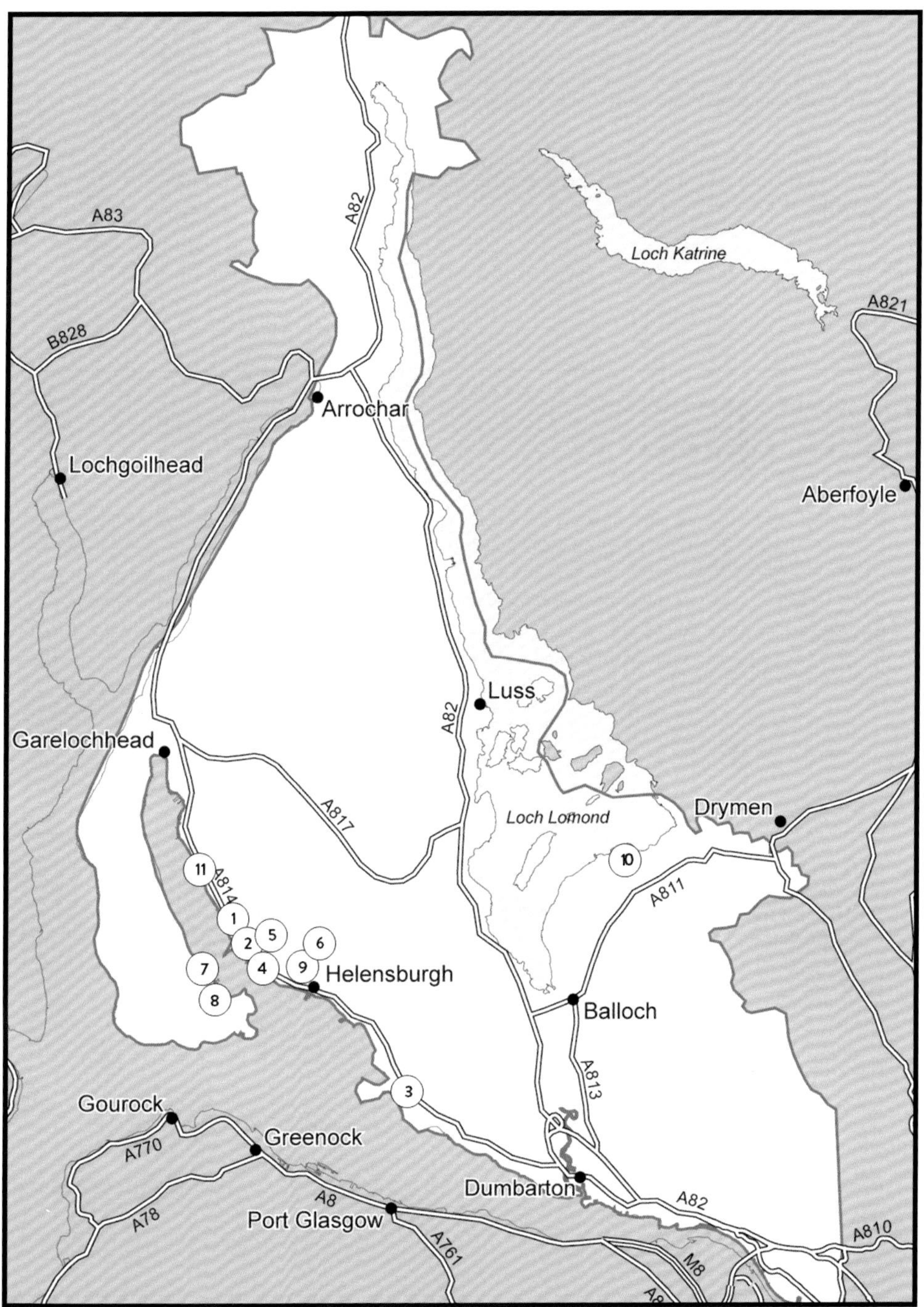

## 8 LAGGARY PARK

Rhu, Helensburgh G84 8LY
**Mrs Susan Miller**

This ½ acre garden features a collection of over 50 hydrangeas which should be at their best. Also flowering shrubs and specimen trees. Clematis arbour, pergola, fernery and woodland. Mixed borders with hardy geraniums, violas, penstemons and fuchsias.

**Directions:** Take A814 shore road from Helensburgh to Rhu Marina. Turn right into Pier Road and take second turn right (signposted) into Laggary Park and bear right. Please park in Pier Road.

Disabled Access:
Partial

Opening Times:
Sunday 17 August
2:00pm - 5:00pm

Admission:
£4.00

Charities:
SSPCA receives 40%, the net remaining to SG Beneficiaries.

## 8 LAGGARY PARK PLANT SALE

Rhu, Helensburgh G84 8LY
**Susan Miller T: 01436 821314**
**E: susan.miller17@btinternet.com**

Large plant sale comprising perennials and shrubs propagated from the collection growing in the garden, including hardy geraniums, penstemons, meconopsis, delphiniums and violas.

**Other Details:** Please note the garden will not be open during the Plant Sale.

**Directions:** Take A814 shore road from Helensburgh to Rhu Marina. Turn right into Pier Road and take second turn right (signposted) into Laggary Park and bear right. Please park in Pier Road.

Disabled Access:
Partial

Opening Times:
Sunday 15 June
2:00pm - 5:00pm

Admission:
Free

Charities:
SSPCA receives 40%, the net remaining to SG Beneficiaries.

## GEILSTON GARDEN

Main Road, Cardross G82 5HD
**The National Trust for Scotland T: 0844 4932219**
**E: jgough@nts.org.uk www.nts.org.uk**

Enjoy a fruit-laden 'Berry Day' at Geilston to promote its delicious range of soft fruits, in support of Scotland's Gardens. Geilston Garden has many attractive features including the walled garden with the herbaceous border providing summer colour, the tranquil woodland walks along the Geilston Burn and a large working kitchen garden.

**Other Details:** There will be a produce sale offering a range of fresh fruit and vegetables picked from the garden, teas and home baking plus a strawberries and cream stall.

**Directions:** On the A814, 1 mile from Cardross.

Disabled Access:
Partial

Opening Times:
Sunday 3 August
1:00pm - 5:00pm

Admission:
£5.00, children under 12 free
N.B. Prices correct at time of going to print.

Charities:
Donation to SG Beneficiaries.

## GLENARN

Glenarn Road, Rhu, Helensburgh G84 8LL
**Michael and Sue Thornley T: 01436 820493**
**E: masthome@dsl.pipex.com www.gardens-of-argyll.co.uk**

Glenarn survives as a complete example of a 10 acre garden which spans from 1850 to the present day. There are winding paths through glens under a canopy of oak and lime, sunlit open spaces, a vegetable garden with beehives, and a rock garden with views over the Gareloch. It is famous for its collection of rare and tender rhododendrons but horticulturally there is much more besides.

**Other Details:** Catering for groups by prior arrangement.

**Directions:** On A814, two miles north of Helensburgh. Cars to be left at gate unless passengers are infirm.

Disabled Access:
Partial

Opening Times:
21 March - 21 September
Dawn - Dusk

Admission:
£4.00

Charities:
Donation to SG Beneficiaries.

## GLENARN PLANT SALE

Glenarn Road, Rhu G84 8LL
**Michael and Sue Thornley T: 01436 820493**
**E: masthome@dsl.pipex.com www.gardens-of-argyll.co.uk**

Large plant sale with a selection of rhododendrons and magnolias propagated from the collection of special plants at Glenarn. Also unusual shrubs, woodland and rock garden plants.

**Other Details:** Teas and coffee with homemade scones available. Glenarn honey for sale.

**Directions:** On A814, two miles north of Helensburgh. Cars to be left at gate unless passengers are infirm.

Disabled Access:
Partial

Opening Times:
Sunday 4 May
2:00pm - 5:00pm

Admission:
Free but normal admission of £4.00 will apply for those wishing to go round the garden

Charities:
Donation to SG Beneficiaries.

© Ray Cox

## HILL HOUSE PLANT SALE

Helensburgh G84 9AJ
**The National Trust for Scotland/SG T: 01436 673900**
**E: gsmith@nts.org.uk www.nts.org.uk**

The Plant Sale is held in the garden of The Hill House which has fine views over the Clyde estuary and is considered Charles Rennie Mackintosh's domestic masterpiece. The gardens continue to be restored to the patron's planting scheme with many features that reflect Mackintosh's design.
The sale includes a wide selection of nursery grown perennials and locally grown trees, shrubs, herbaceous, alpine and house plants.

**Directions:** Follow signs to The Hill House.

Disabled Access:
Full

Opening Times:
Sunday 7 September
11:00am - 4:00pm
The garden will also be open

Admission:
Free to plant sale

Charities:
All proceeds to SG Beneficiaries.

## KILARDEN

Rosneath G84 0PU
**Jimmy and Carol Rowe**

Sheltered hilly 10 acre woodland with notable collection of species and hybrid rhododendrons gathered over a period of 50 years by the late Neil and Joyce Rutherford as seen on the "Beechgrove Garden".

**Other Details:** Teas served in the church hall.

**Directions:** A quarter of a mile from Rosneath off B833.

Disabled Access:
Partial

Opening Times:
Sunday 27 April
2:00pm - 5:00pm

Admission:
£3.00, children free

Charities:
Friends of St Modan's receives 40%, the net remaining to SG Beneficiaries.

## PARKHEAD

Rosneath, Helensburgh G84 0QR
**Ian and Susan McKellar T: 01436 831448 e-mail preferred**
**E: imckellaris@gmail.com**

Early 18th century building attached to an older walled garden which was a field by the 1960s. Since then, the current owners have restored the burnt out property and laid out the architectural Italianate garden, featuring box, yew, beech, hornbeam, holly and prunus in hedges parterre and topiary. Pots and bedding plants set off the clipped evergreens. A lily pond, foot maze and sundial garden occupy 3 circular yew "rooms". There is a hen run and walled enclosure for vegetables and soft fruit.

**Directions:** One mile beyond Rosneath on B833 fork left at sign for caravan park for ¼ mile then track on right (sign on tree). Exercise caution. Helensburgh/ Coulport Service bus 316 hourly.

Disabled Access:
Partial

Opening Times:
By arrangement on request

Admission:
By donation: minimum £4.00, children free. Groups by arrangement.

Charities:
Friends of St Modan's receives 40%, the net remaining to SG Beneficiaries.

## QUEEN STREET GARDENS

Queen Street, Helensburgh G84 9LG

**David and Maureen Morton, Tom & Tricia Stewart**

**The Old Coach House**, 22 Queen Street (David and Maureen Morton)
**High Glenan**, 24a Queen Street (Tom and Tricia Stewart)
Two secluded neighbouring gardens offering a contrast of styles, old and new and reclaimed. Wooded area with burn and waterside plants; formal and courtyard gardens, gravel garden, alpine beds and numerous areas for reflection; kitchen gardens with extensive selection of fruit and vegetables.

**Directions:** Gardens are situated in West Helensburgh, approximately half a mile along Queen Street from its junction with Sinclair Street on right hand side.

Disabled Access:
Partial

Opening Times:
Sunday 10 August
2:00pm - 5:00pm

Admission:
£4.00 (includes both gardens) Children free

Charities:
Helensburgh District Girl Guiding receives 40%, the net remaining to SG Beneficiaries.

## ROSS PRIORY

Gartocharn G83 8NL

**University of Strathclyde**

An 1812 Gothic addition by James Gillespie Graham to house of 1693 with glorious views over Loch Lomond. A good selection of rhododendrons, azaleas, selected shrubs and trees can be seen along with an extensive walled garden with glasshouses, pergola and ornamental plantings. There is also a family burial ground as well as nature and garden trails.

**Other Details:** Teas are served in the house. Putting green.
The house is not open to view.

**Directions:** Gartocharn 1½ miles off A811. Bus: Balloch to Gartocharn leaves Balloch at 1:00pm and 3:00pm.

Disabled Access:
Partial

Opening Times:
Sunday 11 May
2:00pm - 5:00pm

Admission:
£5.00, children under 12 free

Charities:
CHAS receives 40%, the net remaining to SG Beneficiaries.

## SHANDON GARDENS

Shandon G84 8HN

**Mrs and Mrs J. Lang & Mr and Mrs R Murray**

**Ardchapel:** Well established 3½ acres with a variety of mature trees overlooking the Gareloch. Retains the rough layout drawn by James Smith in 1854 when the house was built. Rhododendrons, azaleas and camellias. There is also a bank of bluebells, herbaceous and rose garden, an apple orchard and a vegetable garden.
**7 The Birches:** Features include crevice garden, rockery, raised beds, gravel garden, ferns, grasses, roses and richly planted mixed borders. Spring flowering bulbs give a lovely display.

**Directions:** Three and three quarter miles north of Helensburgh on A814. Take Ardchapel exit and park on service road below houses.

Disabled Access:
Partial

Opening Times:
Sunday 18 May
2:00pm - 5:00pm

Admission:
£4.00 (includes both gardens), children free

Charities:
Sight Savers receives 40%, the net remaining to SG Beneficiaries.

# EAST LOTHIAN



## District Organiser

| | |
|---|---|
| Mr W Alder | Granary House, Kippielaw, Haddington EH41 4PY |

## Area Organisers

| | |
|---|---|
| Mr Peter Atkins | Mizzentop, Westerdunes Pk, North Berwick EH39 5HJ |
| Mrs Roz Bruneau | Belhaven House, Edinburgh Road, Dunbar EH42 1NS |
| Mrs J Flockhart | Belton, Hill Road, Gullane EH31 2BE |
| Mr M Hedderwick | Gifford Bank, Gifford EH41 4JE |
| Mr Frank Kirwan | Humbie Dean, Humbie, East Lothian EH36 5PW |
| Mrs J Lindsay | Kirkland, Whittingehame EH41 4QA |
| Mrs Nicholas Parker | Steading Cottage, Stevenson, Haddington EH41 4PU |

## Treasurer

| | |
|---|---|
| Mr S M Edington | Meadowside Cottage, Strathearn Road, North Berwick EH39 5BZ |

## Gardens open on a specific date

| | | | | |
|---|---|---|---|---|
| Shepherd House, Inveresk | Saturday 22 February | 11:00am | - | 4:00pm |
| Shepherd House, Inveresk | Sunday 23 February | 11:00am | - | 4:00pm |
| Winton House, Pencaitland | Sunday 13 April | 12:00pm | - | 4:30pm |
| Shepherd House, Inveresk | Saturday 10 May | 11:00am | - | 4:00pm |
| Shepherd House, Inveresk | Sunday 11 May | 11:00am | - | 4:00pm |
| Tyninghame House, Dunbar | Sunday 11 May | 1:00pm | - | 5:00pm |
| Stenton Village | Sunday 1 June | 2:00pm | - | 5:30pm |
| Dirleton Village | Saturday 7 June | 2:00pm | - | 5:00pm |
| Dirleton Village | Sunday 8 June | 2:00pm | - | 5:00pm |
| Inveresk Village | Sunday 8 June | 2:00pm | - | 5:00pm |
| Longniddry Gardens | Sunday 15 June | 2:00pm | - | 5:00pm |
| East Lothian Garden Trail | Tuesday 17 June | 11:00am | - | 8:00pm |
| East Lothian Garden Trail | Wednesday 18 June | 11:00am | - | 8:00pm |
| East Lothian Garden Trail | Thursday 19 June | 11:00am | - | 8:00pm |
| East Lothian Garden Trail | Friday 20 June | 1:00pm | - | 6:00pm |
| East Lothian Garden Trail | Saturday 21 June | 1:00pm | - | 6:00pm |
| Gifford Village | Sunday 22 June | 1:00pm | - | 6:00pm |
| Tyninghame House, Dunbar | Sunday 29 June | 1:00pm | - | 5:00pm |
| Greywalls, Gullane | Saturday 26 July | 2:00pm | - | 5:00pm |

## Gardens open regularly

| | | |
|---|---|---|
| Inwood, Carberry | 1 May - 30 August (Tues, Thurs and Sats) | 2:00pm - 5:00pm |
| Shepherd House, Inveresk | 18 February - 27 February | 2:00pm - 4:00pm |
| | and 22 April - 10 July (Tues and Thurs) | 2:00pm - 4:00pm |

## Gardens open by arrangement

| | | |
|---|---|---|
| Bowerhouse, Dunbar | 14 April - 27 September | bectyn247@hotmail.co.uk |
| Humbie Dean, Humbie | 17 April - 31 July | 07768 996382 |
| Stobshiel House , Humbie | 17 June - 21 June (mornings) | 01875 833646 |

Winton House, East Lothian © Tony Marsh

## Key to symbols

| | | |
|---|---|---|
|  New in 2014 | Homemade teas |  Accommodation |
|  Teas |  Dogs on a lead allowed |  Plant stall |
| Cream teas |   Wheelchair access |  Scottish Snowdrop Festival |

## Garden locations

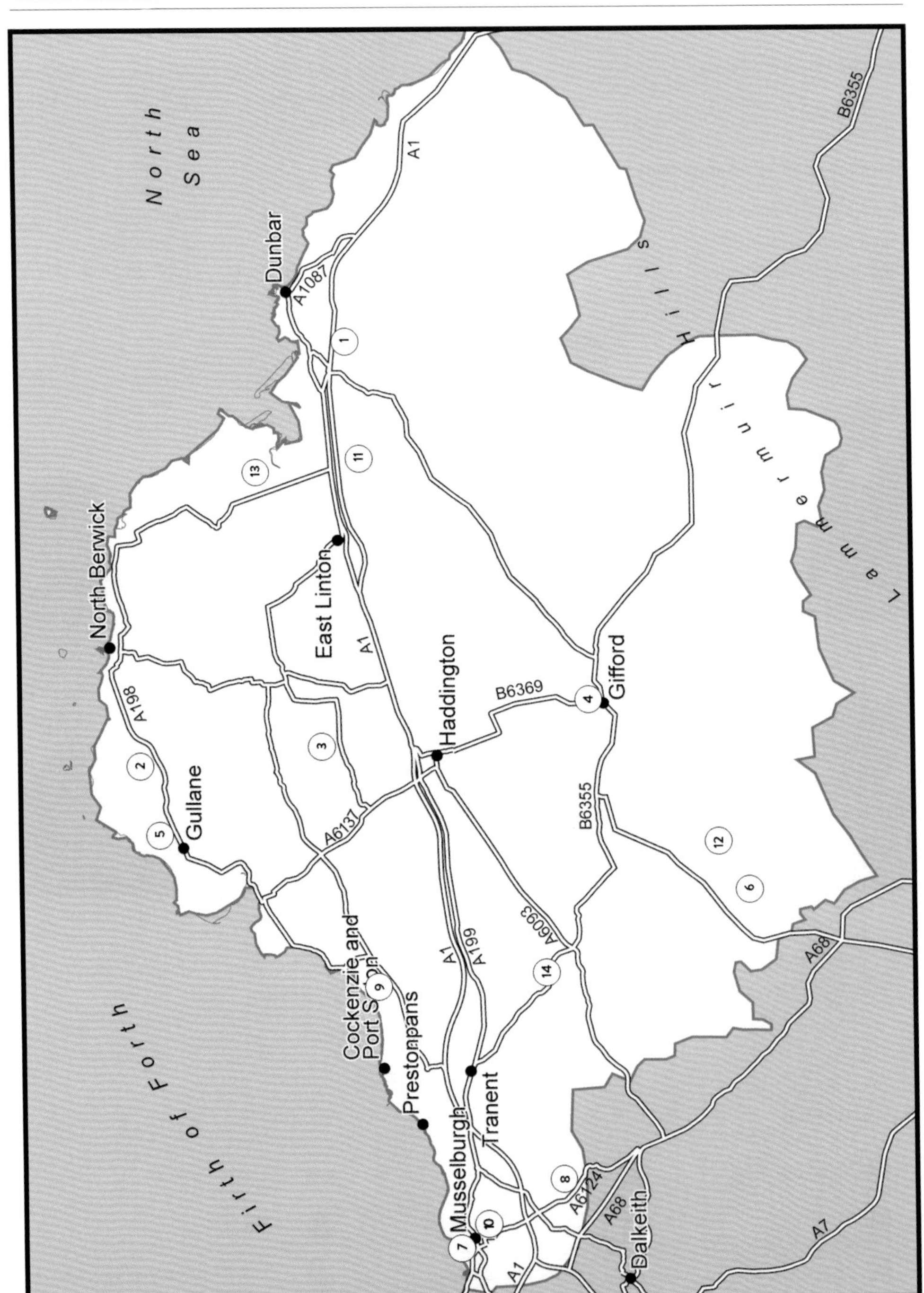

## BOWERHOUSE

Dunbar EH42 1RE

**Mark and Rebecca Tyndall**
**E: bectyn247@hotmail.co.uk**

The formal gardens with courtyards and water features enhance the 1835 David Bryce Mansion House set in 17 acres of parkland, orchard and woodland walks.

**Directions:** One mile south of Dunbar off the westbound carriage of the A1.

Disabled Access:
Partial

Opening Times:
By arrangement
14 April - 27 September

Admission:
£4.00

Charities:
Leuchie House receives 40%, the net remaining to SG Beneficiaries.

## DIRLETON VILLAGE

North Berwick EH39 5EH

**The Gardeners of Dirleton & Historic Scotland**

Dirleton is a beautiful conservation village with a large green, historic church and castle. Gardens of various sizes and types are open throughout the village.

**Other Details:** Parking, tickets and maps are available at the green and teas are served in the Church Hall.

**Directions:** Dirleton Village is 2 miles west of North Berwick off the A198.

Disabled Access:
Partial

Opening Times:
Saturday 7 June
2:00pm - 5:00pm
Sunday 8 June
2:00pm - 5:00pm

Admission:
£4.00, children free

Charities:
RNLI and Dog Rescue receives 40%, the net remaining to SG Beneficiaries.

## EAST LOTHIAN GARDEN TRAIL

East Lothian

**The East Lothian Gardeners**

**Blackdykes** EH39 5PQ (Hew and Janey Dalrymple)
Friday 20 & Saturday 21 June 1:00pm - 6:00pm

**Birrell's House** EH42 1SE (Annabel Younger)
Wednesday 18, Friday 20 & Saturday 21 June 1:00pm - 6:00pm

**Bowerhouse and Bowerhouse Walled Garden** EH42 1RE (Mark & Rebecca Tyndall) and Ian & Moira Marrian)
Tuesday 17 - Saturday 21 June: Tuesday - Thursday 2:00pm - 5:00pm and Friday & Saturday 1:00pm - 6:00pm

**Congalton House** EH39 5JL (Mr and Mrs John Carson)
Friday 20 - Saturday 21 June 1:00pm - 6:00pm

**Frostineb** EH37 5TB (Henry and Caroline Gibson)
Tuesday - Saturday 17 - 21 June: Tuesday - Thursday 11:00am - 4:00pm and Friday & Saturday 1:00pm - 6:00pm

**Humbie Dean** EH36 5PW (Frank Kirwan)
Tuesday 17 - Saturday 21 June: Tuesday - Thursday 3:00pm - 8:00pm and Friday & Saturday 1:00pm - 6:00pm

**Inwood** EH21 8PZ (Irvine and Lindsay Morrison)
Thursday 19 - Saturday 21 June 1:00 - 6:00pm

**Redcliffe** EH41 4QA (Joe and Jenny Harper)
Tuesday 17 - Saturday 21 June: Tuesday - Thursday 11:00am - 5:00pm and Friday & Saturday 1:00pm - 6:00pm

**Stevenson Steading** EH41 4PU (Mr and Mrs Nicholas Parker)
Tuesday - Saturday 17 - 21 June 1:00pm - 6:00pm

**Stobshiel House** EH36 5PD (Mr Maxwell and Lady Sarah Ward)
Tuesday - Saturday 17 - 21 June 1:00pm - 6:00pm

**Other Details:** Plant stalls at Humbie Dean, Inwood and Stobshiel House.
Teas at Stobshiel House.
Further details available in leaflet provided on purchase of tickets.

**Directions:** Details will be shown in leaflet provided on purchase of tickets.

Disabled Access:
Partial

Opening Times:
Tuesday 17 June
11:00am - 8:00pm
Wednesday 18 June
11:00am - 8:00pm
Thursday 19 June
11:00am - 8:00pm
Friday 20 June
1:00pm - 6:00pm
Saturday 21 June
1:00pm - 6:00pm
NOTE: Garden and times vary Tuesday - Thursday.
All gardens are open Friday and Saturday.

Admission:
£20.00 for all 10 gardens, accompanied children under 16 free
Entry to all gardens by presold ticket only. A limited number of tickets are available and can be purchased by credit card from:
**www.eastlothiantrail.org.uk**
or by cheque payable to Scotland's Gardens from:
Bill Alder, Granary House, Kippielaw, Haddington EH41 4PY

Charities:
Leuchie House receives 20%, The Lamp of Lothian Trust receives 20%, the net remaining to SG Beneficiaries.

## GIFFORD VILLAGE

Gifford EH41 4QY

**The Gardeners of Gifford**

Gifford was laid out early in the 18th century and has retained much of its original charm. The village includes a beautiful church built in 1708, the Lime Avenue of Yester House, the Goblin Ha' and Tweeddale hotels and a wide range of gardens all within walking distance of each other.
The gardens vary in size and type, from the compact and the informal, to the large and formal with a wide range of plants, shrubs and trees.

**Other Details:** Tickets and garden maps available from the village hall.

**Directions:** Gifford sits between the A1 and A68 roads about 5 miles south of Haddington. The village is well signposted from Haddington, Pencaitland and Duns.

Disabled Access:
Partial

Opening Times:
Sunday 22 June
1:00pm - 6:00pm

Admission:
£5.00

Charities:
Local Charities will receive 40%, the net remaining to SG Beneficiaries.

## GREYWALLS

Gullane EH31 2EG

**Mr and Mrs Giles Weaver**

**www.greywalls.co.uk**

Six acres of formal garden attributed to Gertrude Jekyll complements the Edwardian house built by Sir Edwin Lutyens in 1901. Formal garden, shrub and annual borders.

**Directions:** Signposted on the A198 southeast of Gullane. From Edinburgh take A1 south, then A198 to Gullane last turning on left side. From south take A1 north to Haddington, Gullane is signposted. Further information on our website.

Disabled Access:
None

Opening Times:
Saturday 26 July
2:00pm - 5:00pm

Admission:
£4.00, accompanied children free

Charities:
All proceeds to SG Beneficiaries.

© Ray Cox

© Ray Cox

## HUMBIE DEAN

Humbie EH36 5PW

**Frank Kirwan T: 07768 996382**

**E: frank.kirwan@which.net www.humbiedean.com**

A 2 acre ornamental and woodland garden at 600 feet under single-handed renovation and major extension since 2008 - tree clearance; creation of light and access to the woodland; replanting; construction of paths, steps, and an elevated walkway/bridge. A limited palette of plants with extensive primula, meconopsis and spring bulbs; bluebell meadow; mature and recent azalea and rhododendron planting. Featured in 'Scotland for Gardeners' 2nd Edition.

**Other Details:** Access-exit to the woodland is via steps.

**Directions:** Enter Humbie from A68, pass school and village hall on left then immediately turn right into lane . Take second left, Humbie Dean is on left between 2 small bridges.

Disabled Access:
None

Opening Times:
By arrangement
17 April - 31 July

Admission:
£4.00

Charities:
Oxfam receives 40%, the net remaining to SG Beneficiaries.

## INVERESK VILLAGE

Musselburgh EH21

**The Gardeners of Inveresk**

A collection of walled gardens in an historic village. Each has its own individual character displaying a wide variety of interesting and unusual trees, shrubs and plants.

**Directions:** South side of Musselburgh, Inveresk Village Road - A6124.

**Disabled Access:**
Full

**Opening Times:**
Sunday 8 June
2:00pm - 5:00pm

**Admission:**
£6.00, children free

**Charities:**
Lamp of Lothian Trust receives 40%, the net remaining to SG Beneficiaries.

## INWOOD

Carberry, Musselburgh EH21 8PZ

**Mr and Mrs I Morrison T: 0131 665 4550**

**E: lindsay@inwoodgarden.com www.inwoodgarden.com**

Created from scratch, Inwood Garden sits snugly around the house, with a fine Cornus contraversa 'Variagata' at the centre and a sheltering backdrop of mature woodland. This acre enthusiast's garden is packed with interesting plants in generously proportioned island beds. It's worth a visit at any time during the season with massed tulips and rhododendrons in spring, rambling roses and clematis in high summer and hydrangeas and late flowering perennials in early autumn. Greenhouses with begonias and streptocarpus collections and a pond invite further exploration. An "RHS Partner Garden".

**Other Details:** Toilet available.

**Directions:** From the A1 take A6094 exit signed Wallyford and Dalkeith. At roundabout turn left on A6124. Continue uphill for 1½ miles. Turn left at Inwood sign on left.

**Disabled Access:**
Partial

**Opening Times:**
1 May - 30 August
2:00pm - 5:00pm Tuesdays, Thursdays and Saturdays.
Groups welcome by prior arrangement

**Admission:**
£4.00, children free

**Charities:**
Donation to SG Beneficiaries.

## LONGNIDDRY GARDENS

EH32 0QS

**The Gardeners of Longniddry**

A selection of mature and charming gardens with an impressive diversity of trees, shrubs, roses and herbaceous borders set in attractive surroundings with sea views.

**Other Details:** Tickets will be available at all open gardens which will be signposted.

**Directions:** On A198.

**Disabled Access:**
Partial

**Opening Times:**
Sunday 15 June
2:00pm - 5:00pm

**Admission:**
£5.00 children free

**Charities:**
Garden Owner's Charity to be advised and will receive 40%, the net remaining to SG Beneficiaries.

## SHEPHERD HOUSE

Inveresk, Musselburgh EH21 7TH

**Sir Charles and Lady Fraser T: 0131 665 2570**

**E: annfraser@talktalk.net www.shepherdhousegarden.co.uk**

Shepherd House and its 1 acre garden form a walled triangle in the middle of the 18th century village of Inveresk. The main garden is to the rear of the house where the formality of the front garden is continued with a herb parterre and two symmetrical potagers. A formal rill runs the length of the garden, beneath a series of rose and clematis arches and connects the 2 ponds. The snowdrops are mainly grown in beds and borders. However there is a growing collection of "specialist snowdrops" around 50 different cultivars at present some of which will be displayed in our "Snowdrop Theatre".
An addition to the garden in 2013 is a Shell House, designed by Lachie Stewart, also Charles and Ann have published a book 'Shepherd House Garden' which is for sale at Open Days, by application to Shepherd House or the web site.

**Other Details:** The garden will also open as part of The Inveresk Village on 8 June. No teas will be served on any of the open days except 8 June.

**Directions:** Near Musselburgh. From A1 take A6094 exit signed Wallyford and Dalkeith and follow signs to Inveresk.

Disabled Access:
Partial

Opening Times:
Saturday 22 February and
Sunday 23 February
11:00am - 4:00pm
for the Snowdrop Festival
Saturday 10 May and
Sunday 11 May
11:00am - 4:00pm
Also 18 - 27 February and
2 April - 10 July
2:00pm - 4:00pm
Tuesday and Thursdays only

Admission:
£5.00, children free

Charities:
Lamp of Lothian receives 40%, the net remaining to SG Beneficiaries.

## STENTON VILLAGE

East Lothian EH42

**The Gardeners of Stenton Village**

Stenton is a lovely conservation village at the edge of the Lammermuir hills with a great variety of gardens.

**Directions:** Follow signs from A199/A1.

Disabled Access:
Full

Opening Times:
Sunday 1 June
2:00pm - 5:30pm

Admission:
£4.00 children free

Charities:
Maggie's Centres receives 40%, the net remaining to SG Beneficiaries.

## STOBSHIEL HOUSE

Humbie EH36 5PD

**Mr Maxwell and Lady Sarah Ward T: 01875 833646**
**E: stobshiel@gmail.com**

A large garden to see for all seasons. Walled garden adjacent to the house, box-edged borders filled with bulbs, roses and lavender beds. There is also a rustic summerhouse, glasshouse, formal lily pond and castellated yew hedge. The shrubbery has rhododendrons, azaleas and bulbs. Growing in the water and woodland garden are meconopsis and primulas. Enjoy the beautiful woodland walks.

**Directions:** B6368 Haddington/Humbie road; sign to Stobshiel 1 mile.

**Disabled Access:**
None

**Opening Times:**
By arrangement for group bookings 17 June - 21 June 9.00am - 1.00pm
Also open on these dates as part of the East Lothian Garden trail 1:00pm - 6:00pm

**Admission:**
£4.00, children under 12 free

**Charities:**
Camphill Blair Drummond receives 40%, the net remaining to SG Beneficiaries.

## TYNINGHAME HOUSE

Dunbar EH42 1XW

**Tyninghame Gardens Ltd**

Splendid 17th century pink sandstone Scottish baronial house, remodelled in 1829 by William Burn, rises out of a sea of plants. Herbaceous border, formal rose garden, Lady Haddington's secret garden with old fashioned roses, formal walled garden with sculpture and yew hedges. The "wilderness" spring garden with magnificent rhododendrons, azaleas, flowering trees and bulbs. Grounds include one mile beech avenue to sea, "apple walk", Romanesque ruin of St Baldred's Church, views across the Tyne estuary and Lammermuir Hills. Tyninghame is one of only seven estates in Scotland to have been awarded 'Outstanding' for every category in the Inventory of Gardens & Designed Landscapes of Scotland.

**Directions:** Gates on A198 at Tyninghame Village.

**Disabled Access:**
Full

**Opening Times:**
Sunday 11 May
1:00pm - 5:00pm
Sunday 29 June
1:00pm - 5:00pm

**Admission:**
£5.00 children free

**Charities:**
May: Lynton Day Centre receives 40%.
June: Marie Curie Cancer Care receives 40%, the net remaining to SG Beneficiaries.

## WINTON HOUSE

Pencaitland EH34 5AT

**Sir Francis Ogilvy Winton Trust T: 01875 340222**
**www.wintonhouse.co.uk**

The gardens continue to develop and improve. In addition to the natural areas around Sir David's Loch and the Dell, extensive mixed borders are taking shape for the terrace borders and walled garden. In spring a glorious covering of daffodils makes way for cherry and apple blossoms. Enjoy an informative tour of this historic house and walk off delicious lunches and home baking around the estate.

**Directions:** Entrance off B6355 Tranent/Pencaitland Road.

**Disabled Access:**
Full

**Opening Times:**
Sunday 13 April
12:00pm - 4:30pm

**Admission:**
£4.00
Guided House Tours: £5.00/£3.00, children under 10 free

**Charities:**
Bethany Christian Trust receives 40%, the net remaining to SG Beneficiaries.

# EDINBURGH & WEST LOTHIAN



## District Organiser

| | |
|---|---|
| Mrs Victoria Reid Thomas | Riccarton Mains Farmhouse, Currie EH14 4AR |

## Treasurer

| | |
|---|---|
| Mr Charles Welwood | Kirknewton House, Kirknewton EH27 8DA |

## Gardens open on a specific date

| | | | | |
|---|---|---|---|---|
| 101 Greenbank Crescent, Edinburgh | Sunday 27 April | 2:00pm | - | 5:00pm |
| Dean Gardens , Edinburgh | Sunday 27 April | 2:00pm | - | 5:00pm |
| Redcroft, Edinburgh | Sunday 4 May | 2:00pm | - | 5:00pm |
| Roscullen, Edinburgh | Saturday 10 May | 2:00pm | - | 5:00pm |
| Roscullen, Edinburgh | Sunday 11 May | 2:00pm | - | 5:00pm |
| Redcroft, Edinburgh | Saturday 17 May | 10:00am | - | 1:00pm |
| Moray Place and Bank Gardens, Edinburgh | Sunday 18 May | 2:00pm | - | 5:00pm |
| The Glasshouses at the Royal Botanic Garden, Edinburgh | Sunday 1 June | 10:00am | - | 5:30pm |
| Rocheid Garden, Edinburgh | Sunday 8 June | 2:00pm | - | 6:00pm |
| Dr Neil's Garden, Duddingston Village | Saturday 14 June | 2:00pm | - | 5:00pm |
| Dr Neil's Garden, Duddingston Village | Sunday 15 June | 2:00pm | - | 5:00pm |
| Merchiston Cottage, Edinburgh | Sunday 22 June | 2:00pm | - | 5:00pm |
| 4 Harelaw Road, Edinburgh | Sunday 13 July | 2:00pm | - | 5:00pm |
| Hunter's Tryst, Edinburgh | Sunday 20 July | 2:00pm | - | 5:00pm |
| 45 Northfield Crescent, Longridge | Saturday 26 July | 2:00pm | - | 5:00pm |
| 9 Braid Farm Road, Edinburgh | Saturday 26 July | 2:00pm | - | 5:00pm |
| 45 Northfield Crescent, Longridge | Sunday 27 July | 2:00pm | - | 5:00pm |
| 9 Braid Farm Road, Edinburgh | Sunday 27 July | 2:00pm | - | 5:00pm |

## Gardens open regularly

| | | | | |
|---|---|---|---|---|
| Newliston, Kirkliston | 1 May - 4 June<br>(closed Mons and Tues) | 2:00pm | - | 6:00pm |

## Gardens open by arrangement

| | | |
|---|---|---|
| 101 Greenbank Crescent, Edinburgh | 1 March - 31 October | 0131 447 6492 |
| 61 Fountainhall Road, Edinburgh | 1 August - 31 October | 0131 667 6146 |
| Hunter's Tryst, 95 Oxgangs Road, Edinburgh | 1 January - 31 December | 0131 477 2919 |
| Laverockdale House, Edinburgh | 1 August - 31 August | 0131 441 7936 |
| Rocheid Garden, Edinburgh | 1 January - 31 December | 0131 311 7000 |

Merchiston Cottage

## Key to symbols

 New in 2014

 Teas

 Cream teas

 Homemade teas

 Dogs on a lead allowed

 Wheelchair access

 Accommodation

 Plant stall

 Scottish Snowdrop Festival

## Garden locations

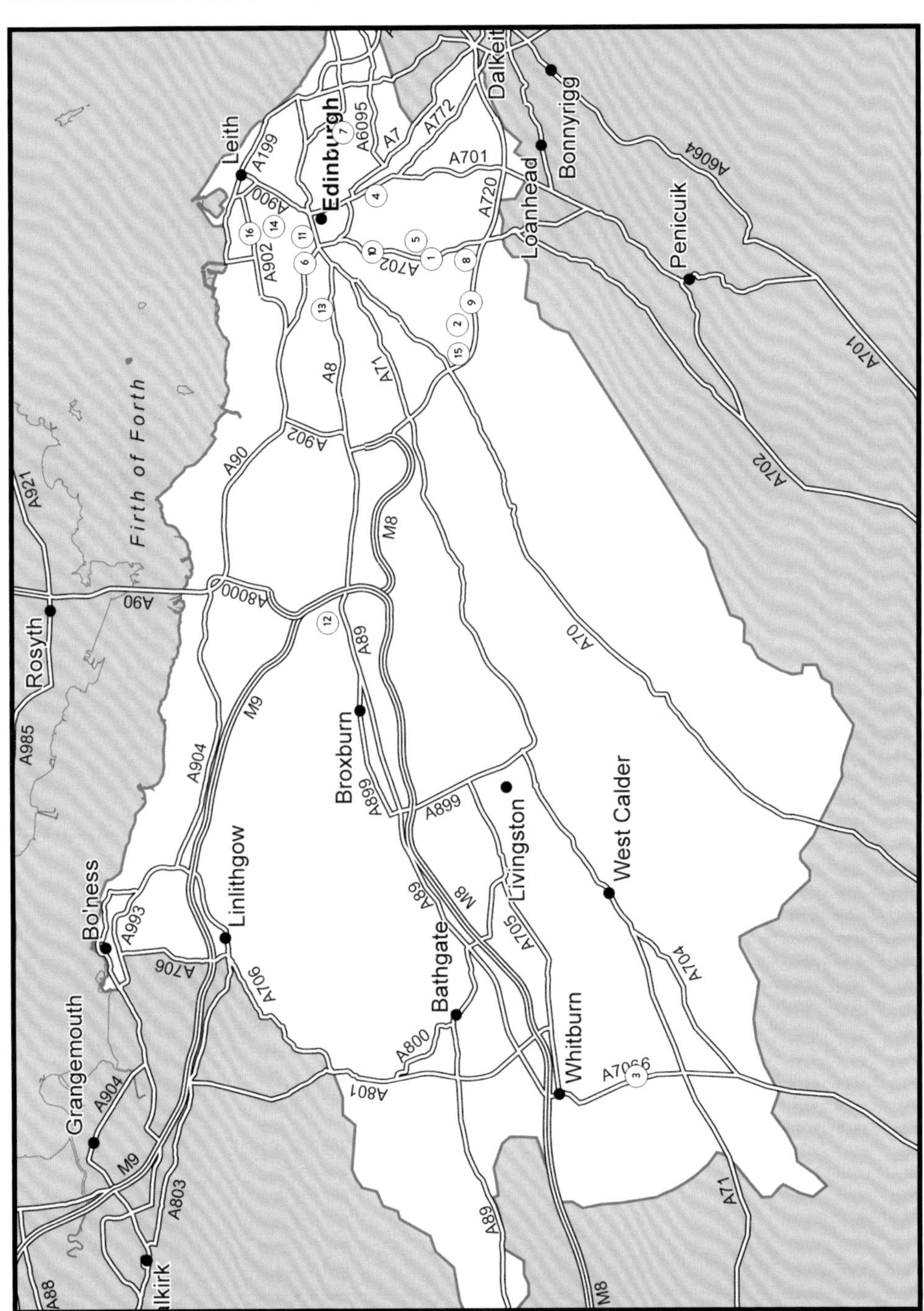

## 101 GREENBANK CRESCENT

Edinburgh EH10 5TA
**Mr and Mrs Jerry and Christine Gregson T: 0131 447 6492**
**E: jerry_gregson@yahoo.co.uk**

The front of the house is on a busy town bus route, but the back of the house is in the country. This is a terraced garden including water feature, a variety of shrubs and trees, and wandering paths and steps - with fine views of hills and the neighbouring park.

**Directions:** From Edinburgh centre, via Morningside Station. Turn right at Greenbank Church crossing. Nos 16 and 5 buses. Stop opposite Greenbank Row.

Disabled Access:
Partial

Opening Times:
Sunday 27 April
2:00pm - 5:00pm
Also by arrangement
1 March - 31 October

Admission:
£3.00

Charities:
Macmillan Cancer Support receives 40%, the net remaining to SG Beneficiaries.

## 4 HARELAW ROAD

Edinburgh EH13 0DR
**Mr and Mrs George Tait T: 0131 441 4802**
**E: tait825@btinternet.com**

An attractive, well designed garden featuring a delightful pond and statuary with a collection of unusual ferns and herbaceous plants.

**Directions:** From city take left fork at traffic lights at top of Colinton village. Bus Route N0 10.

Disabled Access:
Partial

Opening Times:
Sunday 13 July
2:00pm - 5:00pm

Admission:
£4.00

Charities:
The Motor Neurone Disease Society receives 40%, the net remaining to SG Beneficiaries.

## 45 NORTHFIELD CRESCENT

Longridge, Bathgate EH47 8AL
**Mr Jamie Robertson T: 07885 701642**
**E: jamierobertson04@hotmail.co.uk**

A delightful garden with a wide variety of shrubs and herbaceous plants. Large pond with a small waterfall and a colourful decked area with an attractive selection of bedding plants. Good vegetable patch and a 12 foot x 8 foot greenhouse. The owner has won the "West Lothian Gardener of the Year" prize 3 times.

**Directions:** From A71: turn right after Breith at traffic lights, go about a mile and turn right into the Crescent. From Whitburn: take A706 Longridge Road to Longridge and last left into Crescent.

Disabled Access:
Partial

Opening Times:
Saturday 26 July
2:00pm - 5:00pm
Sunday 27 July
2:00pm - 5:00pm

Admission:
£3.00

Charities:
World Cancer Research Fund receives 40%, the net remaining to SG Beneficiaries.

## 61 FOUNTAINHALL ROAD

Edinburgh EH9 2LH

**Mrs Annemarie Hammond T: 0131 667 6146**

**E: froglady@blueyonder.co.uk www.froglady.pwp.blueyonder.co.uk**

Large walled town garden in which trees and shrubs form an architectural backdrop to a wide variety of flowering plants. The growing collection of hellebores and trilliums and a large variety of late blooming flowers provide interest from early March to late October. In addition, there are now several alpine beds which include a large collection of Sempervivums. Three ponds, with and without fish, have attracted a lively population of frogs.

**Directions:** See "Contact Details" on Website.

Disabled Access:
Full

Opening Times:
By arrangement
1 August - 31 October

Admission:
£4.00

Charities:
Froglife receives 40%, the net remaining to SG Beneficiaries.

## 9 BRAID FARM ROAD

Edinburgh EH10 6LG

**Mr and Mrs R Paul T: 0131 447 3482**

**E: raymondpaul@btinternet.com**

A fabulous medium sized town garden of different styles. Cottage garden with pond. Mediterranean courtyard and colourful decked area with water feature and exotic plants. Mosaics and unusual features throughout.

**Directions:** Near Braid Hills Hotel, on the 11 and 15 bus routes.

Disabled Access:
Partial

Opening Times:
Saturday 26 July
2:00pm - 5:00pm
Sunday 27 July
2:00pm - 5:00pm

Admission:
£4.00, children free

Charities:
Alzheimer Scotland receives 40%, the net remaining to SG Beneficiaries.

## DEAN GARDENS

Edinburgh EH4 1QE

**Dean Gardens Management Committee**

**www.deangardens.org**

Nine acres of semi-woodland garden with spring bulbs on the steep banks of the Water of Leith in central Edinburgh. Founded in the 1860s by local residents, the Dean Gardens contains part of the great structure of the Dean Bridge, a Thomas Telford masterpiece of 1835. Lawns, paths, trees, and shrubs with lovely views to the weir in the Dean Village and to the St Bernard's Well. Children's play area.

**Directions:** Entrance at Ann Street or Eton Terrace.

Disabled Access:
Partial

Opening Times:
Sunday 27 April
2:00pm - 5:00pm

Admission:
£3.00, children free

Charities:
All proceeds to SG Beneficiaries.

## DR NEIL'S GARDEN

Duddingston Village EH15 3PX
**Dr Neil's Garden Trust**
**E: info@drneilsgarden.co.uk www.drneilsgarden.co.uk**

Wonderful secluded landscaped garden on the lower slopes of Arthur's Seat including conifers, heathers, alpines, physic garden, herbaceous borders and ponds. Thompson's Tower with the Museum of Curling and beautiful views across Duddingston Loch.

**Directions:** Kirk car park on Duddingston Road West. Then follow signposts through the Manse garden.

Disabled Access:
Partial

Opening Times:
Saturday 14 June
2:00pm - 5:00pm
Sunday 15 June
2:00pm - 5:00pm

Admission:
£3.00

Charities:
Dr Neils Garden Trust receives 40%, the net remaining to SG Beneficiaries.

## HUNTER'S TRYST

95 Oxgangs Road, Edinburgh EH10 7BA
**Jean Knox T: 0131 477 2919**
**E: jean.knox@blueyonder.co.uk**

Well stocked, mature, medium sized town garden comprising herbaceous/shrub beds, lawn, vegetables and fruit, water feature, seating areas and trees.

**Directions:** From Fairmilehead crossroads head down Oxgangs Road to Hunter's Tryst roundabout, last house on the left. Buses 4, 5, 18, 27. Bus Stop at Hunter's Tryst. Garden opposite Hunter's Tryst.

Disabled Access:
Partial

Opening Times:
Sunday 20 July
2:00pm - 5:00pm
Also by arrangement on request

Admission:
£3.00

Charities:
Lothian Cat Rescue receives 40%, the net remaining to SG Beneficiaries.

## LAVEROCKDALE HOUSE

66 Dreghorn Loan, Edinburgh EH13 0DB
**Susan Plag T: 01314417936**
**E: smplag@gmail.com www.laverockdalehouse.com**

The garden at the Sir Robert Lorimer designed Laverockdale House sits on the boundary between city and countryside with the Pentland Hills as a backdrop. From the terrace the view of the garden is very special as the sweeping lawn leads to the spectacular pond and waterfalls fed from the Bonaly Burn. The garden features large areas of planting with herbaceous perennials, shrubs, annuals, a raised vegetable garden and mixed mature woodland.

**Other Details:** Homemade teas available on request.

**Directions:** Top of Dreghorn Loan, carry on straight ahead up lane.

Disabled Access:
Partial

Opening Times:
By arrangement for groups only
1 August - 31 August

Admission:
£4.00

Charities:
Scottish Love in Action (SLA) receives 40%, the net remaining to SG Beneficiaries.

## MERCHISTON COTTAGE

16 Colinton Road, Edinburgh EH10 5EL

**Esther Mendelssohn**

Small, walled, urban wildlife friendly, organic, bee keeper's garden. This eco friendly tapestry of wildlife habitats encourages birds, insects and frogs as pest control. In addition, the bees not only provide honey, but also act as pollinators, for the many fruit trees including blueberries and mulberries. When possible the bees can be seen at close quarters in an observation hive.

**Other Details:** Plant stall by Binny Plants.

**Directions:** Near Holy Corner, opposite Watson's College School. Buses 11 and 16.

Disabled Access:
Partial

Opening Times:
Sunday 22 June
2:00pm - 5:00pm

Admission:
£4.00

Charities:
Alyn Children's Hospital receives 40%, the net remaining to SG Beneficiaries.

## MORAY PLACE AND BANK GARDENS

Edinburgh EH3 6BX

**The Residents of Moray Place and Bank Gardens**

**Moray Place**: Private garden of 3½ acres in Georgian New Town recently benefited from five-year programme of replanting. Shrubs, trees and beds offering atmosphere of tranquillity in the city centre.
**Bank Gardens**: Nearly 6 acres of secluded wild gardens with lawns, trees and shrubs with banks of bulbs down to the Water of Leith. Stunning vistas across Firth of Forth.

**Other Details:** Disabled access Moray Place only.

**Directions:** Moray Place: Enter by north gate in Moray Place.
Bank Gardens: Enter by gate at top of Doune Terrace.

Disabled Access:
Partial

Opening Times:
Sunday 18 May
2:00pm - 5:00pm

Admission:
£3.50

Charities:
The Euan Macdonald Centre for Motor Neurone Disease Research receives 40%, the net remaining to SG Beneficiaries.

## NEWLISTON

Kirkliston EH29 9EB

**Mr and Mrs R C Maclachlan T: 0131 333 3231**
**E: mac@newliston.fsnet.co.uk**

18th century designed landscape with good rhododendrons and azaleas. The house, designed by Robert Adam, is open.

**Directions:** Four miles from Forth Road Bridge, entrance off B800.

Disabled Access:
Partial

Opening Times:
1 May - 4 June
2:00pm - 6:00pm not Mondays and Tuesdays

Admission:
£3.00

Charities:
Children's Hospice Association. receives 40%, the net remaining to SG Beneficiaries.

## REDCROFT

23 Murrayfield Road, Edinburgh EH12 6EP
**James and Anna Buxton T: 0131 337 1747**
**E: annabuxtonb@aol.com**

A walled garden surrounding an Arts and Crafts villa which provides an unexpected haven off a busy road. Interest in Spring comes from many different features - the herbaceous border just coming into growth, the rockery with its pond and cloud pruned conifer, the orchard covered in daffodils, shrubberies and a working greenhouse. Planted and maintained with form and texture in mind. A fine display of spring bulbs, flowering shrubs, rhododendrons and blossom.

**Other Details:** Plant stalls, teas and coffee.

**Directions:** Murrayfield Road runs North from Corstorphine Road to Ravelston Dykes. Easy parking, free. Nos 26, 31 and 38 buses.

© Sheila Sim

Disabled Access:
Full

Opening Times:
Sunday 4 May
2:00pm - 5:00pm
Saturday 17 May
10:00am - 1:00pm

Admission:
£4.00

Charities:
4 May: The Church of the Good Shepherd, Murrayfield receives 20% and the Royal Caledonian Horticultural Society receives 20%
17 May: The MS Trust receives 40%, the net remaining to SG Beneficiaries.

## ROCHEID GARDEN

Rocheid House, 20 Inverleith Terrace, Edinburgh EH3 5NS
**Mrs Anna Guest T: 0131 311 7000**
**E: anna@afguest.co.uk**

A young but rapidly maturing garden with an impressive diversity of plants, shrubs, trees, including native, exotic and rare, providing a tranquil retreat in the midst of the city. The transition from Eastern leads one through ribbons of bamboo and ornamental grasses into the Mediterranean. The natural swimming pond forms a dramatic focus and is surrounded by rich planting and overlooked by olive trees. The planted tunnel leads to the woodland by the river. Mature trees above an exciting variety of planting, creating a mosaic of colour, diversity and interest. Award-winning compost shed with a roof creating waves of ornamental grasses.

**Other Details:** Groups by arrangement only. Teas will be dependent on weather.

**Directions:** The garden is on the southern side of the Royal Botanic Garden, Edinburgh.

Disabled Access:
Partial

Opening Times:
Sunday 8 June
2:00pm - 6:00pm
Also by arrangement on request

Admission:
£4.50

Charities:
Alzheimer Scotland receives 40%, the net remaining to SG Beneficiaries.

## ROSCULLEN

1 Bonaly Road, Edinburgh EH13 0EA
**Mrs Anne Duncan T: 0131 441 2905**

Fabulous spring garden with numerous varieties of tulips. Also rhododendrons and azaleas.

**Directions:** From city take left fork at traffic lights at top of Colinton village. Bonaly Road is 3rd road along on the left. Parking best on Grant Avenue. Bus Route No 10.

Disabled Access:
Partial

Opening Times:
Saturday 10 May
2:00pm - 5:00pm
Sunday 11 May
2:00pm - 5:00pm

Admission:
£4.00

Charities:
Brooke Hospital for Animals receives 40%, the net remaining to SG Beneficiaries.

## THE GLASSHOUSES AT THE ROYAL BOTANIC GARDEN EDINBURGH

20A Inverleith Row, Edinburgh EH3 5LR
**Royal Botanic Gardens T: 0131 552 7171**
**www.rbge.org.uk**

The Glasshouses with 10 climatic zones are a delight all year round. The Orchids and Cycads House brings together primitive Cycads which dominated the land flora some 65 million years ago, and a diverse range of orchids, the most sophisticated plants in the world. In summer, giant water lillies, Victoria amazonica, are the star attraction in the Tropical Aquatic House. Plants with vibrant flowers and fascinating foliage thrive in the Rainforest Riches House and the complex ecosystems of life in the world's deserts are explored in the Arid Lands House. A large collection of gingers, (Zingiberaceae), one of the largest collections of Vi reya rhododendrons in the world and a case housing carnivorous plants are among other attractions.

**Directions:** Located off the A902, 1 mile north of city centre. Entrances at Inverleith Row and Arboretum Place.
Lothian Buses 8, 23 and 27 stop close to the East Gate entrance on Inverleith Row. The Majestic Tour Bus stops at Arboretum Place.

Disabled Access:
Full

Opening Times:
Sunday 1 June
10:00am - 5:30pm

Admission:
£5.00, concessions £4.00, children under 16 free (prices include a small donation to Scotland's Gardens, for admission prices without donation please check our website)

Charities:
Donation to SG Beneficiaries.

# ETTRICK & LAUDERDALE

Scotland's Gardens 2014 Guidebook is sponsored by **INVESTEC WEALTH & INVESTMENT**

## District Organiser

To be appointed

## Area Organisers

| | |
|---|---|
| Mrs M Kostoris | Wester Housebyres, Melrose TD6 9BW |
| Mrs P Litherland | Laidlawstiel, Nr. Clovenfords, Galashiels TD1 1TJ |
| Mrs D Warre | Peace Cottage, Synton Parkhead, Ashkirk TD7 4PB |

## Treasurer

| | |
|---|---|
| Mrs D Muir | Torquhan House, Stow TD1 2RX |

## Gardens open on a specific date

| | | |
|---|---|---|
| 2 Whytbank Row, Clovenfords | Sunday 15 June | 1:00pm - 5:00pm |
| Harmony Garden, Melrose | Sunday 22 June | 1:00pm - 4:00pm |
| Laidlawstiel, Clovenfords | Sunday 22 June | 2:00pm - 5:00pm |
| Priorwood Gardens, Melrose | Sunday 22 June | 1:00pm - 4:00pm |
| Carolside, Earlston | Wednesday 2 July | 11:00am - 5:00pm |
| Carolside, Earlston | Wednesday 9 July | 11:00am - 5:00pm |
| Carolside, Earlston | Wednesday 16 July | 11:00am - 5:00pm |
| Carolside, Earlston | Wednesday 23 July | 11:00am - 5:00pm |
| Carolside, Earlston | Wednesday 30 July | 11:00am - 5:00pm |

## Key to symbols

 New in 2014

 Homemade teas

 Accommodation

 Teas

 Dogs on a lead allowed

 Plant stall

 Cream teas

 Wheelchair access

 Scottish Snowdrop Festival

## Garden locations

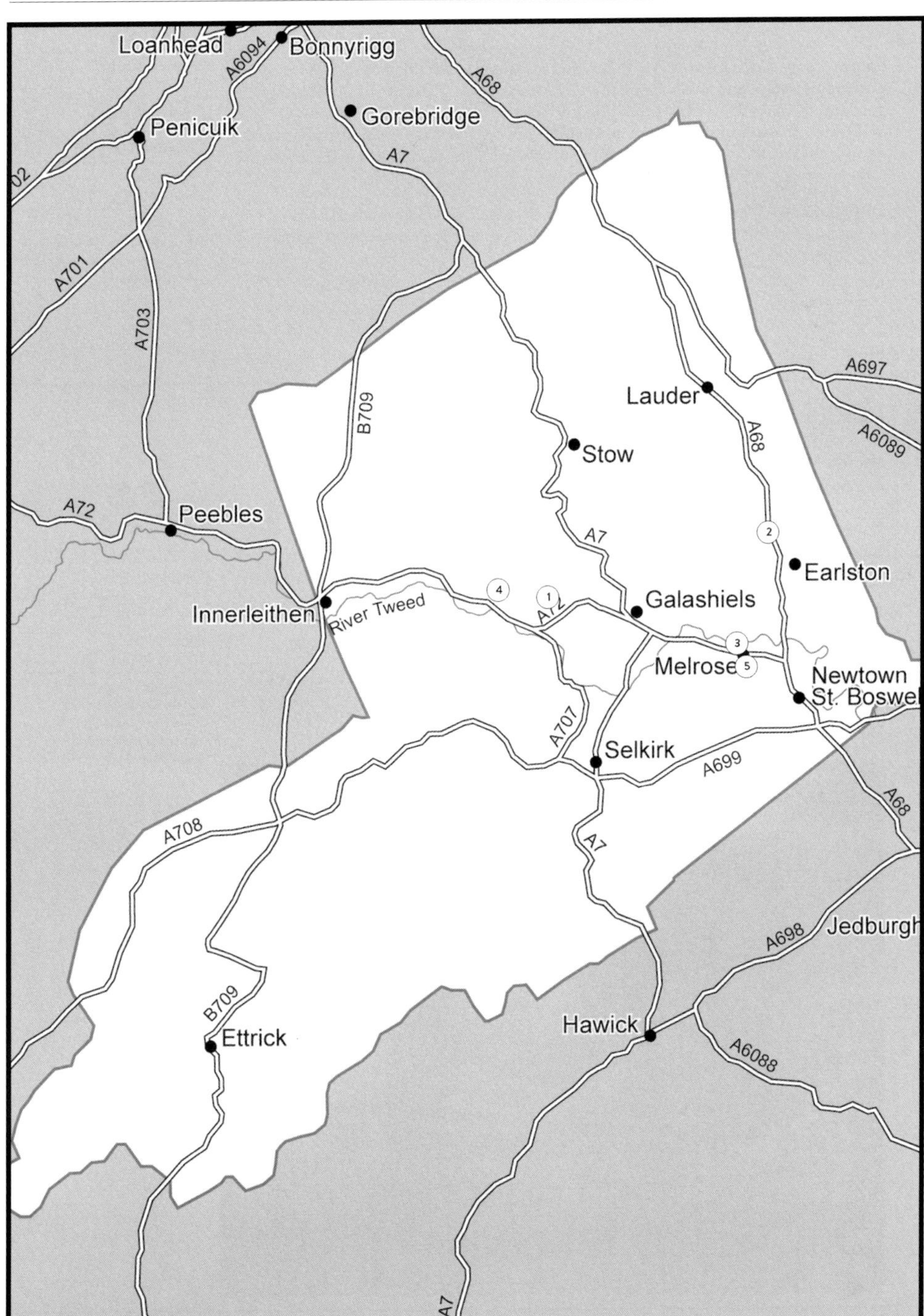

## 2 WHYTBANK ROW

Clovenfords, Galashiels TD1 3NE

**Mr and Mrs A Martin**

Large rural garden (1.4 acres) with fruit trees, raised vegetable beds, greenhouses, polytunnel, pond and an active beehive. Various types of layout with cottage garden borders, shrub beds, container planting. All of the features have been designed and created by the owners and are good examples of organic gardening and what can be done with a bit of imagination and some hard work. The garden was featured on the "Beechgrove Garden".

**Directions:** A72 Galashiels to Peebles road, 3 miles from Galashiels. At the roundabout in the village centre turn up the hill behind the hotel and Whytbank Row is 2nd street on the left.

**Disabled Access:**
None

**Opening Times:**
Sunday 15 June
1:00pm - 5:00pm

**Admission:**
£3.00, children free

**Charities:**
Alzheimers Scotland receives 40%, the net remaining to SG Beneficiaries.

## CAROLSIDE

Earlston TD4 6AL

**Mr and Mrs Anthony Foyle T: 01896 849272**
**E: info@carolside.com www.carolsidegardens.com**

A traditional and romantic garden set in a beautiful 18th century landscape, comprising lawns, shrubberies, mixed borders, a secret garden, a winter garden and an oval walled garden containing herbaceous borders, fruits, vegetables, parterres and an historically important collection of roses that has been carefully assembled over 23 years. Kenneth Cox in his book "Scotland for Gardeners" describes Carolside as "one of Scotland's finest private gardens".

**Other Details:** National Plant Collection®: The National Collection of pre 1900 Gallica Roses for the UK.

**Directions:** One mile north of Earlston on A68. Entrance faces south.

**Disabled Access:**
Full

**Opening Times:**
Wednesdays 2, 9, 16, 23 & 30 July 11:00am - 5:00pm

**Admission:**
£5.00, children free

**Charities:**
Marie Curie Cancer Care receives 40%, the net remaining to SG Beneficiaries.

## HARMONY GARDEN (WITH PRIORWOOD GARDEN)

St. Mary's Road, Melrose TD6 9LJ
**The National Trust for Scotland T: 01896 822493**
**E: ggregson@nts.org.uk www.nts.org.uk**

Wander through this tranquil garden, wonderful herbaceous borders, lawns, fruit and vegetable plots, and enjoy fine views of the Abbey and Eildon Hills. Seasonal fruits and vegetable sales on trolley at entrance.

**Other Details:** Plant stall and dried flowers are available at Priorwood.

**Directions:** Road: Off A6091, in Melrose, opposite the Abbey.
Bus: First from Edinburgh and Peebles.

Disabled Access:
Full

Opening Times:
Sunday 22 June
1:00pm - 4:00pm

Admission:
£6.50 for both gardens.
N.B. Price correct at time of going to print.

Charities:
Donation to SG Beneficiaries

## LAIDLAWSTIEL

Clovenfords, Galashiels TD1 1TJ
**Mr and Mrs P Litherland**

Walled garden containing herbaceous border, fruit, and vegetables in raised beds. Splendid views down to the River Tweed.

**Directions:** A72 between Clovenfords and Walkerburn, turn up hill signed Thornielee. The house is on the right at the top of the hill.

Disabled Access:
None

Opening Times:
Sunday 22 June
2:00pm - 5:00pm

Admission:
£4.00, OAPs £3.00, children free

Charities:
CLIC Sargent receives 40%, the net remaining to SG Beneficiaries.

## PRIORWOOD GARDENS (WITH HARMONY GARDEN)

Abbey Road, Melrose TD6 9PX
**The National Trust for Scotland T: 01896 822493**
**E: ggregson@nts.org.uk www.nts.org.uk**

In Melrose, overlooked by the Abbey ruins, this unique garden produces plants for a superb variety of dried flower arrangements made and sold here. The orchard contains many historic apple varieties.

**Other Details:** Dried flowers available.

**Directions:** Road: Off A6091, in Melrose opposite the Abbey.
Bus: First from Edinburgh and Peebles.

Disabled Access:
Full

Opening Times:
Sunday 22 June
1:00pm - 4:00pm

Admission:
£6.50 for both gardens
N.B. prices correct at the time of going to print

Charities:
Donation to SG Beneficiaries.

# FIFE



## District Organiser

| | |
|---|---|
| Lady Erskine | Cambo House, Kingsbarns KY16 8QD |

## Area Organisers

| | |
|---|---|
| Mrs Jeni Auchinleck | 2 Castle Street, Crail KY10 3SQ |
| Mrs Lisa Bremner | Grey Craig House, Bridge Street, Saline KY12 9TS |
| Mrs Jayne Clarke | Marine House, Ordnance Road, Crombie KY12 8JZ |
| Mrs Evelyn Crombie | West Hall, Cupar KY15 4NA |
| Mrs Lisa Hall | Old Inzievar House, Oakley, Dunfermline KY12 8HA |
| Mrs Lindsay Murray | Craigfoodie, Dairsie KY15 4RU |
| Ms Louise Roger | Chesterhill, Boarhills, St Andrews KY16 8PP |
| Mrs April Simpson | The Cottage, Boarhills, St Andrews KY16 8PP |
| Mrs Fay Smith | 37 Ninian Fields, Pittenweem, Anstruther KY10 2QU |
| Mrs Julia Young | South Flisk, Blebo Craigs, Cupar KY15 5UQ |

## Treasurer

| | |
|---|---|
| Mrs Sally Lorimore | Willowhill, Forgan, Newport-on-Tay DD6 8RA |

## Gardens open on a specific date

| | | |
|---|---|---|
| Lindores House, by Newburgh | Friday 7 March | 11:00am - 3:00pm |
| Cambo House, Kingsbarns | Sunday 13 April | 11:00pm - 4:00pm |
| Rofsie Arts Garden, by Collessie | Sunday 27 April | 1:00pm - 4:00pm |
| Falkland's Small Gardens | Saturday 10 May | 11:00am - 5:00pm |
| Falkland's Small Gardens | Sunday 11 May | 11:00am - 5:00pm |
| Northwood Cottage, Newport-on-Tay | Sunday 18 May | 1:00pm - 5:00pm |
| St Monans Village Gardens | Sunday 18 May | 2:00pm - 5:00pm |
| Tayfield, Forgan | Sunday 18 May | 1:00pm - 5:00pm |
| Willowhill, Forgan | Sunday 18 May | 1:00pm - 5:00pm |
| Tayport Gardens | Saturday 24 May | 12:00pm - 5:00pm |
| Tayport Gardens | Sunday 25 May | 12:00pm - 5:00pm |
| Wemyss Castle Gardens, Coaltown of Wemyss | Sunday 25 May | 2:00pm - 5:00pm |
| Special Evening Openings, South Flisk and Willowhill | Thursday 29 May | 3:00pm - 8:00pm |
| Earlshall Castle, Leuchars | Saturday 31 May | 12:00pm - 5:00pm |
| Newton Mains and Newton Barns, Auchtermuchty | Saturday 31 May | 11:00am - 4:00pm |
| Lindores House, by Newburgh | Sunday 1 June | 2:00am - 6:00pm |
| Newton Mains and Newton Barns, Auchtermuchty | Sunday 1 June | 11:00am - 4:00pm |

| | | | |
|---|---|---|---|
| Northwood Cottage, Newport-on-Tay | Sunday 1 June | 11:00am | - 4:00pm |
| Special Evening Openings, South Flisk and Willowhill | Thursday 5 June | 3:00pm | - 8:00pm |
| Fife Garden Festival | Sat 7 and Sun 8 June | 11:00am | - 5:00am |
| Special Evening Openings, South Flisk and Willowhill | Thursday 12 June | 3:00pm | - 8:00pm |
| Blebo Craigs Village Gardens, Cupar | Saturday 14 June | 12:00pm | - 5:00pm |
| Blebo Craigs Village Gardens, Cupar | Sunday 15 June | 12:00pm | - 5:00pm |
| Freuchie Plant Sale and the Garden at Karbet | Sunday 15 June | 12:00pm | - 4:00pm |
| Culross Palace Garden, Culross | Sunday 22 June | 10:00am | - 5:00pm |
| Greenhead Farm and Blair Adam House | Sunday 22 June | 2:00pm | - 5:30pm |
| Wormit Village Gardens | Sunday 22 June | 11:00am | - 5:00pm |
| Crail: Small Gardens in the Burgh | Saturday 28 June | 1:00pm | - 5:30pm |
| Crail: Small Gardens in the Burgh | Sunday 29 June | 1:00pm | - 5:30pm |
| Earlshall Castle, Leuchars | Sunday 29 June | 2:00pm | - 5:00pm |
| Logie House, Crossford | Sunday 13 July | 2:00pm | - 5:00pm |
| Northwood Cottage, Newport-on-Tay | Sunday 20 July | 2:00pm | - 5:00pm |
| Willowhill, Forgan | Sunday 20 July | 2:00pm | - 5:00pm |
| Balcaskie, Pittenweem | Sunday 27 July | 12:00pm | - 5:00pm |
| Kellie Castle Garden, Pittenweem | Sunday 27 July | 12:00pm | - 5:00pm |
| Falkland Palace and Garden | Sunday 10 August | 1:00pm | - 5:00pm |
| Hill of Tarvit Plant, Cupar | Sunday 5 October | 10:30am | - 4:00pm |
| Northwood Cottage, Newport-on-Tay | Saturday 25 October | 1:00pm | - 4:00pm |
| Northwood Cottage, Newport-on-Tay | Sunday 26 October | 1:00pm | - 4:00pm |

## Gardens open regularly

| | | | |
|---|---|---|---|
| Cambo House, Kingsbarns | 1 January - 31 December | 10:00am | - 5:00pm |
| Glassmount House, by Kirkcaldy | 1 April - 30 Sept (Mon - Fri) | 12:00pm | - 4:00pm |
| Willowhill, Forgan | 4 June - 27 August (Weds) | 2:00pm | - 5:00pm |

## Gardens open by arrangement

| | | |
|---|---|---|
| Barham, Bow of Fife | 1 April - 31 July | 01337 810227 |
| Earlshall Castle, Leuchars | On request | 01334 839205 |
| Glassmount House, by Kirkcaldy | 1 April - 30 September | 01592 890214 |
| Helensbank, Kincardine | 1 June - 30 June | 07739 312912 |
| Kirklands, Saline | 1 April - 30 September | 01383 852737 |
| Logie House, Crossford | 1 April - 30 September | sarah@logiehunt.co.uk |
| Northwood Cottage, Newport-on-Tay | 1 May - 31 October | 07974083110 |
| Rosewells, Pitscottie | 1 April - 30 September | birgittamac@hotmail.co.uk |
| South Flisk, Blebo Craigs, Cupar | 1 May - 30 June | 01334 850859 |
| Strathairly House, Upper Largo, Leven | 1 April - 31 August | Alex: 01333 352936<br>Alison: 01333 360422<br>or M:07594 097052 |
| Teasses Gardens, near Ceres | On request | 01334 828048 |
| The Tower, Wormit | 1 April - 30 September | 01382 541635<br>M: 07768 406946 |
| Willowhill, Forgan | 2 June - 29 August | 07948 286031 |
| Wormiston House, Crail | 1 April - 30 September | 01333 450356 |

## Plant sales

| | | | | |
|---|---|---|---|---|
| Cambo House Spring Plant and Craft Fair, Kingsbarns | Sunday 13 April | 11:00am | - | 4:00pm |
| Freuchie Plant Sale and the Garden at Karbet | Sunday 15 June | 12:00pm | - | 4:00pm |
| Hill of Tarvit Plant Sale and Autumn Fair, Cupar | Sunday 5 October | 10:30am | - | 4:00pm |

Wormistoune, Fife

## Key to symbols

| | | | | | |
|---|---|---|---|---|---|
|  | New in 2014 |  | Homemade teas |  | Accommodation |
|  | Teas |  | Dogs on a lead allowed |  | Plant stall |
|  | Cream teas |  | Wheelchair access |  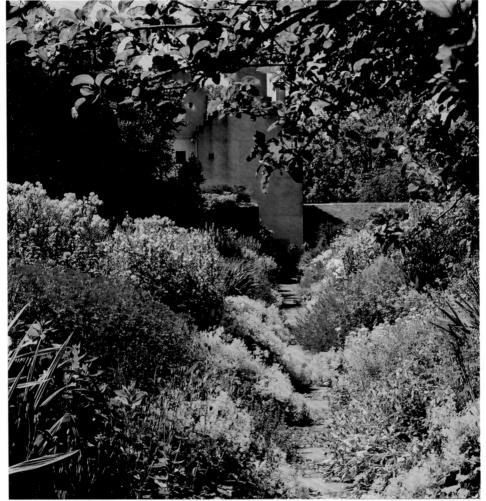 | Scottish Snowdrop Festival |

## Garden locations

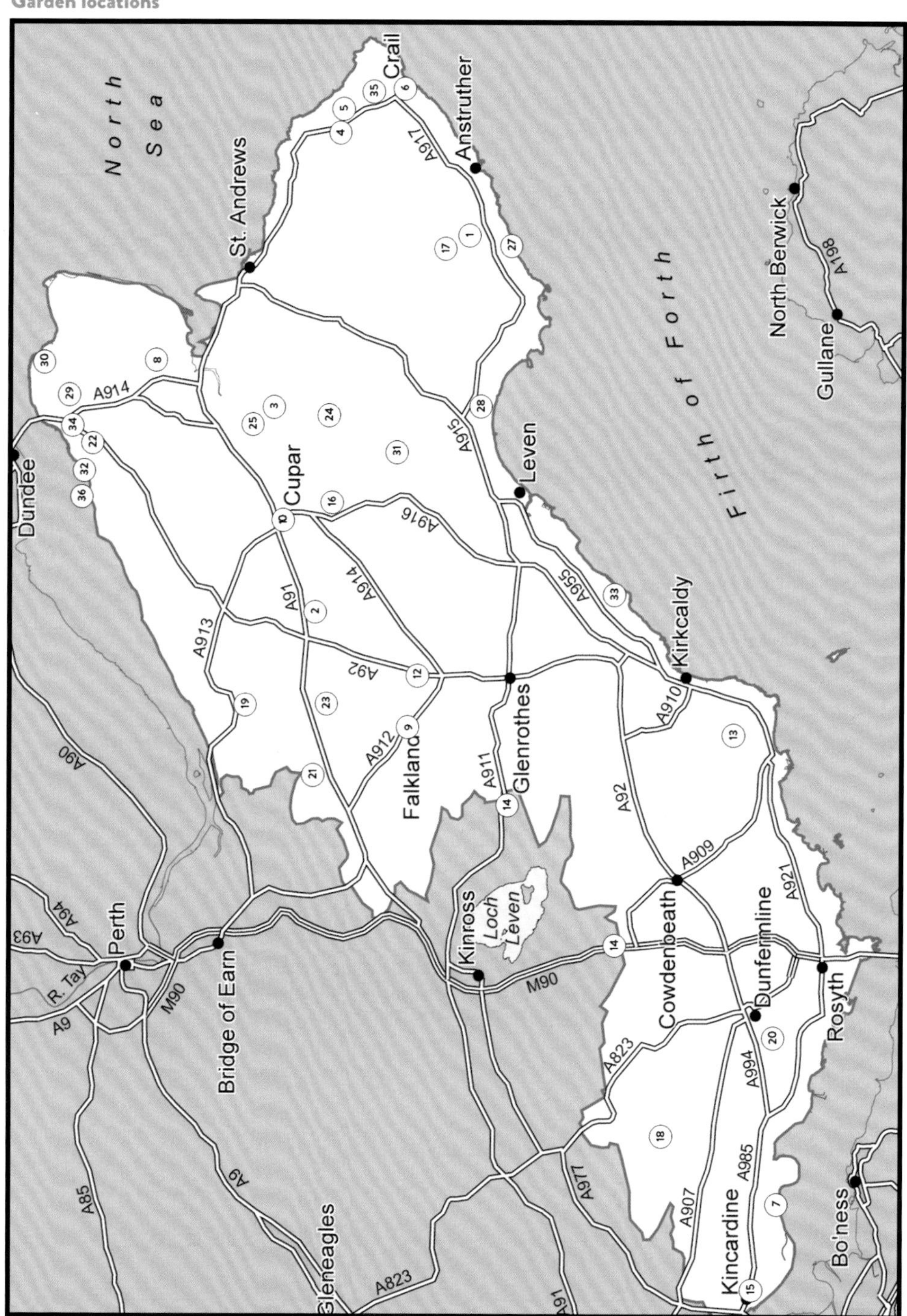

## BALCASKIE (WITH KELLIE CASTLE GARDEN)

Pittenweem KY10 2RD

**The Anstruther Family**

In 1905 George Elgood wrote that Balcaskie was 'one of the best and most satisfying gardens in the British Isles'. Over the centuries the gardens have seen input from Gilpin, Bryce & Nesfield. Today the gardens are at the start of a period of restoration with help from the National Trust for Scotland.

**Directions:** Access is via Kellie Castle only and transport will take visitors from Kellie Castle to Balcaskie. Road: B9171, 3 miles NNW of Pittenweem. Bus: Flexible from local villages by pre-booking.

Disabled Access:
Partial

Opening Times:
Sunday 27 July
12:00pm - 5:00pm

Admission:
£8.00 includes both gardens.

Charities:
Donation to SG Beneficiaries.

## BARHAM

Bow of Fife KY15 5RG

**Sir Robert & Lady Spencer-Nairn T: 01337 810227**

A small woodland garden with snowdrops, spring bulbs, trilliums, rhododendrons and ferns. Also a summer garden with rambler roses, herbaceous borders, island beds and a well stocked vegetable garden.

**Other Details:** Small nursery of rare and unusual plants grown from seed collected or plants divided from the garden.

**Directions:** A914 miles west of Cupar.

Disabled Access:
None

Opening Times:
By arrangement
1 April - 31 July

Admission:
£3.00, OAP's £2.50, children free

Charities:
Pain Association Scotland receives 40%, the net remaining to SG Beneficiaries.

## BLEBO CRAIGS VILLAGE GARDENS

Cupar KY15 5UF

**The Gardeners of Blebo Craigs**

A wide variety of gardens, including some new ones, will be open in this beautifully situated former quarry and farm village with stunning views over the Fife countryside.

**Other Details:** Wheelchair access is limited but parking is available near the village hall. Disabled toilet in the village hall.

**Directions:** From St Andrews: B939 for 4 miles. Small sign on left pointing to right hand turn. From Cupar: B940 and take left at Pitscottie then after 2 miles left at sign onto B939.

Disabled Access:
Partial

Opening Times:
Saturday 14 June
12:00pm - 5:00pm
Sunday 15 June
12:00pm - 5:00pm

Admission:
£4.50

Charities:
Blebo Craigs Village Hall receives 40%, the net remaining to SG Beneficiaries.

## CAMBO HOUSE

Kingsbarns KY16 8QD
**Sir Peter and Lady Erskine T: 01333 450313**
**E: cambo@camboestate.com www.camboestate.com**

Best known for snowdrops (mail order February), but exciting throughout the year, this Victorian walled garden features constantly evolving, magnificent herbaceous borders featuring rare and unusual plants, many of which are propagated for sale at Cambo. Head Gardener, Elliott Forsyth, aided by students and volunteers, creates irresistible planting combinations of bold perennials and grasses, including his much-loved, outrageous ornamental potager garden. The garden is renowned too for its tulips and a stunning rose collection. Outside the main garden an inspiring Winter Garden and North American prairie continue to be developed. Woodland walks to the sea.

**Other Details:** National Plant Collection®: Snowdrops. Champion Trees: Bundle Beech. Tea room and plants for sale throughout the year.
Check our website for events throughout the year.

**Directions:** A917 between Crail and St Andrews.

Disabled Access:
Full

Opening Times:
1 January - 31 December
10:00am - 5:00pm
open for the Snowdrop Festival 1 February - 16 March

Admission:
£5.00, children free

Charities:
Donation to SG Beneficiaries

## CAMBO HOUSE SPRING PLANT AND CRAFT FAIR

Kingsbarns KY16 8QD
**Sir Peter and Lady Erskine T: 01333 450313**
**E: cambo@camboestate.com www.camboestate.com**

Invited nurseries will join Cambo to provide a wide ranging and interesting plant sale.
Local craft and food stalls have also been invited.
The gardens and woodland walks will be open.

**Other Details:** National Plant Collection®: Snowdrops. Champion Trees: Bundle Beech. Tea room.
Money is being raised on this day for the Cambo Stables Project to provide a training and education centre on the estate.

**Directions:** A917 between Crail and St Andrews.

Disabled Access:
Full

Opening Times:
Sunday 13 April
11:00am - 4:00pm
Garden also open

Admission:
£2.50, children free

Charities:
Cambo Stables Project receives 40%, the net remaining to SG Beneficiaries.

## CRAIL: SMALL GARDENS IN THE BURGH

KY10 3SQ
**The Gardeners of Crail**

A number of small gardens in varied styles: cottage, historic, plantsman's and bedding.

**Other Details:** Tickets and maps available from Mrs Auchinleck, 2, Castle Street and Kathleen and Jim Main 17, Marketgate North KY10.
Teas served in British Legion Hall.

**Directions:** Approach Crail from either St Andrews or Anstruther by A917. Park in the Marketgate.

Disabled Access:
None

Opening Times:
Saturday 28 June
1:00pm - 5:30pm
Sunday 29 June
1:00pm - 5:30pm

Admission:
£5.00, children free

Charities:
1st Crail Brownies receives 10%, Crail Preservation Society receives 30%, the net remaining to SG Beneficiaries.

7

## CULROSS PALACE GARDEN

Culross KY12 8JH

**The National Trust for Scotland T: 0844 493 2189**

**E: mjeffery@nts.org.uk www.nts.org.uk**

Relive the domestic life of the 16th and 17th centuries amid the old buildings and cobbled streets of this Royal Burgh on the River Forth. A model 17th-century garden has been recreated behind Culross Palace to show the range of plants available and includes vegetables, culinary and medicinal herbs, soft fruits and ornamental shrubs. Don't miss the adorable Scots Dumpy chickens!

**Other Details:** Fruit and vegetable stalls from produce grown at Culross Palace. Admission includes tea/coffee and cakes.

**Directions:** Off A985, 3 miles east of Kincardine Bridge, 6 miles west of Dunfermline. Stagecoach, Stirling to Dunfermline or First, Edinburgh to Dunfermline. Falkirk station 12 miles, Dunfermline station 6 miles.

Disabled Access:
None

Opening Times:
Sunday 22 June
10:00am - 5:00pm

Admission:
£5.00 including NTS members.
N.B. prices correct at time of going to print.

Charities:
Donation to SG Beneficiaries.

## EARLSHALL CASTLE

Leuchars KY16 0DP

**Paul & Josine Veenhuijzen T: 01334 839205**

Garden designed by Sir Robert Lorimer. Topiary lawn, for which Earlshall is renowned, rose terrace, croquet lawn with herbaceous borders, shrub border, box garden, orchard, kitchen and herb garden.

**Directions:** On Earlshall road, ¾ of a mile east of Leuchars Village (off A919).

Disabled Access:
Partial

Opening Times:
Saturday 31 May
12:00pm - 5:00pm
Sunday 29 June
2:00pm - 5:00pm
By arrangement on request

Admission:
£5.00, children free

Charities:
May: RAF Benevolent Fund receives 40%
June: St Athermase Church, Leuchars receives 40%, the net remaining to SG Beneficiaries.

## FALKLAND PALACE AND GARDEN

Falkland KY15 7BU

**The National Trust for Scotland T: 0844 493 2186**

**E: gardens@nts.org.uk www.nts.org.uk**

Set in a medieval village, the Royal Palace of Falkland is a superb example of Renaissance architecture. Garden enthusiasts will appreciate the work of Percy Cane, who designed and cultivated the gardens between 1947 and 1952.

**Other Details:** Champion Trees: Acer platanoides 'Crimson King'.
On 10 August the garden will be dedicated to families and children. You are invited to bring a picnic and spend an afternoon in the garden having fun. There will be a quiz, and other activities to enjoy. See NTS website for full details.

**Directions:** Road: A912, 10 miles from M90, junction 8, 11 miles north of Kirkcaldy. Bus: Stagecoach Fife stops in High Street (100 metres). OS Ref: NO253075

Disabled Access:
Partial

Opening Times:
Sunday 10 August
1:00pm - 5:00pm

Admission:
£6.00, concessions £5.00, NTS members free
N.B. Prices correct at the time of going to print.

Charities:
Donation to SG Beneficiaries.

## FALKLAND'S SMALL GARDENS

Falkland KY15

**The Gardeners of Falkland**

A wonderful selection of small, secret and private gardens in this interesting, historic village.

**Directions:** On A912 and B936.

Disabled Access:
Partial

Opening Times:
Saturday 10 May
11:00am - 5:00pm
Sunday 11 May
11:00am - 5:00pm

Admission:
£4.50

Charities:
Alzheimer Scotland receives 20%, British Heart Foundation receives 20%, the net remaining to SG Beneficiaries.

## FIFE GARDEN FESTIVAL

Fife

**The Fife Gardeners**

**www.fifegardenfestival.org.uk**

Cedar Cottage, Craigrothie KY15 5PZ (Ian and Rena Douglas)

Fairbairn, Craigrothie KY15 5QA (Ewan and Jane Allan)

Kenly Green Farm KY16 8PP (Frank and Bernice Roger)

Kinaldy House, near St. Andrews KY16 8NA (David and Lynne King)

Old Inzievar House KY12 8HA (Tim and Lisa Hall)

Rofsie Arts Garden, by Collessie KY15 7UZ (Caroline and Andrew Thomson)

Seaview KY16 8PP (Alan and Ann Cairns)

Southern Hemisphere Botanics, near Torryburn KY12 8LH (Lorna McHardy),

Strathkiness Community Trust Garden, Bonfield Road, KY16 9RS (Strathkinness Community Trust)

The Cottage KY16 8PP (Bobby and April Simpson)

**Other Details:** Plant sales will be held at Rofsie Arts Gallery, Kenly Green Farm and Old Inzievar House. Teas will be available on Saturday and Sunday at The Cottage, Fairbairn and Southern Hemisphere Botanics and on Sunday only at Old Inzievar House.

**Directions:** Details will be shown in booklet provided on purchase of ticket(s).

Disabled Access:
Partial

Opening Times:
Saturday 7 June
11:00am - 5:00am
Sunday 8 June
11:00am - 5:00pm

Admission:
£20.00 for all gardens, accompanied children under 16 free. Tickets (limited in number) and are available only in advance from: www.fifegardenfestival.org.uk by credit card, or by cheque payable to Scotland's Gardens from S. Lorimore, Willowhill, Forgan, Newport-on-Tay, Fife DD6 8RA.

Charities:
AICR (The Association for International Cancer Research) receives 40%, the net remaining to SG Beneficiaries.

## FREUCHIE PLANT SALE AND THE GARDEN AT KARBET

KY15 7EY

**Major and Mrs A B Cran**

A good plant sale with a wide selection for garden and container.

**Directions:** In the centre of Freuchie on the B936.

Disabled Access:
Partial

Opening Times:
Sunday 15 June
12:00pm - 4:00pm
Garden also open.

Admission:
£1.50

Charities:
SSAFA Forces Help receives 40%, the net remaining to SG Beneficiaries.

## GLASSMOUNT HOUSE

by Kirkcaldy KY2 5UT

**James and Irene Thomson T: 01592 890214**
**E: peterlcmclaren@yahoo.co.uk www.petermclarenfineart.com**

Intriguing densely planted walled garden with surrounding woodland. An A-listed sun dial, Mackenzie & Moncur greenhouse and historical doocot are complemented by newer structures including an atmospheric water feature/fish pond. Snowdrops and daffodils are followed by a mass of candelabra and cowslip primula, meconopsis and Cardiocrinum giganteum. The hedges & topiary form backdrops for bulbs, clematis, rambling roses and perennials, creating interest through the summer into September. Featured in 'Country Living', 'The English Garden' 2012,' The Scottish Field' 2013. Winner The Times/Fetzer Back Gardens of the Year 2008 Green garden category.

**Other Details:** Artists studio, gallery, woodpiles and wild garden.

**Directions:** West from Kirkcaldy on B9157, left after 2 miles up steep hill signed Kinghorn. Turn right uphill at crossroads. Glassmount drive is 200 yards uphill on right. From Kinghorn take B923 follow signs past EcoCentre for 1 mile under the kissing trees to the crossroads. Turn left uphill. Glassmount drive is 200 yards uphill on your right.

Disabled Access:
None

Opening Times:
1 April - 30 September
12:00pm - 4:00pm
Monday to Friday
and for other times by arrangement 1 April - 30 September

Admission:
£3.00

Charities:
Parkinson's UK receives 40%, the net remaining to SG Beneficiaries.

## GREENHEAD FARM AND BLAIR ADAM HOUSE

Greenhead of Arnot KY6 3JQ and Kelty KY4 QJF

**Malcolm & Maggie Strang Steel and Keith & Elizabeth Adam T: 01592 840459**
**www.fife-bed-breakfast-glenrothes.co.uk**

**Greenhead Farm:** The south facing garden combines a sense of formality in its symmetrical layout with an informal look of mixed herbaceous borders planted "cottage" style. There are roses, a small vegetable plot and a polytunnel in its second year of use. **Blair Adam House:** The walled garden was established by the Adam architects as part of a designed landscape in 1750. The garden comprises an arboretum together with a productive area for flowers, fruit and vegetables which is sheltered by a high north wall that was originally heated. The 1834 layout is still in evidence and recently a regeneration project which includes allotments for local use, got under way.

**Other Details:** Teas at Greenhead Farm. Allow 15 mins drive between the 2 gardens.

**Directions:** Greenhead Farm: 10 mins off M90, exit 5 for Glenrothes. A911 between Auchmuir Bridge and Scotlandwell. Blair Adam: From M90 exit 5, take B996 south for Cowdenbeath. Right for Maryburgh, through village, right through pillars onto long drive, under bridge, then ½ mile on up to house.

Disabled Access:
None

Opening Times:
Sunday 22 June
2:00pm - 5:30pm

Admission:
£5.00 for both gardens, children under 12 free

Charities:
Epilepsy Research receives 40%, the net remaining to SG Beneficiaries.

## HELENSBANK

Kincardine FK10 4QZ

**David Buchanan-Cook and Adrian Miles T: 07739 312912**
**E: Helensbank@aol.com**

Small 18th c. walled garden occupying approximately ½ an acre. The main feature of the garden is a Cedar of Lebanon which was reputedly planted as a sapling brought back from the Holy Land in 1750 by the sea captain who built the house. The tree dominates the garden providing challenges for planting in terms of shade and needle fall. One side of the garden is terraced with subdivided hedges to form distinctive garden 'rooms', including a perennial blue and white cottage garden, formal rose garden and 'Italian' garden with citrus trees in pots. Large conservatory/greenhouse with various climbing plants including 7 varieties of passiflora. A 'hot' courtyard near the garden entrance contains exotics such as bananas, acacias, Iochromas, melianthus and brugmansia. The gardens main body is surrounded by mixed borders 1 of which is backed by a shaded and planted with cardiocrinums, meconopsis, euphorbia, ligularia, rheum and kirengeshoma.

**Other Details:** Homemade teas available for groups on request.

**Directions:** On request.

Disabled Access:
None

Opening Times:
By arrangement
1 June - 30 June

Admission:
£3.00

Charities:
The Sick Kids Friends Foundation receives 40%, the net remaining to SG Beneficiaries.

## HILL OF TARVIT PLANT SALE AND AUTUMN FAIR

Hill of Tarvit, Cupar KY15 5PB

**The National Trust for Scotland**

Generous divisions of herbaceous plants plus a large selection of potted alpines, shrubs etc. A wide range of stalls selling local foods and crafts. Games for all ages. Guided walks around the estate by fungi and wild food experts. Mansion House open (reduced entry fee) 1.00-5.00pm, Hatters Edwardian Tearoom open 11.00am- 5.00pm. A great day out for all the family!

**Other Details:** The Hill of Tarvit gardens will also be open, normal entrance fee applies. Spectacular gardens designed by Robert Lorimer, woods, open heath and parkland to explore. For the energetic, a walk to the monument situated on the hill behind the house is rewarded with spectacular views over the Fife countryside. Monument at the top of the hill

**Directions:** Two miles south of Cupar off A916.

Disabled Access:
Partial

Opening Times:
Sunday 5 October
10:30am - 4:00pm
Garden also open.

Admission:
Plant sale: £2.50, children under 16 free

Charities:
All proceeds to SG Beneficiaries.

## KELLIE CASTLE GARDEN (WITH BALCASKIE)

Pittenweem KY10 2RF

**The National Trust for Scotland T: 0844 4932184**
**E: marmour@nts.org.uk www.nts.org.uk**

This superb garden, around 400 years old, was sympathetically restored by the Lorimer family in the late 19th century. The Arts and Crafts style garden has a selection of old-fashioned roses and herbaceous plants, cultivated organically and hosts an amazing 30 varieties of rhubarb and 75 different types of apple.

**Other Details:** Access to Balcaskie and Kellie Castle via Kellie Castle only, a free minibus will transport visitors between gardens. There will be an exciting mix of artist and craft stalls on offer.

**Directions:** Road: B9171, 3 miles NNW of Pittenweem. Bus: Flexible from local villages by pre-booking.

Disabled Access:
Partial

Opening Times:
Sunday 27 July
12:00pm - 5:00pm

Admission:
£8.00 includes both gardens.

Charities:
Donation to SG Beneficiaries.

## KIRKLANDS

Saline KY12 9TS
**Peter & Gill Hart T: 01383 852737**
**E: gillhart@globalnet.co.uk www.kirklandshouseandgarden.co.uk**

Kirklands has been developed and restored over the last 36 years, although the house dates from 1832 and is on the site of an earlier building. Herbaceous borders, bog garden, woodland garden and terraced walled garden with raised beds and espalier fruit trees. Saline Burn divides the garden from the ancient woodland and the woodland walk.

**Directions:** Junction 4, M90, then B914. Parking in the centre of the village.

Disabled Access:
Partial

Opening Times:
By arrangement
1 April - 30 September

Admission:
£4.50, children free

Charities:
Prospect Burma receives 40%, the net remaining to SG Beneficiaries.

## LINDORES HOUSE

by Newburgh KY14 6JD
**Mr and Mrs R Turcan**

Stunning lochside position with snowdrops, leucojums, rhododendrons, trilliums and herbaceous borders. Woodland walks and amazing seventeenth century yew believed to be the largest in Fife.

**Other Details:** Champion Trees: Yew.
**March**: Open for the Snowdrop Festival. Soup and homemade bread served in the conservatory. Snowdrops and Leucojum for sale.
**June:** Homemade teas and plant stall.

**Directions:** Off A913 2 miles east of Newburgh.

Disabled Access:
Partial

Opening Times:
Friday 7 March
11:00am - 3:00pm
Sunday 1 June
2:00am - 6:00pm

Admission:
March: £3.00
June: £4.50
children free on both dates

Charities:
Garden Owners Choice of Charity to be advised and will receive 40%, the net remaining to SG Beneficiaries.

## LOGIE HOUSE

Crossford KY12 8QN
**Mr and Mrs John Hunt**
**E: sarah@logiehunt.co.uk**

Originally a traditional formal walled garden with a path through the superb double mixed border but extended to include fruit and vegetables possibly by Robert Lorimer when altering the house. There is a Mackenzie & Moncur greenhouse in working order along with glorious climbers against the house, roses, shrubs, annuals and lawns.

**Other Details:** Fresh strawberries from the garden and cream also available.

**Directions:** M90 exit 1 for Rosyth and Kincardine Bridge (A985). After about 2 miles turn right to Crossford. At traffic lights in Crossford turn right and the drive opening is on the right at the end of the village main street.

Disabled Access:
Full

Opening Times:
Sunday 13 July
2:00pm - 5:00pm
By arrangement
1 April - 30 September

Admission:
£5.00, children free

Charities:
July opening Juvenile Diabetic Research Fund receives 40%, the net remaining to SG Beneficiaries.

## NEWTON MAINS AND NEWTON BARNS

Auchtermuchty KY14 7HR

**Ruth and Tony Lear and John and Jess Anderson**

Work started on the Newton Mains garden in 2008 when the owners faced hundreds of self-sown ash saplings and more than a thousand tons of builder's spoil. These were removed and a garden evolved with retaining walls, a large rockery, borders and lawns. Development continued in 2012 with dry stone walling, paths and plants merging into the naturalised field. This area is now fully planted and beginning to mature and develop alongside the first wave of planting.
Newton Barns was created 13 years ago. The borders are planted with choice shrubs, trees and rhododendrons at their best in May. Central to the garden is a huge rockery with a stream surrounded by sweeping lawns and generous borders sloping steeply up and away from the house towards Pitmedden Wood. There are breathtaking views across the top of the garden south towards the Lomond Hills.

**Other Details:** Teas & light meals at the Tannochbrae Tearooms in Auchtermuchty.

**Directions:** A91 from Cupar turn right in Auchtermuchty onto B936. Follow SG signs.

Disabled Access:
None

Opening Times:
Saturday 31 May
11:00am - 4:00pm
Sunday 1 June
11:00am - 4:00pm

Admission:
£5.00 children under 12 free

Charities:
Asbestos Action Tayside receives 40%, the net remaining to SG Beneficiaries.

## NORTHWOOD COTTAGE (WITH TAYFIELD AND WILLOWHILL)

St Fort Farm, Newport-on-Tay DD6 8RE

**Mr and Mrs Andrew Mylius T: 07974083110**

**www.stfort.co.uk**

A visit to Ruskins house and woodland garden at Brantwood, on Lake Coniston in 2000 was the inspiration for creating a woodland garden at St Fort. The existing mature woodland behind our house, formally the estates keepers cottage, seemed a sensible place to start.
Before any planting could commence, a large number of mature trees and scrub had to be removed. The plan was to start slowly by clearing and planting up areas and moving on to new ones as dictated by a mixture of cost, effort and terrain. The paths were formed in a natural and informal way and are dictated by the slope and existing trees and are modified as plants grow and mature.
Brantwood is famous for its azaleas and specimen rhododendrons and it was always the intention to use these two species as the principal plants in the garden here. The acid soil within the wood makes them ideal along with ability to withstand browsing from roe deer. Most of the rhododendrons came from Glendoick in Perthshire and comprise a wide selection of both specimen and hybrids. Most of the azaleas are Azalea ponticum chosen for their excellent scent and good autumn colour. Autumn colour was another consideration in plant selection so many red maples were added to the colourful scene already set by the mature larch, beech, rowans and even some elms.
Mid July is a surprise as the fading rhododendrons are replaced with a carpet of wild foxgloves. The north wood is about 30 acres and is home to a colony of red squirrels, some of the paths lead to view points with the river Tay and Tayrail bridge as a backdrop. In addition to over 200 rhododendrons some of the other plants of interest include Eucryphia, Cerdiphyllum pendulara, tulip tree, various red acers, a wide selection of rowans, liquidambar, metasequoia, magnolias and so on.

**Other Details:** The garden is approached with a woodland walk of about 400metres from the car park and garden entrance. A garden plan is available at the entrance hut.

**Directions:** One and three quarters miles south of the Tay Road Bridge off the A92, between the Forgan and Five Roads roundabouts.

Disabled Access:
None

Opening Times:
Sunday 18 May
1:00pm - 5:00pm
with Willowhill and Tayfield
Sunday 1 June
11:00am - 4:00pm
Northwood Cottage only
Sunday 20 July
2:00pm - 5:00pm
with Tayfield and Willowhill
Sat & Sun 25 /26 October
1:00pm - 4:00pm
Also by arrangement
1 May - 31 October

Admission:
18 May and 20 July: £5.00
Other times: £4.00

Charities:
18 May and 20 July: Forgan Arts Centre receives 40%, By arrangement openings: St Mary's Church receives 40%, the net remaining to SG Beneficiaries.

## ROFSIE ARTS GARDEN

By Collessie KY15 7UZ
**Mr and Mrs Andrew and Caroline Thomson**

The 1¼ acre Victorian Walled Garden has been developed as a 'roofless studio', a private, hidden space in which to explore ideas, philosophies and care for the family's horticultural legacy. The lovely Backhouse Heritage Narcissus, awaiting National Collection Status, is rare, graceful and bred by the family's Backhouse forebears. William Backhouse introduced the first triploid Narcissus cultivars in 1865 N. 'Emperor' and N. 'Empress'. They caused a sensation. Many other plant specimens bred or introduced by the Backhouses can be seen in the garden including, Erica carnea, Lavandula, Dicksonia and Galanthus. There is a woodland walk with daffodils in season to the ruined tomb, interesting collection of hostas and ferns and a long shrub border under cultivation. The garden/Backhouse cultivars have been featured in Period Living, The Garden Magazine, 'Yellow Fever' by Dr David Willis, The Daffodil Society Year Book, numerous academic papers and Horticultural Shows.

**Directions:** Between Auchtermuchty & Collessie on A91. 1 mile east of Auchtermuchty turn right for Charlottetown, turn first right into Rofsie Estate un-melted drive.

Disabled Access:
Partial

Opening Times:
Sunday 27 April
1:00pm - 4:00pm

Admission:
£5.00

Charities:
Garden owner's charity to be decided and will receive 40%, the net remaining to SG Beneficiaries.

## ROSEWELLS

Pitscottie KY15 5LE
**Birgitta and Gordon MacDonald**
**E: birgittamac@hotmail.co.uk**

Designed by Birgitta & Gordon MacDonald, the garden has developed over the last 17 years and continues to evolve. There is an underlying theme that each part of the garden should work in relation to the rest to create one overall effect and it must also be child friendly. The design centres on texture and foliage to provide a lively effect with structure and shape all year round. The winter 'bones' are provided with trees and shrubs with attractive features such as contorted stems and peeling or coloured bark. In spring and summer, texture and coloured foliage of specially selected shrubs and perennials add to the overall design. Birgitta sees flowers as an added bonus with scent and colour being important, combinations of yellow, blue and white colour schemes are preferred. The garden has many varieties of cornus, magnolias, trilliums, meconopsis, agapanthus rhododendrons, auricular primulas, fritillaries, erythroniums and peonies as well as acers.

**Directions:** B940 between Pitscottie and Peat Inn, 1 mile from Pitscottie. Rosewells is the ochre coloured house.

Disabled Access:
Partial

Opening Times:
By arrangement
1 April - 30 September

Admission:
£3.00, children free

Charities:
Save the Children receives 40%, the net remaining to SG Beneficiaries.

## SOUTH FLISK

Blebo Craigs, Cupar KY15 5UQ
**Mr and Mrs George Young T: 01334 850859**
**E: julia@standrewspottery.co.uk www.standrewspottery.co.uk.**

A flooded former quarry is the centrepiece of this enchanting 3 acre garden. The pond supports toads, frogs, newts, dragonflies and golden orfe while water lilies and marginal plants add colour throughout the season.
Spectacular boulders, cliffs and big, mature trees form a backdrop for spring bulbs, rhododendrons, magnolias, azaleas, and carpets of primulas while the woodland area sports meconopsis, trilliums, podophyllums & hellebores - all at their best in May & June. In front of the house (a former smiddy) is a charming, mature walled garden with cottage garden planting offering spectacular views of north Fife, Highland Perthshire and Angus.

**Other Details:** South Flisk is home to a working pottery where you can meet George Young and watch him at work.

**Directions:** Six miles west of St Andrews off the B939 between Strathkinness and Pitscottie. There is a small stone bus shelter opposite the road into the village and a small sign saying Blebo Craigs. Or check out the map on our website.

Disabled Access:
Partial

Opening Times:
By arrangement
1 May - 30 June
Gardens will be open on 14/15 June as part of the Blebo Craigs Village Gardens openings.

Admission:
£4.00, children free

Charities:
RUDA receives 40%, the net remaining to SG Beneficiaries.

## SPECIAL EVENING OPENINGS

South Flisk KY15 5UQ and Willowhill DD6 8RA

**George & Julia Young and Eric Wright & Sally Lorimore**

South Flisk, Blebo Craigs and Willowhill, Forgan are opening for 3 Thursdays in May and June in the afternoon and into the long summer evenings for visitors who are busy during the day and have many commitments at weekends. Visitors will be able to unwind in the tranquillity of a garden at the end of a long busy day when the garden is often at its best with soft light through the flowers and foliage and when the wind drops.

**Other Details:** For garden details and positions on the map see entries for South Flisk and Willowhill, numbers 25 and 34.

**Directions:** See entries for South Flisk and Willowhill.

Disabled Access:
Partial

Opening Times:
Thursdays 29 May, 5 June & 12 June 3:00pm - 8:00pm

Admission:
£4.00 for each garden or £5.00 for both gardens, children under 16 free

Charities:
Charity to be advised and will receive 40%, the net remaining to SG Beneficiaries.

## ST MONANS VILLAGE GARDENS

KY10 2BX

**The Gardeners of St. Monans T: 01333 730792**

Several gardens will be opening, many for the first time in this picturesque seaside village. The medieval church welcomes visitors.

**Directions:** Enter village, drive to harbour, turn right and follow road to top of hill where tickets can be bought from Mr and Mrs Gardner at Inverie. Large church car park is just beyond.

Disabled Access:
None

Opening Times:
Sunday 18 May
2:00pm - 5:00pm

Admission:
£4.00

Charities:
Auld Kirk, St Monans receives 40%, the net remaining to SG Beneficiaries.

## STRATHAIRLY HOUSE

Upper Largo, Leven KY8 6ED

**Mr and Mrs Andrew Macgill T: Alison:01333360422, 07594097052 Alex:01333352936 E: strathairly@btconnect.com**

A recently restored walled garden. Herbaceous and mixed planting schemes. Parkland and woodlands with views over Largo Bay.

**Other Details:** Teas available for groups

**Directions:** Located outside the village of Upper Largo on the A917 Leven to Elie coast road.

Disabled Access:
Partial

Opening Times:
By arrangement
1 April - 31 August

Admission:
£4.00, children under 16 free

Charities:
SSAFA Forces Help receives 40%, the net remaining to SG Beneficiaries.

## TAYFIELD (WITH NORTHWOOD COTTAGE AND WILLOWHILL)

Forgan, Newport-on-Tay DD6 8RA

**William and Elizabeth Berry**

A wide variety of shrubs and fine trees, many to mark celebrations of the family who have lived here for over 200 years. Some trees are of great age and Tayfield has the tallest beech tree recorded in Scotland at 39 metres. A picturesque approach to Tayfield House is enhanced by wonderful large tree rhododendrons in May and views across the Tay all year round. The grounds are wildlife rich and contain 2 large ponds. Look out for red squirrels which are often seen.

**Directions:** See Willowhill

**Disabled Access:**
Partial

**Opening Times:**
Sunday 18 May
1:00pm - 5:00pm

**Admission:**
£5.00 (includes entry to Northwood Cottage and Willowhill)

**Charities:**
Forgan Arts Centre receives 40%, the net remaining to SG Beneficiaries.

## TAYPORT GARDENS

Tayport DD6 9HX

**The Gardeners of Tayport T: 07777 671150**

Located at the mouth of the river Tay, Tayport is an historic harbour town with attractive views of the Broughty Ferry coastline and the Tentsmuir Forest. Several gardens of varied ages and styles will open.

**Other Details:** Tickets, maps and refreshments available in the village. Toilets available at the Tayport harbour area.

**Directions:** On the south of the Tay Road Bridge take the B946 to Tayport.

**Disabled Access:**
None

**Opening Times:**
Saturday 24 May
12:00pm - 5:00pm
Sunday 25 May
12:00pm - 5:00pm

**Admission:**
£5.00

**Charities:**
Tayport Community Trust receives 40%, the net remaining to SG Beneficiaries.

## TEASSES GARDENS

near Ceres KY8 5PG

**Sir Fraser and Lady Morrison T: 01334 828048**
**E: kate@teasses.com**

Teasses Gardens have been developed by the present owners for 12 years and now extend to approximately 60 acres. In addition to the traditional oval walled garden with fruit, vegetables, cut flowers and a large greenhouse, there are formal and informal areas of garden linked by numerous woodland walks with many woodland gardens. There are also extensive areas of spring bulbs.

**Other Details:** Please allow 2 hours for a tour with a member of the gardening staff to enjoy these large and peaceful gardens. The garden is open for individuals or groups.

**Directions:** Between Ceres and Largo. Enter by farm entrance 2 miles west of New Gilston village. Follow tarmac road to Estate Office.

**Disabled Access:**
None

**Opening Times:**
By arrangement on request

**Admission:**
£5.00 (includes tour)

**Charities:**
All proceeds to SG Beneficiaries.

32

## THE TOWER

1, Northview Terrace, Wormit DD6 8PP
**Peter and Angela Davey T: 01382 541635 M: 07768406946**

Situated 4 miles south of Dundee, this 1 acre Edwardian landscaped garden has panoramic views over the river Tay. Special features include rhododendron walk, rockeries, informal woodland planting schemes using native and exotic plants, offering year round interest. Original raised paths lead to a granite grotto with waterfall pool. A boardwalk leads to four further ponds joined by a stream. Of additional interest are raised vegetable beds made from granite sets.

**Other Details:** Garden set into a hill with steep paths, therefore not suitable for those with poor mobility.

**Directions:** From B946 park on Naughton Road outside Spar shop and walk up path left following signs.

Disabled Access:
None

Opening Times:
By arrangement
1 April - 30 September

Admission:
£3.00

Charities:
Barnados receives 40%, the net remaining to SG Beneficiaries.

33

## WEMYSS CASTLE GARDENS

Wemyss Castle, Coaltown of Wemyss KY1 4TE
**Mr and Mrs Michael Wemyss, Wemyss Estates Trustees T: 01592 651327**
**E: charlotte@wemyss-em.com wemysscastlegardens.com**

At barely 50 feet above sea level with an annual rainfall of circa 23 inches, the south facing ground has proved an interesting and challenging site for the establishment of a garden.
The proximity of the Forth and exposure to winter easterly winds result in little frost but the challenge of salt laden gales. The grounds have been gardened since the 17th c. and consist of a circa 15 acres spring woodland garden with a fine display of Erythronium revolutum followed by bluebells and narcissi.
Since 1994 the contiguous redundant 6 acre walled garden has been substantially overhauled and redesigned by the present owners with new planting and landscaping featuring clematis, roses and ornamental trees.

**Directions:** In village of Coaltown of Wemyss (3 miles east of Kirkcaldy on A955). Drive entrance opposite bowling green, ½ mile down drive bear left at fork and follow drive through stable yard, parking in field on right approximately 200 yards after stable yard.

Disabled Access:
Full

Opening Times:
Sunday 25 May
2:00pm - 5:00pm

Admission:
£5.00, children under 12 free
The castle is not open to the public.

Charities:
Fife Scouts receive 40%, the net remaining to SG Beneficiaries.

## WILLOWHILL (WITH NORTHWOOD COTTAGE AND TAYFIELD)

Forgan, Newport-on-Tay DD6 8RA
**Eric Wright & Sally Lorimore T: 07948 286031**

An evolving 3 acre garden featured in "Scotland for Gardeners" and "Scotland on Sunday". The house is surrounded by a vegetable plot and a series of mixed borders designed with different vibrant colour combinations for effect all season. Newly developed area containing borders of bulbs, roses and perennials. A stepped terrace of alpines leads to a wildlife pond in grassland planted with trees, bulbs and herbaceous perennials through which wide sweeping paths are mown.

**Other Details:** Plants stalls with perennials from Willowhill and other Fife gardens. Craft stalls at Forgan Arts Centre and teas 18 May and 20 July.
**Joint openings:** with Northwood Cottage & Tayfield Sundays 18 May and 20 July
**Willowhill only**: 4 June - 27 August and By Arrangement dates.
For full charity details see website.

**Directions:** 1 ½ miles south of Tay Road Bridge. Take B995 to Newport off the Forgan roundabout. Willowhill is first house on left hand side next to Forgan Arts Centre.

**Disabled Access:**
Partial

**Opening Times:**
Sunday 18 May
1:00pm - 5:00pm
Sunday 20 July
2:00pm - 5:00pm
Wednesdays 4 June - 27 Aug.
2:00pm - 5:00pm
By arrangement 2 Jun - 29 Aug.

**Admission:**
Joint Openings: £5.00
Willowhill Openings: £4.00

**Charities:**
40% Forgarn Arts Centre & Rio Comm. Centre (see left).

## WORMISTON HOUSE

Crail KY10 3XH
**Baron and Lady Wormiston T: 01333 450356**
**E: Ktaylor.home@googlemail.com (Head Gardener)**

This 17th century Scots tower house and gardens have been painstakingly restored over the last 20 years. The charming 1.5 acre walled garden is a series of 'rooms', each one with its own individual enchantment. These include a wildlife meadow, productive potager, intricate formal parterre, magical Griselinia garden and recently planted late-season perennial borders. The garden's backbone is the splendid midsummer herbaceous border – as featured on the cover of Kenneth Cox's 'Scotland for Gardeners'. The walled garden also contains two award-winning Georgian-style garden pavilions. Outside the walled garden enjoy woodland walks around the newly re-landscaped lochan.

**Other Details:** Owing to building works, this year Wormiston will be opening by arrangement only to individuals and groups. You are welcome to contact us in advance, when planning your visit, to find out what's looking good in the garden.

**Directions:** One mile north of Crail on the A917 Crail to St Andrews road.

**Disabled Access:**
None

**Opening Times:**
By arrangement
1 April - 30 September

**Admission:**
£5.00 Children free

**Charities:**
CHAS receives 40%, the net remaining to SG Beneficiaries.

## WORMIT VILLAGE GARDENS

Wormit DD6 8LW
**The Gardeners of Wormit**

A selection of gardens varying from large and Edwardian to small and modern in a picturesque setting on the river Tay, aside the historic Tay Rail Bridge. Several are designed by their artist owners, including an award-winning 'wild-life' garden. Beautiful walks, beach, harbour and stunning views provide further interest.

**Other Details:** Tickets and maps available from 21 Riverside Road, Wormit DD6 8LP. Refreshments (2-4pm) and toilet facilities in West Hall, Bay Road, Wormit. Guide dogs only.

**Directions:** On south side of Tay road Bridge follow signs to Newport-on-Tay then on to Wormit.

**Disabled Access:**
None

**Opening Times:**
Sunday 22 June
11:00am - 5:00pm

**Admission:**
£4.00 Children under 16 free with accompanying adult

**Charities:**
Music in Hospitals Scotland receives 20%, The Trussell Trust Foodbank (local branch) receives 20%, the net remaining to SG Beneficiaries.

# GLASGOW & DISTRICT

Scotland's Gardens 2014 Guidebook is sponsored by **INVESTEC WEALTH & INVESTMENT**

## District Organiser

| | |
|---|---|
| Mrs J Millar | 3 Cochrane Court, Milngavie G62 6QT |

## Area Organisers

| | |
|---|---|
| Mrs S Elliot | 46 Corrour Road, Newlands G43 2DX |
| Mrs A Murray | 44 Gordon Road, Netherlee G44 3TW |
| Mrs Sandra Wilson | Robinsfield Gatehouse, Bardowie G62 6ER |

## Treasurer

| | |
|---|---|
| Mr J Murray | 44 Gordon Road, Netherlee G44 3TW |

## Gardens open on a specific date

| | | |
|---|---|---|
| Holmwood, Cathcart | Saturday 19 April | 12:00pm - 4:00pm |
| Holmwood , Cathcart | Sunday 20 April | 12:00pm - 4:00pm |
| Kew Terrace Secret Gardens, Glasgow | Saturday 7 June | 2:00pm - 5:00pm |
| Crossburn, Milngavie | Sunday 8 June | 2:00pm - 5:00pm |
| Greenbank Garden, Clarkston | Sunday 15 June | 11:00am - 5:00pm |
| Kilsyth Gardens, Kilsyth | Sunday 3 August | 2:00pm - 5:00pm |
| Watch Us Grow, Palacerigg Visitor Centre | Sunday 3 August | 1:00pm - 4:00pm |

## Gardens open by arrangement

| | | |
|---|---|---|
| Kilsyth Gardens, Kilsyth | 1 April - 30 September | 01236 821983 |

## Key to symbols

 New in 2014
 Homemade teas
 Accommodation
 Teas

Dogs on a lead allowed
 Plant stall
Cream teas
 Wheelchair access
 Scottish Snowdrop Festival

## Garden locations

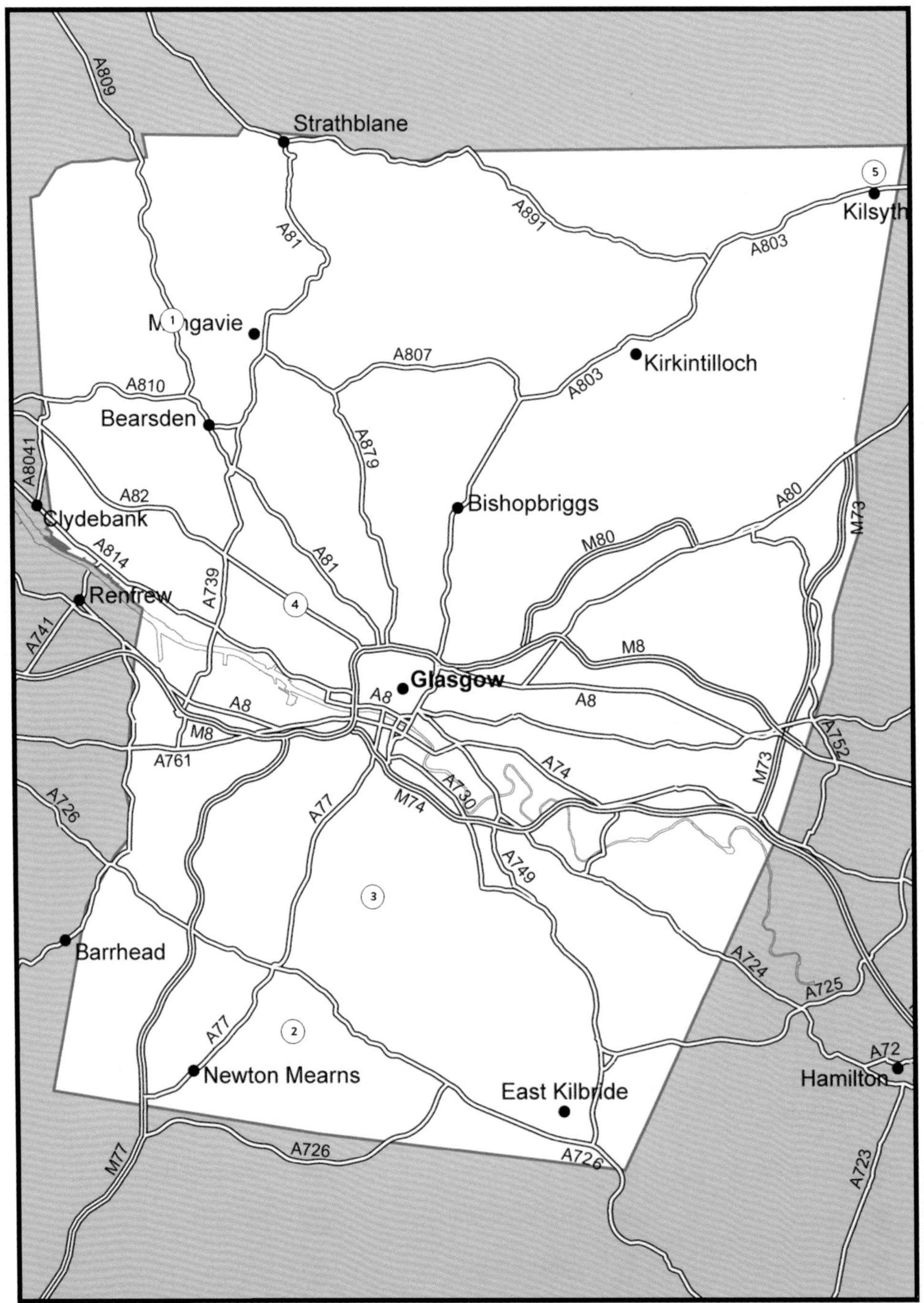

## CROSSBURN

Stockiemuir Road, Milngavie G62 7HJ

**Annika Sandell & Robert Johnston and Willie & Pat Anderson T: 0141 955 1789**
**E: mail@robertjohnston-architects.co.uk**

Two neighbouring gardens set around a converted farm steading.
One a south facing wooded garden dominated by a large pond, the banks of which are left for natural growth. There is a fruit and vegetable plot within the cultivated garden plus a number of mixed borders with a good variety of plants.
The other a 1 acre garden with mature woodland, a lily pond and bog garden, mixed and herbaceous borders with choice plants: hardy geraniums, irises, paeonies, oriental poppies and others.

**Directions:** From Glasgow take A739 to Bearsden, Drymen Road, turn right on to A809 Stockiemuir Road, signposted Drymen, go straight through Baljaffrey Roundabout, continue to Crossburn Roundabout, take first left road to Douglasmuir Quarry.
Bus: Glasgow City Bus 15 travels through Mains Estate opposite; First Bus 60A terminates in Mains Estate.

Disabled Access:
None

Opening Times:
Sunday 8 June
2:00pm - 5:00pm

Admission:
£6.00 including teas

Charities:
Allergy UK receives 40%, the net remaining to SG Beneficiaries.

## GREENBANK GARDEN

Flenders Road, Clarkston G76 8RB

**The National Trust for Scotland T: 0844 493 2201**
**E: dferguson@nts.org.uk www.nts.org.uk**

A unique walled garden with plants and designs of particular interest to suburban gardeners. There are also fountains and a woodland walk. The wheelbarrow gardens planted up by local schoolchildren will be on the lawn for judging by visitors and the Head Gardener will also do a guided walk of the garden at 2.30pm.

**Other Details:** National Plant Collection®: Bergenia cvs. & spp.

**Directions:** Flenders Road, off Mearns Road, Clarkston. Off M77 and A727, follow signs for East Kilbride to Clarkston Toll. Bus: No. 44a, Glasgow to Newton Mearns. Rail: Clarkston station 1¼miles.

Disabled Access:
Full

Opening Times:
Sunday 15 June
11:00am - 5:00pm

Admission:
£6.50, concessions £5.00, guided tour £2.00.
N.B. Prices correct at time of going to print.

Charities:
Donation to SG Beneficiaries.

## HOLMWOOD

61-63 Netherlee Road, Cathcart G44 3YU

**The National Trust for Scotland T: 0844 493 2204**
**E: holmwood@nts.org.uk www.nts.org.uk**

Kitchen garden planted with a range of Victorian fruits, herbs and vegetables. There are 5 acres of landscaped grounds to explore.

**Other Details:** Lots of Easter family fun and games. See NTS website for full details.

**Directions:** Netherlee Road, off Clarkston Road, B767 or Rhannan Road 4 miles south of Glasgow city centre. Frequent bus service from city centre.

Disabled Access:
Partial

Opening Times:
Saturday 19 April
12:00pm - 4:00pm
Sunday 20 April
12:00pm - 4:00pm

Admission:
By donation

Charities:
Donation to SG Beneficiaries.

## KEW TERRACE SECRET GARDENS

Kew Terrace Lane, Glasgow G12 0TE

**Professor George G Browning and other owners**

Kew Terrace is one of the grand terraces that line Great Western Road and, when built in 1845-1849, only one of the 20 houses had a mews, the others had back gardens. Using them as car storage spaces has been resisted and now there is a series of secret gardens. This year additional ones to the rear of Huntly Gardens will be open. They all enhance green living in a town environment. A walk along the shrub border in the Glasgow City owned front garden of Kew Terrace is suggested. This border has been replanted and maintained for the public by the Kew Terrace Assoc. The cost of this comes from their funds and the charitable sums raised by the garden openings.

**Directions:** From M8 take junction 17 (A82), turn right onto Great Western Road. Continue 1 mile to cross over the Great Western Road/Byres Road junction. Kew Terrace is on the left and access is 250 yards beyond traffic lights.
Car parking may be difficult in the adjacent streets. The Kirklee area on the north side of Great Western Road usually has ample spaces and is a short walk away. Access to the gardens is from tree-lined, cobbled Kew Terrace Lane.

Disabled Access:
None

Opening Times:
Saturday 7 June
2:00pm - 5:00pm

Admission:
£6.00 includes entry to several private gardens and teas with home baking served from a marquee.

Charities:
Kew on Great Western Road Fund receives 40%, the net remaining to SG Beneficiaries.

## KILSYTH GARDENS

Allanfauld Road, Kilsyth G65 9DE

**Mr and Mrs George Murdoch and Mr and Mrs Alan Patrick T: 01236 821983**

**Aeolia** (Mr and Mrs G Murdoch): A ⅓ acre garden developed since 1960 by the owners. Mature specimen trees and shrubs, a large variety of rhododendrons, primulas, hardy geraniums and herbaceous plants.
**Blackmill** (Mr and Mrs Alan Patrick): Across the road from Aeolia. An acre of mature and recent planting of specimen trees and shrubs on the site of an old mill. There is an ornamental pond and rock pool built into the remains of an old mill building. A further acre of natural woodland glen. Paths along the Garrel Burn with views to the cascading waterfalls.

**Directions:** A803 to Kilsyth, through main roundabout. Turn left into Parkburn Road up to the crossroads. Short walk up Allanfauld Road. Buses: no. 27 Glasgow-Falkirk, no. 24 Glasgow-Stirling, no. X86 Glasgow-Kilsyth (not Sunday).

Disabled Access:
Partial

Opening Times:
Sunday 3 August
2:00pm - 5:00pm
By arrangement
1 April - 30 September

Admission:
£6.00 includes both gardens and homemade teas.

Charities:
Strathcarron Hospice receives 40%, the net remaining to SG Beneficiaries.

## WATCH US GROW

Palacerigg Visitor Centre, Palacerigg Country Park, Cumbernauld G67 3HU

**Watch Us Grow T: 01236 727970**

**E: info@watchusgrow.org.uk www.watchusgrow.org.uk**

An organic community garden situated within the Palacerigg Country Park, Watch us Grow works with adults with support needs growing a range of delicious vegetables and fruit. Our lovely garden is a peaceful haven in the countryside outside the busy new town of Cumbernauld.

**Other Details:** There is a cafe in the Country Park and our garden is accessible to all.

**Directions:** From M80 Junction 6 at Old Inns roundabout take 3rd exit on to A8011 then at Kildrum South roundabout 2nd exit on B8054. Follow signs to Country Park which is on the left hand side.

Disabled Access:
Full

Opening Times:
Sunday 3 August
1:00pm - 4:00pm

Admission:
£4.00, children free

Charities:
Watch Us Grow receives 40%, the net remaining to SG Beneficiaries.

# ISLE OF ARRAN



## District Organiser

| | |
|---|---|
| Mrs S C Gibbs | Dougarie, Isle of Arran KA27 8EB |

## Treasurer

| | |
|---|---|
| Mrs E Adam | Bayview, Pirnmill, Isle of Arran KA27 8HP |

## Gardens open on a specific date

| | | | | |
|---|---|---|---|---|
| Brodick Castle & Country Park, Brodick | Sunday 4 May | 10:00am | - | 4:30pm |
| Hazelbank, Pirnmill | Friday 9 May | 11:00am | - | 4:00pm |
| Hazelbank, Pirnmill | Saturday 10 May | 11:00am | - | 4:00pm |
| Dougarie | Sunday 29 June | 2:00pm | - | 5:00pm |
| Brodick Castle & Country Park, Brodick | Sunday 6 July | 10:00am | - | 4:30pm |

Dougarie, Isle of Arran

## Key to symbols

| | | | | | |
|---|---|---|---|---|---|
|  | New in 2014 | | Homemade teas | | Accommodation |
|  | Teas |  | Dogs on a lead allowed |  | Plant stall |
| | Cream teas |   | Wheelchair access |  | Scottish Snowdrop Festival |

## BRODICK CASTLE & COUNTRY PARK

Brodick KA27 8HY
**The National Trust for Scotland T: 0844 493 2152**
**E: brodickcastle@nts.org.uk www.nts.org.uk**

At any time of year the gardens are well worth a visit, though especially in spring when the internationally acclaimed rhododendron collection bursts into full bloom. There are exotic plants and shrubs, a walled garden and a woodland garden to be enjoyed by garden enthusiasts, families and children. Venture out into the country park and discover wildflower meadows where Highland cows graze, woodland trails and tumbling waterfalls.There is something for everyone.

**Other Details:** National Plant Collection®: Three Rhododendron collections. Champion Trees: Embothrium coccineum.

**Directions:** Brodick 2 miles. Service buses from Brodick Pier to Castle. Regular sailings from Ardrossan and Claonaig (Argyll).
Information from Caledonian MacBrayne, Gourock. T: 01475 650100.

Disabled Access:
Partial

Opening Times:
Sunday 4 May
10:00am - 4:30pm
Sunday 6 July
10:00am - 4:30pm

Admission:
£5.50, concessions £4.50, family £15.00 including NTS members.
N.B. Prices are correct at time of going to print.

Charities:
Donation to SG Beneficiaries.

## DOUGARIE

KA27 8EB
**Mr and Mrs S C Gibbs**
**E: office@dougarie.com**

Most interesting terraced garden in castellated folly built in 1905 to celebrate the marriage of the 12th Duke of Hamilton's only child to the Duke of Montrose. Good selection of tender and rare shrubs, herbaceous border, kitchen garden. Small woodland area with interesting trees including Azara, Abutilon, Eucryphia, Hoheria and Nothofagus.

**Other Details:** Teas in 19th century boathouse.

**Directions:** Blackwaterfoot 5 miles. Regular ferry sailing from Ardrossan and Claonaig (Argyll).
Information from Caledonian MacBrayne, Gourock. T: 01475 650100.

Disabled Access:
None

Opening Times:
Sunday 29 June
2:00pm - 5:00pm

Admission:
£3.50

Charities:
Pirnmill Village Association receives 40%, the net remaining to SG Beneficiaries.

## HAZELBANK

Pirnmill KA27 8HP
**Gordon and Susan Furzer**

Natural coastal garden backed by a wooded bank/cliff. Around 2 acres of planting has been done over the past 7 years with specimens suited to the west coast environment, featuring many natives from the warmer climates of South America and New Zealand. This garden usually has a project on the go, however small.

**Other Details:** Morning coffee and afternoon teas with home baking available.

**Directions:** C147, 5 miles south of Lochranza, eleven miles north of Blackwaterfoot.
Information from Caledonian MacBrayne, Gourock. T: 01475 650100.

Disabled Access:
Partial

Opening Times:
Friday 9 May
11:00am - 4:00pm
Saturday 10 May
11:00am - 4:00pm

Admission:
£2.00

Charities:
Pirnmill Village Association receives 40%, the net remaining to SG Beneficiaries.

# KINCARDINE & DEESIDE

Scotland's Gardens 2014 Guidebook is sponsored by **INVESTEC WEALTH & INVESTMENT**

## District Organisers

| | |
|---|---|
| Tina Hammond | Bardfield, Inchmarlo, Banchory AB31 4AT |
| Julie Nicol | Bogiesheil, Ballogie, Aboyne AB34 5DU |

## Area Organisers

| | |
|---|---|
| Mrs Andrea Bond | Rosebank, Crathes, Banchory AB31 5JE |
| Mrs Wendy Buchan | |
| Mr Gavin Farquhar | Ecclesgreig Castle, St Cyrus DD10 0DP |
| Mrs Helen Jackson | |
| Mrs Catherine Nichols | Bridge of Canny, Banchory AB31 4AT |
| Mr and Mrs David Younie | Bealltainn, Ballogie, Aboyne AB34 5DL |

## Treasurer

| | |
|---|---|
| Lesley Mitchell | 8 Ashley Lodge Gardens, 253 Great Western Road, Aberdeen AB10 6PP |

## Gardens open on a specific date

| | | | | |
|---|---|---|---|---|
| Crathes Castle Garden, Banchory | Saturday 15 February | 10:00am | | |
| Ecclesgreig Castle, St Cyrus | Sunday 2 March | 1:00pm | - | 4:00pm |
| Woodend House, Banchory | Sunday 25 May | 1:30pm | - | 4:30pm |
| Inchmarlo House Garden, Banchory | Sunday 8 June | 1:30pm | - | 4:30pm |
| Kincardine, Kincardine O'Neil | Sunday 15 June | 1:00pm | - | 5:00pm |
| Ecclesgreig Castle, St Cyrus | Sunday 22 June | 1:00pm | - | 5:00pm |
| Findrack, Torphins | Sunday 6 July | 2:00pm | - | 5:00pm |
| Douneside House, Tarland | Sunday 13 July | 2:00pm | - | 5:00pm |
| Mill of Benholm Project, Benholm | Sunday 20 July | 10:00am | - | 5:00pm |
| Crathes Castle Garden, Banchory | Saturday 26 July | 7:00pm | | |
| Mallamauch, Banchory | Sunday 27 July | 1:00pm | - | 5:00pm |
| Glenbervie House, Drumlithie | Sunday 3 August | 2:00pm | - | 5:00pm |
| Fasque House, Fettercairn | Sunday 7 September | 1:00pm | - | 5:00pm |
| Drum Castle Garden, Drumoak | Sunday 21 September | 11:00pm | - | 5:00pm |
| Inchmarlo House Garden, Banchory | Sunday 19 October | 1:30pm | - | 4:30pm |

## Gardens open regularly

| | | |
|---|---|---|
| Drum Castle Garden, Drumoak | 2 July - 30 July Wednesdays: | 2:00pm - 3:30pm |
| | Fridays: | 6:00pm - 7:30pm |

## Gardens open by arrangement

| | | |
|---|---|---|
| 14 Arbeadie Avenue, Banchory | 1 June - 31 July | 01330 823615 |

14 Arbeadie Avenue, Banchory

## Key to symbols

| | | |
|---|---|---|
|  New in 2014 | Homemade teas |  Accommodation |
| Teas |  Dogs on a lead allowed |  Plant stall |
| Cream teas |  Wheelchair access |  Scottish Snowdrop Festival |

## Garden locations

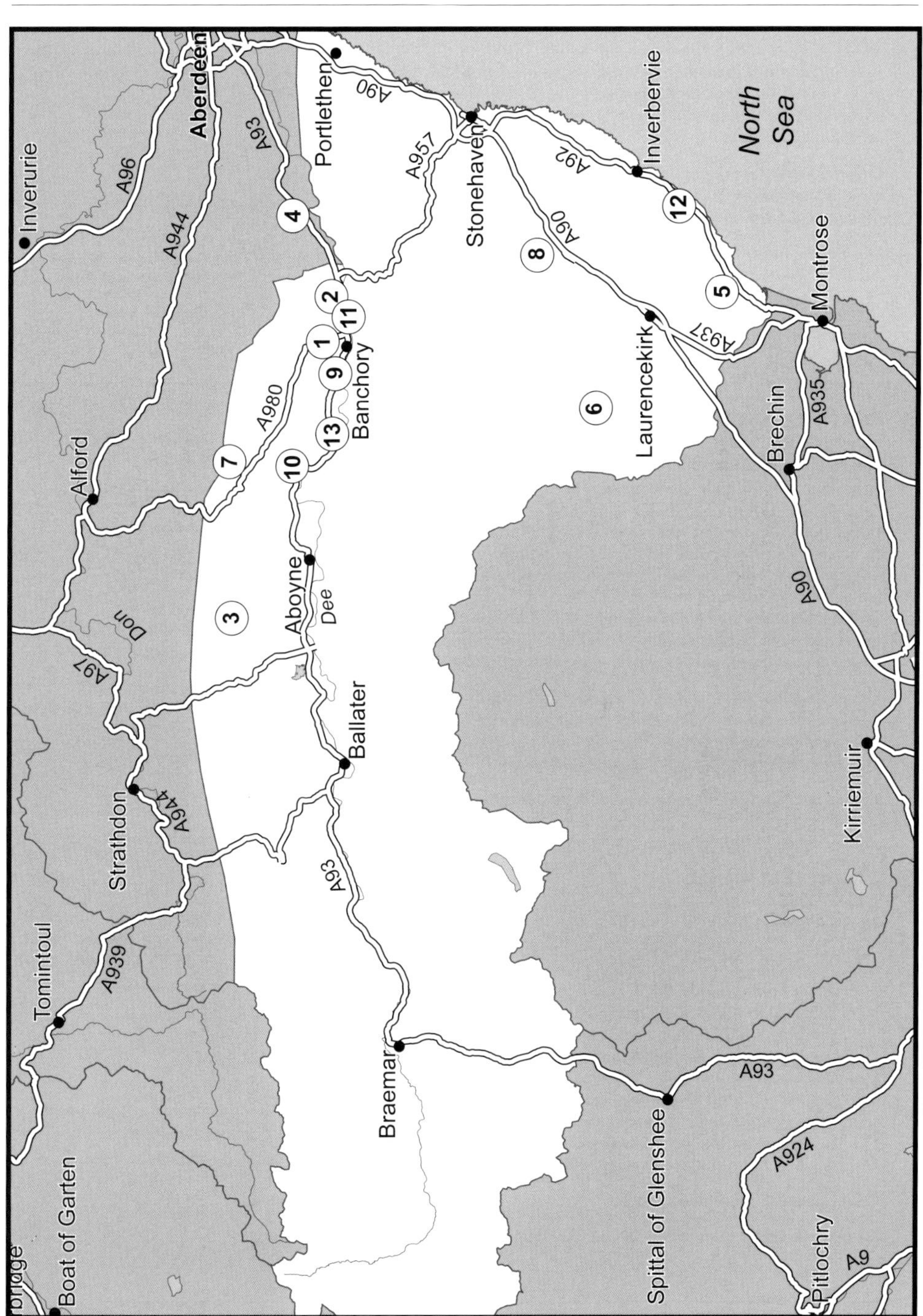

## 14 ARBEADIE AVENUE

Banchory AB31 4EL

**Mr and Mrs Alisdair Harrison T: 01330 823615**

**E: alisdair.harrison@btinternet.com**

A delightful small garden designed to be maintenance free. Water features, lighting and a traditional Japanese garden with a wooden walkway, pergolas, ponds, running stream and use of slate and natural stones and lighting features all add to the atmosphere and interest.

**Other Details:** Groups of up to 12 people welcome as are evening visits. Alasdair is more than happy to discuss and give advice to anyone considering transforming their own garden, building a water feature or installing garden lighting.

**Directions:** From Station Road, Banchory (main road) go up Arbeadie Road and Arbeadie Avenue is on the left near the top of the hill.

Disabled Access:
None

Opening Times:
By arrangement
1 June - 31 July
Thursdays only

Admission:
£3.00

Charities:
Forget Me Not Children's Hospice receives 40%, the net remaining to SG Beneficiaries.

## CRATHES CASTLE GARDEN

Banchory AB31 5QJ

**The National Trust for Scotland T: 0844 493 2166**

**E: crathes@nts.org.uk www.nts.org.uk**

**15 February:** Join our expert Head Gardener for a full day to learn about the principles of pruning within the beautiful setting of the gardens at Crathes Castle. This practical, hands-on workshop will cover general formative pruning as well as looking at how to prune most roses, trees and shrubs.
**26 July:** Gather in the great hall and learn about how the gardens were shaped by generations of the Burnett family over 400 years. Then follow in the footsteps of the family as you leave the castle and explore the gardens through their eyes.

**Other Details:** National Plant Collection®: Dianthus (Malmaison).
Booking essential via NTS website for both events. Places are limited.
**February Pruning workshop:** Price includes tea/coffee and a light lunch.
**July Evening event:** Price includes refreshments.

**Directions:** On A93, 15 miles west of Aberdeen and 3 miles east of Banchory.

Disabled Access:
Full

Opening Times:
Saturday 15 February
10:00am
Saturday 26 July 7:00pm

Admission:
February event: £50.00
July event: £25:00
Admission also applicable to NTS members.

Charities:
Donation to SG Beneficiaries.

## DOUNESIDE HOUSE

Tarland AB34 4UD

**The MacRobert Trust**

The former home of Lady MacRobert who designed and developed the gardens from farmland in the early to mid 1900s. The house and gardens are now in Trust and from March to October are used exclusively by retired and serving officers of the armed forces, and as a conference centre in the winter months. Overlooking the Deeside Hills, ornamental terraced borders, woodland and water gardens surround a spectacular elevated lawn. The garden also boasts a large walled garden which supplies vegetables and cut flowers and also houses a large ornamental greenhouse. The Trust offers horticultural training placements each year and the gardens are accredited as a 'Royal Horticultural Society Approved Learning Centre'.

**Other Details:** Local pipe band, raffle.

**Directions:** B9119 towards Aberdeen. Tarland 1½ miles.

Disabled Access:
Partial

Opening Times:
Sunday 13 July
2:00pm - 5:00pm

Admission:
£4.00, concessions £2.00, children free

Charities:
Perennial receives 40%, the net remaining to SG Beneficiaries.

Douneside House, Tarland

## DRUM CASTLE GARDEN

Drumoak, by Banchory AB31 5EY
**The National Trust for Scotland T: 0844 493 2161**
**www.nts.org.uk**

Each Wednesday at 2:00pm and Fridays at 6:00pm in July join the Head Gardener for a walk through the historic rose garden: The Trust has established a collection of old-fashioned roses, at its peak for blossom and colour during July.
On 21 September there is a guided walk theme 'The colours of autumn' with tea in the garden and plants for sale. Open to visitors all season and evening guided tours available on request throughout the year. See the Trust's website or telephone for further information.

**Other Details: Guided walks**: are with the Head Gardener. As places are limited advance booking is essential. 10% discount will be given on plant purchases.
**Wednesdays:** Guided walks £5.00. Guided walks and refreshments £8.00.
**Fridays:** teas in the garden available for groups at £2.50 per head. Booking advised.

**Directions:** Three miles west of Peterculter on A93. Ten miles west of Aberdeen and 8 miles east of Banchory.

Disabled Access:
Partial

Opening Times:
Sunday 21 September
11:00pm - 5:00pm
Weds 2 - 30 July 2:00pm - 3:30pm for guided walks.
Fris 4 - 25 July 6:00pm - 7:30pm for guided walks.

Admission:
July Guided walks £5.00
September: £4.00
Including NTS members.

Charities:
Donation to SG Beneficiaries.

## ECCLESGREIG CASTLE

St Cyrus DD10 0DP
**Mr Gavin Farquhar T: 01674 850 100**
**E: enquiries@ecclesgreig.com www.ecclesgreig.com**

Ecclesgreig Castle, Victorian Gothic on a 16th century core, is internationally famous as an inspiration for Bram Stoker's Dracula. The snowdrop walk starts at the castle, meanders around the estate, along woodland paths and the pond, ending at the garden. The woodlands contain some very interesting trees and shrubs. Herbaceous borders 10 feet wide 140 feet long in Italian balustraded gardens. The garden has classical statues and stunning shaped topiary with views across St Cyrus to the sea. Started from a derelict site, development continues.

**Directions:** Ecclesgreig will be signposted from the A92 Coast Road and from the A937 Montrose / Laurencekirk Road.

Disabled Access:
Partial

Opening Times:
Sunday 2 March
1:00pm - 4:00pm
for the Snowdrop Festival
Sunday 22 June
1:00pm - 5:00pm

Admission:
£4.00, accompanied children free

Charities:
Scottish Civic Trust receives 20%, Montrose Guides receives 20%, the net remaining to SG Beneficiaries.

## FASQUE HOUSE

Fettercairn, Laurencekirk AB30 1DN
**Mr and Mrs Douglas Dick-Reid**
**www.fasquehouse.co.uk**

Fasque House is situated within the finely landscaped Fasque House Estate with the foothills of the Grampians behind and rolling parkland to the front. The house remained in the ownership of the Gladsone family until 2007. The current owners purchased it in 2010 and are currently restoring the house and gardens to their former glory. Landscaping of the West Garden took place in 2013 with a sunken terrace garden containing a formal pond and a mixture of formal and herbaceous plants. There are some magnificent trees in the surrounding woodlands. The grandiose walled garden and old Apple Store are also being restored but the planting has not yet begun.

**Other Details:** Self catering accommodation.

**Directions:** Off B974 Cairn O'Mount road 1¼ miles north of Fettercairn.

**Disabled Access:**
Partial

**Opening Times:**
Sunday 7 September
1:00pm - 5:00pm

**Admission:**
£4.00, children free

**Charities:**
Fettercairn Community Allotments receives 20%, Home Start Stonehaven receives 20%, the net remaining to SG Beneficiaries.

## FINDRACK

Torphins AB31 4LJ
**Mr and Mrs Andrew Salvesen**

The gardens of Findrack are set in beautiful wooded countryside and are a haven of interesting plants and unusual design features. There is a walled garden with circular lawns and deep herbaceous borders, a stream garden leading to a wildlife pond, vegetable garden and woodland walk.

**Directions:** Leave Torphins on A980 to Lumphanan after ½ mile turn off signposted Tornaveen. Stone gateway 1 mile up on the left.

© Ray Cox

**Disabled Access:**
Partial

**Opening Times:**
Sunday 6 July
2:00pm - 5:00pm

**Admission:**
£4.50, children under 12 £1.00

**Charities:**
The Breadmaker receives 40%, the net remaining to SG Beneficiaries.

## GLENBERVIE HOUSE

Drumlithie, Stonehaven AB39 3YB

**Mr and Mrs A Macphie**

Nucleus of present day house dates from 15th century with additions in 18th and 19th centuries. A traditional Scottish walled garden on a slope with roses, herbaceous and annual borders along with fruit and vegetables. One wall is taken up with a Victorian style greenhouse with many species of pot plants and climbers including peach and figs. A woodland garden by a burn is punctuated with many varieties of plants, primula to name but one.

**Directions:** Drumlithie 1 mile. Garden 1½ miles off A90.

Disabled Access:
None

Opening Times:
Sunday 3 August
2:00pm - 5:00pm

Admission:
£4.50, children under 12 free

Charities:
Friends of Anchor (Haematology and Oncology Dept ARI) receives 40%, the net remaining to SG Beneficiaries.

## INCHMARLO HOUSE GARDEN

Inchmarlo, Banchory AB31 4AL

**Skene Enterprises (Aberdeen) Ltd T: 01330 826242**

**E: info@inchmarlo-retirement.co.uk www.inchmarlo-retirement.co.uk**

An ever-changing 5 acre Woodland Garden, featuring ancient Scots pines, Douglas firs and silver firs, some over 42 metres tall, beeches and rare and unusual trees, including pindrow firs, Pere David's maple, Erman's birch and a mountain snowdrop tree. The Oriental Garden features a Kare Sansui, a dry slate stream designed by Peter Roger, a RHS Chelsea gold medal winner. The Rainbow Garden, within the keyhole-shaped purple Prunus cerasifera hedge, has been designed by Billy Carruthers, an 8 times gold medal winner at the RHS Scottish Garden Show.

**Directions:** From Aberdeen via North Deeside Road on A93, one mile west of Banchory turn right at the main gate to the Inchmarlo Estate.

Disabled Access:
Full

Opening Times:
Sunday 8 June
1:30pm - 4:30pm
Sunday 19 October
1:30pm - 4:30pm

Admission:
£5.00, OAP £4.00, children 14 and under free

Charities:
June: Alzheimer Scotland receives 40% October: Forget Me Not Children's Hospice receives 40% , the net remaining to SG Beneficiaries.

## KINCARDINE

Kincardine O'Neil AB34 5AE

**Mr and Mrs Andrew Bradford**

A woodland or wilderness garden in development with some mature rhododendrons and azaleas and new planting amongst mature trees. Sculpture by Lyman Whittaker of Utah. A walled garden with a mixture of herbaceous and shrub borders, a sensational laburnum walk, vegetables and fruit trees. Extensive lawns and wild-flower meadows and a thought-provoking Planetary Garden. All with a background of stunning views across Royal Deeside.

**Other Details:** Children's treasure trail.

**Directions:** Kincardine O'Neil on A93. Gates and lodge are opposite the village school.

Disabled Access:
Partial

Opening Times:
Sunday 15 June
1:00pm - 5:00pm

Admission:
£5.00, children £2.00 including entry to the treasure trail

Charities:
Children 1st receives 20%, Kincardine O'Neil Village Hall receives 20%, the net remaining to SG Beneficiaries.

## MALLAMAUCH

Banchory AB31 6HY

**Mr and Mrs J Stripling**

Situated in a challenging north facing quarry this is a relatively new garden which has been developed from scratch over the last 8 years. The garden boasts a huge array of herbaceous plants and shrubs to suit the different soil conditions in the quarry. There is a large pond and the beginnings of a collection of unusual trees. The garden is a true plantsman's garden. A small but interesting Alpine garden adjoins Mallamauch garden alongside a vegetable plot with raised beds, fruit and a polytunnel. The garden is still developing and has the potential to keep its owners busy over the coming years.

**Directions:** Situated on the B9077 travel 1 mile east of the Feugh Bridge on the right or approx 3 miles west from Crathes Bridge on the left. The road entrance is marked with a sign Maryfield Farm and Tilquhillie puddings and has a picture of a Christmas pudding and chicken on it.

**Disabled Access:**
Partial

**Opening Times:**
Sunday 27 July
1:00pm - 5:00pm

**Admission:**
£4.00, children free

**Charities:**
Stonehaven Renal Unit receives 40%, the net remaining to SG Beneficiaries.

## MILL OF BENHOLM PROJECT

Benholm by Johnshaven DD10 0HT

**Mill of Benholm Project T: 01561 362466**

**E: mill_of_benholm@btconnect.com**

The Project provides training and work experience in catering, crafts, landscape maintenance and horticulture for adults with additional needs. There are student gardens and a cottage garden and a delightful river and woodland walk through Millbrae Wood where there is an abundance of wildlife. There are mill wheel demonstrations and guided tours of the mill as well as plants for sale, raised by the students. This is a work in progress which warrants an annual visit to follow the efforts of students, staff, volunteers and members.

**Directions:** Turn off the A92 onto the Kirk of Benholm road. We are south of Inverbervie and north of Johnshaven. Large visitors parking area with disabled parking for 2 cars directly by tearoom.

**Disabled Access:**
None

**Opening Times:**
Sunday 20 July
10:00am - 5:00pm

**Admission:**
£3.00

**Charities:**
Mill of Benholm receives 40%, the net remaining to SG Beneficiaries.

## WOODEND HOUSE

Banchory AB31 4AY

**Mr and Mrs J McHardy**

Tucked away in a secluded woodland location. Mature rhododendrons and azaleas with extensive lawns create a stunning backdrop for Woodend House set on the banks of the River Dee. There is a small walled cottage garden and a glorious riverside walk amongst the cowslips and wildflowers giving way to ancient and majestic beech trees.

**Directions:** Four miles west of Banchory on the A93 (Banchory to Aboyne road).

**Disabled Access:**
Partial

**Opening Times:**
Sunday 25 May
1:30pm - 4:30pm

**Admission:**
£4.00

**Charities:**
Sandpiper Trust receives 40%, the net remaining to SG Beneficiaries.

# KIRKCUDBRIGHTSHIRE



## District Organiser

| | |
|---|---|
| Dr Janet Brennan | Barholm Castle, Gatehouse of Fleet DG7 2EZ<br>T: 01557 840327 |

## Area Organisers

| | |
|---|---|
| Mrs Val Bradbury | Glenisle, Jubilee Path, Kippford DG5 4LW |
| Mrs W N Dickson | Chipperkyle, Kirkpatrick, Durham DG7 3EY |
| Mrs M McIlvenna | Braeneuk, Balmaclellan, Castle Douglas DG7 3QS |
| Mrs C McIver | Loxley, Abercrombie Road, Castle Douglas DG7 1BA |
| Mrs Lesley Pepper | Anwoth Old Schoolhouse, Gatehouse of Fleet DG7 2EF |
| Mrs K Ross | Slate Row, Auchencairn, Castle Douglas DG7 1QL |
| Mrs C V Scott | 14 Castle Street, Kirkcudbright DG6 4JA |

## Treasurer

| | |
|---|---|
| Mr Duncan Lofts | Balcary Tower, Auchencairn, Castle Douglas DG7 1QZ |

## Gardens open on a specific date

| | | | | |
|---|---|---|---|---|
| Brooklands, Crocketford | Sunday 16 February | 12:00pm | - | 4:00pm |
| Threave Garden, Castle Douglas | Sunday 11 May | 10:00am | - | 5:00pm |
| Netherhall, Glenlochar | Sunday 18 May | 2:00pm | - | 5:00pm |
| Corsock House, Corsock | Sunday 25 May | 2:00pm | - | 5:00pm |
| Broughton House Garden, Kirkcudbright | Thursday 12 June | 6:00pm | - | 9:00pm |
| The Limes, Kirkcudbright | Saturday 28 June | 1:00pm | - | 5:00pm |
| Brooklands, Crocketford | Sunday 29 June | 2:00pm | - | 5:00pm |
| Cally Gardens, Gatehouse of Fleet | Sunday 29 June | 10:00am | - | 5:30pm |
| Seabank, Rockcliffe | Sunday 6 July | 2:00pm | - | 7:30pm |
| Southwick House, Southwick | Sunday 13 July | 2:00pm | - | 5:00pm |
| Southwick House, Southwick | Monday 14 July | 2:00pm | - | 5:00pm |
| Southwick House, Southwick | Tuesday 15 July | 2:00pm | - | 5:00pm |
| Southwick House, Southwick | Wednesday 16 July | 2:00pm | - | 5:00pm |
| Southwick House, Southwick | Thursday 17 July | 2:00pm | - | 5:00pm |
| Southwick House, Southwick | Friday 18 July | 2:00pm | - | 5:00pm |
| Anwoth House, Anwoth | Sunday 20 July | 2:00pm | - | 5:00pm |
| Anwoth Old Schoolhouse, Anwoth | Sunday 20 July | 2:00pm | - | 5:00pm |
| Glensone Walled Garden, Southwick | Sunday 27 July | 2:00pm | - | 5:00pm |

| | | |
|---|---|---|
| Crofts, Kirkpatrick Durham | Sunday 10 August | 2:00pm - 5:00pm |
| Threave Garden, Castle Douglas | Sunday 10 August | 10:00am - 5:00pm |
| Cally Gardens, Gatehouse of Fleet | Sunday 17 August | 10:00am - 5:30pm |

## Gardens open by arrangement

| | | |
|---|---|---|
| Barholm Castle, Gatehouse of Fleet | 1 February - 1 September | 01557 840327 |
| Corsock House, Castle Douglas | 1 April - 30 June | 01644 440250 |
| Cosy Cottage, Borgue | 1 July - 31 August | 01557 870648 |
| Steadstone, Dalbeattie | 1 January - 30 November | 01556 611565 |
| Stockarton, Kirkcudbright | 1 April - 31 August | 01557 330430 |
| The Mill House at Gelston, Gelston | 13 July - 14 September | 01556 503955 |
| The Waterhouse Gardens at Stockarton, Kirkcudbright | 1 April - 30 September | 01557 331266 |

Anwoth Old Schoolhouse, Gatehouse of Fleet

## Key to symbols

| | | | | | |
|---|---|---|---|---|---|
|  | New in 2014 |  | Homemade teas |  | Accommodation |
|  | Teas |  | Dogs on a lead allowed |  | Plant stall |
|  | Cream teas |  | Wheelchair access |  | Scottish Snowdrop Festival |

## Garden locations

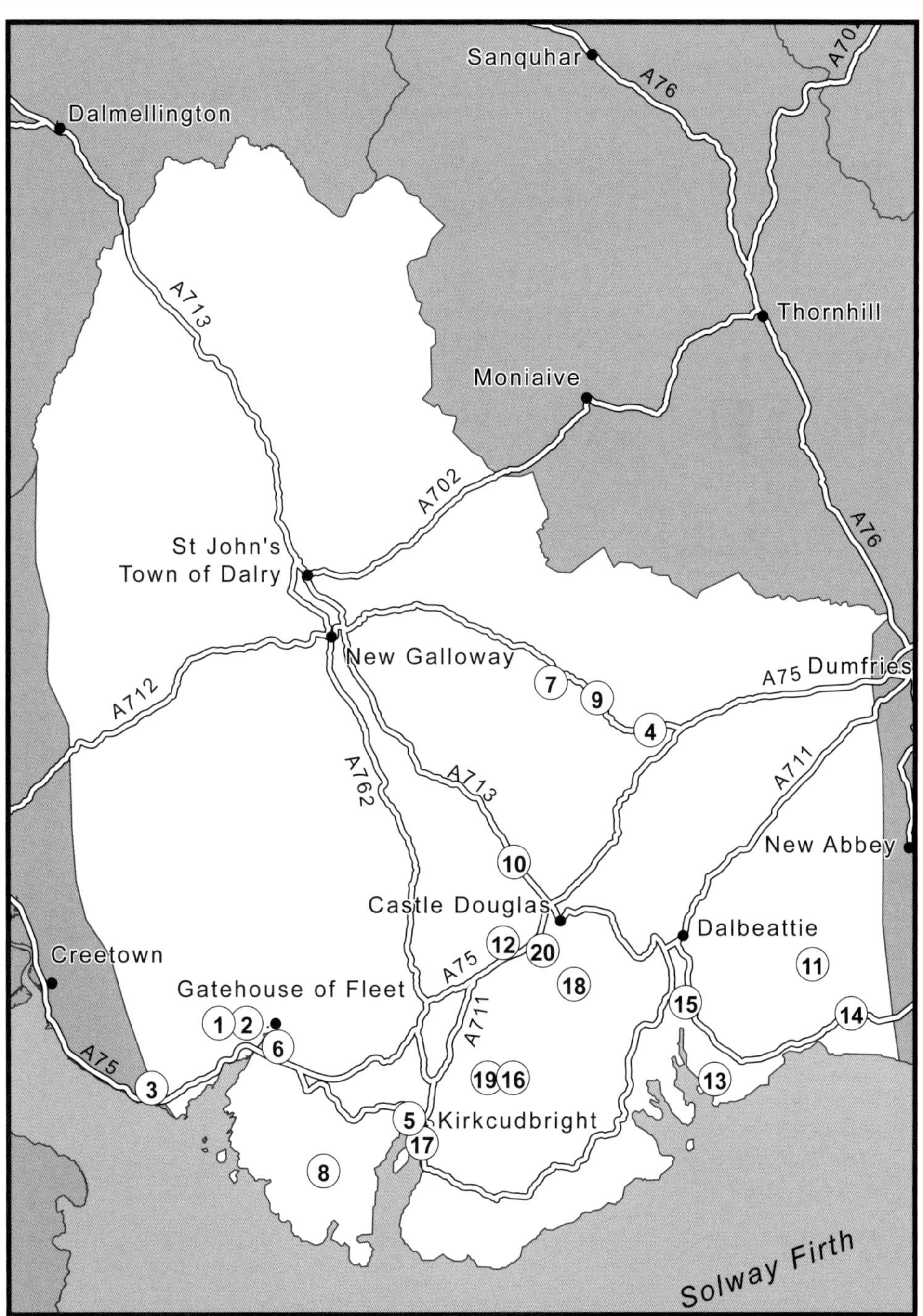

## ANWOTH HOUSE (WITH ANWOTH OLD SCHOOLHOUSE)

Anwoth, Gatehouse of Fleet DG7 2EF
**Major Willy Peto T: 01557 814517**
**E: wgpeto@btinternet.com**

Two acres of formal and woodland gardens surrounding a charming 18th century house. Croquet lawn, romantic doocot, semi-walled garden with yew hedge and long herbaceous border, lochan and woodland stream, all developed within the last 10 years. Fine views.

**Other Details:** Teas in Anwoth Church, adjacent to Anwoth House.
Plant stall at Anwoth Old Schoolhouse.
Parking available outside Anwoth Church for Anwoth House and outside Anwoth Old (ruined) Church for Anwoth Old Schoolhouse. Short walk between the 2 venues.

**Directions:** Driving west on the A75, take the Anwoth turnoff about ½ a mile after Gatehouse of Fleet. Anwoth Church and Anwoth House are about ½ a mile along the road on the right and Anwoth Old Schoolhouse is a little further along opposite the ruined church.

**Disabled Access:**
Partial

**Opening Times:**
Sunday 20 July
2:00pm - 5:00pm

**Admission:**
£4.00 (includes entry to both gardens)

**Charities:**
Marie Curie Cancer Care receives 40%, the net remaining to SG Beneficiaries.

## ANWOTH OLD SCHOOLHOUSE (WITH ANWOTH HOUSE)

Anwoth, Gatehouse of Fleet DG7 2EF
**Mr & Mrs Pepper T: 01557 814444**
**E: mlesleypepper@hotmail.com**

Two acres of delightful cottage-style gardens behind the old schoolhouse and cottage in a picturesque setting opposite Anwoth old church (ruinous) and graveyard. Winding paths alongside burn, informally planted with unusual woodland perennials and shrubs. Wildlife pond, fish pond, rock garden, wildflower area and viewpoint, vegetable garden.

**Other Details:** Teas in Anwoth Church, adjacent to Anwoth House.
Plant stall at Anwoth Old Schoolhouse.
Parking available outside Anwoth Church for Anwoth House and outside Anwoth Old (ruined) Church for Anwoth Old Schoolhouse. Short walk between the 2 venues.

**Directions:** Driving west on the A75, take the Anwoth turnoff about ½ a mile after Gatehouse of Fleet. Anwoth Church and Anwoth House are about ½ a mile along the road and Anwoth Old Schoolhouse is a little further along.

**Disabled Access:**
None

**Opening Times:**
Sunday 20 July
2:00pm - 5:00pm

**Admission:**
£4.00 (includes entry to both gardens)

**Charities:**
Marie Curie receives 40%, the net remaining to SG Beneficiaries.

## BARHOLM CASTLE

Gatehouse of Fleet DG7 2EZ
**Dr John and Dr Janet Brennan T: 01557 840327**
**E: barholmcastle@gmail.com**

Barholm Castle, a 16th century tower, was restored from a ruin in 2006 and the owners moved in permanently in 2011. Since the restoration, the 3 acre gardens surrounding the tower have been slowly developing from scratch. There is a small walled garden, a wooded ravine, a greenhouse and newly developing shrub borders, ponds, rockeries and herbaceous beds. Good snowdrop display in February. Much colour March - September. The views over Wigtown Bay are magnificent.

**Directions:** Off the A75 at the Cairn Holy turn-off, fork right 3 times up a steep narrow road for ½ mile.

**Disabled Access:**
Partial

**Opening Times:**
By arrangement
1 February - 1 September

**Admission:**
£4.00

**Charities:**
Lepra receives 40%, the net remaining to SG Beneficiaries.

## BROOKLANDS

Crocketford DG2 8QH

**Mr and Mrs Robert Herries**

Large old walled garden, richly planted with a wide variety of perennials, including many unusual species, soft fruit and vegetables. Mature woodland garden full of rhododendrons and carpeted with snowdrops in spring.

**Directions:** Turn off the A712 Crocketford to New Galloway road 1 mile outside Crocketford at the Gothic gatehouse (on the right travelling north).

Disabled Access:
Partial

Opening Times:
Sunday 16 February
12:00pm - 4:00pm
for the Snowdrop Festival
Sunday 29 June
2:00pm - 5:00pm

Admission:
£4.00

Charities:
Paediatric Rheumatology Discretionary Fund receives 20%, The Crocketford Village Hall receives 20%, the net remaining to SG Beneficiaries.

## BROUGHTON HOUSE GARDEN

12 High Street, Kirkcudbright DG6 4JX

**The National Trust for Scotland T: 01557 330 437**

**E: broughtonhouse@nts.org.uk www.nts.org.uk**

This event will offer visitors an evening of live music, gardens walks and refreshments. It is a chance to see the garden by a different light! Broughton House Garden is a fascinating town house garden that belonged to E A Hornel - artist, collector and one of the 'Glasgow boys'. Full of colour, mostly herbaceous, old apple trees, greenhouse with old pelargonium varieties, fruit and vegetable garden and the newly named Dactylorhiza 'Tizzy Hornell'.

**Other Details:** Self-catering accommodation available.

**Directions:** In Kirkcudbright High Street.

Disabled Access:
Partial

Opening Times:
Thursday 12 June
6:00pm - 9:00pm

Admission:
£4.00 including NTS members. Refreshments included in admission price.

Charities:
Donation to SG Beneficiaries.

## CALLY GARDENS

Gatehouse of Fleet DG7 2DJ

**Mr Michael Wickenden T: 01557 814703**

**E: info@callygardens.co.uk www.callygardens.co.uk**

A specialist nursery in a fine 2.7 acre 18th century walled garden with old vinery and bothy, all surrounded by the Cally Oak Woods. Our collection of 3,500 varieties of plants can be seen and a selection will be available pot-grown. Excellent range of rare herbaceous perennials.

**Directions:** From Dumfries take the Gatehouse turning off A75 and turn left through the Cally Palace Hotel gateway from where the gardens are well signposted.

Disabled Access:
Full

Opening Times:
Sunday 29 June
10:00am - 5:30pm
Sunday 17 August
10:00am - 5:30pm

Admission:
£2.50

Charities:
ROKPA Tibetan Charity receives 40%, the net remaining to SG Beneficiaries.

## CORSOCK HOUSE

Corsock, Castle Douglas DG7 3DJ
**The Ingall Family T: 01644 440250**

Rhododendrons, woodland walks with temples, water gardens and loch. One acre formal walled garden under development. David Bryce turretted "Scottish Baronial" house in background.

**Directions:** Off A75 Dumfries 14 miles, Castle Douglas 10 miles, Corsock village ½ mile on A712.

**Disabled Access:**
Partial

**Opening Times:**
Sunday 25 May
2:00pm - 5:00pm
Also by arrangement
1 April - 30 June

**Admission:**
£4.00, concessions £3.00, children free

**Charities:**
Corsock and Kirkpatrick Durham Church receives 40%, the net remaining to SG Beneficiaries.

## COSY COTTAGE

Borgue DG6 4SH
**Mr and Mrs A Broome T: 01557 870648**
**E: j.broome676@btinternet.com**

Village garden with herbaceous borders, rockeries, greenhouse and alpine troughs. A polytunnel with fruit and vegetables has recently been added and there is a new orchard.

**Directions:** Borgue Village is on the B727 between Kirkcudbright and Gatehouse of Fleet 3 miles off the A75 route Carlisle to Stranraer. Cosy Cottage is at the side of the village hall, up a track.

**Disabled Access:**
Full

**Opening Times:**
By arrangement
1 July - 31 August

**Admission:**
£2.00

**Charities:**
Help for Heroes receives 40%, the net remaining to SG Beneficiaries.

## CROFTS

Kirkpatrick Durham, Castle Douglas DG7 3HX
**Mrs Andrew Dalton T: 01556 650235**

Victorian garden with mature trees, a walled garden with fruit and vegetables and glass houses, hydrangea garden and a water garden.
Woodland walk with stream.

**Directions:** A75 to Crocketford, then 3 miles on A712 to Corsock & New Galloway.

**Disabled Access:**
Partial

**Opening Times:**
Sunday 10 August
2:00pm - 5:00pm

**Admission:**
£4.00

**Charities:**
Kirkpatrick Durham Church receives 40%, the net remaining to SG Beneficiaries.

## DANEVALE PARK

Crossmichael DG7 2LP

**Mrs M R C Gillespie T: 01556 670223**
**E: danevale@tiscali.co.uk**

Disabled Access:
Partial

Opening Times:
Date for the snowdrop opening to be advised, see SG website for details.

Admission:
£2.50

Charities:
Poppy Scotland receives 40%, the net remaining to SG Beneficiaries.

Mature policies with woodland walk alongside the River Dee. One of the finest displays of snowdrops in Scotland. We also get great praise for our teas.

**Directions:** On the A713. Crossmichael 1 mile, Castle Douglas 2 miles.

## GLENSONE WALLED GARDEN

Southwick DG2 8AW

**William and Josephine Millar T: 01387 780215**
**E: millar.josephine@gmail.com**

Disabled Access:
Full

Opening Times:
Sunday 27 July
2:00pm - 5:00pm

Admission:
£3.50

Charities:
Combat Stress receives 40%, the net remaining to SG Beneficiaries.

A restored walled garden complete with central water feature. Borders of perennials; shrubs with beds interspersed through the lawn. Large kitchen garden with a variety of vegetables; fruit occupies a section of the garden. Bee Bowls, a unique feature, are positioned in two opposite corners of the wall. Set in an idyllic valley with views of the Solway Firth and the Cumbrian hills.

**Other Details:** Ample parking available. Plant stall.

**Directions:** Off the A710 Dumfries to Dalbeattie coast road at Caulkerbush. Take the B793 to Dalbeattie for two miles then turn right and follow the arrows.

## NETHERHALL

Glenlochar, Castle Douglas DG7 2AA

**Sir Malcolm and Lady Ross T: 01556 680208**
**E: susieross@netherhall.com**

Disabled Access:
Partial

Opening Times:
Sunday 18 May
2:00pm - 5:00pm

Admission:
£4.00, concessions £3.00, children free

Charities:
RNLI Kirkcudbright branch receives 40%, the net remaining to SG Beneficiaries.

Traditional landscaped country house garden with shrub borders, surrounding a charming 19th c. house. Wonderful views across the River Dee to Threave Castle and beyond, with riverside walk. Miniature Shetland ponies. Ospreys, red kites and many species of wildfowl are regular visitors.

**Directions:** Travelling west along the A75, take the turnoff for Glenlochar (opposite the turnoff for Bridge of Dee) shortly after the second Castle Douglas roundabout. Netherhall is about ¾ mile along the Glenochar road on the right.

## SEABANK

Merse Road, Rockcliffe DG5 4QH

**Julian and Theodora Stanning T: 01556 630244**

The 1½ acre gardens extend to the high water mark with fine views across the Urr estuary, Rough Island and beyond. Herbaceous borders surround the house and there is a new walled garden for fruit and vegetables. A plantswoman's garden with a range of interesting and unusual plants.

**Directions:** Park in the public car park at Rockcliffe. Walk down the road about 50 metres towards the sea and turn left along The Merse, a private road. Seabank is the sixth house on the left.

Disabled Access:
Partial

Opening Times:
Sunday 6 July
2:00pm - 7:30pm

Admission:
£3.50

Charities:
Marie Curie (Solway Group) receives 40%, the net remaining to SG Beneficiaries.

## SOUTHWICK HOUSE

Southwick DG2 8AH

**Mr and Mrs R H L Thomas**

Traditional formal walled garden with greenhouses and potager containing fruit, vegetables and cutting flowers. Roses now a prominent feature together with herbaceous borders, shrubs and a lily pond. A water garden with trees, shrubs, ponds and lawns running alongside the Southwick Burn.

**Directions:** On A710 near Caulkerbush. Dalbeattie 7 miles, Dumfries 17 miles.

Disabled Access:
Partial

Opening Times:
Sunday 13 July
2:00pm - 5:00pm
14 July - 18 July
9:00am - 5:00pm

Admission:
£4.00

Charities:
Loch Arthur Community receives 40%, the net remaining to SG Beneficiaries.

## STEADSTONE

Colvend Road, Dalbeattie DG5 4QT

**Mr and Mrs R Kinnaird T: 01556 611565**
**E: rg.kinnaird@live.co.uk**

A garden in a quarry, originally created in the 1950s. Especially lovely in spring and autumn with a large variety of shrubs and seas of mecanopsis and primulas.

**Directions:** One and a half miles out of Dalbeattie on the A710 towards Kippford.

Disabled Access:
Partial

Opening Times:
By arrangement
1 January - 30 November

Admission:
£3.00

Charities:
Colliston Youth Club receives 40%, the net remaining to SG Beneficiaries.

## STOCKARTON

Kirkcudbright DG6 4XS

**Lt. Col. and Mrs Richard Cliff T: 01557 330430**

We began the garden in 1994. Our aim has been to create small informal gardens around a Galloway farmhouse, leading down to a lochan, where there are a number of unusual small trees and shrubs. In 1996 we planted a small arboretum of oak, including some very rare ones, as a shelter belt.

**Directions:** On B727 Kirkcudbright to Gelston Road. Kirkcudbright 3 miles, Castle Douglas 7 miles.

Disabled Access:
Partial

Opening Times:
By arrangement
1 April - 31 August

Admission:
£3.00

Charities:
Friends of Loch Arthur Community receives 40%, the net remaining to SG Beneficiaries.

## THE LIMES

Kirkcudbright DG6 4XD

**Mr and Mrs McHale**

Six years ago this 1¼ acre garden was mainly lawn, a few mature trees and some shrubs. After much blood, sweat and tears there is now a large rock garden, gravel garden, mixed perennial and shrub borders and 2 woodland areas. A large fruit and vegetable area keeps the family almost self-sufficient. The greenhouse is used for propagating and protecting tender plants in winter, and tomatoes are grown in summer.

**Directions:** From the A75 follow the signs for Kirkcudbright. In Kirkcudbright go straight along St Mary Street towards Dundrennan. The Limes is on the right, just on the edge of the town.

Disabled Access:
Partial

Opening Times:
Saturday 28 June 1:00pm - 5:00pm

Admission:
£4.00

Charities:
Friends of Kirkcudbright Swimming Pool receives 40%, the net remaining to SG Beneficiaries.

## THE MILL HOUSE AT GELSTON

Gelston DG7 1SH
**Malcolm and Sheila McEwan T: 01556 503955**
**E: sheilamcewan@yahoo.co.uk**

Large cottage garden on several levels surrounding former Mill House, with adjacent stream and path along former mill lade. The garden is owned by a retired wildlife ranger who has recently planted swathes of colourful perennials especially to attract wildlife. It is now a haven for insects, butterflies and birds. Some of the conifers, planted by the previous owner, remain; in addition, large numbers of flowering plants, shrubs and trees have been planted during the past four years, giving this garden, which was previously opened by the former owner, a new emphasis and layout.

**Directions:** Travelling west along the A75, take the turnoff for Castle Douglas at the second Castle Douglas roundabout, then follow signs for Gelston. The Mill House is the last/first house in the village within the 30mph limit.

Disabled Access:
Partial

Opening Times:
By arrangement
13 July - 14 September

Admission:
£2.50

Charities:
World Wide Fund for Nature (WWF) receives 40%, the net remaining to SG Beneficiaries.

## THE WATERHOUSE GARDENS AT STOCKARTON

Kirkcudbright DG6 4XS
**Martin Gould & Sharon O'Rourke T: 01557 331266**
**E: waterhousekbt@aol.com www.waterhousekbt.co.uk**

One acre of densely planted terraced cottage style gardens attached to a Galloway cottage. Three ponds surround the oak framed eco-polehouse 'The Waterhouse' available to rent 52 weeks a year. Climbing roses, clematis and honeysuckles are a big feature as well as pond-side walk. Over 50 photos on our website. Featured on BBC Scotland's 'Beechgrove Garden' 2007.

**Directions:** On B727 Kirkcudbright to Gelston - Dalbeattie road. Kirkcudbright 3 miles, Castle Douglas 7 miles.

Disabled Access:
None

Opening Times:
By arrangement
1 April - 30 September

Admission:
£3.00

Charities:
Loch Arthur Community receives 40%, the net remaining to SG Beneficiaries.

## THREAVE GARDEN

Castle Douglas DG7 1RX
**The National Trust for Scotland T: 01556 502 575**
**E: sinnes@nts.org.uk www.nts.org.uk**

Home of the Trust's School of Heritage Gardening. Spectacular daffodils in spring, colourful herbaceous borders in summer, striking autumn trees, interesting water features and a heather garden. There is also a working walled garden. For more information on the Scotland's Gardens event, please contact the property or visit http://www.nts.org.uk/events/.

**Other Details:** Champion Trees: Acer platanoides 'Princeton Gold'. Self-catering accommodation available. Restaurant open daily.

**Directions:** Off A75, 1 mile west of Castle Douglas.

Disabled Access:
Full

Opening Times:
Sunday 11 May
10:00am - 5:00pm
Sunday 10 August
10:00am - 5:00pm

Admission:
£6.50, Concessions £6.00. Event admission charge applicable to NTS members. N.B. Prices correct at time of going to print.

Charities:
Donation to SG Beneficiaries.

# LANARKSHIRE



## District Organiser

Mrs M Maxwell Stuart — Baitlaws, Lamington, Biggar ML12 6HR

## Treasurer

To be appointed.

## Gardens open on a specific date

| | | |
|---|---|---|
| Cleghorn, by Lanark | Sunday 23 February | 2:00pm - 4:00pm |
| Dippoolbank Cottage, Carnwath | Sunday 15 June | 2:00pm - 6:00pm |
| Allium Croft, Braehead | Sunday 22 June | 1:00pm - 5:00pm |
| Covington House, Thankerton | Sunday 13 July | 2:00pm - 6:00pm |
| Lindsaylands, Biggar | Sunday 13 July | 2:00pm - 6:00pm |
| Dippoolbank Cottage, Carnwath | Sunday 20 July | 2:00pm - 6:00pm |
| Wellbutts, Elsrickle | Sunday 27 July | 1:00pm - 5:00pm |
| Culter Allers, Coulter | Sunday 17 August | 2:00pm - 5:00pm |

## Gardens open by arrangement

| | | |
|---|---|---|
| Baitlaws, Lamington | 1 June - 31 August | 01899 850240 |
| Biggar Park, Biggar | 1 May - 31 July | 01899 220185 |
| Carmichael Mill, Hyndford Bridge | On request | 01555 665880 |
| The Scots Mining Company House, Leadhills | On request | 01659 74235 |

## Key to symbols

 New in 2014

 Teas

 Cream teas

 Homemade teas

 Dogs on a lead allowed

 Wheelchair access

 Accommodation

 Plant stall

 Scottish Snowdrop Festival

## Garden locations

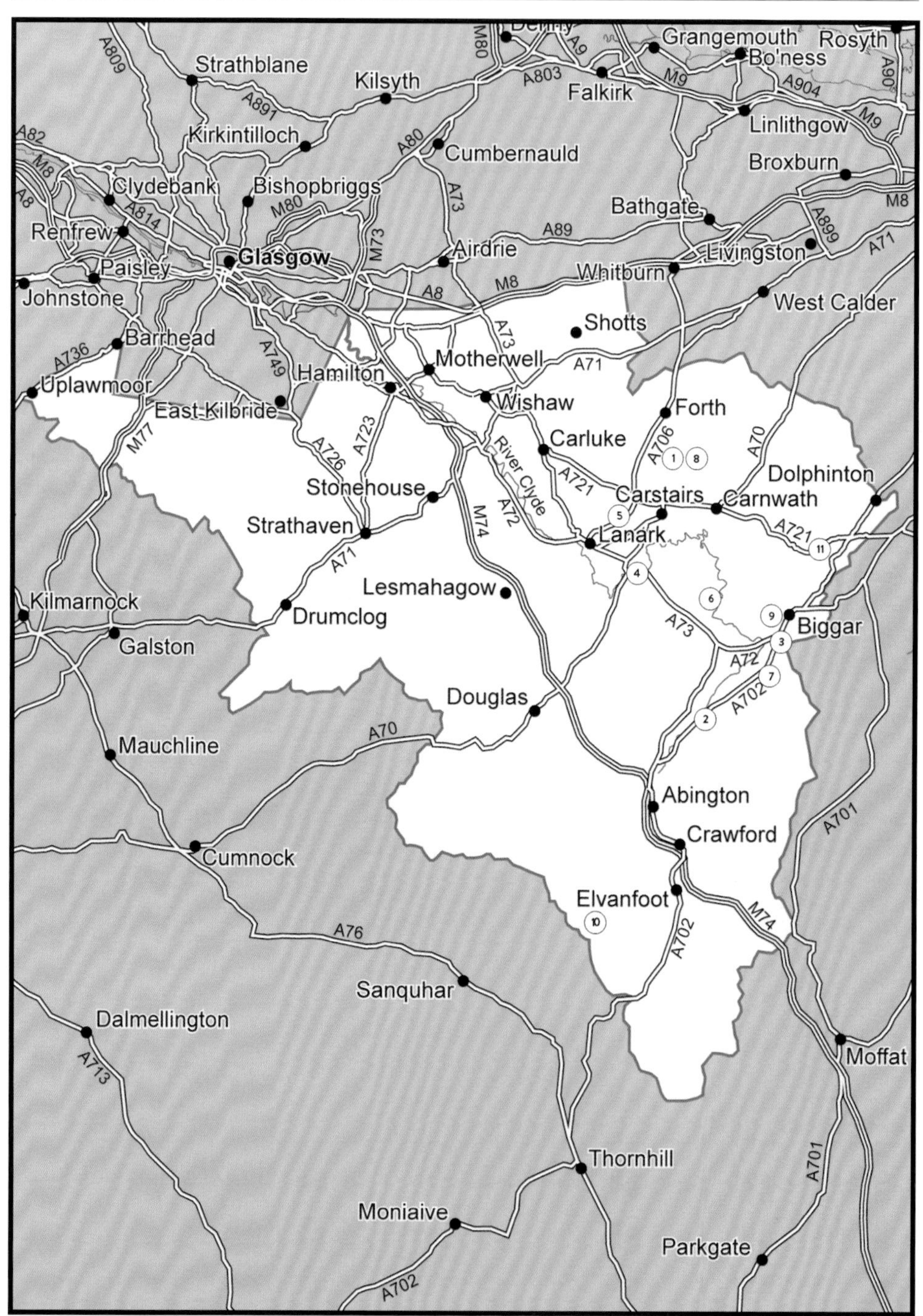

## ALLIUM CROFT

21 Main Street, Braehead ML11 8EZ
**David and Pat Onions T: 01555 812843**
**E: pat@alliumcroft.plus.com**

This is a new garden established only 4 years ago, with new plants and over 700 brought in our own furniture van from our previous garden in Perthshire. This garden is an example of what can be achieved in a very windy and wet location and in only a short time.

**Directions:** The garden is in Main Street off the B7016 (Forth - Carnwarth), turn opposite Last Shaft Inn and Restaurant.

Disabled Access:
None

Opening Times:
Sunday 22 June
1:00pm - 5:00pm

Admission:
£3.00

Charities:
Braehead Village Fund receives 40%, the net remaining to SG Beneficiaries.

## BAITLAWS

Lamington, Biggar ML12 6HR
**Mr and Mrs M Maxwell Stuart T: 01899 850240**
**E: ms.kirsty@gmail.com**

The garden is set at over 900 ft. above sea level and has been developed over the past 25 years with a particular emphasis on colour combinations of shrubs and herbaceous perennials which flourish at that height. A small pond is a recent addition. The surrounding hills make an imposing backdrop. Featured in "Good Gardens' Guide".

**Other Details:** Groups welcome.

**Directions:** Off A702 above Lamington Village. Biggar 5 miles, Abington 5 miles, Lanark 10 miles.

Disabled Access:
None

Opening Times:
By arrangement
1 June - 31 August

Admission:
£4.00

Charities:
Biggar Museum Trust, Lamington Chapel Restoration Fund receives 40%, the net remaining to SG Beneficiaries.

## BIGGAR PARK

Biggar ML12 6JS
**Mr David Barnes T: 01899 220185**

Ten acre garden starred in "Good Gardens Guide", featured on "The Beechgrove Garden" and in "Country Life", "Scottish Field" and many others. Incorporating traditional walled garden with long stretches of herbaceous borders, shrubberies, fruit, vegetables and a potager. Lawns, walks, pools, small Japanese garden and other interesting features. Glades of rhododendrons, azaleas and blue poppies in May and June. Good collection of old fashioned roses in June and July; interesting young trees.

**Other Details:** Groups welcome.

**Directions:** On A702, ¼ mile south of Biggar.

Disabled Access:
Partial

Opening Times:
By arrangement
1 May - 31 July

Admission:
£5.00

Charities:
ZANE receives 40%, the net remaining to SG Beneficiaries.

## CARMICHAEL MILL

Hyndford Bridge, Lanark ML11 8SJ
**Chris, Ken and Gemma Fawell T: 01555 665880**
**E: ken.fawell@btinternet.com**

Riverside gardens surrounding the only remaining workable water powered grain mill in Clydesdale. Admission includes entry to the mill which will be turning, river levels permitting. Diverse plant habitats from saturated to bone dry allow a vast range of trees and shrubs, both ornamental and fruit, with a vegetable garden. Herbaceous perennials, annuals and biennials with ornamental/wildlife pond complementing the landscape. Also, archaeological remains of medieval grain mills from c. 1200 and foundry, lint mill and threshing mill activity within the curtilage of the Category B Listed Building.

**Other Details:** Teas and light refreshments by prior arrangement.

**Directions:** Just off A73 Lanark to Biggar road ½ mile east of the Hyndford Bridge.

**Disabled Access:**
Partial

**Opening Times:**
By arrangement on request

**Admission:**
£4.00, children over 12 £2.00

**Charities:**
Donation to SG Beneficiaries.

## CLEGHORN

Stable House, Cleghorn Farm, Lanark ML11 7RN
**Mr and Mrs R Eliott-Lockhart T: 01555 663792**
**E: info@cleghornestategardens.com www.cleghornestategardens.com**

18th century garden which is currently being renovated. Mature trees and shrubs, with masses of snowdrops spread around. Beautiful views to the south of Tinto Hill and the Cleghorn Glen.

**Directions:** Cleghorn Farm is situated 2 miles north of Lanark on the A706.

**Disabled Access:**
None

**Opening Times:**
Sunday 23 February
2:00pm - 4:00pm
for the Snowdrop Festival

**Admission:**
By Donation

**Charities:**
Marie Curie Cancer Care receives 40%, the net remaining to SG Beneficiaries.

## COVINGTON HOUSE (WITH LINDSAYLANDS)

Covington Road, Thankerton, Biggar ML12 6NE
**Angus and Angela Milner-Brown**

A 3 acre old manse garden, including a walled garden, within the historic conservation area of Covington. The garden consists of lawns, an ornamental pond, herbaceous borders, species trees and shrubs, as well as a small amount of broadleaf woodland. The 18th century walled garden has a developing potager with vegetables and flowers.

**Other Details:** Champion Trees: Large Wellingtonia. Homemade teas will be served at Lindsaylands.

**Directions:** One mile along Covington Road from Thankerton on the left.

**Disabled Access:**
Full

**Opening Times:**
Sunday 13 July
2:00pm - 6:00pm

**Admission:**
£6.00 for both gardens
£4.00 for Covington only

**Charities:**
St Columba's Hospice receives 40%, the net remaining to SG Beneficiaries.

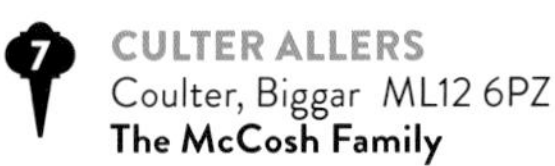

## CULTER ALLERS
Coulter, Biggar ML12 6PZ
**The McCosh Family**

Culter Allers, a late Victorian baronial house, has maintained its traditional one-acre walled kitchen garden, half with fruit and vegetables, the other half with mainly cut flowers and herbaceous. The policies of the house are open and include woodland walks and an avenue of 125 year old lime trees leading to the village church.

**Directions:** In the village of Coulter, 3 miles south of Biggar on A702.

Disabled Access:
Partial

Opening Times:
Sunday 17 August
2:00pm - 5:00pm

Admission:
£4.00, children free

Charities:
Coulter Library Trust receives 40%, the net remaining to SG Beneficiaries.

## DIPPOOLBANK COTTAGE
Carnwath ML11 8LP
**Mr Allan Brash**

Artist's intriguing cottage garden. Vegetables grown in small beds. Herbs, fruit, flowers, pond in woodland area with tree house and summer house. Fernery completed in 2007. This is an organic garden mainly constructed with recycled materials.

**Directions:** Off B7016 between Forth and Carnwath near the village of Braehead on the Auchengray road. Approximately 8 miles from Lanark. Well signposted.

Disabled Access:
None

Opening Times:
Sunday 15 June
2:00pm - 6:00pm
Sunday 20 July
2:00pm - 6:00pm

Admission:
£4.00

Charities:
The Little Haven receives 40%, the net remaining to SG Beneficiaries.

## LINDSAYLANDS (WITH COVINGTON HOUSE)
Biggar ML12 6NR
**Steve and Alison Crichton**

The garden at Lindsaylands, a William Leiper house dating from 1869, is opening again for the first time in 30 years. The garden is situated within a collection of mature specimen trees and features an herbaceous border, a working kitchen garden and woodland walks.

**Directions:** On Lindsaylands Road ½ mile south west of Biggar.

Disabled Access:
Full

Opening Times:
Sunday 13 July
2:00pm - 6:00pm

Admission:
£6.00 for both gardens
£4.00 for Lindsaylands only

Charities:
St Columba's Hospice receives 40%, the net remaining to SG Beneficiaries.

## THE SCOTS MINING COMPANY HOUSE

Leadhills, Biggar ML12 6XP

**Charlie and Greta Clark T: 01659 74235**

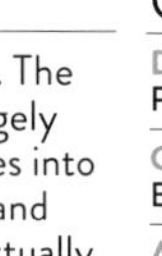

The site is c.400 metres above sea level, which is high for a cultivated garden. The surrounding landscape is open moorland with sheep grazing. The garden is largely enclosed by dense planting, but the various walks allow views through the trees into the surrounding countryside. Historic Scotland in their register of "Gardens and designed landscapes" describe the garden as "An outstanding example of a virtually unaltered, small, 18th c. garden layout connected with James Stirling, the developer of the profitable Leadhills mining enterprise, and possibly William Adam." Say goodbye to spring walking among what must be amongst the last daffodils of the year.

**Other Details:** Homemade teas may be available by prior request.

**Directions:** On Main Street, Leadhills (B797) 6 miles from M74 Junction 13 (Abington).

Disabled Access:
Partial

Opening Times:
By arrangement on request

Admission:
£3.50, children free

Charities:
Scots Mining Company Trust receives 40%, the net remaining to SG Beneficiaries.

## WELLBUTTS

Elsrickle, by Biggar ML12 6QZ

**Mr and Mrs N Slater**

Started in 2000 from a bare brown site around a renovated croft cottage, with additional field ground obtained in 2005, the garden is now approximately 2 acres. Due to the exposed and elevated (960 ft.) position the ongoing priority is hedge and shrub planting to give some protection for the many and varied herbaceous borders leading to the duckhouse, 2 large ponds and 'boggery'.

**Directions:** Parking on main road (A721) near to bus stop. Walk to garden (approximately 200 yards).

Disabled Access:
None

Opening Times:
Sunday 27 July
1:00pm - 5:00pm

Admission:
£4.00

Charities:
CHAS receives 40%, the net remaining to SG Beneficiaries.

# LOCHABER & BADENOCH

Scotland's Gardens 2014 Guidebook is sponsored by **INVESTEC WEALTH & INVESTMENT**

## District Organiser

| | |
|---|---|
| Norrie and Anna Maclaren | Ard-Daraich, Ardgour, Nr. Fort William PH33 7AB |

## Area Organisers

| | |
|---|---|
| Lynn Blair | West Lodge, Roshven, Lochailort PH38 4NB |
| Emma MacKenzie | Glenkyllachy, Tomatin IV13 7YA |
| Anne Moore | Polgreggan, Newtonmore PH20 1BD |

## Treasurer

| | |
|---|---|
| Norrie Maclaren | Ard-Daraich, Ardgour, Nr. Fort William PH33 7AB |

## Gardens open on a specific date

| | | |
|---|---|---|
| Canna House Walled Garden, Isle of Canna | Saturday 3 May | 10:00am - 4:30pm |
| Aberarder, Kinlochlaggan | Sunday 25 May | 2:00pm - 5:30pm |
| Ardverikie, Kinlochlaggan | Sunday 25 May | 2:00pm - 5:30pm |
| Arisaig House, Beasdale | Saturday 14 June | 11:00am - 4:00pm |
| Craigmore Mill, Nethybridge | Sunday 22 June | 1:00pm - 5:00pm |
| Glenkyllachy Lodge, Tomatin | Saturday 26 July | 2:00pm - 5:30pm |
| Glenkyllachy Lodge, Tomatin | Sunday 27 July | 2:00pm - 5:30pm |
| Canna House Walled Garden, Isle of Canna | Wednesday 13 August | 10:30am - 4:00pm |
| Roshven House, Lochailort | Sunday 7 September | 1:00pm - 4:00pm |

## Gardens open regularly

| | | |
|---|---|---|
| Ardtornish, By Lochaline | 1 January - 31 December | 10:00am - Dusk |

## Gardens open by arrangement

| | | |
|---|---|---|
| Ard-Daraich, Ardgour | On request | 01855 841384 |

## Key to symbols

 New in 2014
  Homemade teas
 Accommodation
 Teas

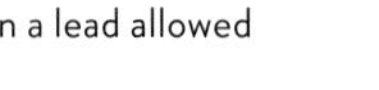 Dogs on a lead allowed
 Plant stall
 Cream teas
Wheelchair access
 Scottish Snowdrop Festival

## Garden locations

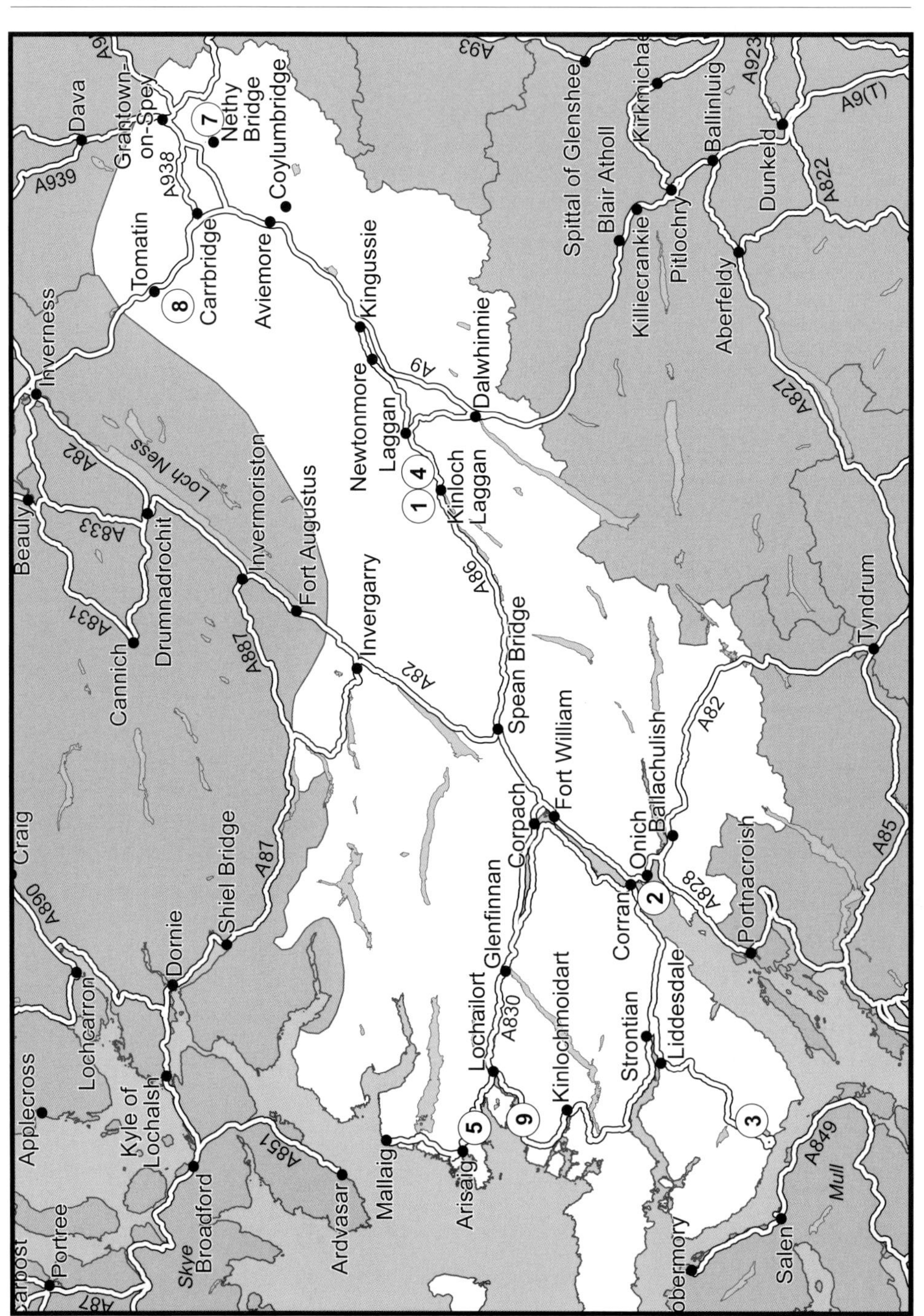

## ABERARDER (WITH ARDVERIKIE)

Kinlochlaggan PH20 1BX
**The Feilden Family T: 01528 544300**

The garden has been laid out over the last 20 years to create a mixture of spring and autumn plants and trees, including rhododendrons, azaleas and acers. The elevated view down Loch Laggan from the garden is exceptional.

**Directions:** On A86 between Newtonmore and Spean Bridge at east end of Loch Laggan.

Disabled Access:
Partial

Opening Times:
Sunday 25 May
2:00pm - 5:30pm

Admission:
£5.00 includes entrance to Ardverikie

Charities:
Marie Curie Cancer Care receives 20%, Laggan Church receives 20%, the net remaining to SG Beneficiaries.

## ARD-DARAICH

Ardgour, by Fort William PH33 7AB
**Norrie and Anna Maclaren T: 01855 841384**
**www.arddaraich.co.uk**

Seven acre hill garden, in a spectacular setting, with many fine and uncommon rhododendrons, an interesting selection of trees and shrubs and a large collection of camellias, acers and sorbus.

**Directions:** West from Fort William, across the Corran Ferry, turn left and a mile on the right further west.

Disabled Access:
None

Opening Times:
By arrangement on request

Admission:
£4.00

Charities:
Donation to SG Beneficiaries.

## ARDTORNISH

By Lochaline, Morvern PA80 5UZ
**Mrs John Raven**

Wonderful gardens of interesting mature conifers, rhododendrons, deciduous trees, shrubs and herbaceous, set amid magnificent scenery.

**Directions:** A884 Lochaline 3 miles.

Disabled Access:
None

Opening Times:
1 January - 31 December
10:00am - 6:00pm or Dusk

Admission:
£4.00

Charities:
Donation to SG Beneficiaries.

## ARDVERIKIE (WITH ABERARDER)

Kinlochlaggan PH20 1BX
**Mrs P Laing and Mrs E T Smyth-Osbourne T: 01528 544300**

Lovely setting on Loch Laggan with magnificent trees. Walled garden with large collection of acers, shrubs and herbaceous. Architecturally interesting house (not open). Site of the filming of the TV series "Monarch of the Glen".

**Other Details:** Teas at Aberarder.

**Directions:** On A86 between Newtonmore and Spean Bridge. Entrance at east end of Loch Laggan by gate lodge over bridge.

Disabled Access:
Partial

Opening Times:
Sunday 25 May
2:00pm - 5:30pm

Admission:
£5.00 includes entrance to Aberarder

Charities:
Marie Curie Cancer Care receives 20%, Laggan Church receives 20%, the net remaining to SG Beneficiaries.

## ARISAIG HOUSE

Beasdale, Arisaig PH39 4NR
**Ms. Emma Weir T: 01687 450730**
**E: sarahwi@arisaighouse.co.uk www.arisaighouse.co.uk**

Arisaig House, designed in 1864 by Philip Webb, is a luxurious guest house offering dinner, bed and breakfast. Wander through 20 acres of well-established and cared for woodlands and gardens. Extensive collection of specimen trees and rhododendrons. Exquisite terrace with formal rose and herb beds. Visit the kitchen garden - an orchard, soft fruit cages, productive polytunnel, and vegetable beds. Whatever can be found in the garden that day is on the menu that night!

**Other Details:** Live music on the terrace. Delicious homemade teas in the Dining Room. Works by local artists for sale within the house. Extensive collection of Victorian shrubs and trees. Birds and wildlife abound.

**Directions:** Arisaig House is 32 miles from Fort William on the A830 road to Mallaig. Approx. 1.2 miles from Beasdale train station turn left into junction sign posted Arisaig House and Cottages.

Disabled Access:
None

Opening Times:
Saturday 14 June
11:00am - 4:00pm

Admission:
£4.00

Charities:
Local Feis receives 20%, Cancer Research receives 20%, the net remaining to SG Beneficiaries.

## CANNA HOUSE WALLED GARDEN

Isle of Canna PH44 4RS
**National Trust for Scotland T: 01687 462998**
**E: sconnor@nts.org.uk www.nts.org.uk**

Formerly derelict 2 acre walled garden brought back to life following a 5 year restoration project. There is soft fruit, top fruit, vegetables, ornamental lawns and flower beds. There is also a stunning 80ft Escallonia arch. The garden has been replanted to attract bees, butterflies and moths. The woodland walks outside walls are not to be missed along with the spectacular views of neighbouring islands. Don't miss your chance to see this gem.

**Directions:** Access Isle of Canna via Calmac ferry from Mallaig pier.

Disabled Access:
Partial

Opening Times:
Saturday 3 May
10:00am - 4:30pm
Wednesday 13 August
10:30am - 4:00pm

Admission:
£3.00 including NTS members.
N.B. Prices correct at the time of going to print.

Charities:
Donation to SG Beneficiaries.

## CRAIGMORE MILL

Dorback Road, Nethybridge PH25 3ED
**Chris and Harry Jamieson**

Half acre garden set outside Nethybridge village surrounded by Scots Pines, silver birches and fields mostly on a sloping terrain facing east. The Aultmore Burn borders the garden and feeds a natural pond containing bog plants. Mixed borders, rockeries and paths have evolved over the years since the Old Meal Mill was converted into a house by the present owners in 1976. Wide range of shrubs and herbaceous plants including meconopsis, incarvillea, primulas, celmisias, hostas etc. with the main focus on foliage.

**Other Details:** Teas available in workshop, garage or garden. Toilets are available.

**Directions: From A9**: Take B970 to Boat of Garton then Nethybridge. Over humpback bridge, turn right before Nethybridge Hotel. Continue uphill on Dorback/Tomintoul road, over next crossroads. A minute later sign for PARKING on left at Woodside. **From East:** Near Grantown take B970 to Nethybridge, after Nethybridge Hotel turn left (before bridge) and follow directions from Dorback/Tomintoul road as above.

Disabled Access:
None

Opening Times:
Sunday 22 June
1:00pm - 5:00pm

Admission:
£3.50

Charities:
Marie Curie Cancer Care receives 40%, the net remaining to SG Beneficiaries.

## GLENKYLLACHY LODGE

Tomatin IV13 7YA
**Mr and Mrs Philip Mackenzie**
**E: emmaglenkyllachy@gmail.com**

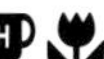

In a remote highland glen and at an altitude of 1150 feet this is a glorious garden of shrubs, herbaceous, rhododendrons and trees planted round a pond with a backdrop of a juniper and birch covered hillside. There is also a vegetable garden, a polytunnel and a short wooded walk with stunning views down the Findhorn. A wild flower meadow and wondrous stone wall folly are new this year. Various original sculptures are situated around the garden.

**Directions:** Turn off the A9 at Tomatin and take the Coignafearn and Garbole single track road down north side of River Findhorn, cattle grid and gate on right after sign to Farr.

Disabled Access:
Partial

Opening Times:
Saturday 26 July
2:00pm - 5:30pm
Sunday 27 July
2:00pm - 5:30pm

Admission:
£4.00, children free

Charities:
26 July: Macmillan Cancer Support receives 40%,
27 July: Marie Curie Cancer Care the net remaining to SG Beneficiaries.

## ROSHVEN HOUSE

Lochailort PH38 4NB
**Mr and Mrs Angus MacDonald**

Roshven House, a recently restored large, historic house spectacularly sited overlooking one of the great romantic views of the west towards a pattern of islands including Eigg, Muck and Rhum. The house is surrounded by nearly 30 acres of grounds. The formal garden is the most recent creation, joining mature trees, box edged shrubbery, azaleas, rhododendrons, and unusual species extending the flowering season from summer into autumn color. Woodland walks under construction.

**Other Details:** Tea location - outside seating under a canopy.

**Directions:** From Fort William, take the A830 to Lochailort. Left at Lochailort Inn onto A861, 5 miles to Roshven signpost, a further 400 meters turn right at stone pillar entrance.

Disabled Access:
None

Opening Times:
Sunday 7 September
1:00pm - 4:00pm

Admission:
£4.00

Charities:
Royal National Lifeboat Institution receives 40%, the net remaining to SG Beneficiaries.

# MIDLOTHIAN

Scotland's Gardens 2014 Guidebook is sponsored by **INVESTEC WEALTH & INVESTMENT**

## District Organiser

| | |
|---|---|
| Mrs Sarah Barron DL | Laureldene, Kevock Road, Lasswade EH18 1HT |

## Area Organisers

| | |
|---|---|
| Mrs Margaret Drummond | Pomathorn House, Penicuik EH26 8PJ |
| Mrs R Hill | Law House, 27 Biggar Road, Silverburn EH26 9LJ |
| Mrs Eilidh Liddle | 21 Craigiebield Crescent, Penicuik EH26 9EQ |

## Treasurer

| | |
|---|---|
| Mrs Margaret Drummond | Pomathorn House, Penicuik EH26 8PJ |

## Gardens open on a specific date

| | | |
|---|---|---|
| Kevock Garden, Lasswade | Sunday 2 March | 12:00pm - 3:00pm |
| Kevock Garden, Lasswade | Saturday 14 June | 2:00pm - 5:00pm |
| Kevock Garden, Lasswade | Sunday 15 June | 2:00pm - 5:00pm |
| The Old Sun Inn, Newbattle | Sunday 22 June | 2:00pm - 5:00pm |
| Broomieknowe Gardens, Lasswade | Sunday 29 June | 2:00pm - 5:30pm |
| Pomathorn Gardens, Penicuik | Sunday 20 July | 2:00pm - 5:00pm |
| Newhall, Carlops | Sunday 27 July | 2:00pm - 5:00pm |

## Gardens open by arrangement

| | | |
|---|---|---|
| Newhall, Carlops | 1 May - 31 August | 01968 660206 |

## Plant sale

| | | |
|---|---|---|
| Vogrie Plant Sale (with Midlothian Council), Gorebridge | Saturday 24 May | 10:00am - 4:00pm |

## Key to symbols

 New in 2014

Homemade teas

 Accommodation

 Teas

 Dogs on a lead allowed

 Plant stall

Cream teas

 Wheelchair access

Scottish Snowdrop Festival

## Garden locations

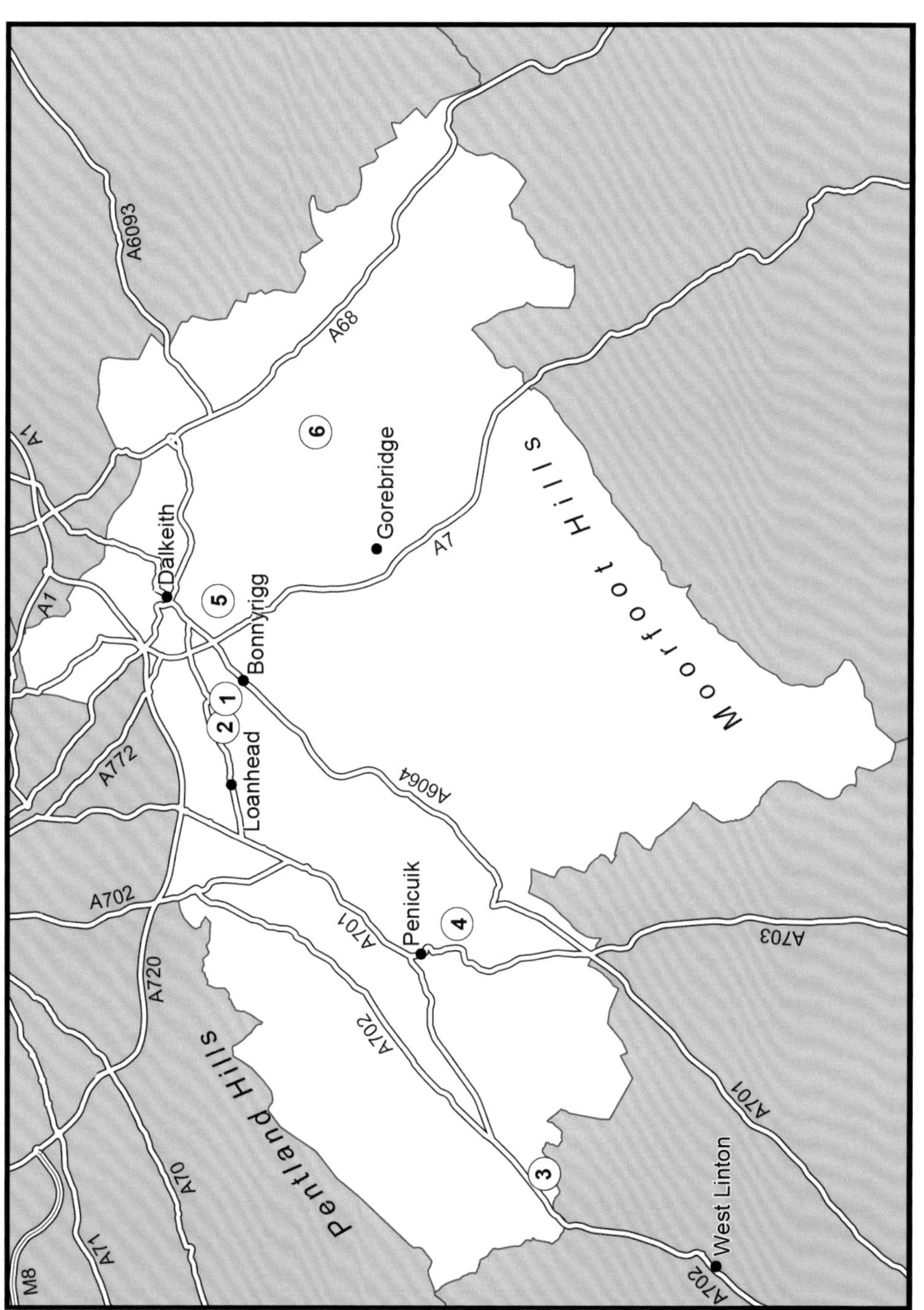

## BROOMIEKNOWE GARDENS

Lasswade EH18 1LN

**The Gardeners of Broomieknowe T: 0131 663 8700**
**E: ruthmehlsen@googlemail.com**

Several charming and individual gardens are to be found in the Broomieknowe Conservation Area of Lasswade. They all differ in size and design, yet are complementary in style, witness to the skill and imagination of their owners. Many interesting trees and shrubs, with a variety of unusual herbaceous and bedding plants, brilliant colour, foliage and form. Lots of ideas and unusual garden features to interest the keen gardener.

**Other Details:** We are supporting the Marie Curie "Ann Spence Memorial Fund" as Ann Spence lived in Broomieknowe, loved gardens and was a keen supporter of Scotland's Gardens.
There will be a good quality plant stall.

**Directions:** Broomieknowe is signposted off B704 between Lasswade and Bonnyrigg. Lothian Region Transport Bus No. 31 to Cockpen. Get off at Nazareth House Nursing Home at Hillhead.

Disabled Access:
Partial

Opening Times:
Sunday 29 June
2:00pm - 5:30pm

Admission:
£5.00 for all gardens, children free

Charities:
Marie Curie 'Ann Spence Memorial Fund' receives 40%, the net remaining to SG Beneficiaries.

## KEVOCK GARDEN

16 Kevock Road, Lasswade EH18 1HT

**David and Stella Rankin T: 0131 454 0660**
**E: info@kevockgarden.co.uk www.kevockgarden.co.uk**

A wonderful compact hillside garden overlooking the North Esk Valley with rockeries and a pond with damp-loving plants. Several mature specimen trees, azaleas, rhododendrons and unusual shrubs are interplanted with a range of rare woodland plants. Kevock Garden has featured in many magazine articles and gardening programmes and was a Gold Medal winner at the 2013 Chelsea Flower Show. The garden is open in March for spring bulbs and other plants including daphnes and in the summer for interesting perennials and rhododendrons.

**Other Details:** Soup and rolls available in March and homemade teas in June.

**Directions:** Kevock Road lies to the south of A678 Loanhead/Lasswade Road. 5 minutes from the city by-pass Lasswade Junction and on the 31 Lothian Bus route to Polton/Bonnyrigg. Parking available in Drummond Grange Nursing Home. Only disabled parking on Kevock Road please.

Disabled Access:
None

Opening Times:
Sunday 2 March
12:00pm - 3:00pm
Saturday 14 June
2:00pm - 5:00pm
Sunday 15 June
2:00pm - 5:00pm

Admission:
£4.00, children free

Charities:
Building for the Future of Nepal receives 40%, the net remaining to SG Beneficiaries.

## NEWHALL

Carlops EH26 9LY

**John and Tricia Kennedy T: 01968 660206**
**E: tricia.kennedy@newhalls.co.uk**

Traditional 18th century walled garden with huge herbaceous border, shrubberies, fruit and vegetables. Many unusual plants for sale. Stunning glen running along the North Esk river in process of restoration (stout shoes recommended). Large pond with evolving planting. Young arboretum and collection of Rosa pimpinellifolia. As in "Good Gardens Guide 2010", "Scottish Field", "Gardens Monthly", "Scotland on Sunday".

**Other Details:** 27 July: Homemade teas and plant stall.
By Arrangement dates, 1 May - 31 August: Light lunches and teas available for arranged visits if organised in advance.

**Directions:** On A702 Edinburgh/Biggar, a ¼ of a mile after Ninemileburn and a mile before Carlops. Follow signs.

Disabled Access:
Partial

Opening Times:
Sunday 27 July
2:00pm - 5:00pm
By arrangement
1 May - 31 August

Admission:
£5.00

Charities:
William Steel Trust receives 40%, the net remaining to SG Beneficiaries.

4

## POMATHORN GARDENS

Pomathorn Road, Penicuik EH26 8PJ
**Mrs. Margaret Drummond T: 01968 674046**
**E: med1002@btinternet.com**

Several small country gardens set high above Penicuik with lovely views of the Pentland Hills. All are different in design, but face similar challenges from wind and snow in the winter. The gardens are all within walking distance of each other. There will be a plant and secondhand book stall. Teas served in Pomathorn House.

**Directions:** From Edinburgh City by-pass take A701 to Gowkley Moss roundabout, exit for Penicuik then take slip road to Auchendinny on B7026 and after Loanstone turn right onto B6372 Pomathorn Road, where gardens and parking are signposted. Parking at Pomathorn Mill and where directed for disabled.

Disabled Access:
Partial

Opening Times:
Sunday 20 July
2:00pm - 5:00pm

Admission:
£4.00 includes all gardens, children free

Charities:
RDA : Riding For The Disabled receives 40%, the net remaining to SG Beneficiaries.

5

## THE OLD SUN INN

Newbattle, Dalkeith EH22 3LH
**Mr and Mrs James Lochhead T: 0131 663 2648**
**E: randjlochhead@uwclub.net**

An interesting and beautifully designed, half acre garden of island and raised beds, containing a collection of species lilies, rock plants and some unusual bulbs. There are also two small interconnecting ponds and a conservatory.

**Other Details:** Homemade teas £3.00

**Directions:** B703 (Newtongrange) from Eskbank Toll. Garden is immediately opposite Newbattle Abbey College entrance. First bus 95 & 95X to Eskbank Toll only. Parking at Newbattle Abbey College.

Disabled Access:
Partial

Opening Times:
Sunday 22 June
2:00pm - 5:00pm

Admission:
£3.50, children free

Charities:
All proceeds to SG Beneficiaries.

6

## VOGRIE PLANT SALE (IN CONJUNCTION WITH MIDLOTHIAN COUNCIL)

Vogrie Walled Garden, Vogrie Country Park, Gorebridge EH23 4NU
**Midlothian Council T: 01875 821986 E: ld9kevock@aol.com**

Stock up your gardens with a wide variety of interesting plants from the Midlothian Council and Scotland's Gardens Plant Sale, held within Vogrie Walled Garden in the beautiful grounds of Vogrie Country Park. A range of plants will include bedding, baskets, herbaceous, and shrubs with some unusual plants from local gardens and Vogrie Nursery. For beginner and connoisseur gardeners alike.

**Other Details:** Cash and cheque sales only please. BBQ available from 11.00am. Fun for the family with woodland walks, adventure playground, picnic area, 9 hole golf course, pony rides, scavenger hunt with Countryside Ranger and miniature railway running 12:00pm-2:00pm. Garden accessories available.

**Directions:** From Edinburgh travel south along A68 through Dalkeith towards Jedburgh. Just before Pathhead, turn right onto B6372 signposted Vogrie Country Park continue for approximately 2 kilometres, main park entrance gates on left.

Disabled Access:
Full

Opening Times:
Saturday 24 May
10:00am - 4:00pm
Grounds also open

Admission:
Free
Parking: £1.00

Charities:
Marie Curie Edinburgh receives 20%, Cancer Research UK receives 20%, the net remaining to SG Beneficiaries.

# MORAY & NAIRN



## District Organiser

| | |
|---|---|
| Mr James Byatt | Lochview Cottage, Scarffbanks, Pitgaveny IV30 5PQ |

## Area Organisers

| | |
|---|---|
| Mrs Lorraine Dingwall | 10 Pilmuir Road West, Forres IV36 2HL |
| Mrs Rebecca Russell | 12 Duff Avenue, Elgin, Moray IV30 1QS |
| Mrs Annie Stewart | 33 Albert Street, Nairn IV12 4HF |

## Treasurer

| | |
|---|---|
| Mr Michael Barnett | Drumdelnies, Nairn IV12 5NT |

## Gardens open on a specific date

| | | |
|---|---|---|
| Brodie Castle, Brodie | Saturday 12 April | 10:30am - 4:30pm |
| Brodie Castle, Brodie | Sunday 13 April | 10:30am - 4:30pm |
| Newbold House, Forres | Sunday 18 May | 2:00pm - 6:00pm |
| Carestown Steading, Deskford | Saturday 14 June | 10:00am - 4:00pm |
| Cuddy's Well, Clephanton | Saturday 28 June | 12:30pm - 8:30pm |
| Cuddy's Well, Clephanton | Sunday 29 June | 12:30pm - 8:30pm |
| 1 Sanquhar Drive, Forres | Sunday 13 July | 2:00pm - 6:00pm |
| 10 Pilmuir Road West, Forres | Sunday 13 July | 2:00pm - 6:00pm |
| Newbold House, Forres | Sunday 13 July | 2:00pm - 6:00pm |
| Castleview, Auchindoun | Sunday 3 August | 2:00pm - 5:00pm |
| Glenrinnes Lodge, Dufftown | Sunday 3 August | 2:00pm - 5:00pm |
| Gordonstoun, Duffus | Sunday 7 September | 2:00pm - 4:30pm |

## Gardens open by arrangement

| | | |
|---|---|---|
| 10 Pilmuir Road West, Forres | 1 June - 30 August | 01309 674634 |
| Bruntlands Bungalow, Alves | 1 May - 30 September | 07999 817715 |

## Key to symbols

 New in 2014

 Homemade teas

 Accommodation

 Teas

 Dogs on a lead allowed

 Plant stall

 Cream teas

 Wheelchair access

 Scottish Snowdrop Festival

## Garden locations

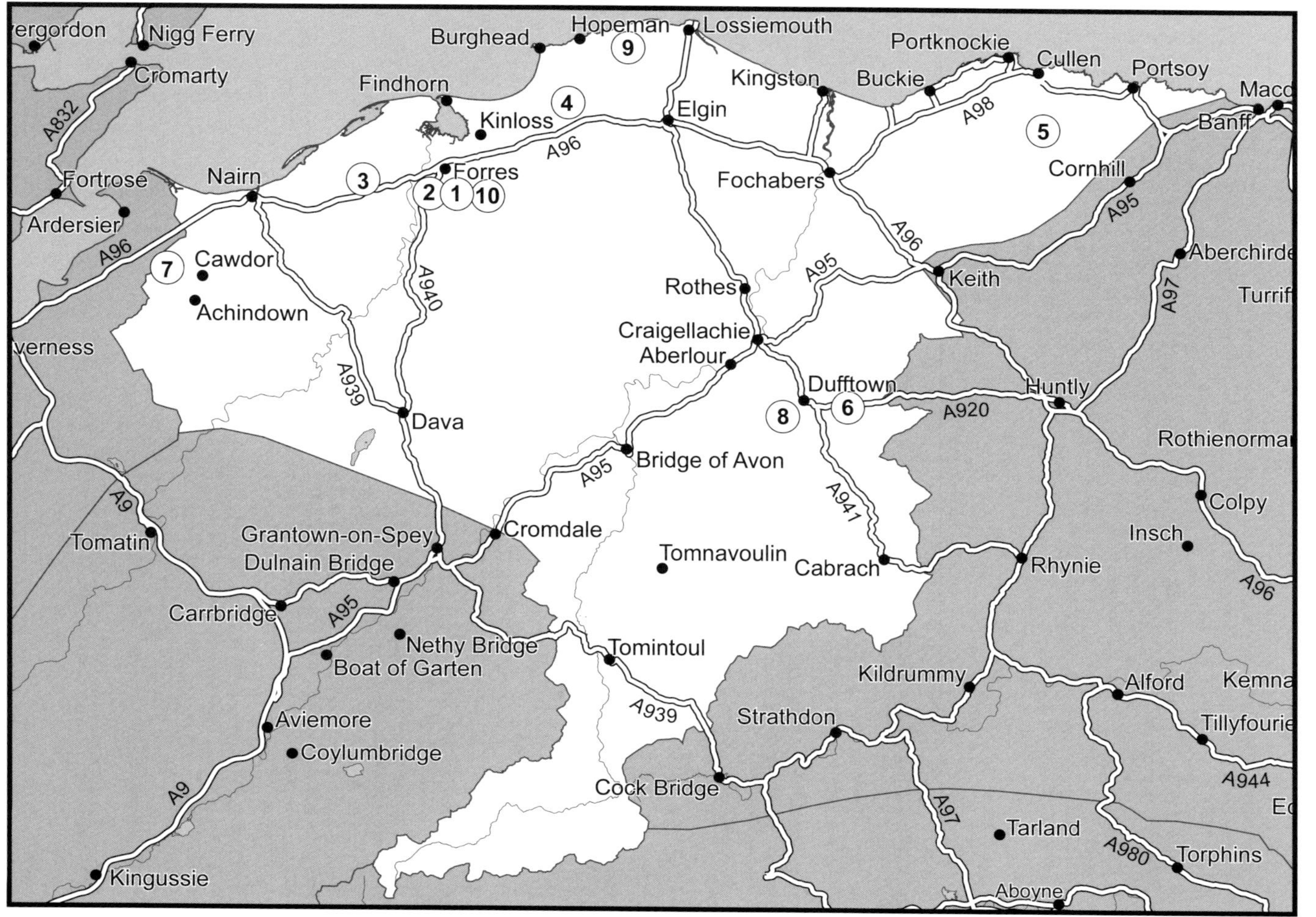

## 1 SANQUHAR DRIVE (WITH 10 PILMUIR ROAD WEST AND NEWBOLD HOUSE)

Forres IV36 1DQ
**Mr and Mrs George Paul**

Informal cottage-style garden with mixed borders, vegetables and fruit. It is gardened without artificial fertilizer and chemicals and provides habitats and food for wildlife.

**Other Details:** Plant stalls at 1 Sanquhar Drive and 10 Pilmuir Road West. Teas at Newbold House.

**Directions:** From Forres High Street turn down Tolbooth Street which is by the clock tower, take the 3rd exit on the roundabout onto Sanquhar Road. Sanquhar Drive is opposite the swimming pool.

Disabled Access:
None

Opening Times:
Sunday 13 July
2:00pm - 6:00pm

Admission:
£5.00 (all 3 gardens)

Charities:
CHECT (Childhood Eye Cancer Trust) receives 40%, the net remaining to SG Beneficiaries.

## 10 PILMUIR ROAD WEST (WITH 1 SANQUHAR DRIVE & NEWBOLD)

Forres IV36 2HL
**Mrs Lorraine Dingwall T: 01309 674634**
**E: fixandig@aol.com www.simplesite.com/hosta**

Plantsman's small town garden with over 300 cultivars of hostas, an extensive collection of hardy geraniums together with many other unusual plants. Managed entirely without the use of artificial fertilizers or chemicals, the owner encourages hedgehogs, toads and wild birds to control slugs.

**Other Details:** 13 July: Plant stalls at 1 Sanquhar Drive and 10 Pilmuir Road West. Teas at Newbold House.

**Directions:** From Tesco roundabout at Forres continue along Nairn Road. Take first left onto Ramflat Road, then right at the bottom, then first left onto Pilmuir Road West.

Disabled Access:
None

Opening Times:
Sunday 13 July 2:00pm - 6:00pm (Joint opening)
Also by arrangement 1 June - 30 August : (10 Pilmuir Road West only)

Admission:
13 July: £5.00 (all 3 gardens)
By Arrangement dates: £3.00

Charities:
Macmillan Cancer Support receives 40%, the net remaining to SG Beneficiaries.

## BRODIE CASTLE

Brodie, Forres IV36 2TE
**The National Trust for Scotland T: 0844 4932156**
**E: sferguson@nts.org.uk www.nts.org.uk**

In springtime the grounds are carpeted with the daffodils for which the castle is rightly famous. Bred by Ian Brodie, these daffodils are internationally significant. Some are found nowhere else in the world but the castle grounds! There is also a shrubbery garden with rhododendrons and a good tree collection plus wildflowers.

**Other Details:** National Plant Collection®: Narcissus (Brodie cvs.)
On these special days the garden team will lead guided walks in support of Scotland's Gardens. There will also be a plant stall selling pots of daffodils. Contact property for further information.

**Directions:** Off A96 4½ miles west of Forres and 24 miles east of Inverness.

Disabled Access:
Full

Opening Times:
Saturday 12 April
10:30am - 4:30pm
Sunday 13 April
10:30am - 4:30pm
both dates for daffodil tea day

Admission:
Garden tour £3.00 (including NTS members).
N.B. price correct at the time of going to print.

Charities:
Donation to SG Beneficiaries.

## BRUNTLANDS BUNGALOW

Alves, Elgin IV30 8UZ
**Mitch and Colin Buss T: 07999 817715**
**E: buss.shelter@virgin.net http://in-the-buss-shelter.webs.com**

Newly landscaped garden, with further landscaping to be added, features a circular pagoda as a centrepiece and gives definition to the raised beds and curving paths, in what is, essentially a rural cottage style planting, and planted with exuberance! Huge collection of daylilies compliment choice plants for seasonal interest, colour and impact.
The owners have transformed a dull, lifeless, uninteresting flat area within 8 months, into an exciting, lively, imaginatively designed space, full of motion and vibrancy.

**Other Details:** Teas on request, well stocked plant stall.

**Directions:** A96, Alves, turn into road next to Crooked Inn, Burghead Road. Go 1½ miles, passing cemetery and over crossroads, passing Bruntlands Farm on the right, slow down to turn left into drive (next to track) with big wooden gate and low white wall along roadside.

Disabled Access:
None

Opening Times:
By arrangement
1 May - 30 September

Admission:
£3.00, children not admitted

Charities:
Macmillan Nurses, Raigmore Hospital receives 40%, the net remaining to SG Beneficiaries.

## CARESTOWN STEADING

Deskford, Buckie AB56 5TR
**Tom and Cherie Timney-Gunn T: 01542 841245**
**E: cherietg@sky.com**

The Garden History Society in Scotland paid this garden the best compliment in describing it a "garden history in the making". It was started in 1990 and has received press, TV and web accolades ever since. Every year a new addition is made, the latest, the epitome of the modern vegetable plot which is proving very successful, 4 year rotation, raised beds, seeping irrigation. The "pearl" of the garden, the courtyard with knot beds and topiary is now fully mature.

**Other Details:** Toilet facilities available. Parking in the field next to the house. Teas will be served in the Garden Room.

**Directions:** East of B9018 Cullen/Keith (Cullen 3 miles, Keith 9½ miles). Follow SG signs towards Milton and Carestown.

Disabled Access:
Partial

Opening Times:
Saturday 14 June
10:00am - 4:00pm

Admission:
£4.00

Charities:
Scottish Autism receives 40%, the net remaining to SG Beneficiaries.

## CASTLEVIEW (WITH GLENRINNES LODGE)

Auchindoun, Dufftown AB55 4DY
**Mr and Mrs Ian Sharp T: 01340 820941**
**E: castleview10@hotmail.com**

A small secluded riverside garden, created on 3 levels from scrub land by 2 enthusiastic beginners in 2005. The garden consists of 2 interconnected ponds, 1 formal, 1 natural and an abundance of herbaceous plants and shrubs. There are several sitting areas where you can admire the garden from many viewpoints.

**Directions:** From Dufftown on the A920, travel approximately 3 miles towards Huntly. Drive until a small cluster of houses is reached, garden on the left is approximately 20 yards off the main road.

Disabled Access:
None

Opening Times:
Sunday 3 August
2:00pm - 5:00pm

Admission:
£3:00
or £6:00 for both Castle View and Glenrinnes

Charities:
All proceeds to SG Beneficiaries.

## CUDDY'S WELL

Clephanton, Inverness IV2 7QS
**Jim and Jacque Smith T: 01667 493639**
**E: jimjacq1@btinternet.com**

A relatively young family-friendly garden (started in 2005) designed to blend in with the surrounding rural woodland setting and to provide colour and interest throughout the year. There are colourful mixed herbaceous borders enclosing lawns, with ponds, rockeries and a herb garden to provide interest. A raised terrace contains productive rotational vegetable plots, a fruit garden and a well-stocked polytunnel.

**Other Details:** Families and children welcome.

**Directions:** From the A96 Inverness-Nairn road take the B9090 road south towards Cawdor. Clephanton is 1 mile up the hill. Cuddy's Well is the last house on the left going towards Cawdor.

Disabled Access:
Partial

Opening Times:
Saturday 28 June
12:30pm - 8:30pm
Sunday 29 June
12:30pm - 8:30pm

Admission:
£3.00, children free

Charities:
Save the Children receives 20%, Raigmore Renal Unit receives 20%, the net remaining to SG Beneficiaries.

## GLENRINNES LODGE (WITH CASTLEVIEW)

Dufftown, Keith, Banffshire AB55 4BS
**Mrs Kathleen Locke T: 01340 820384**
**www.glenrinnes.com**

The garden and policies surrounding Glenrinnes Lodge are typical of a Victorian Lodge. There is a formal garden which lends itself to quiet reflection and views up the glen. A large walled garden with a large heated greenhouse both of which supply plants, cut flowers and fruit and vegetables. In addition, there is a lovely walk around the pond or along the woodland "azalea walk". There are lovely views of the surrounding countryside from all areas. Some major works have been undertaken recently so much of the garden is still a "work in progress". In keeping with the rest of the estate, Glenrinnes Lodge is gardened organically.

**Directions:** In the centre of Dufftown at the Clock Tower take the B9009 road to Tomintoul for about 1 mile. After passing Dufftown Golf Club on your right there is a lane to the left which leads to 2 stone pillars to Glenrinnes Lodge.

Disabled Access:
Partial

Opening Times:
Sunday 3 August
2:00pm - 5:00pm

Admission:
£4:00
or £6:00 for both Glenrinnes and Castle View, children free

Charities:
All proceeds to SG Beneficiaries.

## GORDONSTOUN

Duffus, near Elgin IV30 5RF
**Gordonstoun School T: 01343 837837**
**E: richardss@gordonstoun.org.uk www.gordonstoun.org.uk**

The gardens consist of good formal herbaceous borders around lawns, a terrace and an orchard.
The school grounds include Gordonstoun House, a Georgian House of 1775/6 incorporating an earlier 17th century house built for 1st Marquis of Huntly, and the school chapel, both of which will be open to visitors. There is also a unique circle of former farm buildings known as the Round Square and a scenic lake.

**Directions:** Entrance off B9012, 4 miles from Elgin at Duffus Village.

Disabled Access:
Full

Opening Times:
Sunday 7 September
2:00pm - 4:30pm

Admission:
£4.00, children £2.00

Charities:
All proceeds to SG Beneficiaries.

## NEWBOLD HOUSE (WITH 1 SANQUHAR DRIVE & 10 PILMUIR ROAD W)

111 St Leonards Road, Forres IV36 2RE
**Newbold Trust T: 01309 672659**
**E: office@newboldhouse.org www.newboldhouse.org**

The Newbold House Garden nestles within the structure of a late 19th century mansion and its now mature conifer plantings and glorious rhododendrons. It features a beautiful walled garden combining vegetables, fruit and flowers together with an original glasshouse. The main part of the garden contains a variety of herbaceous and annual plantings and is being consciously developed as a wildlife friendly space. To this end, a butterfly garden has been planted and parts of the lawns are being managed to increase their wild flower content. Apple trees are a particular feature with nearly a 100 trees of more than 30 varieties. The house is a listed building in recognition of the original conservatory by Mackenzie and Moncur and is planted with a variety of tender plants and fruit.

**Other Details:** 18 May: open for rhododendrons and apple blossom (Newbold House only)
13 July: joint opening with 1 Sanquhar Drive and 10 Pilmuir Road West.
Teas served in the Newbold House conservatory. Plant stalls at 1 Sanquhar Drive and 10 Pilmuir Road West.

**Directions:** From Forres High Street turn down Tolbooth Street. Take the 2nd exit on the roundabout onto St Leonard's Road. Continue past Leanchoil Hospital, Newbold House is on the left.

Disabled Access:
None

Opening Times:
Newbold House : Sunday 18 May 2:00pm - 6:00pm
Joint openings: Sunday 13 July 2:00pm - 6:00pm

Admission:
18 May: £3.00
13 July £5.00 (includes entry to all 3 gardens)

Charities:
The Newbold Trust receives 40%, the net remaining to SG Beneficiaries.

# PEEBLESSHIRE



## District Organiser

| | |
|---|---|
| Mrs Mary Carrel | 14 Leeburn View, Cardrona, Peebles EH45 9LS |

## Area Organisers

| | |
|---|---|
| Mr J Bracken | Gowan Lea, Croft Road, West Linton EH46 7DZ |
| Mr Graham Buchanan-Dunlop | The Potting Shed, Broughton Pl, Broughton ML12 6HJ |
| Mr Mathew Godfrey-Faussett | Tor Hill House, Wester Happrew, Peebles EH45 8PU |
| Ms R Hume | Llolans, Broughton ML12 6HJ |
| Mrs R Parrott | An Sparr, Medwyn Road, West Linton EH46 7HA |
| Mr K St C Cunningham | Hallmanor, Peebles, Tweeddale EH45 9JN |
| Mr Brian Taylor | 5 Fawnburn Crescent, Cardrona EH45 9LG |

## Treasurer

| | |
|---|---|
| Mr J Birchall | The Old Manse, Drumelzier, Biggar ML12 6JD |

## Gardens open on a specific date

| | | |
|---|---|---|
| Kailzie Gardens, Peebles | Sunday 2 March | 2:00pm - 4:00pm |
| Haystoun, Peebles | Sunday 25 May | 1:30pm - 5:00pm |
| Portmore, Eddleston | Wednesday 2 July | 10:00am - 4:00pm |
| Portmore, Eddleston | Wednesday 9 July | 10:00am - 4:00pm |
| Drumelzier Old Manse, Drumelzier | Sunday 13 July | 2:00pm - 5:00pm |
| Portmore, Eddleston | Wednesday 16 July | 10:00am - 4:00pm |
| 8 Halmyre Mains, West Linton | Sunday 20 July | 2:00pm - 5:00pm |
| Portmore, Eddleston | Wednesday 23 July | 10:00am - 4:00pm |
| Portmore, Eddleston | Wednesday 30 July | 10:00am - 4:00pm |
| Glen House, Innerleithen | Sunday 3 August | 1:30pm - 5:00pm |
| Portmore, Eddleston | Wednesday 6 August | 10:00am - 4:00pm |
| West Linton Village Gardens | Sunday 10 August | 2:00pm - 5:00pm |
| Portmore, Eddleston | Wednesday 13 August | 10:00am - 4:00pm |
| Portmore, Eddleston | Wednesday 20 August | 10:00am - 4:00pm |
| Portmore, Eddleston | Wednesday 27 August | 10:00am - 4:00pm |
| Dawyck Botanic Garden, Stobo | Sunday 5 October | 10:00am - 5:00pm |

## Gardens open regularly

| | | | | |
|---|---|---|---|---|
| Dawyck Botanic Garden, Stobo | 1 April - 30 September | 10:00am | - | 6:00pm |
| | February and November | 10:00am | - | 4:00pm |
| | March and October | 10:00am | - | 5:00pm |
| Kailzie Gardens, Peebles | 1 January - 24 March | Dawn | - | Dusk |
| | 25 March - 31 October | 11:00am | - | 5:00pm |
| | 1 November - 31 December | Dawn | - | Dusk |

## Gardens open by arrangement

| | | |
|---|---|---|
| Portmore, Eddleston | 1 June - 30 September | 07825 294388 |
| Stobo Japanese Water Garden, Stobo | 1 May - 31 October | 01721 760245 |

Haystoun, Peeblesshire

## Key to symbols

 New in 2014

 Teas

 Cream teas

 Homemade teas

 Dogs on a lead allowed

 Wheelchair access

 Accommodation

 Plant stall

 Scottish Snowdrop Festival

## Garden locations

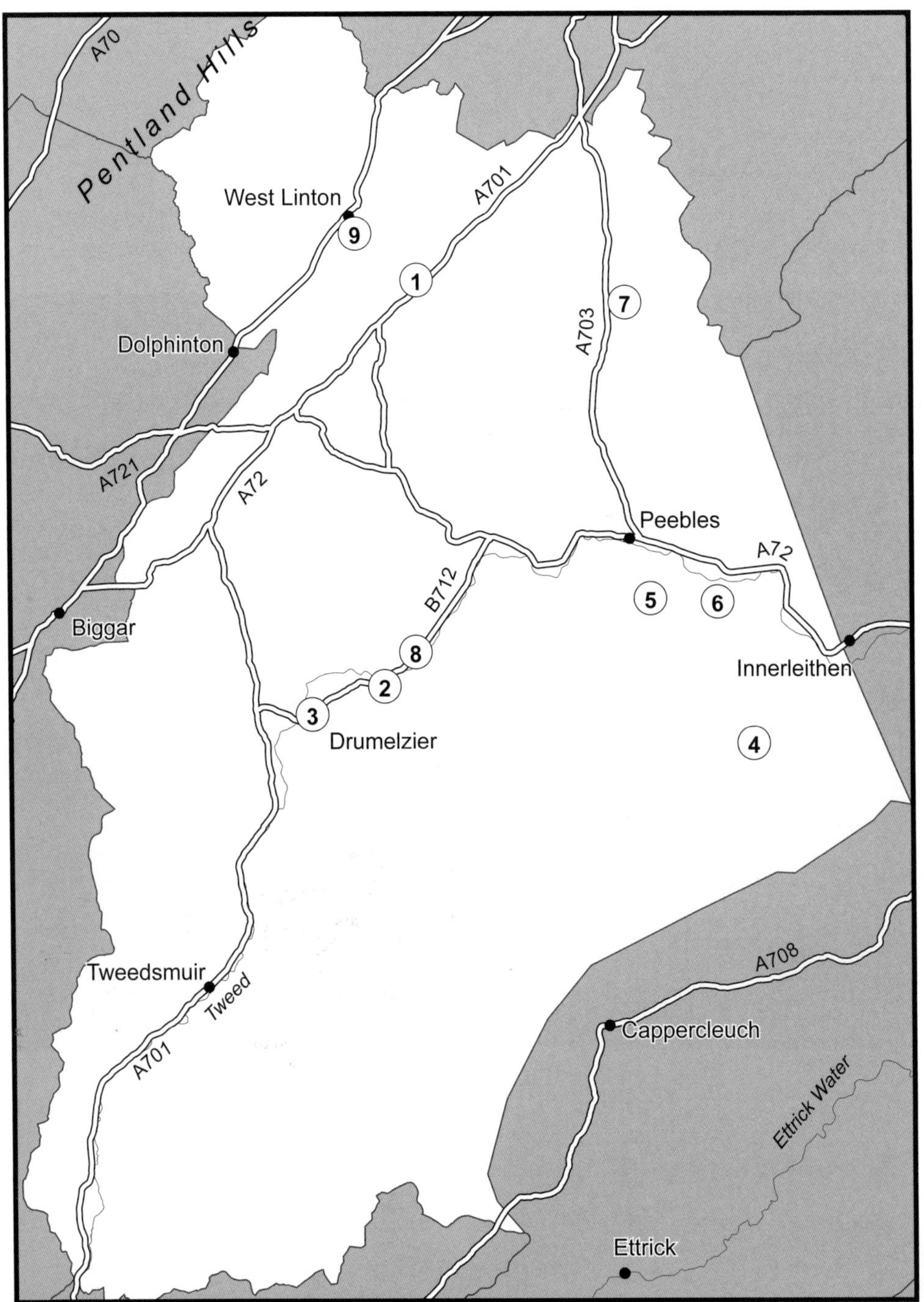

## 8 HALMYRE MAINS

West Linton, Borders EH46 7BX
**Joyce Andrews and Mike Madden T: 07774 609 547**
**E: romanno@btinternet.com**

Half-acre organic garden, formal beds, large pond, vegetable plot, greenhouse, keder house, gazebo and polytunnel, 25 foot pergola to large composting area. Further developments since last year.

**Other Details:** Teas will be provided in The Hub at Lamancha.

**Directions:** Five miles South of Leadburn Junction on the A701 (Moffat). Signposted Newlands Hall.

Disabled Access:
Full

Opening Times:
Sunday 20 July
2:00pm - 5:00pm

Admission:
£4.00, children free

Charities:
Whitmuir Project receives 40%, the net remaining to SG Beneficiaries.

## DAWYCK BOTANIC GARDEN

Stobo EH45 9JU
**Royal Botanic Gardens Edinburgh T: 01721 760 254**
**www.rbge.org.uk/dawyck**

Stunning collection of rare trees and shrubs. With over 300 years of tree planting, Dawyck is a world famous arboretum with mature specimens of Chinese conifers, Japanese maples, Brewer's spruce, the unique Dawyck beech and Sequoiadendrons from North America which are over 45 metres tall. Bold herbaceous plantings run along the burn. Range of trails and walks. Fabulous autumn colours.

**Other Details:** National Plant Collection®: Larix and Tsuga.
Open for the Snowdrop Festival 1 February - 16 March.
Autumn magic guided walk on 5 October at 2:00pm, costs £3.50 plus admission charge (Please book with Dawyck Botanics).
Homemade teas and interesting lunches are available in our restaurant.
Sorry no dogs are allowed.

**Directions:** Eight miles south west of Peebles on B712.

Disabled Access:
Partial

Opening Times:
Sunday 5 Oct. 10:00am - 5:00pm for Scotland's Gardens
1 Feb - 31 Oct 10:00am - 6:00pm but closes Feb/Nov 4:00pm & Mar/Oct 5:00pm

Admission:
£6.00, conc. £5.00, under 16's free (prices include a donation to the Garden. Check our website for prices without donation).

Charities:
Donation to SG Beneficiaries.

## DRUMELZIER OLD MANSE

Drumelzier, Near Broughton, ML12 6JD
**Mr and Mrs Julian Birchall**

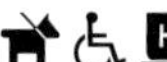

A traditional Manse garden in attractive Upper Tweed Valley. Colourful herbaceous border within walled garden. Unusual selection of plants throughout the garden including rare Meconopsis Hensol Violet. There is a rock border and kitchen garden. Wide variety of shrubs planted in the last 15 years in lower garden leading down to path along burn with primulas and hostas. Beautiful setting and surrounding walks.

**Directions:** It is on the B712, 10 miles west of Peebles. Broughton 2 miles.

Disabled Access:
Partial

Opening Times:
Sunday 13 July
2:00pm - 5:00pm

Admission:
£4.00, children free

Charities:
John Buchan Museum, Peebles receives 20%, Stobo and Drumelzier Church receives 20%, the net remaining to SG Beneficiaries.

## GLEN HOUSE

Glen Estate, Innerleithen EH44 6PX
**The Tennant Family T: 01896 830210**
**E: info@glenhouse.com www.glenhouse.com**

Surrounding the outstanding Scots Baronial mansion designed by David Bryce in the mid-19th century, Glen House gardens are laid out on a series of shallow terraces overhanging the glen itself, which offers one of the loveliest 'designed landscapes' in the Borders. The garden expands from the formal courtyard through a yew colonnade, and contains a fine range of trees, long herbaceous border and pool garden with pergola, all arranged within the curve of slopes sheltering the house.

**Directions:** Follow B709 out of Innerleithen for approx. 2½ miles. Right turn at signpost for Glen Estate.

Disabled Access:
Partial

Opening Times:
Sunday 3 August
1:30pm - 5:00pm

Admission:
£5.00, children free

Charities:
Global Cool Foundation receives 40%, the net remaining to SG Beneficiaries.

## HAYSTOUN

Peebles EH45 9JG
**Mrs David Coltman**

A 16th century house (not open) has a charming walled garden with an ancient yew tree, herbaceous beds and vegetable garden. There is a wonderful burnside walk, created since 1980, with azaleas, rhododendrons and primulas leading to a small ornamental loch (cleared in 1990), with stunning views up Glensax valley.

**Directions:** Cross River Tweed in Peebles to south bank and follow garden open sign for approximately 1 mile.

Disabled Access:
Partial

Opening Times:
Sunday 25 May
1:30pm - 5:00pm

Admission:
£5.00, children free

Charities:
St Columba's Hospice receives 40%, the net remaining to SG Beneficiaries.

## KAILZIE GARDENS

Peebles EH45 9HT
**Lady Buchan-Hepburn T: 01721 720007**
**E: angela.buchanhepburn@btinternet.com www.infokailziegardens.com**

Semi-formal walled garden with shrubs and herbaceous borders, rose garden, well stocked Victorian greenhouses, chicken village, including rare poultry breeds. Woodland and burnside walks amongst spring bulbs, rhododendrons and azaleas. The garden is set among fine old trees including an old larch planted in 1725. Osprey watch with live CCTV recordings of Ospreys nesting in the recently extended nature centre. Kailzie has been featured on Landward and the Beechgrove Garden.

**Other Details:** There is a restaurant and tearoom open throughout the year.
**1 Jan - 24 Mar**: for wild garden & woodland walks (Snowdrop Festival 1 Feb-16 Mar).
**25 Mar - 31 Oct**: for walled, wild gardens and woodland walks.
**1 Nov - 31 Dec**: for wild garden and woodland walk.
Admission shows adult prices only for concessions, children and groups see website.

**Directions:** 2½ miles on B7062 east of Peebles.

Disabled Access:
Partial

Opening Times:
Sunday 2 March 2:00pm - 4:00pm, 1 Jan - 24 Mar and 1 Nov - 31 Dec Dawn - Dusk 25 Mar - 31 Oct 11:00am - 5:00pm

Admission:
**1 Nov - 14 Mar:** £2.50
**15 Mar - 31 May:** £3.50
**1 Jun - 31 Oct:** £4.50

Charities:
Erskine Hospital receives 40%, the net remaining to SG Beneficiaries.

## PORTMORE

Eddleston EH45 8QU

**Mr and Mrs David Reid T: 07825 294388**

Lovingly created by current owners over the past 20 years the gardens surrounding the David Bryce mansion house contain mature trees and offer fine views of the surrounding countryside. Large walled garden with box-edged herbaceous borders planted in stunning colour harmonies, potager, rose garden, pleached lime walk and ornamental fruit cages. The Victorian glasshouses contain fruit trees, roses, geraniums, pelargoniums and a wide variety of tender plants. Italianate grotto. Water garden with shrubs and meconopsis and woodland walks lined with rhododendrons, azaleas and shrub roses. Starred in "Good Gardens Guide".

**Other Details:** Cream teas for groups by prior arrangement. DIY refreshments on Wednesday openings July - August.

**Directions:** Off A703 1 mile north of Eddleston. Bus no.62.

Disabled Access:
Partial

Opening Times:
Wednesdays:
2, 9, 16, 23 & 30 July and
6, 13,20,27 August
10:00am - 4:00pm
Also by arrangement 1 June - 30 September for groups.

Admission:
£5.00

Charities:
Tweeddale Youth Action receives 40%, the net remaining to SG Beneficiaries.

## STOBO JAPANESE WATER GARDEN

Home Farm, Stobo EH45 8NX

**Hugh and Charles Seymour T: 01721 760245**

**E: hugh.seymour@btinternet.com**

The Stobo Japanese Water Garden has just had its 100th birthday! Magnificent trees dominate the garden and, along with some of the shrubs, provide vibrant autumn colours, especially the cercidiphyllum and acers. The rhododendrons and azaleas are the main feature in early summer, once the bank of primroses and wood anenomes have faded. The Japanese artefacts, such as lanterns, a tea house, oriental style bridges, stepping stones, a large cascading waterfall and many smaller rills, make up the Japanese style of this tranquil woodland garden.

**Other Details:** Teas, coffee, lunches available on request. B&B at Home Farm. Please wear appropriate footwear.

**Directions:** Seven miles west of Peebles on the B712. 1½ miles from Dawyck Botanical Garden.

Disabled Access:
Partial

Opening Times:
By arrangement
1 May - 31 October

Admission:
£5.00, children free

Charities:
Donation to SG Beneficiaries.

## WEST LINTON VILLAGE GARDENS

West Linton EH46 7EL

**West Linton Village Gardeners**

At least 4 gardens will be opening this year, of which 2 are in the main part of the village and 2 at a higher altitude near the golf course! One of the gardens will be opening for the first time in many years, featuring a fine selection of roses. Another being an eco-friendly garden using novel techniques; the others are more traditional gardens enjoying fine borrowed views.

**Other Details:** Teas served in the village hall.

**Directions:** A701 or A702 and follow signs.

Disabled Access:
Partial

Opening Times:
Sunday 10 August
2:00pm - 5:00pm

Admission:
£4.00

Charities:
The Ben Walton Trust receives 40%, the net remaining to SG Beneficiaries.

# PERTH & KINROSS



## District Organisers

| | |
|---|---|
| Mrs Miranda Landale | Clathic House, By Crieff PH7 4JY |
| Mrs Judy Nichol | Rossie House, Forgandenny PH2 9EH |

## Area Organisers

| | |
|---|---|
| Mrs Sonia Dunphie | Wester Cloquhat, Bridge of Cally, Perthshire PH10 7JP |
| Mrs Margaret Gimblett | Croftcat Lodge, Grandtully PH15 2QS |
| Miss Henrietta Harland | Easter Carmichael Cottage, Forgandenny Road, Bridge of Earn PH2 9EZ |
| Mrs Tim Holcroft | Glenbeich, Lochearnhead FK19 8PZ |
| Mrs Celia Innes | Kilspindie Manse, Kilspindie PH2 7RX |
| Lady Lavinia Macdonald Lockhart | Thornton Hill, Fossoway, Kinross KY13 7PB |
| Mrs Lizzie Montgomery | Burleigh House, Milnathort, Kinross KY13 7PB |
| Miss Judy Norwell | Dura Den, 20 Pitcullen Terrace, Perth PH2 7EG |
| Miss Bumble Ogilvy Wedderburn | Garden Cottage, Lude, Blair Atholl PH18 5TR |

## Treasurer

| | |
|---|---|
| Mr Michael Tinson | Parkhead Hse, Parkhead Gdns, Burghmuir Rd PH1 1JF |

## Gardens open on a specific date

| | | | | |
|---|---|---|---|---|
| Kilgraston School, Bridge of Earn | Sunday 23 February | 2:00pm | - | 4:30pm |
| Rossie House, Forgandenny | Thursday 6 March | 2:00pm | - | 5:00pm |
| Rossie House, Forgandenny | Thursday 10 April | 2:00pm | - | 5:00pm |
| Megginch Castle, Errol | Sunday 13 April | 2:00pm | - | 5:00pm |
| Rossie House, Forgandenny | Thursday 1 May | 2:00pm | - | 5:00pm |
| Branklyn Garden, Perth | Sunday 4 May | 10:00am | - | 4:00pm |
| Hollytree Lodge, Dollar | Sunday 11 May | 2:00pm | - | 5:00pm |
| Rossie House, Forgandenny | Thursday 15 May | 2:00pm | - | 5:00pm |
| Briglands House, Rumbling Bridge | Sunday 18 May | 2:00pm | - | 5:00pm |
| Wester House of Ross, Comrie | Sat/Sun 24 & 25 May | 1:30pm | - | 4:30pm |
| Rossie House, Forgandenny | Thursday 29 May | 2:00pm | - | 5:00pm |
| Pitcurran House, Abernethy | Sunday 1 June | 2:00pm | - | 6:00pm |
| Tullichettle, Comrie | Wednesday 4 June | 11:00am | - | 4:00pm |
| Blair Castle Gardens, Blair Atholl | Saturday 7 June | 9:30am | - | 5:30pm |
| Explorers Garden, Pitlochry | Sunday 8 June | 10:00am | - | 5:00pm |
| Tullichettle, Comrie | Wednesday 11 June | 11:00am | - | 4:00pm |

| | | |
|---|---|---|
| The Old Manse, Caputh | Sunday 15 June | 2:00pm - 5:00pm |
| Tullichettle, Comrie | Wednesday 18 June | 11:00am - 4:00pm |
| Bonhard Garden, Perth | Sunday 22 June | 10:00am - 4:00pm |
| Carig Dhubh, Bonskeid | Sunday 22 June | 2:00pm - 5:30pm |
| Hollytree Lodge, School Road, Muckhart | Sunday 22 June | 2:00pm - 5:00pm |
| Tullichettle, Comrie | Wednesday 25 June | 11:00am - 4:00pm |
| The Bield at Blackruthven, Tibbermore | Saturday 28 June | 2:00pm - 5:00pm |
| Cloichfoldich, Strathtay | Sunday 29 June | 2:00pm - 5:00pm |
| Pitnacree House, Ballinluig | Sunday 29 June | 2:00pm - 5:00pm |
| Wester Cloquhat , Bridge of Cally | Saturday 12 July | 2:00pm - 5:00pm |
| Auchleeks House, Calvine | Sunday 20 July | 2:00pm - 5:30pm |
| Croftcat Lodge, Grandtully | Sunday 27 July | 11:00am - 5:00pm |
| Kincarrathie House, Perth | Sunday 27 July | 10:00am - 4:30pm |
| Drummond Castle Gardens, Crieff | Sunday 3 August | 1:00pm - 5:00pm |
| The Walled Garden, Perth | Sunday 3 August | 11:00am - 5:00pm |
| Mill of Fyall Cottage, Alyth | Sunday 31 August | 10:30am - 5:00pm |

## Gardens open regularly

| | | |
|---|---|---|
| Ardvorlich, Lochearnhead | 1 May - 1 June | 9:00am - Dusk |
| Blair Castle Gardens, Blair Atholl | 1 April - 31 October | 9:30am - 5:30pm |
| Bolfracks, Aberfeldy | 1 April - 31 October | 10:00am - 6:00pm |
| Braco Castle, Braco | 1 March - 31 October | 10:00am - 5:00pm |
| Cluny House, Aberfeldy | 1 Jan - 15 Mar & Nov/Dec<br>16 March - 31 October | 10:00am - 4:00pm<br>10:00am - 6:00pm |
| Dowhill, Cleish | 1 May - 31 May | 12:00pm - 4:00pm |
| Drummond Castle Gardens, Crieff | 1 May - 31 October | 1:00pm - 6:00pm |
| Glenbeich, Lochearnhead | 21 July - 3 August | 2:00pm - 5:30pm |
| Glenericht House, Blairgowrie | 1 January - 31 December | 9:00am - 7:00pm |
| Glendoick, by Perth | 1 April - 31 May weekdays:<br>weekends: | 10:00am - 4:00pm<br>2:00pm - 5:00pm |

## Gardens open by arrangement

| | | |
|---|---|---|
| Briglands House, Rumbling Bridge | 1 March - 30 June &<br>1 October - 31 December | 01577 840205 |
| Carig Dhubh, Bonskeid | 15 May - 15 October | 01796 473469 |
| Croftcat Lodge, Grandtully | 15 May - 15 October | 01887 840288 |
| Easter Meikle Fardle, Meikleour | 1 January - 31 December | 01738 710330 |
| Little Tombuie, Killiechassie, Aberfeldy | 15 May - 15 October | sallycrystal@gmail.com |
| Parkhead House, Perth | 1 June - 31 August | 01738 625983 |

## Key to symbols

 New in 2014

 Homemade teas

 Accommodation

 Teas

 Dogs on a lead allowed

 Plant stall

Cream teas

 Wheelchair access

 Scottish Snowdrop Festival

## Garden locations

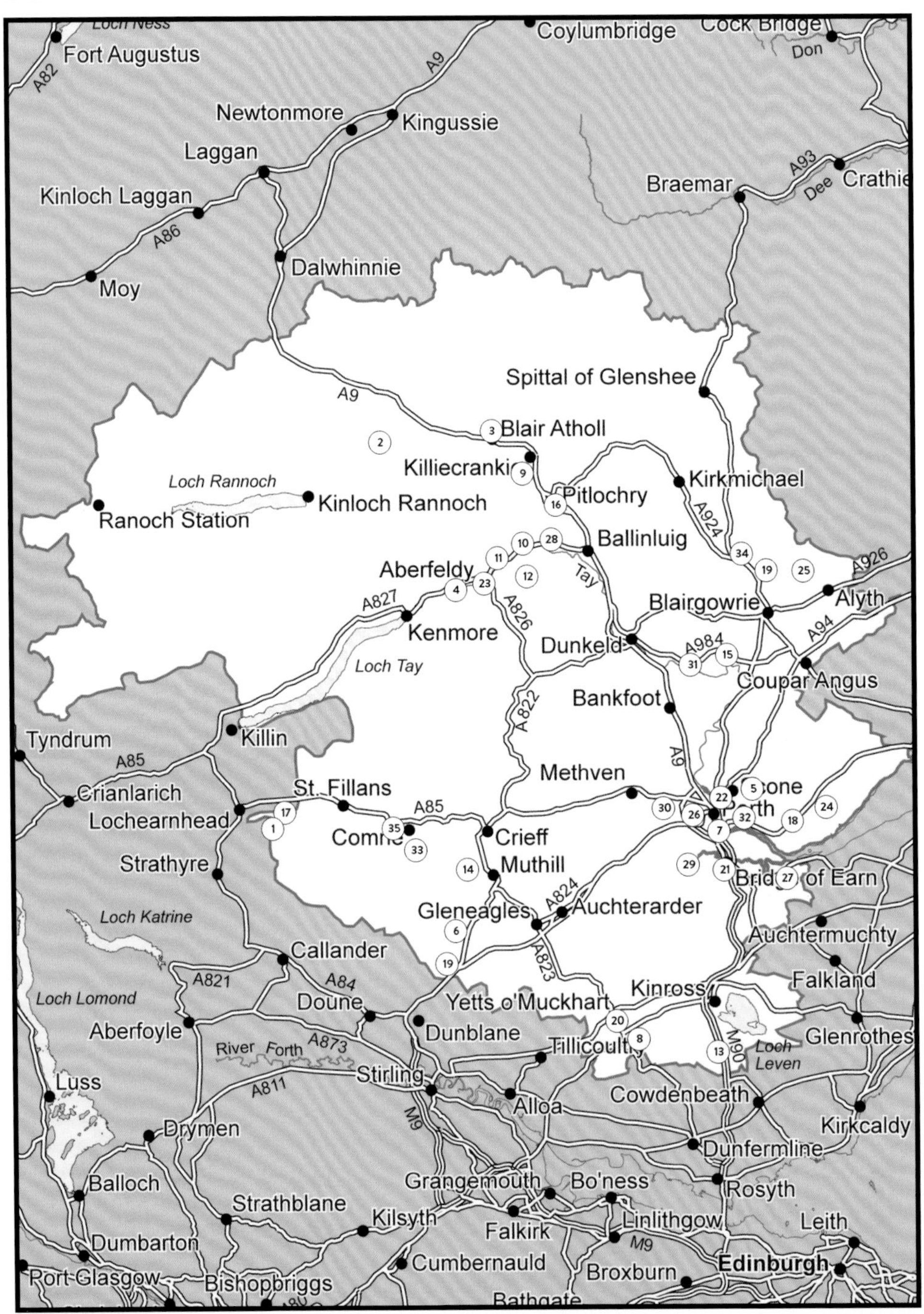

## ARDVORLICH

Lochearnhead FK19 8QE
**Mr and Mrs Sandy Stewart**

Beautiful hill garden featuring over 300 different species and hybrid rhododendrons, grown in a glorious setting of oaks and birches on either side of the Ardvorlich Burn. Quite steep in places. Boots advisable.

**Directions:** On South Loch Earn Road 3 miles from Lochearnhead, 5 miles from St Fillans.

Disabled Access:
None

Opening Times:
1 May - 1 June
9:00am - Dusk

Admission:
£4.00

Charities:
The Ghurka Welfare Trust receives 40%, the net remaining to SG Beneficiaries.

## AUCHLEEKS HOUSE

Calvine PH18 5UF
**Mr and Mrs Angus MacDonald**

On the south facing slopes of Glen Errochty nestles a fine Georgian House which looks down the glen and into the stunning walled garden. There is everything imaginable contained within the walls. Cleverly planted and constantly rejuvenated, this beautiful garden holds its history while new introductions have augmented all the trees and shrubs you could hope to see. The wow factor is the avenue of herbaceous borders tiered to perfection. Take a while to stand above the wall and look down onto the garden and the glen to absorb this spectacle, then walk down the steps and meander along the paths passing espaliered fruit trees, long herbaceous boarders, a well and a burn with damp loving primulas, hostas and meconopsis, classic vegetable garden and appreciate all the plants and shrubs in their perfect place. This garden is the gem of the Glen.

**Directions:** North of Blair Atholl turn off A9 at Calvine. B847 towards Kinloch Rannoch, 5 miles on right.

Disabled Access:
None

Opening Times:
Sunday 20 July
2:00pm - 5:30pm

Admission:
£4.00

Charities:
The Ghurka Welfare Trust receives 40%, the net remaining to SG Beneficiaries.

## BLAIR CASTLE GARDENS

Blair Atholl PH18 5TL
**Blair Charitable Trust T: 01796 481207**
**E: office@blair-castle.co.uk www.blair-castle.co.uk**

Blair Castle stands as the focal point in a designed landscape of some 2,500 acres within a large and traditional estate. Hercules Garden is a walled enclosure of about 9 acres recently restored to its original 18th century form with landscaped ponds, a Chinese bridge, plantings, vegetables and an orchard of more than one hundred fruit trees. The glory of this garden in summer is the herbaceous borders which run along the 275 metre south facing wall. A delightful sculpture trail incorporates contemporary and 18th century sculpture as well as 8 new works, letter-carving on stone from the Memorial Arts Charity's Art and Memory Collection. Diana's Grove is a magnificent stand of tall trees including Grand Fir, Douglas Fir, Larch and Wellingtonia in just two acres.

**Directions:** Off A9, follow signs to Blair Castle, Blair Atholl.

Disabled Access:
Partial

Opening Times:
Saturday 7 June
9:30am - 5:30pm
Charity Day
1 April - 31 October
9:30am - 5:30pm

Admission:
£5.45, children £2.50

Charities:
Donation to SG Beneficiaries.

## BOLFRACKS

Aberfeldy PH15 2EX

**The Douglas Hutchison Trust T: 01887 820344**

**E: athel@bolfracks.com www.bolfracks.com**

Special 3 acre garden with wonderful views overlooking the Tay Valley. Burn garden with rhododendrons, azaleas, primulas, meconopsis in woodland garden setting. Walled garden with shrubs, herbaceous borders, rose rooms with old fashioned roses. Rose and clematis walk. Peony beds underplanted with tulips and Japanese anemone. Great selection of bulbs in spring and good autumn colour. Slippery paths in wet weather.

**Other Details:** Refreshments available for groups by prior arrangement.

**Directions:** Two miles west of Aberfeldy on A827. White gates and Lodge on left. Brown tourist signs.

Disabled Access:
None

Opening Times:
1 April - 31 October
10:00am - 6:00pm

Admission:
£4.50, children under 16 free

Charities:
Donation to SG Beneficiaries..

## BONHARD GARDEN

Perth PH2 7PQ

**Stephen and Charlotte Hay T: 01738 552471**

A marvellous traditional 19th century garden of 5 acres with mature trees, lawns, rhododendrons, azaleas, herbaceous borders, ponds and an oak drive lined with primulas and daffodils. There is also a kitchen garden, Pinetum and wooded area.

**Other Details:** Teas and coffee available from adjacent Bonhard nursery leading to the arboretum. Sensible footwear should be worn.

**Directions: From Perth**: take A94 north to Scone. Turn right at sign to Murrayshall Hotel. Continue about 1 mile. House drive on right where road turns sharp left. **From Balbeggie**: take A94. Turn left signed for Bonhard 1 mile north of Scone and in ½ mile turn right. House drive on left where road turns sharp right shortly after Bonhard Nursery.

Disabled Access:
Partial

Opening Times:
Sunday 22 June
10:00am - 4:00pm

Admission:
£3.50

Charities:
Freedom from Fistula Foundation receives 40%, the net remaining to SG Beneficiaries.

## BRACO CASTLE

Braco FK15 9LA

**Mr and Mrs M van Ballegooijen T: 01786 880437**

A 19th c. landscaped garden with wonderful and interesting trees, shrubs, bulbs and plants. It is an old garden for all seasons that has been expanded over the last 26 years. The partly walled garden is approached on a rhododendron and tree lined path and features an ornamental pond with paths taking you to yet other special corners. Superb spring bulbs, shrub and herbaceous borders, and many ornamental trees are all enhanced by the spectacular views across the park to the Ochils.
From snowdrops through to vibrant autumn colour this garden is a gem. Look out for the Embothrium in June, Hoheria in August, Eucryphia in September and an interesting collection of rhododendrons and azaleas with long flowering season.

**Other Details:** Catering facilities are not available.

**Directions:** 1 to 1½ mile drive from gates at north end of Braco Village, just west of bridge on A822.

Disabled Access:
Partial

Opening Times:
1 March - 31 October
10:00am - 5:00pm
includes opening for the Snowdrop Festival
1 - 16 March

Admission:
£3.50

Charities:
The Woodland Trust receives 40%, the net remaining to SG Beneficiaries.

## BRANKLYN GARDEN

116 Dundee Road, Perth PH2 7BB
**The National Trust for Scotland T: 0844 493 2193**
**E: smcnamara@nts.org.uk www.nts.org.uk**

This attractive garden in Perth was once described as "the finest two acres of private garden in the country". It contains an outstanding collection of plants, particularly rhododendrons, alpine, herbaceous and peat-loving plants, which attract gardeners and botanists from all over the world. This is the perfect time to see the Meconopsis in their glory!

**Other Details:** National Plant Collection®: Cassiope, Lilium, Meconopsis and Rhododendron. Champion Trees: Pinus sylvestris 'Globosa.' Weather permitting, homemade scones will be served on the patio.

**Directions:** On A85 Perth/Dundee road.

Disabled Access:
Partial

Opening Times:
Sunday 4 May
10:00am - 4:00pm

Admission:
£6.50, family £16.50, concessions £5.00 (including NTS members).
N.B. Prices correct at the time of going to print.

Charities:
Donation to SG Beneficiaries.

## BRIGLANDS HOUSE

Rumbling Bridge KY13 0PS
**Mrs Briony Multon T: 01577 840205**
**E: briony@briglands.com**

Lovingly restored by the current owners over the past 35 years, the 9 acre, essentially spring garden was originally designed by Sir Robert Lorimer and surrounds the house, remodelled by him in 1898. There are glorious displays of bulbs, rhododendrons, young trees and shrubs, an historic lime walk, newly planted peony garden, topiary, rockery, and vegetable garden, plus good autumn colour.

**Other Details:** Plant stall with unusual alpines from alpine specialists, Rumbling Bridge Nurseries.

**Directions:** On A977 Kinross to Kincardine Bridge road, on the left just beyond Crook of Devon.

Disabled Access:
Partial

Opening Times:
Sunday 18 May
2:00pm - 5:00pm
Also by arrangement
1 March - 30 June and
1 October - 31 December

Admission:
£4.00

Charities:
Local Animal Rescue Charities will receive 40%, the net remaining to SG Beneficiaries.

## CARIG DHUBH

Bonskeid PH16 5NP
**Jane and Niall Graham-Campbell T: 01796 473469**
**E: niallgc@btinternet.com**

The garden is comprised of mixed shrubs and herbaceous plants with meconopsis and primulas. It extends to about one acre on the side of a hill with some steep paths and uneven ground. The soil is sand overlying rock - some of which projects through the surface. Beautiful surrounding country and hill views.

**Directions:** Take old A9 between Pitlochry and Killiecrankie, midway turn west on the Tummel Bridge Road B8019, ¾ mile on north side of the road.

Disabled Access:
None

Opening Times:
Sunday 22 June
2:00pm - 5:30pm
Also by arrangement
15 May - 15 October

Admission:
£3.50

Charities:
Tenandry Kirk receives 20%, Abbeyfield Society receives 20%, the net remaining to SG Beneficiaries.

## CLOICHFOLDICH (WITH PITNACREE HOUSE)

Strathtay PH9 0LP

**David and Squibbs Noble**

Even the long drive from the road to this garden is interesting. Look out for red squirrels and the giant Monkey Puzzle tree at the top with its big round cones in good years. This is a work in progress garden with new beds being made in front of the early 19th c. house and all the planting in the herbaceous border of the walled garden having been redesigned recently. Follow the path by the side of the house through a green shady garden with a waterfall and pass through a small gate into the walled garden. In addition to the new herbaceous border there is a fruit & vegetable garden and at the back of the walled garden a deep south facing border with roses, clematis, hydrangeas, agapanthus and shrubs chosen for all year round interest. There are wonderful views across the valley to the hills and forests beyond.

**Directions:** From A9 take A827 towards Aberfeldy. In the village of Grandtully, turn right and cross the river. At the T junction turn left and go through Strathtay Village. Cloichfoldich's drive is approx. 1 mile along on the right hand side immediately after a narrow bridge.

**Disabled Access:**
Partial

**Opening Times:**
Sunday 29 June
2:00pm - 5:00pm

**Admission:**
£5.00 (includes entry to both gardens)

**Charities:**
St. Andrews Episcopal Church, Strathtay receives 40%, the net remaining to SG Beneficiaries.

## CLUNY HOUSE

Aberfeldy PH15 2JT

**Mr J and Mrs W Mattingley T: 01887 820795**

**E: wmattingley@btinternet.com www.clunyhousegardens.com**

A wonderful, wild woodland garden overlooking the scenic Strathtay valley. Experience the grandeur of one of Britain's widest trees, the complex leaf variation of the Japanese maple, the beauty of the American trillium or the diversity of Asiatic primulas. A good display of snowdrops. Cluny's red squirrels are usually very easily seen. A treasure not to be missed.

**Other Details:** Plant seeds available for sale.

**Directions:** Three and a half miles from Aberfeldy on Weem to Strathtay Road.

**Disabled Access:**
Partial

**Opening Times:**
1 Jan - 15 Mar and Nov/Dec
10:00am - 4:00pm
16 March - 31 October
10:00am - 6:00pm

**Admission:**
2 February - 15 March: £4.00, children £1.00.
16 March - 31 October: £5.00, children £1.00.
Other dates free, but donations towards squirrel food welcome.

**Charities:**
Donation to SG Beneficiaries.

## CROFTCAT LODGE

Grandtully PH15 2QS

**Margaret and Iain Gimblett T: 01887 840288**

**E: iain@gimblettsmill.plus.com**

An oddly shaped one acre set on a windy, stoney hillside with spectacular views. There is a small walled garden with climbing plants, herbaceous beds and at its centre a mirror pool. Surrounding the house are lawns, an autumn/spring garden, small alpine and rock gardens, rose terraces, heathers, azaleas, clipped beehive laurels, a growing clematis collection and a Japanese water garden with pavilion. The garden has mainly gravel and grass paths. There are garden seats wherever you might like to rest or just sit and look nearby a beautiful bluebell walk. This is a garden for all seasons, created and cared for by its owners. It is welcoming, inspiring and well worth seeing especially if you would like to arrange a visit outwith the opening dates.

**Other Details:** Wheelchair access with help to most of the garden. Outside toilet.

**Directions:** From A9 take A827 signposted Aberfeldy. Through Grandtully village and 1 mile from traffic lights on bridge turn left by cream house set back from road. Croftcat is on left 300 yards up lane.

**Disabled Access:**
Partial

**Opening Times:**
Sunday 27 July
11:00am - 5:00pm
By arrangement
15 May - 15 October

**Admission:**
£4.00

**Charities:**
Chest Heart & Stroke, Scotland receives 40%, the net remaining to SG Beneficiaries.

## 13 DOWHILL

Cleish KY4 0HZ

**Mr and Mrs Colin Maitland Dougall**

A garden set off by the background of Benarty Hill and magnificent old trees. Lovely woodland walks to the ruins of Dowhill Castle. Nine linked ponds. Blue poppies and primulas together with temptingly placed seats make the garden a wonderful place for a picnic in fine weather.

**Directions:** ¾ mile off M90, exit 5, towards Crook of Devon on the B9097 in the trees.

Disabled Access:
None

Opening Times:
1 May - 31 May
12:00pm - 4:00pm

Admission:
£4.00

Charities:
Motor Neurone Disease receives 40%, the net remaining to SG Beneficiaries.

## 14 DRUMMOND CASTLE GARDENS

Crieff PH7 4HZ

**Grimsthorpe & Drummond Castle Trust Ltd**

**www.drummondcastlegardens.co.uk**

The Gardens of Drummond Castle were originally laid out in 1630 by John Drummond, 2nd Earl of Perth. In 1830 the Parterre was changed to an Italian style. One of the most interesting features is the multi-faceted sundial designed by John Mylne, Master Mason to Charles I. The formal garden is said to be one of the finest in Europe and is the largest of its type in Scotland.

**Other Details:** Teas on 3 August only.

**Directions:** Entrance 2 miles south of Crieff on Muthill road (A822).

Disabled Access:
Partial

Opening Times:
Sunday 3 August
1:00pm - 5:00pm
for Scotland's Gardens
1 May - 31 October
1:00pm - 6:00pm

Admission:
£4.00, OAPs £3.00, children £2.00

Charities:
British Limbless Ex-Servicemen's Association receives 40%, the net remaining to SG Beneficiaries.

## 15 EASTER MEIKLE FARDLE

Meikleour PH2 6EF

**Rear Admiral and Mrs John Mackenzie T: 01738 710330**

A delightful old-fashioned 2 acre garden. Herbaceous borders backed by soft sandstone walls or beech hedges. Small enclosed garden with raised beds. There is also a matured water garden and walks through mature woodland.

**Other Details:** Homemade lunches and light refreshments available on request. Groups preferred Monday to Friday, not weekends.

**Directions:** Take A984 Dunkeld to Coupar Angus 1½ miles, from Spittalfield towards Meikleour, third house on left after turning to Lethendy.

**Disabled Access:**
Partial

**Opening Times:**
By arrangement on request

**Admission:**
£4.00

**Charities:**
Seafarers UK receives 40%, the net remaining to SG Beneficiaries.

## 16 EXPLORERS GARDEN

Pitlochry PH16 5DR

**Pitlochry Festival Theatre**

**www.explorersgarden.com**

This 6 acre woodland garden, now 8 years old, is maturing nicely. More and more visitors are coming to see the wonders this four star VisitScotland attraction reveals: art and architecture, wildlife and birds, exotic plants, peat and rock gardens, extraordinary landscaping and magnificent views. Try the guided tours that reveal the stories of the Scottish Plant Hunters who risked their lives travelling the globe in search of new plants and trees. In this garden, which is divided into different parts of the world, you will see the plants they collected for cultivation, commerce and conservation.

**Directions:** A9 to Pitlochry town, follow signs to Pitlochry Festival Theatre.

**Disabled Access:**
Partial

**Opening Times:**
Sunday 8 June
10:00am - 5:00pm

**Admission:**
£4.00
Guided tour including entry
£5.00

**Charities:**
Acting for Others receives 40%, the net remaining to SG Beneficiaries.

## 17 GLENBEICH

Lochearnhead FK19 8PZ

**Mrs Tim Holcroft**

Two acre, contemporary, architectural, green garden in magnificent setting overlooking Loch Earn. Formal planting near the house. Topiary contrasting with grasses and an unusual selection of trees and perennials, giving way to more naturalistic planting along a burnside walk.

**Other Details:** Boots advisable. DIY tea/coffee available.

**Directions:** On A85, 1¾ miles east of Lochearnhead, 5 miles west of St Fillans.

**Disabled Access:**
None

**Opening Times:**
21 July - 3 August
2:00pm - 5:30pm

**Admission:**
£4.00

**Charities:**
The Falls of Dochart Retirement Home, Killin receives 40%, the net remaining to SG Beneficiaries.

## GLENDOICK

by Perth PH2 7NS
**Peter, Patricia, Kenneth and Jane Cox T: 01738 860205**
**E: orders@glendoick.com www.glendoick.com**

Glendoick was included in *The Independent on Sunday's* exclusive survey of Europe's top 50 gardens, boasts a unique collection of plants collected by three generations of Coxes from their plant-hunting expeditions in China and the Himalaya. You can see one of the finest collections of rhododendrons and azaleas, primulas, meconopsis, kalmias and Sorbus in our woodland garden, peat garden and nursery. Many of the Rhododendron and Azalea species and hybrids have been introduced from the wild or bred by the Cox family and the gardens boast a huge range of plants from as far afield as Chile, Tasmania and Tibet. Three new waterfall viewing platforms have been built in the woodland gardens. You can also take a glimpse into the fascinating world of hybridising in the walled garden where you'll find new as yet unnamed hybrids from the Glendoick breeding programme trial beds.

**Other Details:** National Plant Collection®: Rhododendron x 4. For group bookings contact Jane Cox by post at the above address or E: jane@glendoick.com. Refreshments for groups should be pre-booked. The woodland garden is not easily accessible to wheelchairs but some of the gardens by the house are. Disabled toilets at the garden centre only. Peter and Kenneth Cox have written numerous books on rhododendrons and gardens. Kenneth Cox's book *Scotland for Gardeners* describes 500 of Scotland's finest gardens.

**Directions:** Follow brown signs to Glendoick Garden Centre off A90 Perth - Dundee road. Gardens are ½ mile behind Garden Centre. After buying tickets at the garden centre please drive up and park at gardens (free parking).

© Ken Cox

Disabled Access:
None

Opening Times:
1 April - 31 May
weekdays: 10:00am - 4:00pm
weekends: 2:00pm - 5:00pm

Admission:
£5.00, school age children free
Tickets available from the garden centre.
A 32-page guidebook is available at £2.95.

Charities:
Donation to SG Beneficiaries.

## GLENERICHT HOUSE

Blairgowrie PH10 7JD
**Mr William McCosh T: 01250 872092**

Spectacular collection of Victorian planted trees and shrubs which are centred around a Grade 'A' listed suspension bridge (1846). 92 tree varieties, mostly conifers includng a Top Douglas Fir which is 171 ft. and still growing, also a collection of younger trees. In May you will be able to view the wonderful daffodils and the rhododendrons in flower.

**Directions:** Off A93, the Lodge House is 5 miles north of Blairgowrie on right hand side. Follow avenue to house.

**Disabled Access:**
Partial

**Opening Times:**
1 January - 31 December
9:00am - 7:00pm or dusk

**Admission:**
£4.00

**Charities:**
Seafarers UK receives 40%, the net remaining to SG Beneficiaries.

## HOLLYTREE LODGE

School Road, Muckhart, Dollar FK14 7JW
**Liz and Peter Wyatt**

A mature 1 acre garden divided into different areas: A collection of rhododendrons, azaleas and number of other unusual trees and shrubs. A wildlife pond, several areas of bulb planting in grass. A small Japanese garden and some unusual garden sculpture. Recent developments include a mini wildflower meadow and espaliered apples and pears.

**Other Details:** Small amount of disabled parking available at Hollytree Lodge, otherwise please park in the village.

**Directions:** Hollytree lodge is off the A91 down the small lane directly opposite the Inn at Muckhart.

**Disabled Access:**
Full

**Opening Times:**
Sunday 11 May
2:00pm - 5:00pm
Sunday 22 June
2:00pm - 5:00pm

**Admission:**
£4.00, teas £2.50

**Charities:**
RAF Benevolent Fund receives 20%, The Coronation Hall receives 20%, the net remaining to SG Beneficiaries.

## KILGRASTON SCHOOL

Bridge of Earn PH2 9BQ
**Kilgraston School T: 01738 815517**
**E: marketing@kilgraston.com www.kilgraston.com**

Set within the grounds of Kilgraston School, this is a wonderful opportunity to see the snowdrops whilst exploring the woodlands and surroundings of this very unique garden. Kilgraston has been a girls' boarding school since 1930. The house dates from the first decade of the 19th century and was the home of the Grant family. Impressive art sculptures (including work by Hew Lorimer) intermingle with ancient trees, snowdrops and even the resident red squirrels. Spend a Sunday afternoon wandering along wild woodland pathways and through the extensive grounds whilst taking in the surrounding winter landscape. There is also an opportunity to explore the chapel, main hall and artistic works within the school itself.

**Other Details:** Homemade teas available in the main hall.

**Directions:** Bridge of Earn is 3 miles South of Perth on the A912. Kilgraston School is signposted from the main road.

Disabled Access:
Partial

Opening Times:
Sunday 23 February
2:00pm - 4:30pm
for the Snowdrop Festival

Admission:
£4.00, children free

Charities:
Mary's Meals receives 40%, the net remaining to SG Beneficiaries.

## KINCARRATHIE HOUSE

Pitcullen Crescent, Perth PH2 7HX
**The Kincarrathie Trust T: 07402 215555**
**E: susan.eisner@sky.com**

Kincarrathie House was originally the home of the whisky baron and philanthropist A K Bell (1868-1942). It is now a beautiful private residential care home for 44 residents. The house sits in extensive grounds, which incorporates 6.5 acres of parkland, a woodland walk and a walled garden of about 1 acre comprising of herbaceous borders, a small orchard and four large vegetable plots providing seasonal produce for use within the home.

**Directions:** Located on the north east edge of Perth on the A94.
**From Perth**: follow A94 towards Coupar Angus/Scone and the entrance to the House is at the end of the row of guest houses.
**From North-East**: follow A94 towards Perth. The entrance to the House is on the road from Scone to Perth just before the built up area begins on that side. Turn right at Kincarrathie House sign.

Disabled Access:
Full

Opening Times:
Sunday 27 July
10:00am - 4:30pm

Admission:
£3.50

Charities:
The Kincarrathie Trust receives 40%, the net remaining to SG Beneficiaries.

## LITTLE TOMBUIE

Killiechassie, Aberfeldy PH15 2JS
**Mrs Sally Crystal**
**E: sallycrystal@gmail.com**

Perched high up, facing south on the hill overlooking Aberfeldy and the Tay, this is not a garden where everything is finished and perfect. But, if you want to meet a gardener who is diffidently very knowledgeable but warm and welcoming and see a garden which has huge potential, this is the garden for you. The views alone are worth the journey. Mrs. Crystal is not only a compost queen, but builder of dry stone walls, plantswoman and tree planter. Her raised bed vegetable garden would put most of us to shame. The older part of the garden is immaculate with emerald lawns, a wide selection of trees and shrubs and an interesting collection of old stone cheese presses. The newer part is still very much work in progress with a garden being carved out from the hill. In early summer, azaleas and meconopsis are flowering and the autumn colours are wonderful.

**Directions:** From A9 take A827 to Aberfeldy. At traffic lights turn right and take B846 crossing the river. Take 1st road on right to Strathtay. The drive to Tombuie is approx 2 miles along this road opposite a small graveyard on the right and beside a large copper beech tree.

Disabled Access:
Partial

Opening Times:
By arrangement
15 May - 15 October

Admission:
£3.00

Charities:
Cancer Research, UK receives 20%, Prostate Cancer, UK receives 20%, the net remaining to SG Beneficiaries.

## MEGGINCH CASTLE

Errol PH2 7SW

**Mr Giles Herdman and The Hon. Mrs Drummond-Herdman of Megginch**

Fifteenth century turreted castle (not open) with Gothic stable yard and pagoda dovecote. Nineteenth century formal front garden, topiary and ancient yews. Splendid array of daffodils and rhododendrons. There is also a double walled kitchen garden and orchard.

**Directions:** Approach from Dundee only, directly off A90, on south side of carriageway ½ mile on left after Errol flyover, between lodge gatehouses. Seven miles from Perth, 8 from Dundee.

Disabled Access:
Full

Opening Times:
Sunday 13 April
2:00pm - 5:00pm

Admission:
£4.00, children free

Charities:
All Saints Church, Glencarse receives 40%, the net remaining to SG Beneficiaries.

## MILL OF FYALL COTTAGE

Alyth, Blairgowrie PH11 8LB

**Gregg and Lisa Hector T: 01828 633422**
**E: gregg@fyallcottage.com**

Tucked above the Den of Alyth, the small Mill of Fyall Cottage garden is divided into many areas of interest. Colourful courtyard garden with herbaceous borders leading into a productive vegetable with cut flower borders and a quirky vintage greenhouse. Paddock area with interesting hedging, small orchard and wild flower areas. The Alyth Burn borders the garden with hens, ducks and geese free ranging just over the bridge.

**Other Details:** Artists studio in the garden with hand made textiles, ceramics and cards. Plant sale and homemade teas served all day.

**Directions:** Driving through Alyth, continue through the village past the Den of Alyth along tree lined road for approx 2.5 miles. Signposted “Primrose Hill Studio”, white cottage on left. Limited parking on roadside and in driveway.

Disabled Access:
Partial

Opening Times:
Sunday 31 August
10:30am - 5:00pm

Admission:
£3.00

Charities:
Army Benevolent Fund receives 40%, the net remaining to SG Beneficiaries.

## PARKHEAD HOUSE

Parkhead Gardens, Burghmuir Road, Perth PH1 1JF

**Mr & Mrs M.S. Tinson T: 01738 625983**
**E: maddy.tinson@gmail.com**

Parkhead is an old farmhouse sited within an acre of beautiful gardens. Mature trees include an outstanding 300 year old Spanish chestnut. This hidden gem is a garden for all seasons. Gentle terracing and meandering paths lead you past a large variety of unusual and interesting plants and shrubs. Holder of the National Collection of ‘Mylnefield Lilies’ originally developed by Dr Christopher North at the Scottish Horticultural Research Institute, Dundee.

**Other Details:** National Plant Collection®: Mylnefield Lilies, flower in July. Homemade teas by request. Plant stall when available.

**Directions:** Parkhead Gardens is a small lane off the west end of Burghmuir Road in Perth. More detailed directions on request.

Disabled Access:
Partial

Opening Times:
By arrangement
1 June - 31 August

Admission:
£3.50

Charities:
Plant Heritage receives 40%, the net remaining to SG Beneficiaries.

## PITCURRAN HOUSE

Abernethy PH2 9LH

**The Hon Ranald and Mrs Noel-Paton**

Ten year old garden with many interesting and unusual plants. Behind the house, semi-hardy Euphorbia mellifera, Melianthus major and Sophora davidii grow happily amongst cistus and hebes. The garden also includes many ericaceous shrubs, meconopsis, peonies, primulas and Smilacina racemosa. A rose pergola is covered in Blush Noisette, Felicite Perpetue and Paul's Himalayan Musk. A large west facing hydrangea border brightens up the late summer.

**Other Details:** Very good major plant stall.

**Directions:** SE of Perth. From M90 (exit 9) take A912 towards Glenfarg, go left at roundabout onto A913 to Abernethy.
Pitcurran House is at the far eastern end of the village.

Disabled Access:
Partial

Opening Times:
Sunday 1 June
2:00pm - 6:00pm

Admission:
£4.00, children free

Charities:
Juvenile Diabetes Research Foundation (JDRF) receives 40%, the net remaining to SG Beneficiaries.

## PITNACREE HOUSE (WITH CLOICHFOLDICH)

Pitnacree, Ballinluig, Pitlochry PH9 0LW

**Mrs Susan Sherriff**

Mature grounds surround an 18th c. house with fine views south over the Strathtay valley. To the back of the house is a large well maintained walled garden, the main feature of which is a long walk lined with herbaceous planting, roses and tree peonies. Arches and stone sundials draw the eye from one part of the garden to another. Running through the garden is a small burn edged with bog and marginal plants, while to one side of the garden is a formal vegetable parterre. This is a beautiful, peaceful garden, at its best in midsummer and made for slowly meandering through, enjoying the mixture of colours and scents and, on a sunny day, the play of light and shade on the paths.

**Other Details:** There is disabled access to most parts of the garden.

**Directions:** From The A9 take the A827 towards Aberfeldy. Look out for a sign to the right to the village of Strathtay. The entrance to Pitnacree is approximately ½ to ¾ mile along this narrow road on the right.

Disabled Access:
Partial

Opening Times:
Sunday 29 June 2:00pm - 5:00pm

Admission:
£5.00 (includes entry to Cloichfoldich

Charities:
St. Andrews Episcopal Church, Strathtay receives 40%, the net remaining to SG Beneficiaries.

## ROSSIE HOUSE

Forgandenny PH2 9EH

**Mr and Mrs David B Nichol T: 01738 812265**
**E: judynichol@rossiehouse.co.uk**

Rossie House was built by the Oliphant family in 1657. It is set in extensive woodland with burns running through the lower ground of an undulating terrain. Paths and bridges, seats and sculptures are there to explore. Snowdrops and aconites start the season giving way to abundant hellebores, scilla, chinadoxias, early rhododendron and Narcissi in April. May is alive with more rhododendron, blankets of bluebells, trillium, smilacina, solomon seal, rodgersia and when warmer the primula begin to flower on the wet banks by the water as the early Dipelta floribunda, deutzia and weigelia buds are bursting. The Davidia involucrata shows off its hankerchief bracts in competition with the old Cornus kousa chinensis.

**Other Details:** Teas available on 15 May and may also be available by prior request on other open days. 6 March open for the Snowdrop Festival.

**Directions:** Forgandenny is on the B935 between Bridge of Earn and Dunning.

Disabled Access:
Partial

Opening Times:
Thursdays: 6 March, 10 April, 1, 15 and 29 May
2:00pm - 5:00pm

Admission:
£4.00

Charities:
Sandpiper Trust receives 40%, the net remaining to SG Beneficiaries.

## THE BIELD AT BLACKRUTHVEN

Blackruthven House, Tibbermore, Perth PH1 1PY
**The Bield Christian Co. Ltd. T: 01738 583238**
**E: info@bieldatblackruthven.org.uk www.bieldatblackruthven.org.uk**

The Bield is set in extensive grounds comprising well maintained lawns and clipped hedges, a flower meadow and a large collection of specimen trees. Visitors are encouraged to stroll around the grounds and explore the labyrinth cut into the grass of the old orchard. The main garden is a traditional walled garden containing extensive herbaceous borders, manicured lawns and an organic vegetable plot. The walled garden also contains a wide variety of trained fruit trees, a fruit cage, glasshouse and a healing garden.

**Directions:** From Dundee or Edinburgh, follow signs for Glasgow, Stirling Crianlarich which lead onto the Perth bypass. Head west on the A85 signed to Crieff/Crianlarich to West Huntingtower. Turn left at the crossroads to Madderty/ Tibbermore. The entrance is on your left after ½ a mile and is marked by stone pillars and iron gates. Take a left up the tarmac road passing the gate lodge. Turn right to park at the Steading.

Disabled Access:
Full

Opening Times:
Saturday 28 June
2:00pm - 5:00pm

Admission:
£5.00 including refreshments

Charities:
Southton Smallholding receives 40%, the net remaining to SG Beneficiaries.

## THE OLD MANSE

Caputh PH1 4JQ
**Mr and Mrs Charles Arbuthnott**

Charming established garden with areas in the process of replanting. Small walled garden with vegetable potager and herbaceous borders and short camelia hedge. Rose terrace beside the early 18th century house and an old Glasgow Sharman's caravan in the policies. There is a walk down to the river through the fields with wonderful wild flowers along the river bank.

**Directions:** From south or north, follow A9 to Bankfoot, then sign to Murthly/ Caputh. In Caputh turn left to Dunkeld below the Church. Two hundred yards on left amongst trees.

Disabled Access:
Partial

Opening Times:
Sunday 15 June
2:00pm - 5:00pm

Admission:
£4.00

Charities:
The Caputh and Clunie Churches receives 40%, the net remaining to SG Beneficiaries.

## THE WALLED GARDEN

Muirhall Road, Perth PH2 7BH
**PKAVS Mental Wellbeing Services T: 01738 631777**
**www.pkavs.org.uk**

Set in a Victorian walled garden this therapeutic enterprise, supporting adults recovering from mental health issues, began in 1994. Incorporating a fine collection of fan, espalier and cordon-trained fruit trees, a productive vegetable garden, newly renovated herbaceous borders and surrounded by established box hedging. Herb garden which supplies the popular on-site cafe. Also available a gift shop stocking art and craft work and garden furniture produced by clients.

**Directions:** From M90/A90 exit at junction 11, take A85. Approx. 2 miles along Dundee Road turn right onto Back Wynd, right on to Lochie Brae and right to Muirhall Road. From North A93 or A94, at Main Street/West Bridge Street junction turn left onto Lochie Brae follow the road to the right, Muirhall Road. Enter through ornamental gates in central driveway. From city centre follow Dundee and Edinburgh M90 signs. Over West Bridge Street, at junction with Main Street, straight ahead to Lochie Brae and right to Muirhall Road. Enter through ornamental gates in central driveway.

Disabled Access:
Full

Opening Times:
Sunday 3 August
11:00am - 5:00pm

Admission:
£3.00, children free

Charities:
PKAVS Mental Wellbeing Services receives 40%, the net remaining to SG Beneficiaries.

## TULLICHETTLE

Comrie PH6 2HU

**Lady Jauncey**
**E: scjauncey@hotmail.co.uk**

This 1829 walled garden is surrounded by the magnificent Aberuchill hills forming an unusual peaceful setting. Featured on Beechgrove Garden in 2007.
Through the walled garden gate there are herbaceous borders filled with roses and shrubs and paths leading into new areas with distinctive characters including vegetables. Look out for roses Queen of Sweden Phyllis Bide, Crocus, FitzNobis, etc. with unusual and clever under planting. Two impressive and rare Wesselii trees stand in front of the house and large open lawns lead to grass parterres and on over a small burn to a newly made Mount. Continue through a young plantation of Acers, Silver Birch and Prunus trees and look for the grass labyrinth where you could have a meditative walk to connect to the great mystery and benevolence of life which this enchanting piece of land offers.

**Other Details:** Plants for sale when available. Grass paths for wheelchairs.

**Directions:** From Comrie, take road to Braco (B827). 1½ miles from centre of the village, just through the end of the speed limit, the drive to house is on the right.

Disabled Access:
Partial

Opening Times:
Wednesdays 4, 11, 18 and 25 June 11:00am - 4:00pm

Admission:
£4.00

Charities:
RNLI receives 40%, the net remaining to SG Beneficiaries.

## WESTER CLOQUHAT

Bridge of Cally PH10 7JP

**Brigadier and Mrs Christopher Dunphie**

Terraced garden, water garden, lawns, mixed borders with a wide range of shrubs, roses and hebaceous plants. Splendid situation with fine view to the river Ericht.

**Directions:** Turn off A93 just north of Bridge of Cally and follow signs for ½ mile.

Disabled Access:
None

Opening Times:
Saturday 12 July
2:00pm - 5:00pm

Admission:
£5.00

Charities:
ABF, The Soldiers' Charity receives 40%, the net remaining to SG Beneficiaries.

## WESTER HOUSE OF ROSS

Comrie PH6 2JS

**Mrs Sue Young**

Wester House of Ross is an inspiring and delightful 3 acre garden that has something to be seen all year round. It has been developed over the last 13 years by an enthusiastic plantswoman. The garden has many different areas to explore - partly woodland and partly herbaceous with meconopsis and 20 varieties of peonies. There is always something to delight.

**Other Details:** If plants are available, then there will be a plant stall. Weather permitting, the neighbour's passenger carrying miniature railway will be running on the open days.

**Directions:** On A85 drive through Comrie, past the White Church and at the end of the village take a left turn over a small bridge, signposted Ross. Then take first right, signposted Dalchonzie. After ¼ mile turn left at the two large dustbins and follow signs to parking and the garden.

Disabled Access:
None

Opening Times:
Saturday 24 May 1:30pm - 4:30pm
Sunday 25 May 1:30pm - 4:30pm

Admission:
£4.00, children free

Charities:
Maggie's Centres receives 40%, the net remaining to SG Beneficiaries.

# RENFREWSHIRE

Scotland's Gardens 2014 Guidebook is sponsored by **INVESTEC WEALTH & INVESTMENT**

## District Organisers

| | |
|---|---|
| Mrs Rosemary Leslie | High Mathernock Farm, Auchentiber Road, Kilmacolm PA13 4SP T: 01505 874032 |
| Mrs Alexandra MacMillan | Langside Farm, Kilmacolm, Inverclyde PA13 4SA T: 01475 540423 |

## Area Organisers

| | |
|---|---|
| Mrs Helen Hunter | 2 Bay Street, Fairlie, North Ayrshire KA29 0AL |
| Mrs B McLean | 49 Middlepenny Rd, Langbank, Inverclyde PA14 6XE |
| Mr J A Wardrop OBE DL | St Kevins, Victoria Road, Paisley PA2 9PT |

## Treasurer

| | |
|---|---|
| Mrs Jean Gillan | Bogriggs Cottage, Carlung, West Kilbride KA23 9PS |

## Gardens open on a specific date

| | | |
|---|---|---|
| Ardgowan, Inverkip | Sunday 16 February | 2:00pm - 5:00pm |
| Duchal, Kilmacolm | Sunday 18 May | 2:00pm - 5:00pm |
| Carruth, Bridge of Weir | Sunday 25 May | 2:00pm - 5:00pm |
| Newmills Cottage, Nr Lochwinnoch | Sunday 22 June | 2:00pm - 5:00pm |

## Plant sales

| | | |
|---|---|---|
| Kilmacolm Plant Sale, Kilmacolm | Saturday 19 April | 10:00am - 12:30pm |
| St Fillan's Episcopal Church Plant Sale, Kilmacolm | Saturday 13 September | 10:00am - 12:30pm |

## Key to symbols

 New in 2014

 Teas

 Cream teas

 Homemade teas

 Dogs on a lead allowed

 Wheelchair access

 Accommodation

 Plant stall

 Scottish Snowdrop Festival

## Garden locations

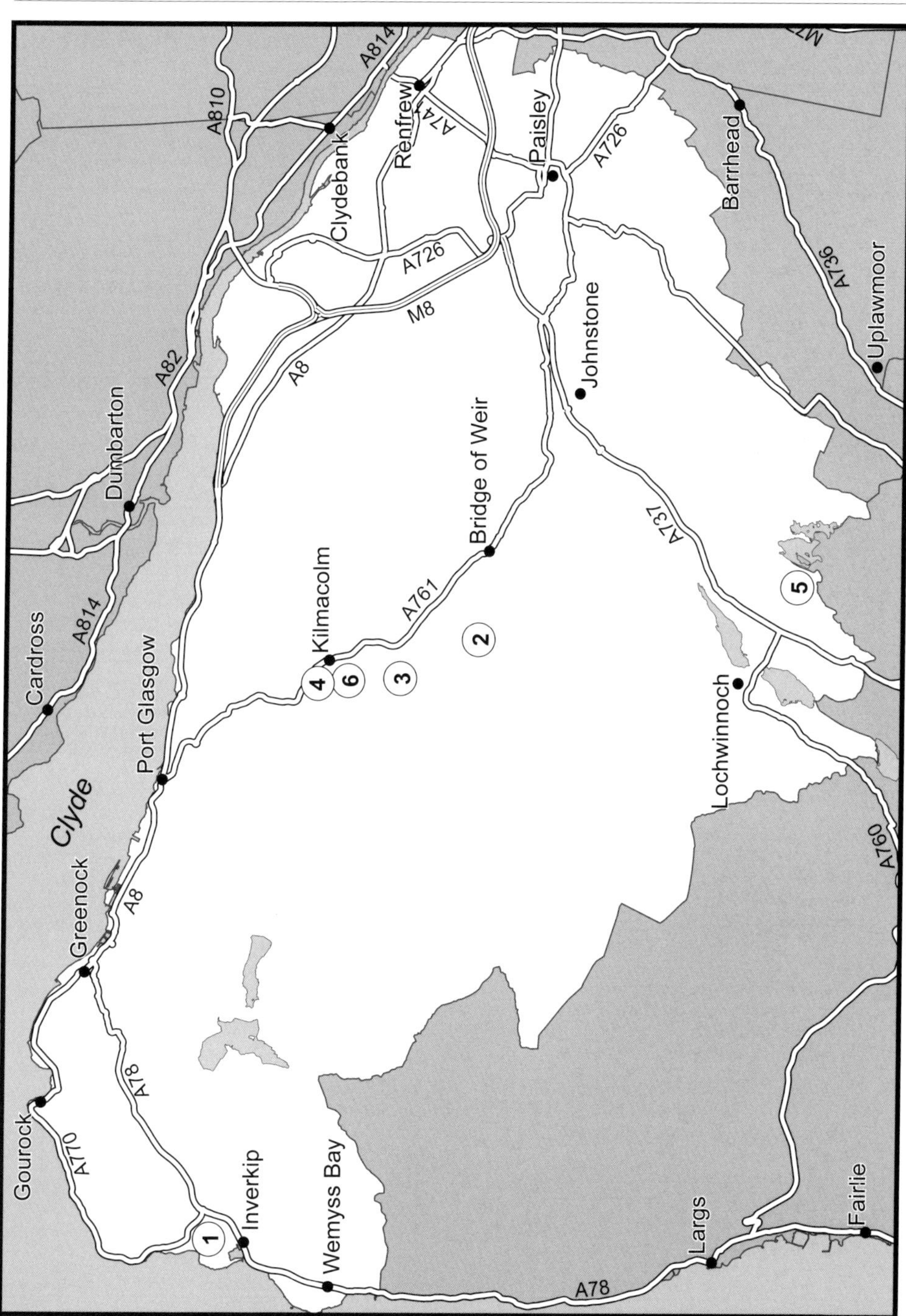

## ARDGOWAN

Inverkip PA16 0DW
**The Hon Mrs Christopher Chetwode T: 01475 521656/226**
**E: info@ardgowan.co.uk**

Woodland walks carpeted with masses of snowdrops in a lovely setting overlooking the River Clyde.

**Other Details:** Strong waterproof footwear/boots advised as some paths may be wet/muddy depending on the weather.
Wheelchair access not advisable in wet weather.
There will be snowdrop plants and bunches of snowdrops for sale.

**Directions:** Inverkip 1½ miles. Glasgow/Largs buses to and from Inverkip Village. Entrance at roundabout or via Marina.

Disabled Access:
Partial

Opening Times:
Sunday 16 February
2:00pm - 5:00pm
for the Snowdrop Festival

Admission:
£2.00

Charities:
Greenock Medical Aid Society receives 40%, the net remaining to SG Beneficiaries.

## CARRUTH

Bridge of Weir PA11 3SG
**Mr and Mrs Charles Maclean**

Over 20 acres of long established rhododendrons, woodland with good bluebells and lawn gardens in lovely landscaped setting. Young arboretum.

**Directions:** Access from B786 Kilmacolm/Lochwinnoch road. From Bridge of Weir take Torr Road until you get to the B786. Turn right and after approximately 100 yards, garden entrance is on the right.

Disabled Access:
Partial

Opening Times:
Sunday 25 May
2:00pm - 5:00pm

Admission:
£4.00, children under 16 free

Charities:
Marie Curie Cancer Care receives 40%, the net remaining to SG Beneficiaries.

## DUCHAL

Kilmacolm PA13 4RS
**Lord Maclay**

Eighteenth century walled garden particularly well planted and maintained, entered by footbridge over the Greenwater. Specie trees, hollies, old fashioned roses, shrubs and herbaceous borders with fruit orchards and vegetable garden. Also in the garden are azaleas and a lily pond.

**Directions:** On B788 1 mile from Kilmacolm (this road links B786 Lochwinnoch Road and A761 Bridge of Weir Road) Greenock/Glasgow bus via Bridge of Weir. Knapps Loch stop is ¼ mile from garden.

Disabled Access:
Partial

Opening Times:
Sunday 18 May
2:00pm - 5:00pm

Admission:
£4.00, children under 16 free

Charities:
Strathcarron Hospice, Denny receives 40%, the net remaining to SG Beneficiaries.

## KILMACOLM PLANT SALE

Outside Kilmacolm Library, Lochwinnoch Road, Kilmacolm PA13 4EL
**Scotland's Gardens**

Spring plant sale in the centre of Kilmacolm.

**Directions:** To be held at the Cross outside the Library and Cargill Centre.

Disabled Access:
Full

Opening Times:
Saturday 19 April
10:00am - 12:30pm

Admission:
Free, donations welcome

Charities:
Kilmacolm Local Association of Guiding receives 40%, the net remaining to SG Beneficiaries.

## NEWMILLS COTTAGE

Nr Lochwinnoch PA12 4JR
**Patricia Allan**

Surviving mill in a series of 5 built in 1864. Well established colourful garden on different levels sloping down to the burn. The garden is divided into different areas with pots and hanging baskets filling areas which cannot be planted. There is also a pond. Steps down the garden are steep but it can be accessed from a gate on the road if needed and can still be seen from the lower level. Lovely colour and planting in very peaceful setting.

**Directions:** Approach from Roadhead roundabout near Lochwinnoch (junction off A760/A737). Take turning by "Powerdoors" onto Auchengrange Hill. At T junction turn left onto Belltrees Road. Drive for 20 seconds then turn right. Single track road, garden on left after 1 mile.

Disabled Access:
Partial

Opening Times:
Sunday 22 June
2:00pm - 5:00pm

Admission:
£3.00, children under 16 free

Charities:
Kilbarchan Old Library receives 40%, the net remaining to SG Beneficiaries.

## ST FILLAN'S EPISCOPAL CHURCH PLANT SALE

Moss Road, Kilmacolm PA13 4LX
**SG Renfrewshire and St Fillan's Episcopal Church**

A wide variety of interesting and good locally grown plants and shrubs.

**Other Details:** The monthly lunch will be available in the Church Hall for a nominal charge or alternatively tea/coffee and homebaking is available for a lesser charge.

**Directions:** Turn off A761 Port Glasgow-Bridge of Weir Road in centre of Kilmacolm into Moss Road.

Disabled Access:
Full

Opening Times:
Saturday 13 September
10:00am - 12:30pm

Admission:
Free, donations welcome

Charities:
St Fillan's Episcopal Church receives 40%, the net remaining to SG Beneficiaries.

# ROSS, CROMARTY, SKYE & INVERNESS

Scotland's Gardens 2014 Guidebook is sponsored by **INVESTEC WEALTH & INVESTMENT**

## District Organiser

| | |
|---|---|
| Lady Lister-Kaye | House of Aigas, Beauly IV4 7AD |

## Treasurer

| | |
|---|---|
| Mrs Sheila Kerr | Lilac Cottage, Struy, By Beauly IV4 7JU |

## Gardens open on a specific date

| | | | | |
|---|---|---|---|---|
| Dundonnell House, Little Loch Broom | Thursday 17 April | 2:00pm | - | 5:00pm |
| Brackla Wood, Culbokie | Monday 21 April | 2:00pm | - | 4:00pm |
| Brackla Wood, Culbokie, | Wednesday 23 April | 2:00pm | - | 4:00pm |
| Brackla Wood, Culbokie | Friday 25 April | 2:00pm | - | 4:00pm |
| Inverewe Garden and Estate, Poolewe | Wednesday 21 May | 10:00am | - | 4:00pm |
| Oldtown of Leys Garden, Inverness | Saturday 24 May | 2:00pm | - | 5:00pm |
| Aultgowrie Mill, Aultgowrie | Sunday 25 May | 1:00pm | - | 5:00pm |
| House of Gruinard, Laide | Wednesday 28 May | 2:00pm | - | 5:00pm |
| Novar, Evanton | Sunday 1 June | 2:30pm | - | 5:00pm |
| Inverewe Garden and Estate, Poolewe | Wednesday 4 June | 10:00am | - | 4:00pm |
| Dundonnell House, Little Loch Broom | Thursday 5 June | 2:00pm | - | 5:00pm |
| Field House, Belladrum, Beauly | Sunday 8 June | 2:00pm | - | 5:00pm |
| Gorthleck , Stratherrick | Wednesday 11 June | 10:30am | - | 4:30pm |
| Hugh Miller's Birthplace Cottage & Museum, Cromarty | Saturday 14 June | 12:00pm | - | 5:00pm |
| Rhuba Phoil Forest Gardens, Ardvasar | Saturday 21 June | 10:30am | - | 5:00pm |
| House of Aigas and Field Centre, By Beauly | Sunday 22 June | 2:00pm | - | 5:00pm |
| Coiltie Garden, Divach, Drumnadrochit | Mon 23 June - Sun 6 July | 12:00pm | - | 5:00pm |
| House of Gruinard, Laide | Wednesday 9 July | 2:00pm | - | 5:00pm |
| House of Aigas and Field Centre, By Beauly | Sunday 27 July | 2:00pm | - | 5:00pm |
| Woodview, Highfield | Sunday 3 August | 2:00pm | - | 5:00pm |
| Aultgowrie Mill, Aultgowrie | Sunday 10 August | 1:00pm | - | 5:00pm |
| Dundonnell House, Little Loch Broom | Thursday 14 August | 2:00pm | - | 5:00pm |
| Cardon, Balnafoich | Sunday 17 August | 1:00pm | - | 5:00pm |
| Dundonnell House, Little Loch Broom | Thursday 11 September | 2:00pm | - | 5:00pm |

## Gardens open regularly

| | | | | |
|---|---|---|---|---|
| Abriachan Garden Nursery, Loch Ness Side | 1 February - 30 November | 9:00am | - | 7:00pm |
| Applecross Walled Garden, Strathcarron | 15 March - 31 October | 11:00am | - | 9:00pm |
| Attadale, Strathcarron | 31 March - 31 Oct not Suns | 10:00am | - | 5:30pm |

| | | | | |
|---|---|---|---|---|
| Balmeanach House, Struan | 5 May - 31 Oct Mons & Thurs | 10:30am | - | 3:30pm |
| Brackla Wood, Culbokie | 21 May - 25 June Weds | 2:00pm | - | 4:00pm |
| Clan Donald Skye, Armadale | 1 January - 31 March | Dawn | - | Dusk |
| | 1 April - 31 October | 9:30am | - | 5:30pm |
| | 1 November - 31 December | Dawn | - | Dusk |
| Dunvegan Castle and Gardens | 1 April - 15 October | 10:00am | - | 5:30pm |
| Highland Liliums, Kiltarlity, | 1 January - 31 December | 9:00am | - | 5:00pm |
| Leathad Ard, Upper Carloway | 2 June - 30 Aug Not Fris & Suns. Also closed 6 & 7 Aug | 1:45pm | - | 6:00pm |
| Leckmelm Shrubbery & Arboretum, By Ullapool | 1 April - 31 October | 10:00am | - | 6:00pm |
| Oldtown of Leys Garden, Inverness | 1 January - 31 December | Dawn | - | Dusk |
| The Lookout, Kilmuir, North Kessock | 1 May - 30 Sept Sats & Suns | 12:00pm | - | 4:00pm |

## Gardens open by arrangement

| | | |
|---|---|---|
| Brackla Wood, Culbokie | 1 April - 30 September | 01349 877765 |
| Dundonnell House, Little Loch Broom | 1 April - 30 November | 07789 390028 |
| Dunvegan Castle and Gardens, Isle of Skye | 6 January - 31 March | 01470 521206 |
| Dunvegan Castle and Gardens, Isle of Skye | 16 October - 31 December | 01470 521206 |
| House of Aigas and Field Centre, By Beauly | 1 March - 25 October | 01463 782443 |
| Leathad Ard, Upper Carloway | 1 April - 30 September | 01851 643204 |
| The Lookout, Kilmuir | 1 January - 31 December | 01463 731489 |

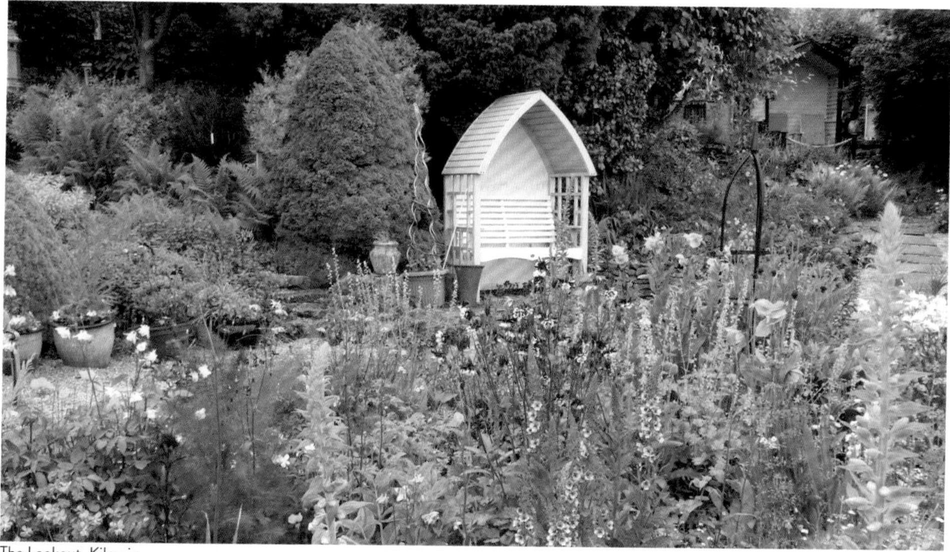

The Lookout, Kilmuir

## Key to symbols

 New in 2014

 Teas

Cream teas

 Homemade teas

 Dogs on a lead allowed

 Wheelchair access

 Accommodation

 Plant stall

 Scottish Snowdrop Festival

## Garden locations

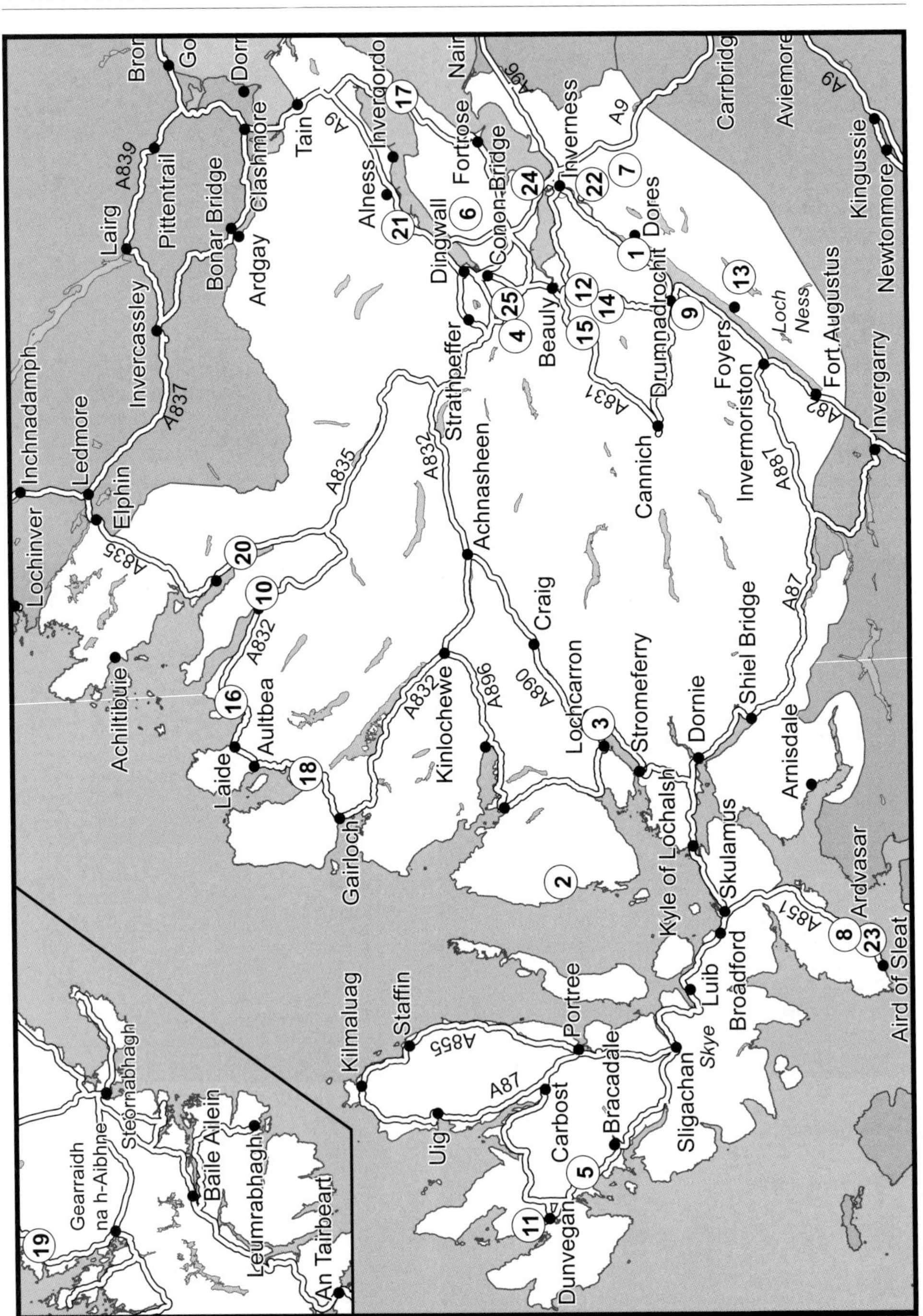

## ABRIACHAN GARDEN NURSERY

Loch Ness Side IV3 8LA
**Mr and Mrs Davidson T: 01463 861232**
**E: info@lochnessgarden.com www.lochnessgarden.com**

An outstanding garden. Over 4 acres of exciting plantings with winding paths through native woodlands. Seasonal highlights - snowdrops, hellebores, primulas, meconopsis, hardy geraniums and colour-themed summer beds. Views over Loch Ness. New path to pond through the Bluebell Wood.

**Other Details:** Working Retail nursery. Drinks machine in nursery.

**Directions:** On A82 Inverness/Drumnadrochit road, approximately 8 miles south of Inverness.

Disabled Access:
Partial

Opening Times:
1 February - 30 November
9:00am - 7:00pm
(includes opening for the Snowdrop Festival 1 February - 16 March)

Admission:
£3.00

Charities:
Highland Hospice receives 40%, the net remaining to SG Beneficiaries.

## APPLECROSS WALLED GARDEN

Strathcarron IV54 8ND
**Applecross Organics T: 01520 744440**

Walled garden of 1¼ acres in spectacular surroundings. Derelict for 50 years but lovingly restored since 2001. Lots of herbaceous borders, fruit trees and raised vegetable beds. We try to have an interesting plant table in this wonderful peaceful setting. Award winning cafe/restaurant within the garden. Open every day from March to October.

**Other Details:** Restaurant open from 11:00am till late, last orders 8:30pm

**Directions:** Take the spectacular Bealach na Ba hill road after Kishorn. At the T-junction in Applecross, turn right for half a mile. Entrance to Applecross House is immediately in front of you.

Disabled Access:
Full

Opening Times:
15 March - 31 October
11:00am - 9:00pm

Admission:
Admission by Donation

Charities:
Smile Train receives 40%, the net remaining to SG Beneficiaries.

## ATTADALE

Strathcarron IV54 8YX
**Mr and Mrs Ewen Macpherson T: 01520 722603**
**E: info@attadalegardens.com www.attadalegardens.com**

The Gulf Stream and surrounding hills and rocky cliffs create a microclimate for 20 acres of outstanding water gardens, old rhododendrons, unusual trees and a fern collection in a geodesic dome. There is also a sunken fern garden developed on the site of an early 19th c. drain, new pool with dwarf rhododendrons, sunken garden and kitchen garden. Other features include a conservatory, Japanese garden, sculpture collection and giant sundial.

**Other Details:** Major collections of meconopsis and ferns. Some plants for sale.

**Directions:** On A890 between Strathcarron and South Strome. Car parking for disabled by the house.

Disabled Access:
Partial

Opening Times:
31 March - 31 October
10:00am - 5:30pm
Closed on Sundays.

Admission:
Adults £6.00, senior citizens £4.00, children £1.00. Wheelchair users free.

Charities:
Howard Doris Centre, Lochcarron & Highland Hospice receives 40%, the net remaining to SG Beneficiaries.

## AULTGOWRIE MILL

Aultgowrie, Urray, Muir of Ord IV6 7XA
**Mr and Mrs John Clegg T: 01997 433699**
**E: john@johnclegg.com**

Aultgowrie Mill is an 18th century converted water mill set in gardens and woodland river walks of 13 acres. Features include a wooded island, a half-acre wildflower meadow and a wildlife pond, all with outstanding views of the surrounding hills. The gardens are being developed with much new landscaping and planting, including terraces, lawns, a mixed orchard and raised vegetable beds.

**Other Details:** Homemade teas on the balcony and millpond lawn. Plans of the gardens, island and river walks will be on display and there is ample field parking. Well behaved dogs on leads are welcome.

**Directions:** From the south, turn left at Muir of Ord Distillery, Aultgowrie Mill is 3.2 miles. From the north and west, after Marybank Primary School, Aultgowrie Mill is 1.7 miles up the hill.

Disabled Access:
Partial

Opening Times:
Sunday 25 May
1:00pm - 5:00pm
Sunday 10 August
1:00pm - 5:00pm

Admission:
£4.00

Charities:
R.N.L.I. receives 40%, the net remaining to SG Beneficiaries.

## BALMEANACH HOUSE

Struan, Isle of Skye IV56 8FH
**Mrs Arlene Macphie T: 01470 572320**
**E: info@skye-holiday.com www.skye-holiday.com**

During the late 1980s, a ⅓ of an acre of croft land was fenced in to create a garden. Now there is a glorious herbaceous border, bedding plants area and a small azalea/rhododendron walk. In addition, there is a woodland dell with fairies, 3 ponds and a small shrubbery.

**Other Details:** Plant stall at Plants 'n Stuff, Atholl Service Station. Teas at Waterside Cafe, Atholl Service Station.

**Directions:** A87 to Sligachan, turn left, Balmeanach is 5 miles north of Struan and 5 miles south of Dunvegan.

Disabled Access:
None

Opening Times:
5 May - 31 October
10:30am - 3:30pm
Mondays & Thursdays

Admission:
£3.00

Charities:
SSPCA receives 40%, the net remaining to SG Beneficiaries.

## BRACKLA WOOD

Culbokie, Dingwall IV7 8GY
**Susan and Ian Dudgeon T: 01349 877765**
**E: smdbrackla@aol.com**

Mature 1 acre plot consisting of woodland, wildlife features, ponds, mixed borders, a kitchen garden, rockery and mini-orchard. Spring bulbs and hellebores, rhododendrons, wisteria and roses followed by crocosmia, clematis and deciduous trees provide continuous colour and interest throughout the season. There is always the chance of seeing red squirrels.

**Other Details:** Homemade teas £2.50.

**Directions: From the north**: Take the A9 and turn off to Culbokie. At the far end of the village, turn right after the playing fields signposted "Munlochy". A mile up the road, turn right into "No Through Road" signposted "Upper Braefindon".
**From the south**: Take the A9 and turn off to Munlochy. At the far end of the village, turn right and then sharp left up road signposted "Culbokie" and "Killen". After about 4½ miles turn left onto road signposted "Upper Braefindon". Brackla Wood is first house on left.

Disabled Access:
Partial

Opening Times:
Monday 21 April
Wednesday 23 April
Friday 25 April
Weds: 21 May - 25 June
all dates 2:00pm - 4:00pm
Also by arrangement
1 April - 30 September

Admission:
£3.00

Charities:
Macmillan Nurses (Black Isle branch) receives 40%, the net remaining to SG Beneficiaries.

## CARDON

Balnafoich, Farr IV2 6XG
**Caroline Smith T: 01808 521389**
**E: csmith@kitchens01.fsnet.co.uk**

The garden is set in approximately 5 acres of woodlands with a feature pond and lawn area. There are also rockeries, wild woodland areas and cottage style plantings.

**Directions:** From Inverness: head south, turn right to Daviot (7 miles) and head to Balnafoich. Cardon 3½ miles. From Inverness Academy: take B861. 4½ miles take left to Daviot & Garden is 400 yds. on left.

Disabled Access:
Full

Opening Times:
Sunday 17 August
1:00pm - 5:00pm

Admission:
£3.00, children free

Charities:
Local Charities will receive 40%, the net remaining to SG Beneficiaries.

## CLAN DONALD SKYE

Armadale, Isle of Skye IV45 8RS
**Clan Donald Lands Trust T: 01471 844305**
**E: office@clandonald.com www.clandonald.com**

Exotic trees, shrubs & flowers, expansive lawns & stunning scenery combine to make this a real treat for garden lovers. The warming influence of the Gulf Stream allows the sheltered gardens to flourish. When the Clan Donald Lands Trust took over, the gardens were overgrown and neglected. Years of hard pruning, rebuilding & planting around the centrepiece of historic Armadale Castle has resulted in 40 acres of stunning woodland gardens & lawns that provide a tranquil place to sit or walk. Specimen trees, some planted in the early 1800s, tower above the gardens. There are woodland walks & nature trails, with beautiful views to the Sound of Sleat, the mountains of Knoydart forming a spectacular backdrop. Children's adventure playground. A new garden interpretation began in 2013.

**Other Details:** Opening times subject to seasonal changes, please check our website.

**Directions:** From Skye Bridge: Head north on A87 and turn left just before Broadford onto A851 signposted Armadale 15 miles. From Armadale Pier: ¼ mile north on A851 to car park.

Disabled Access:
Full

Opening Times:
1 Jan - 31 March Dawn - Dusk
1 April - 31 October
9:30am - 5:30pm
1 Nov - 31 Dec Dawn - Dusk

Admission:
Adults £8.00, concessions/ children £6.50, under 5 free, families £25.00
Admission free Jan - March and Nov - Dec.

Charities:
Donation to SG Beneficiaries.

## COILTIE GARDEN

Divach, Drumnadrochit IV63 6XW
**Gillian and David Nelson T: 01456 450219**

A garden made over the past 35 years from a long neglected Victorian garden, now being somewhat reorganised to suit ageing gardeners. Many unusual trees, shrubs, herbaceous borders, roses, all set in beautiful hill scenery with a fine view of the 100 feet Divach Falls. Trees planted 30 years ago are showing well now.

**Directions:** Take turning to Divach off A82 in Drumnadrochit village. Proceed 2 miles uphill, passing Falls. 150 metres beyond Divach Lodge.

**Disabled Access:**
Partial

**Opening Times:**
23 June - 6 July
12:00pm - 5:00pm

**Admission:**
£3.00, children free

**Charities:**
Amnesty International receives 40%, the net remaining to SG Beneficiaries.

## DUNDONNELL HOUSE

Dundonnell, Little Loch Broom, Wester Ross IV23 2QW
**Dundonnell Estates T: 07789 390028**

Camellias, magnolias and bulbs in spring, rhododendrons and laburnum walk in this ancient walled garden. Exciting planting in new borders gives all year colour centred around one of the oldest yew trees in Scotland. Midsummer roses, restored Edwardian glasshouse, riverside walk, arboretum - in the valley below the peaks of An Teallach.

**Other Details:** On 5th June homemade teas are available in the house. On other dates teas are available at Maggie's Tearoom 3 miles towards Little Loch Broom.

**Directions:** Off A835 at Braemore on to A832. After 11 miles take Badralloch turn for half a mile.

**Disabled Access:**
Partial

**Opening Times:**
Thursdays: 17 April, 5 June, 14 August & 11 September
2:00pm - 5:00pm
Also by arrangement
1 April - 30 November

**Admission:**
£3.50, children free

**Charities:**
Apr/Aug: Juvenile Diabetes Research receives 40%
Jun/Sept: WWF Save The Snow Leopard receives 40%, the net remaining to SG Beneficiaries.

## DUNVEGAN CASTLE AND GARDENS

Isle of Skye IV55 8WF
**Hugh Macleod of Macleod T: 01470 521206**
**E: info@dunvegancastle.com www.dunvegancastle.com**

Dunvegan Castle's 5 acres of formal gardens began life in the 18th century. In stark contrast to the barren moorland that dominates Skye's landscape, the gardens are a hidden oasis featuring an eclectic mix of plants, woodland glades, shimmering pools fed by waterfalls and streams flowing down to the sea. After experiencing the Water Garden with its ornate bridges and islands replete with a rich and colourful plant variety, wander through the elegant surroundings of the formal Round Garden featuring a Box-wood parterre as its centrepiece. The Walled Garden is well worth a visit to see its colourful herbaceous borders and recently added Victorian style glasshouse. In what was formerly the Castle's vegetable garden, there is a garden museum and a diverse range of plants and flowers which complement the attractive features including a waterlily pond, a neoclassical urn and a Larch pergola. A considerable amount of replanting and landscaping has taken place over the last thirty years to restore and develop the gardens at Dunvegan.

**Directions:** One mile from Dunvegan Village, 23 miles west of Portree.

**Disabled Access:**
Partial

**Opening Times:**
1 April - 15 October
10:00am - 5:30pm
By arrangement 6 Jan. - 31 March & 16 Oct. - 31 Dec. weekends only. Closed Christmas and New Year.

**Admission:**
**Garden:** £8.00, Conc. £7.00, Child 5-15 £5.00.
**Castle and Gardens:** £10.00, Conc. £8.00, Child 5-15 £7.00

**Charities:**
Donation to SG Beneficiaries.

## FIELD HOUSE

Belladrum, Beauly IV4 7BA
**Mr and Mrs D Paterson**
**www.dougthegarden.co.uk**

An informal country garden in a 1 acre site with mixed borders and some unusual plants - a plantsman's garden. Featured in The Beechgrove Garden.

**Directions:** 4 miles from Beauly on A833 Beauly to Drumnadrochit road, then follow signs to Belladrum.

Disabled Access:
None

Opening Times:
Sunday 8 June
2:00pm - 5:00pm

Admission:
£4.00

Charities:
Macmillan Cancer Care receives 40%, the net remaining to SG Beneficiaries.

## GORTHLECK

Stratherrick IV2 6UJ
**Steve and Katie Smith T: 07710325903**
**E: visit@gorthleckgarden.co.uk**

Gorthleck is an unusual 20 acre woodland garden built in an unlikely place, on and around an exposed rocky ridge. The layout of the garden works with the natural features of the landscape rather than against them, with numerous paths, hedges and shelter belts creating clearly defined spaces that enable a large collection of plants and trees to thrive. It has extensive collections of both rhododendrons and bamboos. The challenges presented by the site become a bonus with the ridge offering long views of the surrounding countryside in the 'borrowed landscape' tradition of Japanese gardens. It didn't exist ten years ago and Gorthleck is very much a work-in-progress under the day-to-day control of Head Gardener and Landscaper David Cameron and plantsman Graham Chattington.

**Directions:** From A9, join B862. Go through village of Errogie where there is a sharp left-hand bend. Approx 1 mile after bend there is a small church on left. The Gorthleck drive is directly opposite the church, the house can be seen on the hill to the left as you follow the drive (follow it to the left of new house). Park outside on the gravel.

Disabled Access:
None

Opening Times:
Wednesday 11 June
10:30am - 4:30pm

Admission:
£5.00, children free

Charities:
All proceeds to SG Beneficiaries.

## HIGHLAND LILIUMS

10 Loaneckheim, Kiltarlity, IV4 7JQ
**Neil and Frances Macritchie T: 01463 741365**
**E: neil.macritchie@btconnect.com www.highlandliliums.co.uk**

A working retail nursery with spectacular views over the Beauly valley and Strathfarrar hills. A wide selection of home grown plants available including Alpines, Ferns, Grasses, Herbaceous, Herbs, Liliums, Primulas and Shrubs.

**Other Details:** Open day for charity in August with homemade teas. For details check Scotlands Gardens' and our own website.

**Directions:** Signposted from Kiltarlity village, which is just off the Beauly to Drumnadrochit road (A833), approximately 12 miles from Inverness.

Disabled Access:
Partial

Opening Times:
1 January - 31 December
9:00am - 5:00pm

Admission:
Free

Charities:
Highland Hospice receives 40%, the net remaining to SG Beneficiaries.

## HOUSE OF AIGAS AND FIELD CENTRE

By Beauly IV4 7AD

**Sir John and Lady Lister-Kaye T: 01463 782443**
**E: sheila@aigas.co.uk www.aigas.co.uk**

The House of Aigas has a small arboretum of named Victorian specimen trees and modern additions. The garden consists of extensive rockeries, herbaceous borders, ponds and shrubs. Aigas Field Centre rangers lead regular guided walks on nature trails through woodland, moorland and around a loch.

**Other Details:** Homemade teas in the house on both open days. For the "By Arrangement" openings, lunches/teas are available on request. Check out Aigas website for details of other events.

**Directions:** 4½ miles from Beauly on A831 Cannich/Glen Affric road.

**Disabled Access:**
Partial

**Opening Times:**
Sunday 22 June
2:00pm - 5:00pm
Sunday 27 July
2:00pm - 5:00pm
Also by arrangement
1 March - 25 October

**Admission:**
£3.00, children free

**Charities:**
Highland Hospice (Aird branch) receives 40%, the net remaining to SG Beneficiaries.

## HOUSE OF GRUINARD

Laide, by Achnasheen IV22 2NQ

**The Hon Mrs A G Maclay T: 01445 731235**
**E: office@houseofgruinard.com**

Superb hidden and unexpected garden developed in sympathy with stunning west coast estuary location. Wide variety of interesting herbaceous and shrub borders with water garden and extended wild planting.

**Other Details:** Homemade teas available on Wed 28 May, no teas on 9 July.

**Directions:** On A832 12 miles north of Inverewe and 9 miles south of Dundonnell.

**Disabled Access:**
None

**Opening Times:**
Wednesday 28 May
2:00pm - 5:00pm
Wednesday 9 July
2:00pm - 5:00pm

**Admission:**
£3.50, children under 16 free

**Charities:**
The Camphill Village Trust receives 40%, the net remaining to SG Beneficiaries.

## HUGH MILLER'S BIRTHPLACE COTTAGE & MUSEUM

Church Street, Cromarty IV11 8XA

**The National Trust for Scotland T: 0844 493 2158**
**E: apowersjones@nts.org.uk www.nts.org.uk**

The Garden of Wonders, created in 2008, with its theme of natural history, features fossils, exotic ferns, ornamental letter-cutting and a 'mystery' stone. The sculptural centrepiece of this award-winning small but beautiful area is a scrap metal ammonite created by Helen Denerley. Named after Hugh's wife, Lydia, this new garden was completed in 2010. Walk around the crescent-shaped, sandstone path of fragrant climbing roses, herbs and wild plant areas which reflect Miller's own love of nature and curiosity in the natural landscape.

**Directions:** By road via Kessock Bridge and A832 to Cromarty. Twenty-two miles north east of Inverness.

**Disabled Access:**
None

**Opening Times:**
Saturday 14 June
12:00pm - 5:00pm

**Admission:**
£6.50, concession £5.00, family £16.50.
N.B. Prices correct at time of going to print.

**Charities:**
Donation to SG Beneficiaries.

## INVEREWE GARDEN AND ESTATE

Poolewe, Achnasheen, Ross-shire IV22 2LG
**The National Trust for Scotland T: 0844 493 2225**
**E: inverewe@nts.org.uk www.nts.org.uk**

Magnificent 54 acre Highland garden, surrounded by mountains, moorland and sea-loch. Created by Osgood Mackenzie in the late 19th c., it now includes a wealth of exotic plants from Australian tree ferns to Chinese rhododendrons to South African bulbs.

**Other Details:** National Plant Collection®: Olearia, Rhododendron (subsect. Barbata), Rhododendron (subsect. Glischra), Rhododendron (subsect. Maculifera).
**21 May:** The Head Gardener's walk will focus on Woodland Gardening.
**4 June:** The First Gardener's walk will take in the National Collection planting. Join Inverewe's experts to discover what makes a tree a champion. Marvel at Inverewe's awesome examples of nature's best and learn what makes our champion trees so special.
Meet at Visitor Centre 2:00pm for all walks.
A shop and self-service restaurant are available.

**Directions:** Signposted on A832 by Poolewe, 6 miles northeast of Gairloch.

Disabled Access:
Partial

Opening Times:
Wednesday 21 May
10:00am - 4:00pm
Wednesday 4 June
10:00am - 4:00pm

Admission:
Adult £10.00, concessions £7.00
NT/NTS Members free

Charities:
Donation to SG Beneficiaries.

## LEATHAD ARD

Upper Carloway, Isle of Lewis HS2 9AQ
**Rowena and Stuart Oakley T: 01851 643204**
**E: oakley1a@clara.co.uk www.whereveriam.org/leathadard**

Three quarters of an acre sloping garden with stunning views over East Loch Roag. It has evolved along with the shelter hedges that divide the garden into a number of areas. With shelter and raised beds the different conditions created permit a wide variety of plants to be grown. Beds include herbaceous borders, cutting borders, bog gardens, grass garden, exposed beds, patio, a new pond and vegetable and fruit patches, some of which are grown to show.
A full tour by Stuart takes about 2 hours.

**Directions:** A858 Shawbost - Carloway. First right after Carloway football pitch. First house on right. The Westside circular bus ex Stornoway to road end and ask for the Carloway football pitch.

Disabled Access:
None

Opening Times:
2 June - 30 August 1:45pm - 6:00pm (Closed Fris & Suns also Wed/Thurs 6 & 7 August)
Also by arrangement
1 April - 30 September

Admission:
By donation: recommended minimum donation £4.00 per person, children free

Charities:
Red Cross receives 40%, the net remaining to SG Beneficiaries.

## LECKMELM SHRUBBERY & ARBORETUM

By Ullapool IV23 2RH
**Mr and Mrs J Farmer**

The restored 12 acre arboretum, planted in the 1880s, is full of splendid and rare trees including 2 "Champions", species rhododendrons, azaleas and shrubs. Warmed by the Gulf Stream, this tranquil woodland garden has alpines, palms and bamboos along winding paths which lead down to the sea.

**Other Details:** Champion Trees

**Directions:** Situated by the shore of Loch Broom 3 miles south of Ullapool on the A835 Inverness/Ullapool road. Parking in walled garden.

Disabled Access:
None

Opening Times:
1 April - 31 October
10:00am - 6:00pm

Admission:
£3.00, children under 16 free

Charities:
Local charities will receive 40%, the net remaining to SG Beneficiaries

## NOVAR

Evanton IV16 9XL
**Mr and Mrs Ronald Munro Ferguson T: 01349 831062**

Water gardens with recent restoration and new planting, especially rhododendrons and azaleas. Large, 5 acre walled garden with formal 18th c. oval pond (restored). There is a newly planted apple orchard.

**Other Details:** Disabled access to most areas.

**Directions:** Off B817 between Evanton and junction with A836: turn west up Novar Drive.

Disabled Access:
Partial

Opening Times:
Sunday 1 June
2:30pm - 5:00pm

Admission:
£5.00, children free

Charities:
Diabetes Charities receives 40%, the net remaining to SG Beneficiaries.

## OLDTOWN OF LEYS GARDEN

Inverness IV2 6AE
**David and Anne Sutherland T: 01463 238238**
**E: ams@oldtownofleys.com**

Large garden established 10 years ago, on the outskirts of Inverness and overlooking the town. Herbaceous beds with lovely rhododendron and azalea displays in spring. There are specimen trees, 3 ponds surrounded by waterside planting and a small woodland area.

**Directions:** Turn off Southern distributor road (B8082) at Leys roundabout towards Inverarnie (B861). At T-junction turn right. After 50 metres turn right into Oldtown of Leys.

Disabled Access:
Partial

Opening Times:
Saturday 24 May
2:00pm - 5:00pm
1 January - 31 December
Dawn - Dusk

Admission:
**24 May:** £3.00
**Other days:** by donation

Charities:
Local Charities will receive 40%, the net remaining to SG Beneficiaries.

## RHUBA PHOIL FOREST GARDENS

Armadale Pier Road, Ardvasar, Sleat, Isle of Skye IV45 8RS
**Sandy Masson T: 01471 844700**
**E: bookings@skye-permaculture.org.uk www.skye-permaculture.org.uk**

A wild natural forest garden managed on permaculture principles with a woodland walk to seal and bird islands. Look out for otters and other wildlife! There is an interesting Alchemy Centre with a composting display.

**Other Details:** Accommodation is available in tent/bothy retreat. Follow us on Facebook at: http://www.facebook.com/RubhaPhoil and Skye Permaculture at: http://www.facebook.com/skyepermaculture

**Directions:** Turn right at the car park on Armadale Pier.

Disabled Access:
Partial

Opening Times:
Saturday 21 June
10:30am - 5:00pm

Admission:
£4.00, children free

Charities:
Donation to SG Beneficiaries.

## THE LOOKOUT

Kilmuir, North Kessock IV1 3ZG
**Mr and Mrs David and Penny Veitch T: 01463 731489**
**E: david@veitch.biz**

A ¾ acre elevated coastal garden with incredible views over the Moray Firth which is only for the sure-footed. This award winning garden is created out of a rock base with shallow pockets of ground, planted to its advantage to encourage all aspects of wildlife. There is a small sheltered courtyard, raised bed vegetable area, pretty cottage garden, scree and rock garden, rose arbour, rhododendrons, flowering shrubs, bamboos, trees and lily pond with waterside plants.

**Other Details:** Coffee, tea and homebaking outside if weather permits. Studio with exhibition of landscape pictures for sale.

**Directions: From Inverness:** take North Kessock left turn from A9, and 3rd left at roundabout to go on underpass then sharp left onto Kilmuir road.
**From Tore:** take slip road for North Kessock and immediately right for Kilmuir. Follow signs for Kilmuir (3 miles) until you reach the shore.
The Lookout is near the far end of village with a large palm tree on the grass in front.

Disabled Access:
None

Opening Times:
1 May - 30 September
12:00pm - 4:00pm
Saturdays and Sundays
Also by arrangement on request

Admission:
£3.00, children under 16 free

Charities:
Alzeimers Scotland receives 40%, the net remaining to SG Beneficiaries.

## WOODVIEW

Highfield, Muir of Ord IV6 7UL
**Miss Lynda Macleod T: 01463 871928**
**E: lynwoodview@yahoo.co.uk**

This is an award winning well-stocked mature garden of approximately ⅓ acre containing many unusual trees. It comprises various "rooms", Italian inspired with sculptured trees. There is a pergola clad with golden hop overlooking a water feature and a very calm and relaxing Chinese room with acers. Formal borders of twilight and a large exotic border, a pond with waterside plants, raised vegetable beds, a greenhouse along with new borders and features ongoing every year including a special lawn sculptured chair. The garden has an abundance of colour from spring to autumn. Woodview received the Inverness Courier Garden of the Year Award in 2010 and 2013.

**Directions:** Follow signs to Ord Distillery on the A832 Muir of Ord to Marybank. House opposite Clashwood Forest Walk. Parking in Clashwood.

Disabled Access:
None

Opening Times:
Sunday 3 August
2:00pm - 5:00pm

Admission:
£4.00, children free

Charities:
Munlochy Animal Aid receives 40%, the net remaining to SG Beneficiaries.

# ROXBURGHSHIRE

Scotland's Gardens 2014 Guidebook is sponsored by INVESTEC WEALTH & INVESTMENT

## District Organiser

| | |
|---|---|
| Mrs Sally Yonge | Newtonlees, Kelso TD5 7SZ |

## Area Organiser

| | |
|---|---|
| Mrs Clare Leeming | Loanend, Earlston, Berwickshire TD4 6BD |

## Treasurer

| | |
|---|---|
| Mr Peter Jeary | Kalemouth House, Eckford, Kelso TD5 8LE |

## Gardens open on a specific date

| | | |
|---|---|---|
| Corbet Tower, Morebattle | Saturday 5 July | 2:00pm - 5:00pm |
| St Boswells Village Gardens | Saturday 12 July | 11:00am - 6:00pm |
| Yetholm Village Gardens | Sunday 13 July | 2:00pm - 5:30pm |
| Newcastleton Village Gardens | Saturday 19 July | 2:00pm - 5:00pm |
| West Leas, Bonchester Bridge | Sunday 20 July | 2:00pm - 5:00pm |

## Gardens open regularly

| | | |
|---|---|---|
| Floors Castle, Kelso | 18 April - 31 October | 10:30am - 5:00pm |
| Monteviot, Jedburgh | 1 April - 30 October | 12:00pm - 5:00pm |

## Gardens open by arrangement

| | | |
|---|---|---|
| Lanton Tower, Jedburgh | On request | 01835 863443 |
| West Leas, Bonchester Bridge | On request | 01450 860711 |

## Key to symbols

| | | | | | |
|---|---|---|---|---|---|
|  | New in 2014 |  | Homemade teas |  | Accommodation |
|  | Teas |  | Dogs on a lead allowed |  | Plant stall |
|  | Cream teas |  | Wheelchair access |  | Scottish Snowdrop Festival |

## Garden locations

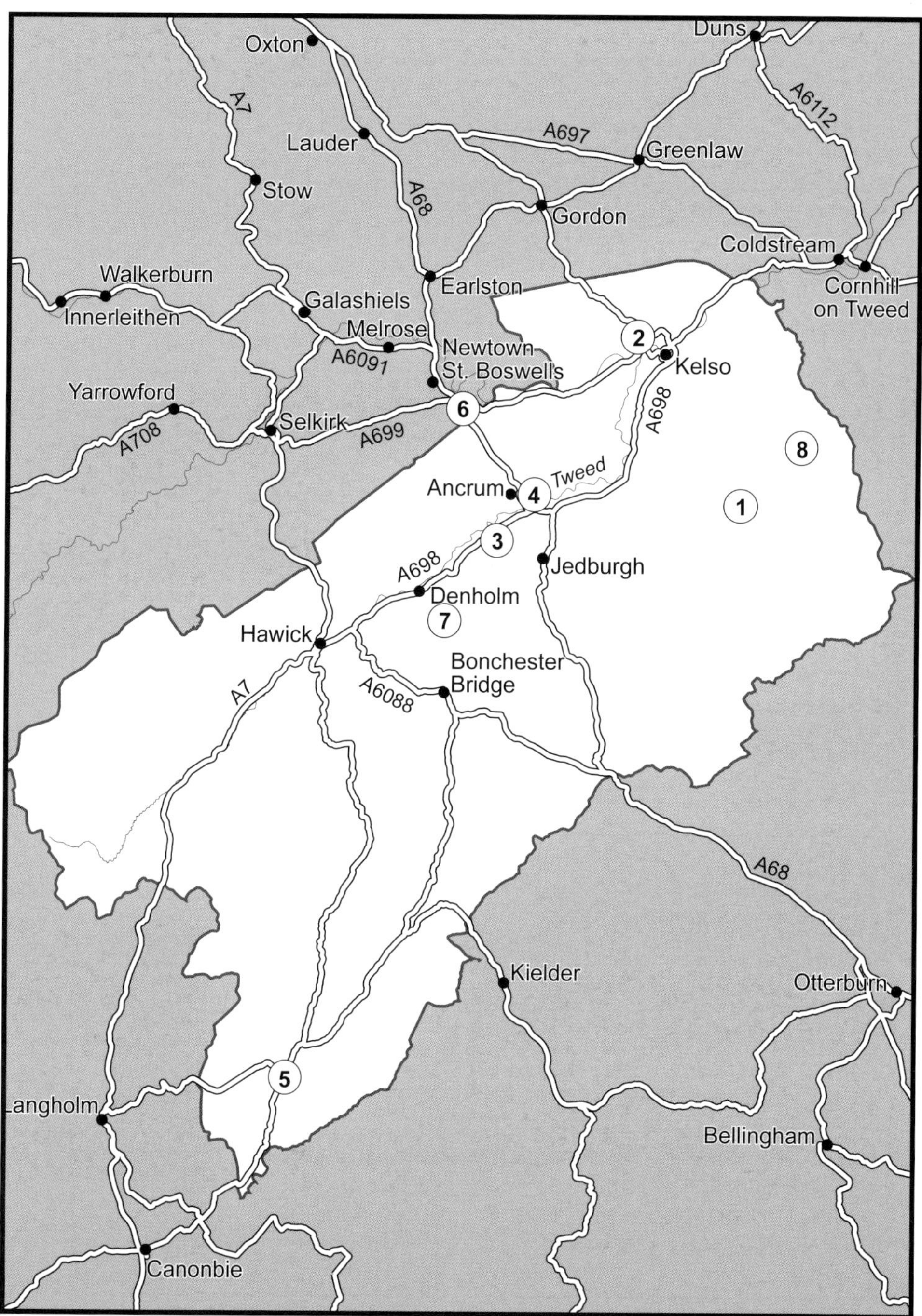

## CORBET TOWER

Morebattle, Nr Kelso TD5 8AQ
**Simon and Bridget Fraser**

Charming Scottish Victorian garden set in parklands in the foothills of the Cheviots. The established garden includes a formal box parterred rose garden with old fashioned roses, a well stocked traditional walled vegetable and cutting garden, terraced lawns around the Victorian house and medieval peel tower. The gardens are approached via an attractive woodland walk with lime avenue.

**Other Details:** Delicious home-made teas and refreshments, cake and produce stall, plant stall and Anne Fraser greetings cards and prints.

**Directions:** From A68 north of Jedburgh take A698 for Kelso. At Kalemouth (Teviot Smokery) follow B6401 to Morebattle, then road marked Hownam to Corbet Tower.

Disabled Access:
Partial

Opening Times:
Saturday 5 July
2:00pm - 5:00pm

Admission:
£4.00

Charities:
The Children's Society receives 40%, the net remaining to SG Beneficiaries.

## FLOORS CASTLE

Kelso TD5 7SF
**The Duke of Roxburghe T: 01573 223333**
**www.floorscastle.com**

The largest inhabited house in Scotland enjoys glorious views across parkland, the River Tweed and the Cheviot Hills. Delightful woodland garden, riverside and woodland walks, formal French style Millennium Parterre and the traditional walled garden. The walled garden contains colourful herbaceous borders, vinery and peach house, and in keeping with tradition, the kitchen garden still supplies vegetables and soft fruit for the Castle.

**Other Details:** Children's adventure playground.

**Directions:** Floors Castle can be reached by following the A6089 from Edinburgh; the B6397 from Earlston or the A698 from Coldstream. Go through Kelso, up Roxburgh Street to the Golden Gates.

Disabled Access:
Partial

Opening Times:
18 April - 31 October
10:30am - 5:00pm
Please check our website for any special closing dates

Admission:
£4.50, OAPs £4.00, Children £2.00

Charities:
Donation to SG Beneficiaries.

## LANTON TOWER

Jedburgh TD8 6SU
**Lady Reid T: 01835 863443**

The garden, divided into 'rooms' by beech, holly and yew hedges and stone walls, is architectural rather than botanical, with an emphasis on shrubs, bulbs and fruit trees. A parterre near the tower, with steps leading to a croquet lawn, is surrounded by shrub borders, with orchards on each side of a beech hedge and wall. An azalea and mixed shrub border is next to a pond surrounded by bog garden. Nearby lies a border of low-growing herbaceous plants with a york stone path leading to a large curved bench, the space contained by hedges of Charles de Mills roses. There is a vegetable garden, and a herb garden near the house. A walk between a holly and Rosa spinosissima hedge towards a large mirror framed in ivy leads to a paddock well-furnished with trees and a fine view towards the Eildon Hills.

**Directions:** Two and a half miles west of Jedburgh.

Disabled Access:
Full

Opening Times:
By arrangement on request

Admission:
£4.00

Charities:
Maggie's Cancer Caring Centres receives 40%, the net remaining to SG Beneficiaries.

## MONTEVIOT

Jedburgh TD8 6UQ

**Marquis & Marchioness of Lothian T: 01835 830380**

**www.monteviot.com**

A series of differing gardens including a herb garden, rose garden, water garden linked by bridges, and river garden with herbaceous shrub borders. There is also the Dene garden featuring ponds and bridges and planted with a variety of foliage plants.

**Directions:** Turn off A68, 3 miles north of Jedburgh B6400.

Disabled Access:
Partial

Opening Times:
1 April - 30 October
12:00pm - 5:00pm

Admission:
£5.00, children under 16 free

Charities:
Donation to SG Beneficiaries.

## NEWCASTLETON VILLAGE GARDENS

Newcastleton TD9 0QS

**The Gardeners of Newcastleton Village**

Newcastleton is a small Borders village with a variety of 'hidden' gardens. In 2010 the village won 'Best Village in Scotland' and was awarded Gold in 'Beautiful Scotland'. In 2011 they achieved Silver Gilt in 'Britain in Bloom' and won Silver Gilt in 'Beautiful Scotland' in 2012.

**Other Details:** As well as cafes and restaurants, teas will be served in the village hall. There will be a scarecrow trail, free parking, recreation park and public toilets.

**Directions:** On B6357 approximately 10 miles from Canonbie (A7).

Disabled Access:
Partial

Opening Times:
Saturday 19 July
2:00pm - 5:00pm

Admission:
£4.00

Charities:
Newcastleton Floral Group and Friends of Newcastleton Park receives 40%, the net remaining to SG Beneficiaries.

## ST BOSWELLS VILLAGE GARDENS

St Boswells TD6 0ET

**St Boswells Gardeners**

St Boswells lies beside the River Tweed in the heart of the Scottish Borders. Much of the charm of the village in summer depends upon the variety, interest and contrast of its many gardens, some of which are normally hidden from view!

**Other Details:** Parking on the Village Green only where tickets and maps will be available.

**Directions:** Off A68 into village on B6404.

Disabled Access:
Partial

Opening Times:
Saturday 12 July
11:00am - 6:00pm

Admission:
£5.00, children free

Charities:
St Boswells Parish Church receives 40%, the net remaining to SG Beneficiaries.

## WEST LEAS

Bonchester Bridge TD9 8TD
**Mr and Mrs Robert Laidlaw T: 01450 860711**
**E: ann.laidlaw@btconnect.com**

The visitor to West Leas can share in the exciting and dramatic project on a grand scale still in the making. At its core is a passion for plants allied to a love and understanding of the land in which they are set. Collections of perennials and shrubs, many in temporary holding quarters, lighten up the landscape to magical effect. New landscaped water features, bog garden and extensive new shrub and herbaceous planting.

**Directions:** Signposted off the Jedburgh/Bonchester Bridge Road.

Disabled Access:
Partial

Opening Times:
Sunday 20 July
2:00pm - 5:00pm
Also by arrangement on request.

Admission:
£4.00

Charities:
Macmillan Cancer Relief, Borders Appeal receives 40%, the net remaining to SG Beneficiaries.

## YETHOLM VILLAGE GARDENS

Town Yetholm TD5 8RL
**The Gardeners of Yetholm Village**

The village of Town Yetholm is situated at the north end of the Pennine Way and lies close to the Bowmont Water in the dramatic setting of the foothills of the Cheviots. A variety of gardens with their own unique features have joined the Yetholm Village Gardens Open Day this year. In addition "The Yew Tree Allotments" running along the High Street will open again, providing an ever popular feature. The day offers visitors the chance to walk through several delightful gardens planted in a variety of styles and reflecting many distinctive horticultural interests. From newly established, developing and secret gardens to old and established gardens there is something here to interest everyone. The short walking distance between the majority of the gardens provides the added advantage of being able to enjoy the magnificence of the surrounding landscape to include "Staerough" and "The Curr" which straddle both the Bowmont and Halterburn Valleys where evidence of ancient settlements remains.

**Other Details:** Tickets will be sold in the Wauchope Hall where there will be plant and produce stalls which will include home baking and garden produce. There will also be bric-a-brac and book stalls. (All donations are welcomed on the day.) In addition at Almond Cottage a craft stall will offer local wood turning products. Home baked cream teas will be served in the Youth Hall during the afternoon. Poetry and Music will again return by popular request.

**Directions:** Equidistant between Edinburgh and Newcastle. South of Kelso in the Borders take the B6352 to Yetholm Village. Ample parking available along the High Street.

Disabled Access:
Partial

Opening Times:
Sunday 13 July
2:00pm - 5:30pm

Admission:
£4.00 (includes all gardens), children under 10 years free

Charities:
Riding for the Disabled Association, Borders Group receives 40%, the net remaining to SG Beneficiaries.

# STIRLINGSHIRE



## District Organiser

| | |
|---|---|
| Carola Campbell | Kilbryde Castle, Dunblane FK15 9NF |

## Area Organisers

| | |
|---|---|
| Gillie Drapper | Kilewnan Cottage, Fintry, By Glasgow G63 0YH |
| Maurie Jessett | The Walled Garden, Doune FK16 6HJ |
| Rosemary Leckie | Auchengarroch, 16 Chalton Rd, Bridge of Allan FK9 4DX |
| Pippa Maclean | Quarter, Denny FK6 6QZ |
| Iain Morrison | Clifford House, Balkerach Street, Doune FK16 6DE |
| Rachel Nunn | 1 Laurelhill Place, Stirling FK8 2JH |
| Douglas Ramsay | The Tors, 2 Slamannan Road, Falkirk FK1 5LG |
| Mandy Readman | Hutchison Farm, Auchinlay Road, Dunblane FK15 9JS |
| Gillie Welstead | Ballingrew, Thornhill FK8 3QD |

## Treasurer

| | |
|---|---|
| John McIntyre | 18 Scott Brae, Kippen FK8 3DL |

## Gardens open on a specific date

| | | | | |
|---|---|---|---|---|
| Kilbryde Castle, Dunblane | Sunday 23 February | 1:00pm | - | 4:00pm |
| West Plean House, by Stirling | Sunday 2 March | 1:00pm | - | 4:00pm |
| The Linns, Sheriffmuir | Sunday 9 March | 10:00am | - | 4:00pm |
| Kilbryde Castle, Dunblane | Sunday 4 May | 2:00pm | - | 5:00pm |
| Roman Camp Hotel and Orchardlea House, Callander | Sunday 11 May | 1:00pm | - | 6:00pm |
| The Pass House, Kilmahog | Sunday 11 May | 2:00pm | - | 5:00pm |
| Thorntree, Arnprior | Wednesday 14 May | 2:00pm | - | 5:00pm |
| Dun Dubh, Aberfoyle | Sunday 18 May | 2:00pm | - | 5:00pm |
| Buchlyvie Gardens | Sunday 25 May | 2:00pm | - | 5:00pm |
| The Linns, Sheriffmuir | Sunday 25 May | 10:00am | - | 4:00pm |
| Arndean, by Dollar | Sunday 1 June | 2:00pm | - | 5:30pm |
| Dunblane Community Gardens | Sunday 8 June | 12:00pm | - | 5:00pm |
| The Linns, Sheriffmuir | Sunday 8 June | 10:00am | - | 4:00pm |
| Stirling Gardens | Sunday 15 June | 2:00pm | - | 5:00pm |
| Settie, Kippen | Sunday 22 June | 2:00pm | - | 5:00pm |
| Thorntree, Arnprior | Sunday 22 June | 2:00pm | - | 5:00pm |
| Bridge of Allan Gardens | Sunday 29 June | 1:00pm | - | 5:00pm |
| Row House, Dunblane | Wednesday 2 July | 2:00pm | - | 5:00pm |

| | | | | |
|---|---|---|---|---|
| Thorntree, Arnprior | Wednesday 16 July | 2:00pm | - | 5:00pm |
| Gean House, Alloa | Tuesday 22 July | 1:30pm | - | 4:30pm |
| The Tors, Falkirk | Sunday 27 July | 2:00pm | - | 5:00pm |
| Row House, Dunblane | Wednesday 30 July | 2:00pm | - | 5:00pm |
| Killearn Village Gardens | Sunday 17 August | 1:30pm | - | 5:30pm |
| Thorntree, Arnprior | Wednesday 20 August | 2:00pm | - | 5:00pm |
| Rowberrow, Dollar | Sunday 24 August | 2:00pm | - | 5:00pm |
| The Pineapple, near Airth, Falkirk | Sunday 31 August | 10:00am | - | 5:00pm |
| Dun Dubh, Aberfoyle | Sunday 14 September | 2:00pm | - | 5:00pm |
| Gargunnock House, Gargunnock | Sunday 21 September | 2:00pm | - | 5:00pm |
| Little Broich, Kippen | Sunday 5 October | 2:00pm | - | 5:00pm |

## Gardens open regularly

| | | | | |
|---|---|---|---|---|
| Gargunnock House, Gargunnock | 1 February - 16 March | 11:00am | - | 3:30pm |
| | 14 April - 13 June Weekdays | 11:00am | - | 3:30pm |

## Gardens open by arrangement

| | | |
|---|---|---|
| Arndean, by Dollar | 15 May - 15 June | 01259 743525 |
| Camallt, Fintry | 1 April - 15 May | 01360 860034 |
| Duntreath Castle, Blanefield | on request | 01360 770215 |
| Kilbryde Castle, Dunblane | 15 February - 31 October | 01786 824897 |
| Milseybank, Bridge of Allan | 1 April - 31 May | 01786 833866 |
| Tamano, By Braco | 29 September - 12 October | 01786 880271 |
| The Tors, Falkirk | 1 May - 30 September | 01324 620877 |

## Plant sales

| | | | | |
|---|---|---|---|---|
| Kilbryde Castle, Dunblane | Sunday 4 May | 2:00pm | - | 5:00pm |
| Gargunnock House, Gargunnock | Sunday 21 September | 2:00pm | - | 5:00pm |

## Key to symbols

 New in 2014

 Teas

 Cream teas

 Homemade teas

 Dogs on a lead allowed

 Wheelchair access

 Accommodation

 Plant stall

 Scottish Snowdrop Festival

## Garden locations

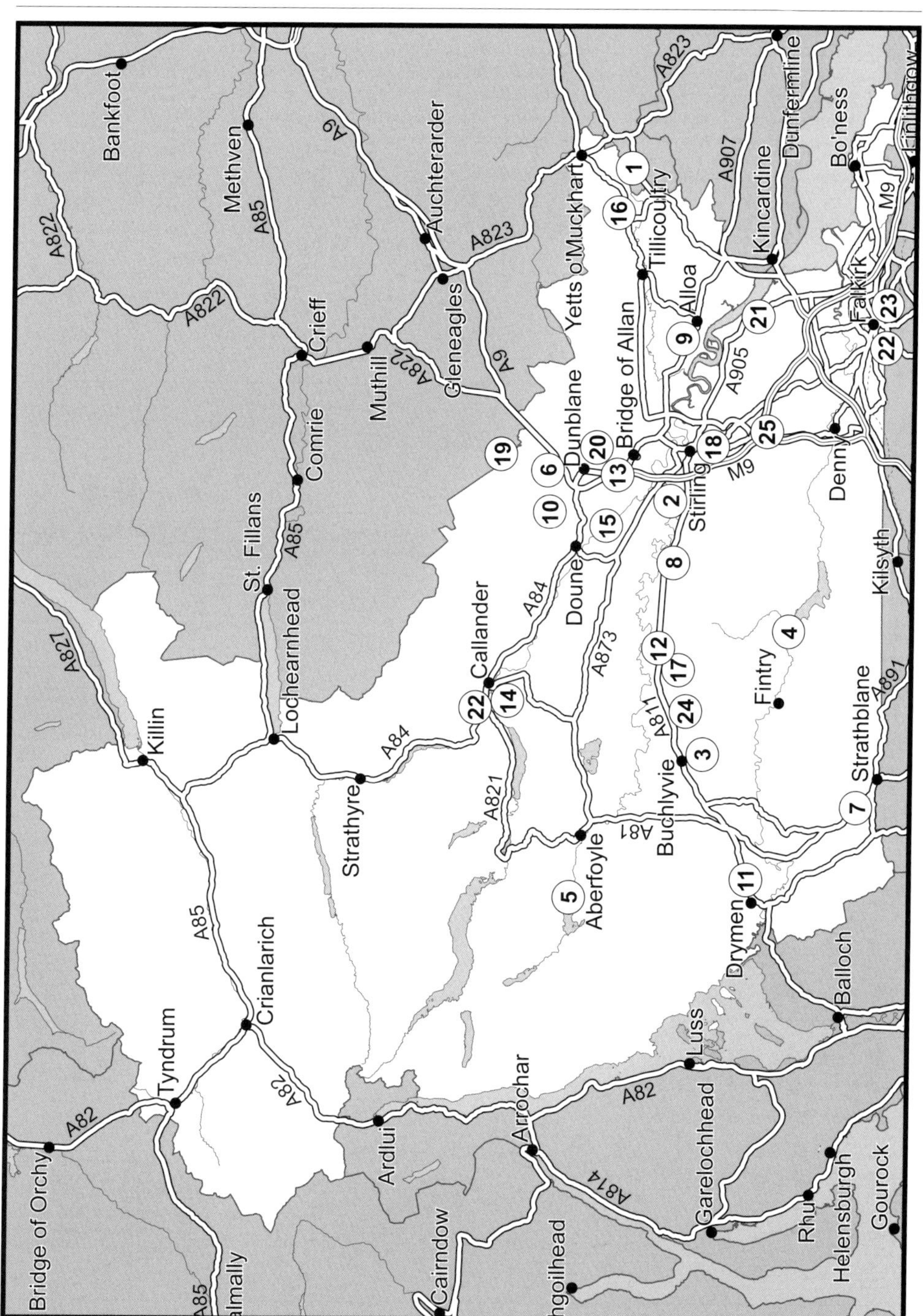

## ARNDEAN

by Dollar FK14 7NH
**Johnny and Katie Stewart T: 01259 743525**
**E: johnny@arndean.co.uk**

This is a beautiful mature garden extending to 15 acres including the woodland walk. There is a formal herbaceous part, a small vegetable garden and orchard. In addition, there are flowering shrubs, abundant and striking rhododendrons and azaleas and many fine specimen trees. There is a tree house for children.

**Directions:** Arndean is well sign posted off the A977.

Disabled Access:
Full

Opening Times:
Sunday 1 June
2:00pm - 5:30pm
Also by arrangement
15 May - 15 June

Admission:
£5.00, children free

Charities:
Marie Curie receives 40%, the net remaining to SG Beneficiaries.

## BRIDGE OF ALLAN GARDENS

Bridge of Allan FK9
**The Bridge of Allan Gardeners**
**E: r.leckie44@btinternet.com**

A delightful selection of gardens, some opening for the first time and some old favourites. A newly designed Japanese garden, terraced gardens to inspire you, and a wonderful selection of specimen trees, shrubs and herbaceous borders.
See the website and posters nearer the time for full details of all the gardens opening.

**Other Details:** Tickets and maps available from all gardens.
Teas will be served in St Saviour's Church Hall, Keir Street.

**Directions:** Signposted from village.

Disabled Access:
Partial

Opening Times:
Sunday 29 June
1:00pm - 5:00pm

Admission:
£5.00, children free

Charities:
St Saviours Church receives 20%, Artlink Central receives 20%, the net remaining to SG Beneficiaries.

## BUCHLYVIE GARDENS

Main Street, Buchlyvie FK8 3LX
**Buchlyvie Gardeners T: 01786 850671**
**E: gillie.welstead@gmail.com**

A variety of gardens, some new, with a wide range of planting, including rhododendrons, azaleas and specimen trees. Herbaceous borders and some vegetable gardens. Also includes Buchlyvie Wildlife Garden which is managed by the primary school children.
More details will be on the website nearer the time.

**Other Details:** Teas in the Village Hall.

**Directions:** Buchlyvie is west of Stirling on the A811. Entry and maps at all gardens which will be signposted from the centre of the village.

Disabled Access:
Partial

Opening Times:
Sunday 25 May
2:00pm - 5:00pm

Admission:
£5.00, children free

Charities:
Crossroads Caring Scotland (West Stirling Branch) receives 20%, Artlink Central receives 20%, the net remaining to SG Beneficiaries.

## CAMALLT

Fintry G63 0XH

**William Acton and Rebecca East T: 01360 860034**
**E: enquiries@camallt.com**

Eight acre garden previously open for its old and interesting daffodil cultivars dating from 1600 which carpet the woodland beside waterfalls and burn, at their best during April and early May. These are followed by bluebells, rhododendrons and azaleas. Herbaceous terraced gardens under continued progression of change meet lawns which run down to the Endrick Water. Other features include ponds and bog garden still under development.

**Directions:** From Fintry village B822 to Lennoxtown, approx 1 mile then turn left to Denny on B818, Camallt entrance on right.

Disabled Access:
None

Opening Times:
By arrangement
1 April - 15 May

Admission:
£3.50, children free

Charities:
Strathcarron Hospice receives 40%, the net remaining to SG Beneficiaries.

## DUN DUBH

Kinlochard Road, Aberfoyle FK8 3TJ

**Callum Pirnie, Head Gardener T: 01877 382698**
**E: callumpirnie@gmail.com**

A late Victorian garden of 6 acres undergoing restoration and development. Set on a series of terraces and slopes which run down to the shores of Loch Ard with superb views west to Ben Lomond framed by stands of mature conifers. There is an enclosed, colour themed formal garden laid out on 3 terraces and a new Victorian style glasshouse overlooking a terraced kitchen and fruit garden. The formal paved terrace at the front of the house overlooks a newly developed rock garden and crag while the lower walk running from the boat house to the main lawn gives views across the Loch. A developing woodland garden leads on to a formal late summer herbaceous border and terraced heather garden.

**Other Details:** Car parking limited to disabled badge holders and helpers, but there will be free transport to and from Aberfoyle car park throughout the afternoon. Parking on the road is dangerous and will be stopped. Guide dogs only.

**Directions:** Follow the signs to the car park in the centre of Aberfoyle, look for a Garden Open sign to show where the minibus will be leaving from.

Disabled Access:
Partial

Opening Times:
Sunday 18 May
2:00pm - 5:00pm
Sunday 14 September
2:00pm - 5:00pm

Admission:
£4.00, children free

Charities:
Help for Heroes receives 40%, the net remaining to SG Beneficiaries.

## DUNBLANE COMMUNITY GARDENS

Dunblane, Perthshire FK15 9JS

**The Gardeners of Dunblane Community Gardens**

A delightful walk along the banks of the Allan Water, the gardens show what can be done by an enthusiastic band of volunteers in a short space of time. In just 4 years the Rock Garden has been created with retaining walls and colourful planting. The Memorial Garden was started in 2011 and the hosta border is in the process of being verified as "the longest hosta border in the world". All areas have followed organic principles and the planting is designed to encourage wildlife.

**Other Details:** Hosta "Andy Murray" will be on display.
Teas available in the many cafes that are open in Dunblane.

**Directions:** Several car parks in Dunblane. Follow the signs towards the Memorial Garden on the south bank of the river and the Rock Garden, at the Haugh on the north side.

Disabled Access:
Partial

Opening Times:
Sunday 8 June
12:00pm - 5:00pm

Admission:
By donation.

Charities:
Dunblane in Bloom receives 20%, Dunblane Development Trust Environment Group receives 20%, the net remaining to SG Beneficiaries.

## DUNTREATH CASTLE

Blanefield G63 9AJ
**Sir Archibald & Lady Edmonstone T: 01360 770215**
**E: juliet@edmonstone.com www.duntreathcastle.co.uk**

Extensive gardens with mature and new plantings. Ornamental landscaped lake and bog garden. Sweeping lawns below formal fountain and rose parterre with herbaceous border leading up to an attractive waterfall garden with shrubs and spring plantings. There is a woodland walk and a 15th century keep and chapel.

**Directions:** A81 north of Glasgow between Blanefield and Killearn.

Disabled Access:
Full

Opening Times:
By arrangement on request
Groups welcome

Admission:
£4.00, children free

Charities:
All proceeds to SG Beneficiaries.

## GARGUNNOCK HOUSE

Gargunnock FK8 3AZ
**The Gargunnock Trustees T: 01786 860392**
**E: william.campbellwj@btinternet.com**

Five acres of mature gardens, woodland walks, walled garden and 18th c. Doocot. Snowdrops in February/March, daffodils in April/May. Glorious display of azaleas and rhododendrons in May/June. Wonderful trees and shrubs, glorious autumn colours. Garden featured in articles in "The Scotsman" and "Scottish Field". Guided tours can be arranged for parties throughout the year, contact the Head Gardener.

**Other Details: 21 September** Major plant sale with a wonderful selection of azaleas and rhododendrons. Homemade teas in Gargunnock House.
**1 February - 16 March** Open for the Snowdrop Festival.
Plant stall always available at rear of Gargunnock House.

**Directions:** On A811 5 miles west of Stirling.

Disabled Access:
Full

Opening Times:
Sunday 21 September
2:00pm - 5:00pm
1 February - 16 March and weekdays 14 April - 13 June
11:00am - 3:30pm

Admission:
21 Sept: £4.00, children free
Other dates: £3, children free

Charities:
Children's Hospice Assoc. & Gargunnock Comm. Centre both receive 20%, the net remaining to SG Beneficiaries.

## GEAN HOUSE

Tullibody Road, Alloa FK10 2EL
**Ceteris (Scotland)**
**E: ebowie@geanhouse.co.uk www.geanhouse.co.uk**

Gean House is an early 20th century Arts & Crafts style mansion. On arrival, the sweeping driveway from the main road takes you through beautiful parkland lined with trees to the mansion set on top of the hill facing north east. The gardens surrounding the house were originally 40 acres and included a Japanese garden in the woods. All that remains now are seven acres on the southern and eastern aspects of the house.

**Other Details:** Cream teas in Gean House. No dogs, except guide dogs.

**Directions:** Gean House is located on the Tullibody Road, Alloa.

Disabled Access:
None

Opening Times:
Tuesday 22 July
1:30pm - 4:30pm

Admission:
£4.00, children free

Charities:
Scottish Society for Autism receives 40%, the net remaining to SG Beneficiaries.

## KILBRYDE CASTLE

Dunblane FK15 9NF
**Sir James and Lady Campbell T: 01786 824897**
**E: kilbryde1@aol.com www.kilbrydecastle.com**

The Kilbryde Castle gardens cover some 12 acres and are situated above the Ardoch Burn and below the castle. The gardens are split into 3 parts: formal, woodland and wild. Huge drifts of snowdrops are in the wild garden during February and March. Natural planting (azaleas, rhododendrons, camellias and magnolias) is found in the woodland garden. There are glorious spring bulbs and autumn colour.

**Other Details: 23 February:** Open for the Snowdrop Festival.
**4 May Gala Day**: Plant stall by Carol Seymour and rhododendrons and azaleas by Willie Campbell, Gargunnock, as well as other stalls. Cream teas served on 4 May only. See website for more details nearer the time.

**Directions:** Three miles from Dunblane and Doune, off the A820 between Dunblane and Doune. On Scotland's Gardens days signposted from A820.

Disabled Access:
Partial

Opening Times:
Sunday 23 February
1:00pm - 4:00pm
Sunday 4 May
2:00pm - 5:00pm
Also by arrangement
15 February - 31 October

Admission:
£5.00 on 4 May, £4.00 on other days, children free

Charities:
Leighton Library receives 40%, the net remaining to SG Beneficiaries.

## KILLEARN VILLAGE GARDENS

G63
**Gardeners of Killearn Village**
**E: glenda.asquith@gmail.com**

Attractive small and medium-sized gardens, the majority of which are within easy walking distance of the centre of Killearn. Some new gardens since the last opening for Killearn. More details of the gardens will be on the website nearer the time.

**Other Details:** Homemade teas in the Hall.
Tickets and maps available at the Hall and at the gardens.

**Directions:** A81 Glasgow to Aberfoyle Road, take A875 turning to Killearn.

Disabled Access:
Partial

Opening Times:
Sunday 17 August
1:30pm - 5:30pm

Admission:
£5.00, children free

Charities:
Crossroads Caring Scotland West (Stirling Branch) receives 40%, the net remaining to SG Beneficiaries.

## LITTLE BROICH

Kippen FK8 3DT
**John Smith T: 01786 870275**

A tree lover's heaven! A hidden arboretum of about 8 acres, planted over the last 20 years, with an extensive collection of native and non-native conifers and broadleaf specimens. Fern leaf oaks, Hungarian oaks, Cercidiphyllom and Glyptostrobus amongst many others around wide, slightly sloping grass paths (can be slippery when wet). Stunning views across the Carse of Stirling and the autumn colours should be outstanding.

**Other Details:** No dogs except guide dogs.

**Directions:** Will be signed off the B8037. Parking in a field at the bottom of the lane or on the road if very wet.

Disabled Access:
Partial

Opening Times:
Sunday 5 October
2:00pm - 5:00pm

Admission:
£4.00 Children free

Charities:
Strathcarron Hospice receives 40%, the net remaining to SG Beneficiaries.

## MILSEYBANK

Bridge of Allan FK9 4NB

**Murray and Sheila Airth T: 01786 833866**
**E: smairth@hotmail.com**

Wonderful and interesting sloping garden with outstanding views, terraced for ease of access. Woodland with bluebells, rhododendrons, magnolias and camellias, and many other unusual plants, a true plantsman's garden.

**Directions:** Situated on A9, 1 mile from junction 11, M9 and ¼ mile from Bridge of Allan. Milseybank is at top of lane at Lecropt Nursery, 250 yards from Bridge of Allan train station.

Disabled Access:
Full

Opening Times:
By arrangement
1 April - 31 May

Admission:
£4.00, children free

Charities:
Strathcarron Hospice receives 40%, the net remaining to SG Beneficiaries.

## ROMAN CAMP COUNTRY HOUSE HOTEL & ORCHARDLEA HOUSE

off Main Street, Callander FK17 8BG

**Eric & Marion Brown and Rod & Hilary Gunkel T: 01877 330003**
**E: mail@romancamphotel.co.uk www.romancamphotel.co.uk**

Set amid 20 acres of grounds the 1625 former Hunting Lodge is now the renowned Roman Camp Country House Hotel. The delightful gardens have evolved over the centuries with much care and attention and incorporate a Victorian semi-walled garden, river side walks, woodland trails and a parterre garden to the rear. The rhododendrons, meconopsis, tulips and early spring herbaceous plants should all be in flower for the open day. Adjoining the Roman Camp is Orchardlea House with its Secret Garden developed over the last 25 years with a wide range of interesting trees and shrubs. These 2 properties were in the same ownership until the early 1970s.

**Other Details:** Approach Orchardlea from the Roman Camp via a special path. Plant stall at Orchardlea. Teas at the Roman Camp Country House Hotel.

**Directions:** Off the A84 at the east end of Callander. Entrance between 2 pink houses off Main Street. Parking available.

Disabled Access:
Partial

Opening Times:
Sunday 11 May
1:00pm - 6:00pm

Admission:
£5.00 Children free

Charities:
Crossroads Caring Scotland(West Stirling Branch) receives 40%, the net remaining to SG Beneficiaries.

## ROW HOUSE

Dunblane, Perthshire FK15 9NZ

**Mr & Mrs P Wordie**
**E: awordie@btinternet.com**

Mature garden with wonderful views to the River Teith and Ben Lomond. Many unusual trees and shrubs and stunning herbaceous borders, including a newly planted lavender bed.

**Directions:** From Keir Roundabout take the B824 to Doune, Row House will be sign posted off the B824.

Disabled Access:
Partial

Opening Times:
Wednesday 2 July
2:00pm - 5:00pm
Wednesday 30 July
2:00pm - 5:00pm

Admission:
£4.00, children free

Charities:
Crossroads Caring Scotland West (Stirling Branch) receives 40%, the net remaining to SG Beneficiaries.

## ROWBERROW

18 Castle Road, Dollar FK14 7BE

**Bill and Rosemary Jarvis T: 01259 742584**

**E: rjarvis1000@hotmail.com**

On the way up to Castle Campbell overlooking Dollar Glen, this colourful garden has several mixed shrub and herbaceous borders, a wildlife pond, two rockeries, alpine troughs, fruit and vegetable gardens, and a mini-orchard. The owner is a plantaholic and likes to collect unusual specimens. Rowberrow was featured on "Beechgrove Garden" in summer 2011.

**Other Details:** The Hillfoot Barbershop singers will entertain you. Parking is limited but transport will be provided from Burnside for people who cannot walk from there.

**Directions:** Pass along the burn side in Dollar, turn right at T junction follow signs for Castle Campbell and Dollar Glen. Park at bottom of Castle Road or in Quarry car park just up from the house.

Disabled Access:
Partial

Opening Times:
Sunday 24 August
2:00pm - 5:00pm

Admission:
£4.00, children free

Charities:
Hillfoot Harmony Barbershop Singers receive 40%, the net remaining to SG Beneficiaries.

## SETTIE (WITH THORNTREE)

Kippen FK8 3HN

**James and Jane Hutchison T: 01786 870428**

**E: plantitdesign@aol.com www.james-hutchison.com**

A 1½ acre country garden located to the south west of Kippen on an exposed site benefitting from wonderful views of the Trossachs. Settie is gaelic for a windy spot and the Hutchisons have divided this garden up into a series of rooms divided by tall random rubble sandstone walls. As a landscape gardener, James has used this challenging site as an opportunity to demonstrate what can be done in either a country garden or an enclosed urban space.

**Other Details:** Homemade teas at Settie, plant stall at Thorntree.

**Directions:** Take the Fintry Road out of Kippen and take the second turn on the right. Settie is approximately ⅓ mile west of the outskirts of Kippen.

Disabled Access:
None

Opening Times:
Sunday 22 June
2:00pm - 5:00pm

Admission:
£6.00 for both gardens

Charities:
Riding for the Disabled receives 40%, the net remaining to SG Beneficiaries.

## STIRLING GARDENS

FK8 2JH

**Stirling Gardeners T: 07758 784732**

**E: rachellnunn@yahoo.co.uk**

A selection of glorious town house gardens with unusual trees, shrubs, herbaceous borders, fruit and vegetables. To include 1 Laurelhill Place, 5 Ogilvie Road, and some new gardens, including 13 Park Avenue, a walled garden with a large pond and water feature and sculptures throughout. Also Carlton Coach House, Gladstone Place, a beautiful courtyard garden with great variety of planting. More details on the website nearer the time.

**Other Details:** Maps and tickets are available at all gardens. Teas are at 1 Laurelhill Place. Plant Stall is at Carlton Coach House.

**Directions:** Most of the gardens are within the King's Park area of Stirling, signposted from St Ninians Road/Snowdon Place junction, and from the north and west from Dumbarton Road/Queen's Road junction.

Disabled Access:
Partial

Opening Times:
Sunday 15 June
2:00pm - 5:00pm

Admission:
£5.00, children free

Charities:
Forth environment link Ltd receives 40%, the net remaining to SG Beneficiaries.

## TAMANO

By Braco FK15 9LP

**Douglas and Tina Lindsay T: 01786 880271**

A very informal woodland and wildlife garden with beautiful views. The garden has evolved, and is still evolving from a bare hillside 600 feet above sea level over the last 30 years. It is mainly planted with trees and shrubs, including a large number of rowans with berries ranging from white through pink, orange and red, which should be at their best at this time. A wildlife pond, stream and bog, mixed borders, some shrub roses, a small vegetable plot and a lovely courtyard area completes a wonderful experience.

**Other Details:** Please phone to arrange a time and book your tea at the same time! Paths are grass and can be slippery and not all are suitable for wheelchairs.

**Directions:** Tamano is about 1½ miles north of Kinbuck.
Coming from south to north on A9 turn on to B8033 from Dunblane to Kinbuck and go through Kinbuck towards Braco. From north to south turn off at the Greenloaning and Braco sign, turn left in Braco following signs for Kinbuck.

Disabled Access:
Partial

Opening Times:
By arrangement
29 September - 12 October

Admission:
£4.00, children free

Charities:
Cancer Research receives 40%, the net remaining to SG Beneficiaries.

## THE LINNS

Sheriffmuir, Dunblane FK15 0LP

**Drs Evelyn and Lewis Stevens T: 01786 822295**
**E: evelyn@thelinns.org.uk**

The Linns is a plantsman's garden of 3½ acres of mature woodland created from scratch since 1984 at the west end of the Ochils. The site demonstrates what is possible, with time and dedication, in what would otherwise be a windswept and bleak location. The layout of trees including beautiful species such as Cercidophyllum japonicum, Acer griseum and Betula albo-sinensis to mention just three, rhododendrons, hedges and walls, has created a wide variety of interesting and attractive garden spaces, giving a real sense of exploration and surprise. The garden display from early January onwards delights with drifts of near 100 forms of "special" snowdrops, a variety of large hellebores and dainty winter aconites. Then come corydalis, trilliums, erythroniums, daffodils etc. The summer display offers a superb collection of Meconopsis and a woodland meander through many other well-loved perennials.

**Other Details:** National Plant Collection®: Meconopsis.
Drs Evelyn and Lewis Stevens are wonderful hosts and are happy to provide a tour or simply let you wander. Plants may be for sale. No dogs except guide dogs.
As parking is limited, it is necessary to phone prior to visiting the garden to book a place. Groups are welcome.

**Directions:** Sheriffmuir by Dunblane. Please phone prior to visit for additional directions.

Disabled Access:
Partial

Opening Times:
Sunday 9 March
10:00am - 4:00pm
for the Snowdrop Festival
Sunday 25 May
10:00am - 4:00pm
Sunday 8 June
10:00am - 4:00pm

Admission:
£4.00, children free

Charities:
Sophie North Charitable Trust receives 40%, the net remaining to SG Beneficiaries.

## THE PASS HOUSE

Kilmahog, Callander FK17 8HD
**Dr and Mrs D Carfrae**

Well planted, medium-sized garden with steep banks down to swift river. The garden paths are not steep. There are lovely displays of camellias, rhododendrons, azaleas, alpines and shrubs. The Scotland's Gardens plaque awarded for 25 years of opening is on display.

**Directions:** Two miles from Callander on A84 to Lochearnhead.

Disabled Access:
None

Opening Times:
Sunday 11 May
2:00pm - 5:00pm

Admission:
£4.00, children free

Charities:
Crossroads receives 40%, the net remaining to SG Beneficiaries.

## THE PINEAPPLE

Near Airth, Falkirk FK2 8LU
**The National Trust for Scotland T: 08444 932189**
**E: mjeffery@nts.org.uk www.nts.org.uk**

The Pineapple is named after the bizarre structure built around 1761 in the shape of a pineapple! This folly once held extensive glasshouses and pineapple pits where a variety of exotic fruits and vegetables were grown. It is now an oasis for wildlife including the rare great crested newt - with a dipping pool, an apple orchard and picnic grounds.

**Other Details:** Join the Pineapple team for a harvest produce and plant sale in this unique setting.

**Directions:** 7 miles east of Stirling, off A905, then off B9124. 1 mile west of Airth.

Disabled Access:
Partial

Opening Times:
Sunday 31 August
10:00am - 5:00pm
for Harvest Produce and Plant Sale

Admission:
By donation

Charities:
All proceeds to SG Beneficiaries

## THE TORS

2 Slamannan Road, Falkirk FK1 5LG
**Dr and Mrs D M Ramsay T: 01324 620877**

The Tors is an award winning Victorian garden of just over 1 acre with a secret woodland garden to the side and a small orchard and wild area to the rear. Many unusual maple trees and rhododendrons are the main interest of this garden and there are several wildlife ponds and water features. The Tors was featured on the 'Beechgrove Garden' for autumn colour in September 2010, but the best time to see this garden is at the end of July or the beginning of August.

**Other Details:** No dogs allowed except guide dogs.

**Directions:** The B803 to the south of Falkirk leads to Glenbrae Road. Turn right at the traffic lights into Slamannan Road and The Tors is a Victorian building immediately on the left.

Disabled Access:
Partial

Opening Times:
Sunday 27 July
2:00pm - 5:00pm
By arrangement
1 May - 30 September

Admission:
£3.50, children free

Charities:
Strathcarron Hospice receives 40%, the net remaining to SG Beneficiaries.

## THORNTREE AND THORNTREE (WITH SETTIE)

Arnprior FK8 3EY
**Mark and Carol Seymour T: 01786 870710**
**E: info@thorntreebarn.co.uk www.thorntreebarn.co.uk**

Charming country garden with flower beds around courtyard. Apple walk, Saltire garden and new mecanopsis bed. Lovely views from Ben Lomond to Ben Ledi. A good display of primroses at the end of April beginning of May.

**Other Details: 22 June:** Joint opening with Settie. Teas at Settie.
**May, July & August:** Thorntree only.

**Directions:** A811. In Arnprior take Fintry Road, Thorntree is second on the right.

Disabled Access:
Full

Opening Times:
Wednesday 14 May
Sunday 22 June
Wednesday 16 July
Wednesday 20 August
All dates 2:00pm - 5:00pm

Admission:
June: £6.00 for both gardens
Other dates: £4.00, children free

Charities:
Riding for the Disabled receives 40%, the net remaining to SG Beneficiaries.

## WEST PLEAN HOUSE

Denny Road, by Stirling FK7 8HA
**Tony and Moira Stewart T: 01786 812208**
**E: moira@westpleanhouse.com www.westpleanhouse.com**

Woodland walks with snowdrops in February and March. Well established garden including site of iron age homestead and panoramic views over seven counties. Woodlands with mature rhododendrons, specimen trees, extensive lawns, shrubs and walled garden with variety of vegetables. Includes woodland walk with planting of azaleas and rhododendrons.

**Directions:** Leave all routes at Junction 9 roundabout where M9/M80 converge. Take A872 for Denny, go less than a mile, turn left at house sign and immediately after lodge cottage. Carry on up the drive.

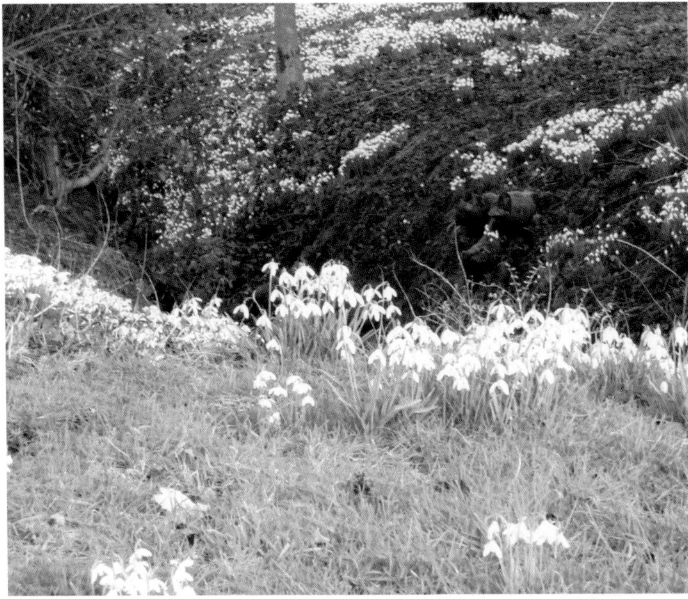

Disabled Access:
Full

Opening Times:
Sunday 2 March
1:00pm - 4:00pm
for the Snowdrop Festival

Admission:
£3.50, children free

Charities:
Scottish Motor Neurone Disease Association receives 40%, the net remaining to SG Beneficiaries.

# WIGTOWNSHIRE

Scotland's Gardens 2014 Guidebook is sponsored by **INVESTEC WEALTH & INVESTMENT**

## District Organiser

| | |
|---|---|
| Mrs Ann Watson | Doonholm, Cairnryan Road, Stranraer DG9 8AT |

## Area Organisers

| | |
|---|---|
| Mrs Terry Brewis | Ardwell House, Stranraer DG9 9LY |
| Mr Giles Davies | Elmlea Plants, Minnigaff, Newton Stewart DG8 6PX |
| Mrs Andrew Gladstone | Craichlaw, Kirkcowan, Newton Stewart DG8 0DQ |
| Mrs Janet Hannay | Cuddyfield, Carsluith DG8 7DS |
| Mrs Vicky Roberts | Logan House, Port Logan, by Stranraer DG9 9ND |

## Treasurer

| | |
|---|---|
| Mr George Fleming | Ardgour, Stoneykirk, Stranraer DG9 9DL |

## Gardens open on a specific date

| | | |
|---|---|---|
| Dunskey Gardens and Maze, Portpatrick | Saturday 15 February | 10:00am - 4:00pm |
| Dunskey Gardens and Maze, Portpatrick | Sunday 16 February | 10:00am - 4:00pm |
| Dunskey Gardens and Maze, Portpatrick | Saturday 22 February | 10:00am - 4:00pm |
| Dunskey Gardens and Maze, Portpatrick | Sunday 23 February | 10:00am - 4:00pm |
| Balker Farmhouse, Stranraer | Sunday 11 May | 2:00pm - 5:00pm |
| Logan House Gardens, Port Logan | Sunday 18 May | 10:30am - 5:00pm |
| Logan Botanic Garden, Port Logan | Sunday 25 May | 10:00am - 5:00pm |
| Claymoddie Garden, Whithorn | Sunday 1 June | 2:00pm - 5:00pm |
| Castle Kennedy and Gardens, Stranraer | Sunday 15 June | 10:00am - 5:00pm |
| Woodfall Gardens, Glasserton | Sunday 22 June | 1:00pm - 5:00pm |
| Damnaglaur Gardens, Drummore | Sunday 20 July | 1:00pm - 5:00pm |
| Lochnaw Castle, Lochnaw | Sunday 27 July | 2:00pm - 5:00pm |
| Balker Farmhouse, Stranraer | Sunday 10 August | 2:00pm - 5:00pm |

## Gardens open regularly

| | | |
|---|---|---|
| Ardwell House Gardens, Ardwell | 1 April - 30 September | 10:00am - 5:00pm |
| Castle Kennedy and Gardens, Stranraer | 1 Feb - 16 March (weekends) and 1 April - 30 October | 10:00am - 5:00pm |
| Claymoddie Garden, Whithorn | 1 April - 30 September (Fris, Sats and Suns) | 2:00pm - 5:00pm |
| Dunskey Gardens and Maze, Portpatrick | 18 April - October | 10:00am - 5:00pm |
| Glenwhan Gardens, Dunragit | 1 April - 31 October | 10:00am - 5:00pm |
| Logan Botanic Garden, Port Logan | 15 March - 31 October | 10:00am - 5:00pm |

## Gardens open by arrangement

| Garden | Dates | Contact |
|---|---|---|
| Castle Kennedy and Gardens, Stranraer | 1 November - 31 December | 01581 400225 |
| Claymoddie Garden, Whithorn | 1 April - 30 September | 01988 500422 |
| Craichlaw, Kirkcowan | 1 January - 31 December | 01671 830208 |
| Dunskey Gardens and Maze, Portpatrick | 2 February - 15 March | 01776 810211 |
| Woodfall Gardens, Glasserton | On request | E: woodfallgardens@btinternet.com |

Logan House, Wigtownshire

## Key to symbols

 New in 2014

Homemade teas

 Accommodation

 Teas

  Dogs on a lead allowed

 Plant stall

Cream teas

 Wheelchair access

 Scottish Snowdrop Festival

## Garden locations

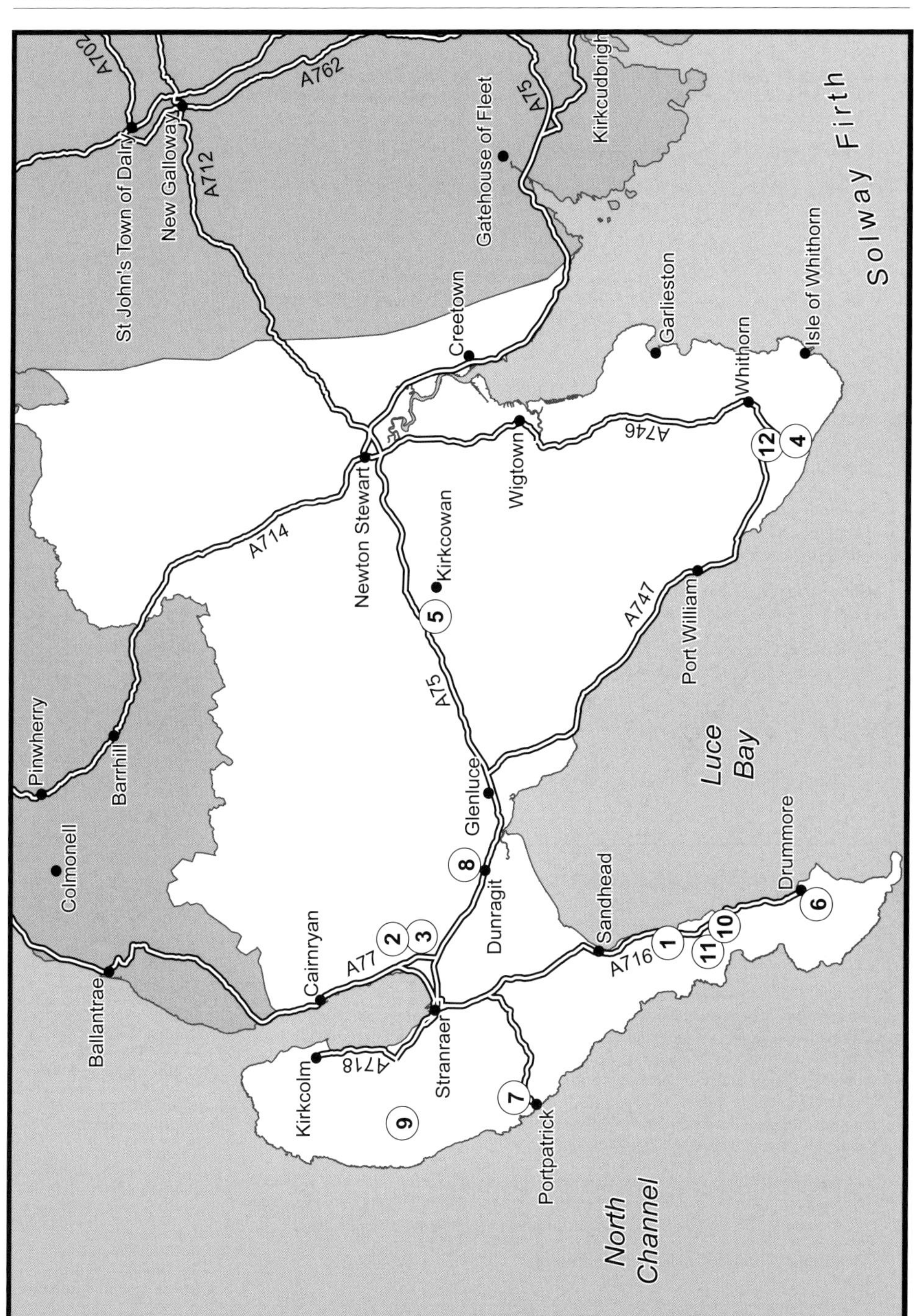

## ARDWELL HOUSE GARDENS

Ardwell, Stranraer DG9 9LY
**Mr and Mrs Francis Brewis**

Daffodils, spring flowers, rhododendrons, flowering shrubs, coloured foliage and rock plants. Moist garden at smaller pond and a walk around larger ponds with views over Luce Bay.

**Other Details:** Collection Box. House not open.

**Directions:** A716 towards Mull of Galloway. Stranraer 10 miles.

Disabled Access:
None

Opening Times:
1 April - 30 September
10:00am - 5:00pm

Admission:
£3.00, concessions £2.00, children under 14 free

Charities:
Donation to SG Beneficiaries

## BALKER FARMHOUSE

Stranraer DG9 8RS
**Davina, Countess of Stair**

The house was restored and the garden, formerly a ploughed field, was started in 2003-4 . It is now full of wonderful shrubs and plants for all seasons.

**Other Details:** Gravel paths on slope so garden is not suitable for wheelchairs. Teas will be available at Castle Kennedy Gardens.

**Directions:** One and a half miles approx off A75, 3 miles from Stranraer - through farmyard to blue gate to garden.

Disabled Access:
None

Opening Times:
Sunday 11 May
2:00pm - 5:00pm
Sunday 10 August
2:00pm - 5:00pm

Admission:
£4.00

Charities:
World Horse Welfare receives 20%, another charity to be advised will receive 20%, the net remaining to SG Beneficiaries.

## CASTLE KENNEDY AND GARDENS

Stranraer DG9 8RT
**The Earl and Countess of Stair T: 01581 400225**

Romantically situated, these famous 75 acres of landscaped gardens are located on an isthmus surrounded by 2 large natural lochs. At one end the ruined Castle Kennedy overlooks a beautiful herbaceous walled garden with Lochinch Castle at the other. With over 300 years of planting there is an impressive collection of rare trees, rhododendrons and exotic shrubs, featuring many spectacular Champion Trees (tallest or largest of their type). The stunning snowdrop walks, daffodils, spring flowers, rhododendron and magnolia displays, and herbaceous borders make this a 'must visit' garden through-out the year.

**Other Details:** Champion Trees: 6 British, 11 Scottish, 25 for Dumfries & Galloway. Wildlife ranger, head gardener guided walks, tree and family trails, charming tea room serving homemade teas and light lunches, plant centre and gift shop.

**Directions:** On A75 5 miles east of Stranraer.

Disabled Access:
Partial

Opening Times:
Sunday 15 June
10:00am - 5:00pm for SG
1 Feb. - 16 March weekends and 1 Apr - 30 Oct 10am - 5pm
By arrangement 1 Nov - 31 Dec

Admission:
£5.00, conc £3.50, children £1.50, disabled free, families £11.00 (2 adults & 3 children)

Charities:
Homestart Wigtownshire receives 40%, the net remaining to SG Beneficiaries

## CLAYMODDIE GARDEN

Whithorn, Newton Stewart DG8 8LX

**Mr and Mrs Robin Nicholson T: 01988 500422**

**E: gallowayplants@aol.com www.gallowayplants.co.uk**

This romantic garden, developed over the last 40 years, with its backdrop of mature trees was designed by the owner, an enthusiastic plantsman. Imaginative hard and soft landscaping provides a wide range of settings, both shady and sunny, for a mass of meticulously placed plants, both old favourites and exotic species, all helped by the proximity of the Gulf Stream. Running through the lower part of the garden is the burn which feeds the pond, all newly planted. There are changes in levels, but most of the garden is accessible to wheelchairs.

**Other Details:** Very good nursery with large collection of rare and interesting plants propagated from the Claymoddie garden. Teas on 11 May only.

**Directions:** Claymoddie is off the A746, 2 miles south of Whithorn.

Disabled Access:
Partial

Opening Times:
Sunday 1 June
2:00pm - 5:00pm
1 April - 30 September
2:00pm - 5:00pm
Fridays, Saturdays & Sundays and by arrangement 1 April - 30 Sept. for other times.

Admission:
£6.00, includes tea

Charities:
Macmillan Cancer Support receives 40%, the net remaining to SG Beneficiaries.

## CRAICHLAW

Kirkcowan, Newton Stewart DG8 0DQ

**Mr and Mrs A Gladstone T: 01671 830208**

Formal garden with herbaceous borders around the house. Set in extensive grounds with lawns, lochs and woodland. A path around the main loch leads to a water garden returning past a recently planted arboretum in the old walled garden.
The best times to visit the garden are early February for snowdrops, May to mid-June for the water garden and rhododendrons and mid-June to August for herbaceous borders.

**Directions:** Take the B733 for Kirkcowan off the A75 at the Halfway House 8 miles west of Newton Stewart. Craichlaw House is the first turning on the right.

Disabled Access:
Partial

Opening Times:
By arrangement on request

Admission:
£4.00, concessions £3.00, children under 14 free

Charities:
Donation to SG Beneficiaries

## DAMNAGLAUR GARDENS

Drummore, Stranraer DG9 9QN

**Mr C & Mrs J D Hadley, Frances Collins and Carol Rennison T: 01776 840636**

**E: chunky.collins@bt.internet.com**

**Ardoch**: Over 1 acre garden, originally planted by John May in the 1990s, containing many mature shrubs in various areas, lawn, veg. & fruit. Views over Luce Bay from the top point of garden. The original planting list is available to view on request.
**Damnaglaur House**: An established garden, landscaping and planting begun in 1991, but still work in progress. Full of trees, shrubs & herbaceous plants, with colour all year and gravel paths useful on wet days. Stunning location and views over farmland and down to Luce Bay, with the Machars of Galloway and the Galloway Hills in the distance.
**The Homestead**: A developing garden around a property completed in 2007, mixed planting, with uninterrupted sea views over Luce Bay.

**Other Details:** Accom. and teas at The Homestead. Locally produced crafts at Ardoch.

**Directions: Ardoch**: From Drummore Village, follow signs for Mull of Galloway. Straight over crossroads at top of hill (left for Mull, right for Port Logan) Ardoch is on your right.
**Damnaglaur House & The Homestead**: 100 yards north of Junction of B7041/B7065.

Disabled Access:
Partial

Opening Times:
Sunday 20 July
1:00pm - 5:00pm

Admission:
£5.00 (includes all 3 gardens)

Charities:
Kirkmaiden Parish Church receives 40%, the net remaining to SG Beneficiaries.

## DUNSKEY GARDENS AND MAZE

Portpatrick, Stranraer DG9 8TJ
**Mr and Mrs Edward Orr Ewing T: 01776 810211**
**E: garden@dunskey.com www.dunskey.com**

Come and enjoy welcoming walled and woodland gardens and woodland snowdrop walks. There are 43 named varieties of snowdrops including: Galanthus 'Dunskey Talia', Galanthus 'Fred's Giant', Galanthus 'Robin Hood', Galanthus 'Sickle'. Featured in The Beechgrove Garden in 2013.

**Other Details:** Gardener led strolls at 2:00pm each Sunday.
Designated dog walk, picnic tables and shaded parking for dog owners. Dogs are allowed on snowdrop walks but not in the gardens. Disabled loos & mobility scooter. Children's games and tree identification. Tearoom with warming soups and tea. Plants for sale have all been raised at Dunskey.
**February Dates**: Open for the snowdrop Festival, admission includes maze. Please refer to website in extreme weather conditions.

**Directions:** One mile from Portpatrick on B738 off A77.

Disabled Access:
Partial

Opening Times:
Sats/Suns 15, 16, 22 & 23 Feb
10:00am - 4:00pm
18 April - October
10:00am - 5:00pm
By arrangement 2 Feb - 15 Mar

Admission:
**Feb. dates**: £4.00, under 16 £0.50, families £12.00
**Other dates**: £5.50, conc. £5.00, under 16 £2.00, families £12.00

Charities:
Donation to SG Beneficiaries

## GLENWHAN GARDENS

Dunragit, by Stranraer DG9 8PH
**Mr and Mrs W Knott**

Glenwhan Garden has been described as one of the best newly created gardens in recent times. 25 years ago there was nothing but bracken, gorse and willows but careful planting has created a 12 acre garden filled with glorious collections of plants from around the world. There is colour in all seasons and the winding paths, well placed seats, sculptures and water all add to the tranquil atmosphere. There is a 17 acre moorland wildflower walk, the chance to see red squirrels and magnificent views over Luce Bay, the Mull of Galloway and the Isle of Man.

**Other Details:** No dogs allowed in the garden but dog walk available. Shop and tea room.

**Directions:** 7 miles east of Stranraer, 1 mile off A75 at Dunragit (follow signs).

Disabled Access:
None

Opening Times:
1 April - 31 October
10:00am - 5:00pm

Admission:
£5.00, season ticket £15.00, family ticket £12.00 (up to 3 children)

Charities:
Donation to SG Beneficiaries

## LOCHNAW CASTLE

Lochnaw, By Leswalt, Stranraer DG9 0RW
**Mr and Mrs Geoffrey Anderson**

The garden is very much a work in progress and presently there is not a great deal of formal garden. We are in the process of designing and restoring what was the Victorian flower garden and a new garden has been created in what was the Victorian wing of the house which was demolished in the 50s. There is a large double walled garden, the largest satellite of the National Apple Collection which was previously at Brogdale (see article in November 2013 issue of "House and Gardens") and also a large selection of red, white & pink currants & gooseberries.

**Other Details:** Access to the walled garden can be on foot through the woodland or by car for those who can't manage the walk. It is also possible to walk around the loch but not in a complete circle as the northern end is near the road.

**Directions:** Turn left at the church in Leswalt and follow Glen Road until Drumlockart Caravan Park (which is on the right). Entrance to the Castle is just after, on the left. Great care should be taken when driving on this road.

Disabled Access:
None

Opening Times:
Sunday 27 July
2:00pm - 5:00pm

Admission:
£4.00, children free

Charities:
Macmillan Nurses receives 20%, Help for Heroes receives 20%, the net remaining to SG Beneficiaries.

## LOGAN BOTANIC GARDEN

Port Logan, by Stranraer DG9 9ND
**The Royal Botanic Gardens Edinburgh**
**www.rbge.org.uk**

At the south western tip of Scotland lies Logan which is unrivalled as the country's most exotic garden. With a mild climate washed by the Gulf Stream, a remarkable collection of bizarre and beautiful plants, especially from the southern hemisphere, flourish out of doors. Enjoy the colourful walled garden with its magnificent tree ferns, palms and borders along with the contrasting woodland garden with its unworldly gunnera bog. Explore the Discovery Centre or take an audio tour.

**Other Details:** National Plant Collection®: Gunnera/Leptospermum/Griselinia. Champion Trees: Polylepis/Eucalyptus. Home baking, botanic shop, Discovery Centre, guided tours and Logan Exhibition studio.

**Directions:** 10 miles south of Stranraer on A716 then 2½ miles from Ardwell village.

Disabled Access:
Full

Opening Times:
Sunday 25 May
10:00am - 5:00pm for SG
15 March - 31 October
10:00am - 5:00pm

Admission:
£6.00, conc £5.00, under 16 free (prices include a small donation to the Garden. For admission prices without donation check our website)

Charities:
RBGE receives 40%, the net remaining to SG Beneficiaries

## LOGAN HOUSE GARDENS

Port Logan, By Stranraer DG9 9ND
**Mr and Mrs Andrew Roberts**

The Queen Ann House is surrounded by sweeping lawns and a spectacular woodland garden. Rare and exotic plants together with champion trees and fine species of rhododendrons provide an excellent habitat for an interesting variety of wildlife.

**Other Details:** Champion Trees: 7 UK and 11 Scottish Champions.
Charity fete day supported by and raising funds for local charities.

**Directions:** On A716 13 miles south of Stranraer, 2½ miles from Ardwell village.

Disabled Access:
Partial

Opening Times:
Sunday 18 May
10:30am - 5:00pm
Charity Fete Day

Admission:
£4.00, children under 16 free

Charities:
Port Logan Hall will receive 40% of the entrance fees, the net remaining to SG Beneficiaries.

## WOODFALL GARDENS

Glasserton DG8 8LY
**Ross and Liz Muir**
**E: woodfallgardens@btinternet.com**

This lovely 3 acre 18th century triple walled garden has been thoughtfully restored to provide year round interest. Many mature trees and shrubs including some less common species; herbaceous borders and shrub roses surround the foundations of original greenhouses; grass borders; a knot garden; extensive beds of fruit and vegetables; a herb garden; woodland walk.
This unusual garden is well worth a visit.

**Directions:** Two miles south-west of Whithorn at junction of A746 and A747 (behind Glasserton Church).

Disabled Access:
Partial

Opening Times:
Sunday 22 June 1:00pm - 5:00pm for SG
By arrangement on request

Admission:
£4:00, children free but must be accompanied by a responsible adult

Charities:
Glasserton Parish Church receives 20%, Macmillan Cancer Support receives 20%, the net remaining to SG Beneficiaries.

# INDEX OF GARDENS

# INDEX OF ADVERTISERS

# WOULD YOU LIKE TO OPEN YOUR GARDEN FOR CHARITY?

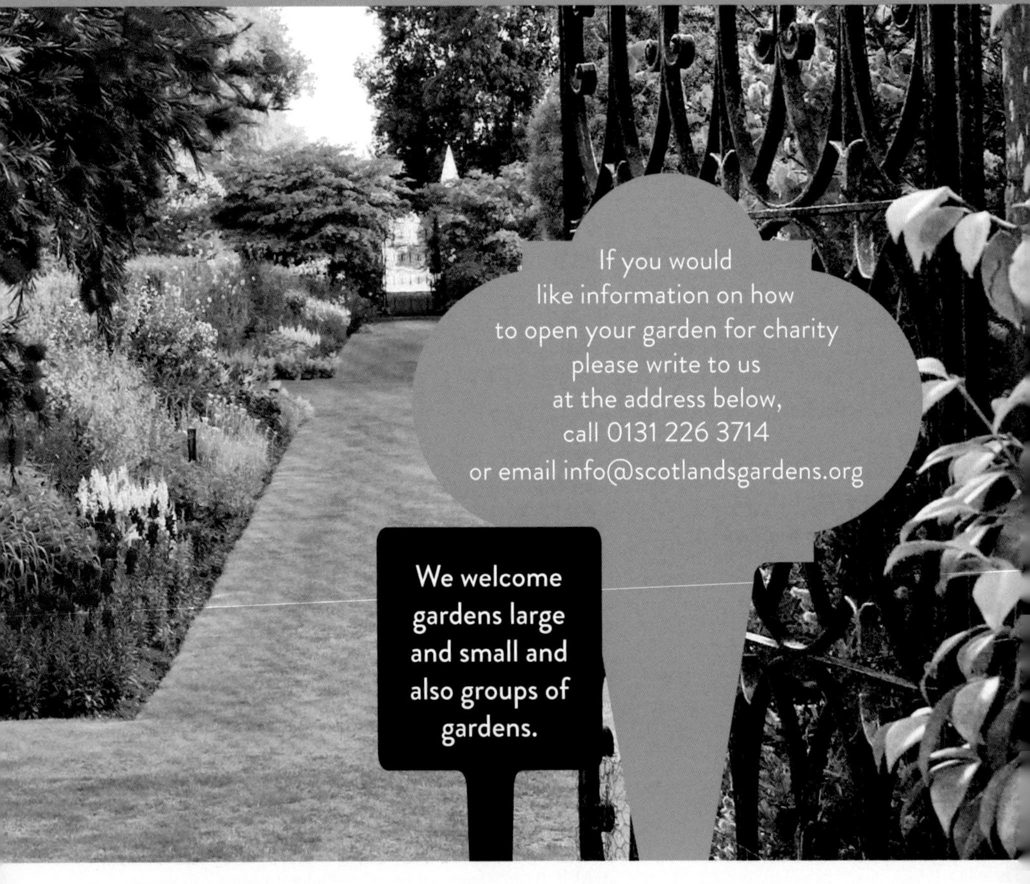
If you would
like information on how
to open your garden for charity
please write to us
at the address below,
call 0131 226 3714
or email info@scotlandsgardens.org
We welcome
gardens large
and small and
also groups of
gardens.

To: Scotland's Gardens, 42a North Castle Street, Edinburgh EH2 3BN

Please send me more information about opening my garden for charity.

Name ________________________________

Address ________________________________

________________________________

Postcode ________________ Tel ________________

Email ________________________________

# NOTES

# OUR GUIDEBOOK FOR 2015

## ORDER NOW

**and your copy will be posted to you on publication in December 2014.**

Send order to:

Scotland's Gardens, 42a North Castle Street, Edinburgh EH2 3BN

Please send me ___ copy / copies of **Our Guide for 2015**,

price £7.50, to include postage and packing, as soon as it is available.

I enclose a cheque / postal order made payable to Scotland's Gardens.

Name ________________________________

Address ________________________________

________________________________

Postcode ________________________________

Copies of Our Guide for 2014 may also be purchased on our website:
**www.scotlandsgardens.org**